THE BLACK HEARTS OF MEN

John Stauffer

The Black Hearts
of Men

RADICAL ABOLITIONISTS AND

THE TRANSFORMATION

OF RACE

HARVARD UNIVERSITY PRESS

CAMBRIDGE, MASSACHUSETTS

AND LONDON, ENGLAND

2002

Library of Congress Cataloging-in-Publication Data

Stauffer, John.
   The black hearts of men : radical abolitionists and the transforma-
tion of race / John Stauffer.
      p. cm.
   Includes bibliographical references and index.
   ISBN 0-674-00645-3 (alk. paper)
      1. Abolitionists—United States—History—19th century.
2. Antislavery movements—United States—History—19th century.
3. Abolitionists—United States—Biography.   4. Smith, James
McCune, 1813–1865.   5. Smith, Gerrit, 1797–1874.   6. Douglass,
Frederick, 1817?–1895.   7. Brown, John, 1800–1859.   8. Radical-
ism—United States—History—19th century.   9. Racism—United
States—Psychological aspects—History—19th century.   10. United
States—Race relations—Moral and ethical aspects.   I. Title.

E449 .S813 2001
973.7'114'0922—dc21

2001039474

For David Brion Davis

Contents

THE BLACK HEARTS OF MEN

Introduction

The white man's unadmitted—and apparently, to him, unspeakable—
private fears and longings are projected onto the Negro. The only
way he can be released from the Negro's tyrannical power over him is
to consent, in effect, to become black himself.

    —JAMES BALDWIN, *THE FIRE NEXT TIME* (1963)

A few days after Christmas in 1846 the black physician James McCune
Smith told his wealthy white friend Gerrit Smith what must be done to
convince Americans of "the eternal equality of the Human race."
"Good Government" would help, he said, particularly "Bible Politics"
and its "first principle" of racial equality. But politics and government
represented only the "outward sign" of "an inward and spirit-owned
conviction." Before equality could be attained, there had to be a profound shift in American consciousness: "The heart of the whites must
be changed, thoroughly, entirely, permanently changed," McCune
Smith said. He went on to suggest that whites had to understand what
it was like to be black. They had to learn how to view the world as if
they were black, shed their "whiteness" as a sign of superiority, and renounce their belief in skin color as a marker of aptitude and social
status. They had to acquire, in effect, a black heart.[1]

This book is about that moral shift. It focuses on James McCune
Smith, Gerrit Smith, and their better-known comrades Frederick
Douglass and John Brown, all of whom embraced an ethic of a black
heart. Their story is remarkable. Together these four men, two black
and two white, forged interracial bonds of friendship and alliance that
were unprecedented in their own time and were probably not dupli-
cated until well into the twentieth century. In a society pervaded by
slavery and racism, they came together to seek equality for all people in
their communities and throughout the country. They offered an alter-

native to an American dream that privileged white men over almost everyone else. As they transformed themselves and overcame existing social barriers, they reimagined their country as a pluralist society in which the standard of excellence depended on righteousness and benevolence rather than on skin color, sex, or material wealth. In one sense they were exemplars of the notion, now quite fashionable in the academy, that race, class, and gender are social constructs. In their time this was a radically new concept.[2]

The rise and fall of these four men's alliance occurred alongside the fragmentation of America from the panic of 1837 to Secession. While the nation virtually doubled in size and dramatically expanded its slave territory and slave population, these men experienced their own extraordinary self-transformations. They saw themselves as prophets preparing for a new and glorious age—a new America that would be free from sin and oppression. They embraced the idea of "sacred self-sovereignty," believing that the kingdom of God was within them and potentially within all individuals. And at a time when the country's two main political parties were fragmenting, they created their own political party. They became Radical Political Abolitionists, and viewed the government as sacred and the appropriate means for pursuing their millennium. But they were overcome by the lack of progress toward a just and moral society. The hearts of whites were *not* being changed, and they felt profoundly alienated from white laws and conventions that defended slavery and racial oppression. In their quest for a perfect society, they accepted righteous violence, which finally resulted in John Brown's disastrous raid on the federal arsenal at Harpers Ferry, Virginia, as part of a scheme to liberate the slaves. The event produced Brown's execution, sent Gerrit Smith to an insane asylum, and destroyed the very alliance that they had so courageously created. It also propelled the nation toward a brutal civil war that had been previewed in Brown's attack on Harpers Ferry and earlier in his efforts to keep Kansas safe from slavery.

A number of other factors united these four men. They corresponded frequently and saw one another as often as possible. In fact they all lived in New York State during their alliance, three of them in upstate New York. They were more successful than any of their peers at collapsing racial barriers, as is revealed by their political and social alliance. And they were instrumental in shaping each other's self-definitions and reform visions. These lines of influence and interconnectedness are revealed in form as well as in content in the story line that unfolds in the following pages, which weaves together the four men's lives by highlighting one at a time. The overall effect is a kind of collective biography, a braiding together of four lives. Only by changing perspectives, listening to multiple voices from different social groups and vantage points, is it possible to understand how racial identities get defined, blurred, and remade.[3]

Gerrit Smith is the lead protagonist. He is the tragic figure who ultimately loses himself and his black heart. He is also the primary thread linking the other three characters. Without him, this biracial quartet could not have existed, for it was through his initiative and generosity that the four men first came together. And without his penchant for saving the letters he received and making copies of those he wrote, their friendship would have been lost to posterity. Most of the letters among the four men run through Smith. The other three corresponded with him far more than they did among themselves. Gerrit Smith's correspondence with Frederick Douglass and James McCune Smith represents the largest extant biracial correspondence in antebellum America, and possibly in the nineteenth century. There are hundreds of letters between them in the Gerrit Smith Papers and the Frederick Douglass Papers, and hundreds more in Douglass' newspapers, providing the raw text of their friendship. As a land baron, Gerrit Smith was also the only character able to connect the world of wealth and power with that of Christian benevolence, militant abolitionism, and the marginalized status of the other three men. And his integrated village of Peterboro, in Madison County, New York, and the black settlement he helped establish at North Elba, New York (which constituted John Brown's permanent residence from 1854 until his death), offer manageable settings in which to view the dynamics of race, religion, class, and gender at the levels of both self and society.

Gerrit Smith, James McCune Smith, Frederick Douglass, and John Brown were in no way "representative" men in antebellum America, even though they were often defined as such by their admirers. They did, however, represent what was possible: they occupied an endpoint on the spectrum of "identity formation," and their self-conceptions and hopes for America depended upon their success in blurring and breaking down distinctions of race, religion, class, and gender. Although they stood apart from their peers in their efforts to imagine and realize a new America, their reform rhetoric resembled the poetic rhetoric of a number of romantic writers. Lord Byron, Walt Whitman, and Ralph Waldo Emerson describe a similar quest for self-transformation and liberation from existing social codes, and the four abolitionists were either inspired by or otherwise connected to these literary figures. Treating their reform work as "art" and comparing it to the work of these more "traditional" artists enhance our understanding of the broader culture of dissent in America by revealing what kinds of protest were permissible, possible, even thinkable.

❧ The story of this interracial alliance offers a number of new insights and perspectives on antebellum reform and the Civil War era. It shows how Americans from different social groups interacted and shaped each other's worldviews—something no other study of antebellum reform has done in depth. Additionally, the links between personal faith and behavior on the one hand and broader historical, political, and literary developments on the other hand have been inadequately addressed, especially among people from different social groups. In the case of this biracial quartet, these links produced an exceptional symbiosis that altered the course of American history, even though two of the characters (Gerrit Smith and James McCune Smith) slipped into an obscurity that itself obscured what they had accomplished.

Together these men also highlight the dynamic interactions between race, religion, class, and gender among moral and social reformers. Beginning in 1933, when the historian Gilbert Barnes published his pathbreaking book on the religious roots of the abolition crusade, scholarship on antebellum reform has evolved from an emphasis on religion and reform to one on religion and class.[4] The current emphasis on gender and race remains limited, for it downplays the diverse aspects of identity and personal behavior. Among these four men, religious belief was the single most important facet of their identities; it was the principal factor that allowed them to befriend and trust one another. Their understanding of God was inseparable from their understanding of themselves, their shared vision of America, and their ability to break down social barriers. The trend in recent scholarship has been to downplay questions of faith, and instead to question why racism and inequalities existed. But beliefs in freedom, equality, democracy, and the very idea that slavery was a sin were still relatively new concepts in the nineteenth century. These men's alliance shows how and why some blacks and whites were able to work together in an effort to overcome these barriers.

As historical actors, Gerrit Smith and James McCune Smith have been downplayed or ignored, even though in their own time they were considered preeminent men. Contemporaries hailed Gerrit Smith as a world-renowned philanthropist and a central figure in reform, but he has received little attention since. Only two full-scale biographies of Smith exist: one was published in 1878, four years after his death, by his friend Octavius Brooks Frothingham; the other, which appeared in 1939, was by Ralph Volney Harlow, who treated his reform efforts as misguided at best and pathological at worst. Yet Smith's papers represent one of the richest collections on nineteenth-century reform, and they are also well indexed and organized. After researching Smith and talking with other historians and critics, I concluded that one reason he has been neglected is that his handwriting appears at first to be illegible—it almost brought tears to my eyes when I tried to read it. Fortunately, I was able to read Smith on microfilm, which allowed me to enlarge his writing by a factor of twenty or more, make copies, and compare words until I had mastered his hand.

The absence of James McCune Smith in the historiographic and critical literature is even more striking. He was a brilliant scholar, writer, and critic, as well as a first-rate physician. In 1882 the black leader Alexander Crummell called him "the most learned Negro of his day," and Frederick Douglass considered him the most important black influence in his life (much as he considered Gerrit Smith the most important white one). Douglass was probably correct when, in 1859, he publicly stated: "No man in this country more thoroughly understands the whole struggle between freedom and slavery, than does Dr. Smith, and his heart is as broad as his understanding."[5] As a prose stylist and original thinker, McCune Smith ranks, at his best, alongside such canonical figures as Emerson and Thoreau. His essays are sophisticated and elegant, his interpretations of American culture are way ahead of his time, and his experimental style and use of dialect anticipate some of the Harlem Renaissance writers of the 1920s. Yet McCune Smith has been completely ignored by literary critics; and aside from one article on him, he has remained absent from the historical record.[6]

Although Frederick Douglass and John Brown have been analyzed at length, important aspects of their characters have been inadequately addressed. No one has emphasized the significance of Gerrit Smith, McCune Smith, and Brown in the development of Douglass' reform work. As a result, scholars have been reluctant to point out the militant and violent nature of his abolitionism in the 1850s.[7] Additionally, historians and especially literary critics have tended to downplay Douglass' millennialist view of America and his self-conception as a prophet, thus ignoring the important links between his personal religious beliefs and his quest to transform his country.[8]

John Brown has typically been described as a thoroughgoing Puritan and Calvinist whose religious views never changed, and he is almost everywhere seen as having no interest in political action. Yet his religion and politics were far more dynamic than scholars have acknowledged, and they shed enormous light on who Brown was in the context of his society. Brown deviated from Puritan and Calvinist theology during the 1850s. He embraced sacred self-sovereignty, harbored perfectionist visions, and looked forward to a heaven on Earth and the end of all sin. Moreover, Brown's reform work in the 1850s was thoroughly political. He played a central role in the formation of the Radical Abolition party and in the development of his three comrades' militancy. Indeed, Brown's participation in the Radical Abolition party helped shape the course of American history. By miscasting Brown as an orthodox Puritan and nonpolitical militant, most scholars have not viewed Brown as he saw himself—as someone who identified so closely with blacks that he chose to live among them and was willing to sacrifice his life for their cause. In other words, they tend to see Brown simply as a white man, and do not take into account his ability to blur racial categories.[9]

Focusing on these men's interracial alliance also sheds light on the origins of a major shift in cultural and intellectual history—one that moved beyond an understanding of "character" as fixed and unchanging, based primarily on heredity and social status, toward a highly subjective notion of the self in a state of continuous flux. At the heart of this shift was an effort to reintegrate cultural dichotomies that had long been present in Western culture—those of black and white, body and soul, sacred and profane, ideal and real, civilization and savagery, and masculine and feminine. The idea of "whiteness" as a sign of superiority and as a justification for racial oppression depended in part on the belief in "character" as static and fixed. The gradual dismantling of these dichotomies relates directly to my characters' alliances and shared visions of America, their radical and ultimately revolutionary means to reform, and the corresponding shifts in their self-conceptions.

The Radical Abolitionist
Call to Arms

For heart of man though mainly right,
Hides many things from mortal sight
Which seldom ever come to light
Except upon compulsion.

— FREDERICK DOUGLASS, "WHAT AM I TO YOU?"

To make a good likeness you must have heart and mind working together. But the heart comes first.

— BARRY UNSWORTH, *SACRED HUNGER* (1992)

It was a fateful convention that brought them together at Syracuse for three days beginning June 26, 1855. The inaugural convention of Radical Abolitionists has been largely forgotten in American history, and the party it launched won few votes and never elected a candidate to office. In fact the party itself lasted only five years and never polled more than a few thousand votes in a single election.[1] But the convention that gave birth to the Radical Abolition party has deep cultural relevance: it marked an unprecedented moment of interracial unity and collapsing of racial brriers. It is the only recorded moment at which Gerrit Smith, James McCune Smith, Frederick Douglass, and John Brown were all in the same place. Despite their close friendship, which began in the late 1840s, they lived in different parts of New York State and had few opportunities to be together. The convention gave tangible shape to their goals for ending slavery, their hopes for their country, and the means for realizing their dreams of a new world. They arrived with high expectations, and left feeling elated by what had transpired. But the convention also marked the crossing of a Rubicon, for the party's platform specifically affirmed violence as a way to end slavery and oppression. The embrace of violence would eventually destroy the four men's alliance.

One week after the convention and a few hundred miles away, another event inaugurated, in an entirely different form, a remarkably similar vision of America. On July 4, 1855, in New York City, Walt Whitman self-published his first edition of *Leaves of Grass*. His revolutionary poem dissolved the boundaries between black and white, rich and poor, sacred and profane, prose and poetry, polite language and slang. In their articulation of a new age, Whitman and the Radical Abolitionists stood apart from almost all their peers. Very few people at the time acknowledged the significance of their work. Yet these two visions, the one political and the other poetic, represent remarkable examples of faith in the possibility of individual and national liberation.

❧ John Brown almost missed the Syracuse convention. Of the four men he had the farthest to travel, some one hundred fifty miles as the crow flies from his home in North Elba, near Lake Placid in the Adirondacks. The actual trip was much longer, for he had to wind his way around "wild summits" by horse and wagon and on foot. The heavens opened with rain, and by the time he reached the soft rolling hills of Onondaga, Madison, and Oneida Counties, the roads felt like "summer butter." He reached the city hall at Syracuse, where the convention was being held, late on the first day, having missed the opening remarks.[2]

On the third day he thanked God for the gift of the convention. It had not only given him the chance to discuss with Gerrit Smith, McCune Smith, and Douglass his recent decision to join five of his sons in Kansas; it had also convinced him that he had made the right decision. He wrote to his wife and family that it "has been one of the most interesting meetings I ever attended in my life." He had received "a most warm reception from all" and "made a great addition to the number of warm-hearted and honest friends." Almost everyone at Syracuse had heartily approved his intentions to go to Kansas and fight for freedom there. The meeting seemed to confirm his faith that God spoke directly to him and guided his actions.[3]

James McCune Smith was no less elated about the convention. He had traveled by train from his home in New York City and arrived the day before it began. His role in organizing the new party was in many respects the most visible and important. He had been asked to chair the convention, and at the close, on a motion from Gerrit Smith, the few hundred men and women attending passed a unanimous resolution of thanks for the "ability, urbanity, and impartiality" with which he had presided over it. It was the first time in American history that a black man chaired a national political convention, and in the eyes of the participants, McCune Smith's role symbolized the great strides being made in race relations.[4] Following the resolution of thanks, McCune Smith declared to the assembly that the convention had fulfilled his "ideal of a glorious enterprise" and the noble yearnings of the "human heart." He felt sure that the party would "advance higher and higher, until all the soil [in the country] shall be consecrated to human freedom." He compared himself and the other Radical Abolitionists to the biracial group of wise men who discovered the Christ child in the manger after following the star westward to Bethlehem. He likened the convention's gospel of freedom and equality to Christ's proclamation of liberty to all captives: "We shall all go hence to proclaim the gospel of liberty—for it is good news, glad tidings of great joy, that we have to tell." Likewise the convention "inaugurate[d] a great movement," proclaiming liberty across the land. "The results thus far, and the promise now before us, fully justify the large hopes of those who looked forward to this gathering." He concluded his remarks, and the convention itself, "amid the most rapturous applause."[5]

Frederick Douglass characterized the Syracuse meeting in similarly lofty terms. He had traveled about eighty miles to Syracuse from his home in Rochester, and in the newspaper that bore his name he characterized the convention as a glorious and grand gathering of the friends of freedom. The men and women attending honored themselves and their new party in thought, word, and deed, he noted. He praised Gerrit Smith's "iron-linked logic" in defining the Constitution as an antislavery document. He called John Brown an "active and self-sacrificing abolitionist." And he urged the people of the country to take special note of McCune Smith's role as chair of the convention. From now on blacks could proudly cite the example of James McCune Smith to refute the "absurd" but widespread belief of their "innate mental inferiority."[6]

For Gerrit Smith, who lived at nearby Peterboro in Madison County, the Syracuse convention satisfied his highest expectations. He was the principal organizer of the event, and he had chosen Syracuse, one of the foremost antislavery cities in the country, partly as a way to honor local abolitionists for their efforts in defending black freedom there. The convention was well attended not only by these locals but by prominent antislavery radicals representing ten states and Canada. It was covered by well-known reform newspapers, from the *New-York Tribune*, *The Liberator*, and the *National Anti-Slavery Standard*, to *Frederick Douglass' Paper*. As a result of this support and coverage, Smith was "in one of his happiest moods," Douglass noted. His euphoria seemed to permeate the meeting. The party's new paper, appropriately called the *Radical Abolitionist*, summarized the general feeling among the few hundred participants by asserting in its first issue that the meeting had surpassed all other abolition conventions. It was "a noble gathering," "spirited, harmonious, thorough, deliberative, determined. It was a time for discussion and action. No *display* speeches—everything said was to some specific point, some definite end."[7]

Not even McCune Smith's biblical analogy could be characterized as showy rhetoric. He and Gerrit Smith often used the term "Bible Politics" to characterize their belief that the government of God and earthly states should be one and the same. They described their platform as "the Jubilee doctrine" to evoke the advent of freedom, and regarded its dissemination "as of more importance than the diffusion of the principle of science" for ending slavery, as McCune Smith told Gerrit Smith in a letter. Not that they ignored science. McCune Smith published numerous articles that drew on his knowledge of medicine and physiology to attack racist doctrines, and Douglass and Gerrit Smith relied on McCune Smith's evidence to formulate their own attacks against antiblack prejudice. But Bible politics was their main weapon against these evils. Their faith in a heaven on Earth, governed by Bible politics, superseded their belief in the principles of science.[8]

The party platform reflected the participants' belief in the millennium and in their roles as prophets. "The same Divine Providence that watched over the anti-slavery cause from the beginning" and "led it out of obscurity into the daylight of national discussion" was "still ruling in the midst of its enemies," Radical Abolitionists declared. From Christ's sepulcher came "pentecostal visitations" (messages from God) to hearten "desponding disciples." Radical Abolitionists saw themselves as God's disciples, receiving His instructions to disseminate Bible politics and to combat all sin. But they also recognized that their success depended, "under God," upon themselves. Their new party fused God's will and their own, like interlocking parts in a vast design. And they followed Christ's example in their willingness to sacrifice themselves for their cause.[9]

Although Gerrit Smith was the main organizer of the new party, Douglass and McCune Smith also played key roles. Both served as delegates, along with Gerrit Smith and five other men. They had discussed the party's doctrine before arriving at Syracuse, and signed the initial "call" for the convention. Douglass had urged Gerrit Smith to write it: "Let us have a strong call," he wrote his friend in March 1855, elated over the prospect of the new party. "No other man must write the call . . . while *Gerrit Smith* lives and is able to wield a pen." Douglass reprinted the call numerous times in his newspaper and besought all truehearted abolitionists to attend:

> We hope to witness a gathering of such men as the solemnity of the hour, and the exigencies of our case, demand. We want men at this crisis who cannot be frightened from the advocacy of our *"radical"* doctrines, because of their unpopularity . . . Let us not, then, grow weary, but believing that "whatever is RIGHT, IS PRACTICABLE," go forth with renewed determination to conquer, though we die in the conflict.[10]

The high point of their excitement occurred on the third and final day. The first two days focused on the discussion and approval of three documents that had already been written: the "Declaration of Sentiments" stipulated that the duty of civil government was to protect human rights and fulfill the government of God; an "Exposition" defined the Constitution as an antislavery document; and a long "Address" outlined the party's primary objective of immediate emancipation. On the third day, however, Radical Abolitionists began to practice what they preached, and in doing so made the implications of their methods for fighting slavery vividly clear.[11]

It started when Gerrit Smith read two letters from John Brown's sons in Kansas. The Kansas territory had recently become a battleground in the national debate over slavery, as a result of the Kansas-Nebraska Act of 1854, which opened the territories of Kansas and Nebraska to slavery if voters there approved it. The letters from Brown's sons described "hundreds and thousands of the meanest and most desperate of men, armed to the teeth with Revolvers, Bowie Knives, Rifles & Cannon," thoroughly organized, and in the pay of slaveholders. Against these stood the friends of freedom, *"not one fourth of them half armed"* and lacking any *"Military Organization."* Brown's sons urged all able-bodied antislavery men to *"immediately"* and *"thoroughly arm* and *organize themselves* in *military companies."* They desperately needed revolvers, rifles, and bowie knives to defend themselves: "We need them more than we do bread," Brown's sons wrote. "Would not Gerrit Smith or someone furnish the money and loan it to us for one, two, or three years . . . until we can raise enough to refund it from the *Free* soil of Kansas?" Gerrit Smith read the letters "with such effect," John Brown noted, "as to draw tears from numerous eyes in the great collection of people present."[12]

Smith's moving speech was followed by one from John Brown, who was far more direct in his call for action. He quoted Hebrews 9.22, reminding his listeners that "without the shedding of blood there is no remission of sin." He then appealed for money and munitions to take with him to Kansas, and his speech galvanized the audience. A handful of people opposed his violent means, but only one delegate—Lewis Tappan—dissented. The vast majority of members agreed that armed aggression was "the only course left to the friends of freedom in Kansas," prompting Frederick Douglass to ask for contributions. "A collection was taken up . . . with much spirit," Douglass recalled, because Brown "spoke for himself; and when he spoke, men believed in the man." Brown received over sixty dollars, twenty from Gerrit Smith.[13]

There are conflicting reports about what happened next. According to *The Liberator*, Radical Abolitionists gave Brown "pistols" along with money. The *National Anti-Slavery Standard* also implied that weapons were among "the objects presented." Richard J. Hinton, a comrade of Brown in Kansas, wrote that Gerrit Smith "presented John Brown with seven muskets and bayonets, seven voltaic repeating pistols, and seven short broadswords," in addition to the sixty dollars that Brown received, but Hinton said the exchanges occurred "the next day," which would have been the day after the convention officially ended. In any case, it seems likely that Radical Abolitionists gave Brown at least some arms as well as money to take with him to Kansas.[14]

❧ Who were these Radical Abolitionists, especially the four men who played such prominent roles at Syracuse? How were they able to forge such alliances and close bonds of friendship despite the social gulfs separating them, and to articulate a shared vision of America? How and why were Gerrit Smith and John Brown able to overcome prevailing social norms and customs, identify themselves as black men, and foster an interracial community within the Radical Abolition party and in their respective villages of Peterboro and North Elba, New York? Similarly, how and why were Frederick Douglass and James McCune Smith able to collaborate with and trust Gerrit Smith and John Brown, and maintain their faith in America when many of their peers, owing to the persistence of slavery and racial oppression, had given up hope and embraced colonization and black nationalism as solutions to racial oppression? These important and complex questions serve as an analytical focal point throughout the following pages. For the present, a summary of principles and key themes offers a way to begin to answer these questions and to understand these men, as well as their successes and failures in overcoming such vast social barriers.

Appreciating the alliance and friendship of these four men requires some knowledge of their differences. Gerrit Smith came from one of the wealthiest families in the country, and as a young man established himself as a land baron and patriarch before making abolitionism his primary vocation. John Brown grew up as an artisan; he started his career as a tanner and, like many of his artisanal peers in antebellum America, held many different jobs. James McCune Smith, the son of a slave and self-emancipated bondwoman, also began his career as an artisan; he was a blacksmith, and owed his liberty to the Emancipation Act of the state of New York, which officially freed its remaining slaves on July 4, 1827. Frederick Douglass was born and bred as a slave. The ranks into which they were born spanned the social spectrum. But a number of factors surrounding the panic of 1837 and subsequent depression coincided with profound changes in their social status and self-conceptions. The panic forced John Brown into bankruptcy and

Gerrit Smith temporarily to the brink of it. While Smith and Brown descended in status, McCune Smith and Douglass ascended. McCune Smith returned to New York City in 1837, after receiving his B.A., M.A., and M.D. degrees from the University of Glasgow, and established himself as the first professionally trained black physician in the United States. Douglass escaped slavery in 1838, moved to Massachusetts to work as a free artisan, and changed his name from Frederick Bailey to Frederick Douglass. Their transformations highlight the unreliable nature of social rank, status, and hierarchy, precipitating a profound shift in the source of their values: they turned inward, away from material conditions and social conventions, and relied instead on their spiritual instincts and passions of the heart.

The 1855 Syracuse convention and the 1850s in general marked the high point of their alliance. It was during this decade that they lived in New York, established the Radical Abolition party, and corresponded more frequently than ever before. They became revolutionaries and self-described "outlaws" who sought to overturn customs that elevated whites above blacks. Douglass and McCune Smith understood that although Gerrit Smith and John Brown were white, they were "in sympathy" colored men. Smith and Brown sought to define themselves according to the standards of their black friends, which were based on moral excellence and spiritual uplift rather than on skin color and the barriers imposed by race. Smith continually sought to "make myself a colored man," as he put it, and so did John Brown. Their efforts to break down racial barriers did not go unnoticed in the black community. In 1846 the editor of the *Ram's Horn*, a black abolitionist newspaper in New York City, praised and "flattered" Smith by declaring: "Gerrit Smith is a colored man!" The black writer Martin Delany considered him one of only two white abolitionists he had ever met who habitually consulted blacks and sought out their opinions and perspectives. Henry Highland Garnet, another friend and black radical, lived with Gerrit Smith briefly in 1848 while teaching near Smith's home in Peterboro, and concluded: "There are yet two places where slaveholders cannot live—Heaven and Peterboro." McCune Smith and Douglass echoed these sentiments, and frequently visited Smith at Peterboro.[15]

The term "passionate outsiders" partly explains the convergence of these men's black and white identities. They were passionate in their desire to reform America, and they were outsiders with regard to both their alienated status in society and the source of their values. They stood totally apart from the status quo, whether through their own volition (as in Gerrit Smith's case) or by virtue of their skin color. Perhaps most important, they defined *themselves* as outsiders. But in fact they were both outsiders and insiders. They acquired insider status through their writings, speeches, and the wealth and generosity of Gerrit Smith. At Syracuse, for instance, they saw themselves as an interracial community of outsiders. But the convention also represented a source of self-empowerment, similar to the ways in which other minority reform groups such as Spiritualists, Mormons, and Christian Scientists used institutional structures to achieve both insider and outsider status.[16]

Gerrit Smith, McCune Smith, Douglass, and Brown relied heavily on "sacred self-sovereignty." For them, the kingdom of God was not some place above or beyond this world, as it was for mainstream Christian groups. God resided within them and theoretically within all people; He was "immanent or indwelling," allowing them to overcome the burden of original sin and to reposition the fundamental locus of value in spiritual passions and emotions rather than in worldly authority and social conventions. They reinterpreted the Golden Rule, as stated in Luke 6:31 and Hebrews 13:3, as a requirement for empathy, and this empathic awareness was central to their reform efforts. By embracing sacred self-sovereignty, they anticipated or followed the religious worldviews of such radicals as William Lloyd Garrison, John Humphrey Noyes, Ralph Waldo Emerson, and Walt Whitman. Both Spiritualists and Garrison's Non-Resistance Society (which owed its founding in part to Noyes's influence) used "self-sovereignty" to denote a state of individual autonomy that was God's intention for every person. Emerson captured something of the idea of sacred self-sovereignty in his 1854 speech "The Fugitive Slave Law": "Divine sentiments," he said, "are always soliciting us, are breathed into us from on high and are a counterbalance to an universe of suffering and crime"; thus, "self-reliance, the height and perfection of man, is reliance on God." Whitman expressed a similar sentiment a year later in his first edition of *Leaves of Grass*: "Divine am I inside and out, and I make holy whatever I touch or am touched from." "In the faces of men and women I see God, and in my own face in the glass." But whereas Garrison and others questioned or condemned the Bible and the Constitution, the Radical Abolitionists regarded them as sacred texts. As Gerrit Smith stated in Douglass' newspaper, a political party should be "emphatically a religious party," with "the Bible" as "its textbook" and "its supreme Constitution."[17]

In their conception of God, Radical Abolitionists resembled the Quaker pioneer abolitionists, as did Emerson and Whitman, who openly acknowledged their kinship with Quakers.[18] Like Quakers, Radical Abolitionists sought deliverance from the depravity of original sin, and they associated moral evil with the institutions of the external world rather than with themselves. Gerrit Smith could not affirm sacred self-sovereignty until he had become "born again" as a sacred being, which brought "membership into the family of Jesus on earth" and the freedom to combat all sin. "To believe in Christ is to be imbued with his spirit," he said, and he acknowledged that his conception of God was similar to "the beautiful Quaker fancy of the 'inner light.'"[19]

There were two key differences between early Quakers, who pioneered the abolition movement during the eighteenth century, and the Radical Abolitionists, Whitman, and Emerson. First, John Woolman and other Quakers felt a profound sense of humility before God that Radical Abolitionists, Emerson, and Whitman lacked. Woolman understood the dangers of self-deification and the depravity that infected human nature, exemplified for him in slaveholding. By contrast, Radical Abolitionists—along with Emerson and Whitman—freed themselves from the fear of an expanding ego. Second, whereas Quakers sought a compromise between their impulse to perfection and their imperfect world, Radical Abolitionists refused to countenance evil. They saw themselves as prophets ushering in a new age. The immediate abolition of every sin was their most passionate desire, and they went to great lengths to effect it. They were profoundly millennialist in their vision of progress, and sought to transcend existing social barriers by abandoning a linear understanding of time and history.

Gerrit Smith, McCune Smith, Frederick Douglass, and John Brown frequently used the tropes of "head" and "heart" to define their status as passionate outsiders. There was a clear distinction between these two realms. The head adhered to reason, logic, law, and authority. The heart was concerned with emotions and spiritual passions; it was the driving force behind their reform efforts. Sacred self-sovereignty resided in the heart. But since their spiritual impulses (and their hearts) were also part of their bodies and the world, they sought to align the head with the heart. Through this delicate balance they could—in theory at least—control the destructive passions of the heart while resisting the oppression of white laws and customs. In practice, however, as the gap between the current reality and their perfectionist visions continued to widen, they abandoned the claims of the head—of existing laws and external restraints—and embraced violent and revolutionary methods to accommodate the passions of the heart. Increasingly, violence became the bridge connecting their perfectionist vision of America with the present, sinful reality.[20]

Their emphasis on the passions of the heart coincided with their efforts to collapse and at times to invert traditional color symbolism. For example, in Gerrit Smith's "Address to the Slaves," a speech that was widely lauded and remembered by blacks, he encouraged slaves to engage in what he admirably called the "black-hearted" measures of "running away" and of "yielding to necessity" by stealing. Frederick Douglass called slave songs "heart songs" that expressed "the finest feelings of human nature." James McCune Smith referred to the religion of blacks as "heart worship," adding that "we [blacks] bow the knee to God alone." In his view, truehearted white abolitionists were those who had achieved a "new birth," had become "awakened to a sense of the sin and shame wherewith Slavery curses the land," and were thus able to view the world as though they were themselves black. "The twain ought to be, but are not, one flesh." For this biracial quartet, the true spiritual heart was a black heart that shared a humanity with all people and lacked the airs of superiority of a white heart.[21]

The "black hearts" of these men thus signify their success at overcoming racial barriers. But the term also carries an ironic and ambivalent meaning that points to the limits of their achievement—particularly their use of violence to effect their sacred society. This ironic connotation parallels their inability to wholly overturn color symbolism, overcome racism, and collapse the meanings of black and white. While Douglass and McCune Smith generally embraced "composite" identities and the "co-mingling" of races, Gerrit Smith and Brown sometimes defined equality in terms of "becoming" black, but without entirely affirming composite identities and an empathic awareness. Douglass and McCune Smith suffered from a similar kind of "dual consciousness"; at times they lapsed into mainstream views and were unable to overturn color symbolism. One month after the Syracuse convention, for instance, Douglass published an article called "The Doom of the Black Power," in which he invoked "black power" to define the evil designs of the men who propagated slavery: "We are conscious that there is a black side to our picture" of society; and it was neither pretty nor laudable. For Douglass, "black power" was synonymous with the "Slave Power." Douglass urged his readers to pursue this "black power" unto death: "Use the proper means, fight with the right weapons, let there be no cessation of the warfare . . . and we shall yet witness the *end of the Black Power in America.*"[22] By using violence to vanquish "the black power," Douglass and his comrades came to resemble their enemies in both method and means, for violence was the very bolt on which the institution of slavery hung. Their use of violence, though temporarily helping to bridge racial divides, ultimately brought a deeper and more lasting form of racism and racial oppression.

In many respects Gerrit Smith, McCune Smith, Douglass, and Brown led the way in the movement to collapse the evangelical Christian cosmos in antebellum America. The historian Robert Abzug has described how, over the first half of the nineteenth century, reform evolved from attacks on drinking and tobacco to rethinking the fundamental theological and social foundations of Western culture. By the 1840s abolitionists and women's-rights reformers were at the center of an effort to literally "rebuild the structure of Heaven and Earth," to fuse the sacred and profane, and to seek "a broad sacralization of the world." The revolutionary ethos these four men shared was rooted in their attempts to dismantle the various cultural dichotomies that posed obstacles to the new age. By attacking the great Aristotelian belief that some men were born to rule and others to serve and do the basic work of society, they were led to question other dichotomies—as opposed to more conservative abolitionists who legitimated the status quo by separating slavery from other institutions.[23]

These four men differed from William Lloyd Garrison, John Humphrey Noyes, and other radicals by encompassing *all* of America in their vision of a sacred, sin-free, and pluralist society, as well as by their willingness to use violence to effect it. Garrison, Noyes, and other radicals limited their vision of a sacred realm to one aspect of society—Noyes's Oneida community, for example, or Garrison's Non-

Resistance Society, and his subsequent notion of "disunion," which separated the sacred from the profane portions of the country. By imposing such limits, they evaded efforts to create an interracial and pluralist society. The relatively few blacks who were part of their societies were relegated to subordinate positions and subject to the white leaders' paternalism. Radical Abolitionists were unique in conceiving of the entire country and the Constitution as sacred. As citizens of this sacred society, they were willing to go to war against their enemies in order to protect it and preserve their Bible politics. Contemporaries called them "mad," but what they were doing in their "madness" was to follow their hearts and explore the possibilities of equality.

❧ On May 28, 1856, almost a year after their inaugural meeting, Radical Abolitionists returned to Syracuse for their National Nominating Convention. Approximately two hundred people attended, including "five ladies arrayed in bloomer costume," according to the *New York Herald*. Gerrit Smith, McCune Smith, and Douglass again served as delegates to the convention and signed the "call" publicizing it.[24] Gerrit Smith and Douglass were among those nominated for office— Smith as the party's presidential candidate, and Douglass as his running mate. Smith confessed that he "would get down upon [his] knees" for the office, because he believed that "nothing short of the election of an abolition President and Congress can save this guilty nation." At the same time, however, he was uncomfortable in the role of a politician, and always felt the sting of "ridicule and malignity" that he suffered for his unpopular beliefs. Consequently, although the party chose him as its presidential candidate, he had to be persuaded to accept the nomination. Frederick Douglass' nomination for vice president did not carry, in part because both Smith and Douglass were New Yorkers; seeking greater geographic diversity, the delegates elected Samuel McFarland of Pennsylvania as Smith's running mate.[25]

The convention was again quite spirited, for six days earlier, Preston Brooks, a young congressman from South Carolina, had bludgeoned Charles Sumner of Massachusetts almost to death in the Senate chamber. Sumner, an outspoken abolitionist, was working at his desk after the Senate adjourned on May 22, when Brooks entered the chamber and began to beat him on the head "as hard as he could" with a gold-headed guttapercha walking stick. Sumner, blinded by blood and trapped at a desk that was bolted to the floor, valiantly struggled to rise, and ripped the desk from the floor before collapsing. Brooks's heavy cane snapped in two during the assault, and people throughout the South were now sending him new canes as congratulatory trophies. Brooks said he had merely intended to "whip" Sumner—the appropriate method for punishing a social inferior, according to the code of Southern gentlemen. He also felt half inclined to "have the throats of every Abolitionist cut." The provocation for this attack was Sumner's "Crime against Kansas" speech on May 19, in which Sumner had accused the South of demanding that Kansas enter the Union as a slave state, of encouraging Missouri thugs to invade Kansas, and of forcing upon the North the Kansas-Nebraska Act of 1854, which repealed the Missouri Compromise and opened northern territories to slavery. Sumner had essentially blamed the South for raping and plundering the virgin territory of Kansas.[26]

Against this background, the nominations of Radical Abolitionists were a mere formality, and most of the discussion focused on how to subdue the Slave Power—a cadre of slaveholders who, in the minds of Radical Abolitionists and many other Northerners, sought to extend slavery throughout the country. In addition to the attack on Sumner, proslavery forces in Kansas had recently burned and pillaged the free-soil settlement of Lawrence. One Radical Abolitionist—James Caleb Jackson, a close friend of Gerrit Smith—characterized the situation in Kansas as one "of *revolution!*" Others called for immediate retaliation: "Slaveholders must be met at the point of the bayonet." There was no other way of reaching them. Frederick Douglass forcefully summarized the prevailing mood of his party: liberty "must either cut the throat of slavery or slavery would cut the throat of liberty," he declared, prompting vigorous applause from the audience.[27]

These were precisely the principles on which John Brown had acted four days earlier at the proslavery settlement of Pottawatomie, Kansas, though Radical Abolitionists did not know it at the time. On the night of May 24, Brown and a group of seven men cut the throats of five unarmed proslavery settlers and hacked them to death with broadswords.[28] Brown's actions need to be understood within the context of the Radical Abolition party and its doctrines. Brown is often described as unique among abolitionists, the *ne plus ultra* of fanatics, but he is seldom associated with political abolitionism. Yet he aligned himself closely with Gerrit Smith, McCune Smith, and Douglass, attended other political conventions with them, and justified his actions under God and the Radical Abolitionist message that whatever was right was practicable, to paraphrase Douglass.[29]

Brown and his comrades were not far removed from Preston Brooks and the thousands of Southerners who sent him canes of congratulation: both sides advocated violent means for realizing wholly different visions of their country. But the two men's uses of violence differed in two ways. First, Brooks used violence to defend his (and the South's) honor, while Brown used violence to defend his (and Radical Abolitionists') vision of social equality. Second, Sumner had challenged and provoked Brooks with his speech; Brown's victims had done nothing *directly* to provoke or challenge Brown and his men.[30]

❧ To understand how Radical Abolitionists legally and morally justified their use of violence, it is necessary to look more closely at the party's origins, influences, and doctrines. Radical Abolitionists identified themselves with their nation's forefathers. They argued for the immediate removal of slavery from the territories and the states according to their understanding of the Declaration of Independence, the Constitution, and the powers vested in them as Americans. The very name of their party (known as both the Radical Abolition party and the Radical Political Abolition party) fitted their intentions and self-descriptions. They advocated a "radical change" in government by tracing the evil of slavery to its constitutional origin, rooting it out, and restoring to America the "original ideas of Civil Government and Civil Law," which were coextensive with God's government and law. The nation's forefathers never attempted "such an absurdity" as to form a government "to establish justice," "insure domestic tranquillity," and "secure the blessings of liberty"—as stated in the Preamble of the Constitution—without the powers to suppress and abolish slaveholding. The signers of the Declaration of Independence had no intention of keeping a portion of the population enslaved while declaring it "self-evident that all men are created equal." Nor did the Founders seek to preserve the "unparalleled wrongs" of slavery while publicly proclaiming the "inalienable rights" of life, liberty, and the pursuit of happiness.

By seeking an immediate end to slavery and interpreting the Constitution as an antislavery document, Radical Abolitionists believed that they were affirming both the *"righteous language"* of the Constitution and the historical objectives of the nation's Founders.[31]

Radical Abolitionists distinguished themselves from all other political parties and abolition societies. They were the only reform organization to advocate immediate abolition through political action. At the 1855 convention they noted that Democrats, Know-Nothings, and Whigs were made up of slaveholders as well as nonslaveholders, and thus refused to attack slavery. They acknowledged that the Free-Soil party (which merged into the Republican party) was an antislavery party seeking the nonextension of slavery and its eventual demise. Yet Free-Soilers denied the right of the federal government to touch slavery in the states; and they supported the Fugitive Slave Act of 1850, which called on state and local governments to aid slaveholders in their efforts to return fugitives to bondage. William Lloyd Garrison's American Anti-Slavery Society sought an immediate end to slavery, but it wielded no political power, focusing exclusively on moral persuasion. Moreover, the doctrine of disunion threatened "to separate the free states from the slave states, and to leave the slave states . . . at perfect liberty to continue their oppression and torture of the black man." Radical Abolitionists insisted that they alone were fit "to wield the political power of the nation for the overthrow . . . of slavery." Garrisonians condemned the Constitution as "a covenant with death" and "an agreement with hell" because they thought it sanctioned slavery. Indeed Garrison had gone so far as to burn the document publicly on Independence Day 1854. By contrast, Radical Abolitionists believed that there was no legal justification for slavery.[32]

Radical Abolitionists stood apart from other antislavery radicals who advocated violence by linking their actions and conceptions of America directly to their political party. New England radicals such as Thomas Wentworth Higginson, Theodore Parker, Franklin Sanborn, Samuel Gridley Howe, and George Luther Stearns were not averse to violent means, and they supported and funded John Brown's raid on Harpers Ferry. But they viewed antislavery violence as taking place outside the realm of politics, and did not define their country and government in such millennialist and pluralist terms. Radical Abolitionists conceived of their country as a heaven on Earth within their very platform, and their party spelled out, through its advocacy of violence, the means for ushering in Christ's advent and achieving their country.[33]

The Radical Abolition party grew out of the Liberty and National Liberty parties. The Liberty party was organized in 1840 after some abolitionists, believing in the validity of political action, defected from Garrison's Anti-Slavery Society and its nonresistance and nonvoting policies. The Liberty party soon splintered into two groups: a conservative wing seeking wide appeal, which evolved into the Free-Soil party in 1848; and the more radical wing advocating the immediate abolition of all sin, which became the National Liberty party in 1848 (after briefly calling itself the National Liberty League) and the Radical Abolition party in 1855. Gerrit Smith was one of the principal founders of all three parties: he gave the Liberty party its name; was instrumental in forming the National Liberty League, National Liberty party, and Radical Abolition party; and ran for president three times—in 1848 as the National Liberty party candidate, and in 1856 and 1860 under the Radical Abolitionist banner.[34]

Radical Abolitionists continued to call themselves "Liberty men," and in many respects the party resembled the National Liberty party and the more radical wing of the Liberty party. Radical Abolitionists (and to a lesser extent the National Liberty party) treated blacks with a far greater degree of equality and respect than did any other abolitionist organization. By the 1850s black leaders overwhelmingly embraced the efficacy of political action. James McCune Smith's appointment as chair of the 1855 Syracuse convention and Douglass' consideration for vice president the following year were only two instances of the party's efforts to act on its principles and to set an example for the rest of the country. The National Liberty party considered running Frederick Douglass for Congress in 1854, and in 1855 it nominated him for secretary of state of New York, thus making him the first black man to be nominated for a political office. Two years later Radical Abolitionists nominated McCune Smith for the same post. These were revolutionary advances in antebellum politics and race relations.[35]

Radical Abolitionists' espousal of equal rights was not limited to blacks. Although they were primarily concerned with the immediate end to slavery, they followed the National Liberty party in recognizing "the broadest principles of democracy," including the right of all individuals, "irrespective of sex, or color, or character," to vote and be citizens. In applying Bible politics to end all sin, they believed that no one was free unless everyone was: "The moral government of God . . . forbids us [from] securing permanently *our own* liberties" until "the liberties of each and all" were secured, delegates at the 1855 Syracuse convention declared. Personal sins had become political.[36]

Radical Abolitionists distinguished themselves from the National Liberty party primarily in their posture of aggression against the Slave Power. The distinction was one of degree rather than an abrupt departure from earlier principles. The National Liberty party had not entirely shunned bloodshed; it had declared in 1849 that "it may be better to resort to revolution than to submit to a government which compels its subjects to pay the debts of their ancestors."[37] But this equivocal statement ("it *may* be better") was as far as the party was willing to go. Radical Abolitionists went a step further, positioning themselves at the far edge of the radical continuum. Although they preferred peaceful means to end slavery, they affirmed armed aggression against the Slave Power as part of their belief in the Constitution as an antislavery document. In their minds, the Slave Power threatened to invade the free states and reduce most Northerners—white and black—to slaves. Not only the fate of blacks and slaves but "the security of NATIONAL liberty, of YOUR liberties and OUR OWN," were at stake.[38]

Radical Abolitionists reinterpreted the writings of the Founding Fathers—especially slaveholders—to justify their antislavery constitutionalism. At their inaugural convention they quoted James Madison, who had written in his famous *Federalist* No. 39 that it was *"essential"* for a republican government to be "derived from the great body of society, not from . . . *a favored class of it.*" They cited Thomas Jefferson as claiming: "The true foundation of republican government is the equal right of every citizen in his person and property," adding that Jefferson had referred to slaves as *"citizens."* They pointed out that Patrick Henry, at the Virginia Convention to ratify the Constitution, had declared that Congress had the "power to pronounce all slaves free." And they said that Virginia Governor Edmund Randolph had predicted an end to slavery should the Constitution be ratified, and had urged his fellow Virginians to honor their state by endorsing ratification. These were gross misstatements, however. Although in theory these slaveowners had considered slavery a sin, in practice they had sought to preserve it (at least during their lifetimes), and had argued that the

Constitution provided fundamental guarantees to the institution. Radical Abolitionists misquoted these slaveowners to accommodate their own, highly subjective view of the Constitution.[39]

John Quincy Adams represented the most important source for Radical Abolitionists' methods to end slavery. They reinterpreted Adams' writings to legally justify their platform of armed aggression. In 1836 Adams had first proposed that Congress, under its war powers, could emancipate slaves in one or more states: "From the instant your slaveholding states become the theatre of war, civil, servile, or foreign," he told Southerners, "from that instant the war powers of Congress extend to interference with the institution of slavery in every way by which it can be interfered with."[40] (He also argued that the president— as commander in chief of the military forces—could apply the war powers to end slavery.) Adams hated slavery and was courted by conservative Liberty men in 1844 to lead their party. But he was also a practical statesman who kept his distance from both political and Garrisonian abolitionists. He believed that the Constitution protected slavery in the states and in the District of Columbia, and according to his biographer Samuel Bemis he confined his antislavery agitation to "four fundamental freedoms of the Constitution: freedom of speech, freedom of petition for the redress of grievances, freedom of debate in Congress, freedom of the press." Until his death in 1848 Adams sought gradual rather than immediate emancipation through patient, diligent action within these parameters.[41]

Nevertheless, Radical Abolitionists latched onto Adams' interpretation of war powers, but with a twist: "John Quincy Adams affirmed the right of Congress to abolish slavery as a means of defense in time of war," they stated at Syracuse in 1855, but added that "until slavery is abolished, we are continually exposed to a state of war." Slavery itself represented a state of war, and slaves "necessarily" became enemies of "the nation that permits it." Congress therefore had the power and duty to "make peace with the slaves by restoring to them their rights." If the government shirked its duty to suppress the present rebellion among roughly four million slaves, it was the "highest obligation" of the people of the free states to abolish slavery, and thus preserve peace.[42]

The existing state of war proclaimed by Radical Abolitionists required armed resistance against the proslavery populace. At their inau-

gural convention they reminded their listeners that the Slave Power—
an "oligarchy" of a few hundred thousand slaveholders—threatened
the liberties of the remaining twenty-four million Americans. They
cited the case of a free white citizen who was seized by slaveholding
brigands in Missouri and *"sold at auction as a slave."* Although they
never abandoned moral suasion—the principle on which abolitionism
had originally been based—they insisted on coupling it with "efficient
action" to give it teeth. In light of the war then raging against blacks—
and by association against all lovers of liberty—they interpreted
"efficient action" to mean armed aggression. It is no wonder, then, that
John Brown "deeply stirred the hearts of the audience," as the convention minutes state, when he told them to combine moral suasion with
the practical measure of bloodshed. No wonder, also, that he received
money and munitions as well as prayers and pleas for godspeed to sustain him in Kansas. Brown explicitly defined slavery as a state of
war, and this definition is central to an understanding of his violent
actions.[43]

The 1855 Syracuse convention was only the first time opponents of
slavery acted on Adams' understanding of war powers. When Confederate troops fired on Fort Sumter, Charles Sumner, who had only recently recovered from Brooks' caning, remembered the advice of Adams, his former friend and mentor. He rushed to the White House to
tell Lincoln "that under the war power the right had come to him to
emancipate the slaves." Union generals John C. Frémont, David Hunter, and Benjamin Butler also tried to use the war-power theory in their
military campaigns. Congress drew on the same source to pass the
Confiscation Acts of 1861 and 1862, which authorized the Union army
to confiscate (and, in the case of the 1862 act, to emancipate) slaves
of disloyal masters. And Lincoln issued the Emancipation Proclamation by the power vested in him "as Commander-in-Chief of the Army
and Navy of the United States in time of actual armed rebellion against
authority and government of the United States, and as a fit and necessary war measure for suppressing said rebellion." Without realizing it,
Radical Abolitionists had established an important precedent.[44]

❧ Radical Abolitionists considered John Quincy Adams an important
forerunner to their own program for ending slavery. It was Adams,

more than any other statesman, who provided them with a way to connect their vision of America to the nation's founding. Both Adams and Radical Abolitionists articulated a sublime vision of America—a darkly romantic vision that embodied both the fulfillment of the nation's sacred ideals and the desolation that would accompany this transformation. But whereas Adams had viewed this vision with horror, Radical Abolitionists embraced it. Frederick Douglass and Gerrit Smith in particular were affected by Adams' antislavery labors and his views on slavery. Adams awakened in them (in very different ways) a new source of hope for fighting slavery that was ultimately connected to their sublime vision. His relationships with Douglass and Smith thus deserve an extended analysis.

In December 1831 a thirteen-year-old slave named Frederick Bailey who would later be known as Frederick Douglass chanced upon an article in the *Baltimore American* that reprinted a speech by John Quincy Adams. The former president was now serving as a congressman and had introduced in the House some petitions from Quakers, who were praying for the abolition of slavery and the slave trade in the District of Columbia (which abolitionists viewed as a stepping-stone to abolition in the states). Douglass had just recently learned how to read. He had often heard the word "abolitionist," and knew it was associated with "fear" as well as "rage" among slaveholders, but did not know its precise meaning. The dictionary did not help; it defined "abolition" as "the act of abolishing." But Adams' speech clarified the meaning of "abolition," gave Douglass "the incendiary information" he was looking for, and changed his life: "There was HOPE in those words," he exclaimed. Because of Adams' efforts, he and countless other slaves understood that they were not alone in their hatred of slavery. "Ever after that, when I heard the words, 'abolition,' or 'abolition movement' mentioned, I felt the matter one of personal concern." He now recognized that "God was angry with the white people because of their slaveholding wickedness," and that His "judgments were abroad in the land." "It was impossible for me not to hope much from the abolition movement, when I saw it supported by the Almighty, and armed with DEATH."[45] The implied object of death for Douglass was obviously slavery, but it was also slaveholders themselves, for he recounted the story in his 1855 autobiography, *My Bondage and My Freedom*, published two months after the 1855 Syracuse convention.[46]

Adams' antislavery efforts had a profound impact on Douglass' own emergence as an abolitionist. Indeed, in *My Bondage and My Freedom* Douglass mentions Adams' speech in the House before describing his own earlier religious conversion. Adams also served as a centerpiece of Douglass' first two recorded speeches. "I well remember getting possession of a speech by John Quincy Adams, made in Congress about slavery and freedom, and reading it to my fellow slaves," he told his Lynn, Massachusetts, audience in November 1841. "Oh! what joy and gladness it produced to know that so great, so good a man was pleading for us, and further, to know that there was a large and growing class of people in the north called abolitionists, who were moving for our freedom." Douglass felt a special bond with Adams throughout his life, even though he never met or corresponded with him. In 1859, by way of illustrating the progress of abolitionists, he asserted that fifteen years previously, "not a single member of Congress dared to stand up and announce himself an abolitionist." Yet he singled out Adams, calling him "the boldest man of all" for standing up for the right of petition.[47]

Gerrit Smith, who had campaigned for Adams' presidency in 1824 and 1828, began a fruitful correspondence with him in February 1837. Smith was forty years old at the time, and a recent convert to abolitionism.[48] Adams was still leading the campaign in the House of Representatives to rescind the "gag rules," a procedure that refused to acknowledge abolitionist petitions brought before the House. Smith submitted two petitions asking for the abolition of slavery in the District of Columbia. (They were among the 150 petitions signed by roughly twelve thousand foes of slavery that Adams had received that month.) "I have always esteemed you," Smith told Adams in his letter accompanying the petitions. "But now, since you have shown the pity of your heart for the enslaved poor—for the down-trodden millions, who are sharers of our common humanity . . . I not only esteem you, but love you."[49]

Adams replied that although he hated slavery, he disagreed with abolitionists' methods of agitation. "I long indulged the hope that the states of Maryland and Virginia, from which the District was taken, would set the example of abolishing slavery within themselves." If Congress were to interfere and "*take the lead* in this process," the "peace of the union would be greatly disturbed." He had long hoped that "public opinion" would serve as the vehicle for ending slavery. Congress should act as an agent of abolition only when "called for by the people." Until recently he had thought that emancipation could best be accomplished through a gradual and peaceful process, without disrupting the "natural" order in society. This was the same view held by his father and most other Founders. But he was no longer so optimistic. Although he still believed that Congress should follow public opinion, he had "abandon[ed] the hope that the states . . . will ever voluntarily surrender their worship of the Moloch of slavery."[50]

The term "Moloch of slavery" wonderfully symbolized for Adams what had gone wrong in America. Moloch was the name of a Canaanite idol to whom children were sacrificed as burnt offerings. God expressly forbids the practice in Leviticus, and in *Paradise Lost* Milton portrays Moloch as one of the devils.[51] Adams' trope for slavery thus links America's attainment of independence from Great Britain to the Israelites' deliverance from bondage in Egypt, and it suggests declension after Americans reached the Promised Land. The Israelites, after conquering Canaan, were forbidden by God to worship Canaanite idols. According to Adams, the children of Israel in the New World, after seizing control, vowed to fulfill "the laws of nature and of nature's God," as stated in the Declaration of Independence, and end the abomination of slavery. Deuteronomy 8 made clear what would happen to future generations who ignored these laws: "And if you forget the Lord your God and go after other gods and serve them and worship them, I solemnly warn you this day that you shall surely perish."[52]

In Adams' view, Americans had abandoned their pledge to fulfill the laws of nature and of nature's God. Instead they sacrificed the children of Africa as "burnt offerings" to the Moloch of slavery, and Adams feared that the nation would dissolve and suffer untold punishment. As he told Gerrit Smith in his February 1837 letter: "This loss of a cherished hope" that the slave states would voluntarily surrender their slaves "has only brought the question of abolition . . . in more fearful aspect before me." All the representatives and senators from the slave states were "arrayed against" abolition and "furious against any man whom they imagine were to favor it." Slaveowners were so furious, in fact, that Adams had just received the first of a steady stream of death threats from the South. Americans North and South now worshipped the false idol of "ambition," the bane of republican governments. As Adams told Smith: "The people of the free states are spellbound by the talisman of ambition to sustain the slavery of the South, and ambition is the most heartless of passions." "Northern servility to Southern servitude" pervaded "*all* the political parties and their leaders."[53]

Adams' tirade against the existing political parties contributed to Smith's decision three years later to help organize the Liberty party. And when Smith himself went to Congress in 1853, he echoed Adams' sentiments by saying that whereas the Founders had considered slavery a "confessed sin" and had "rejoiced in the prospect of its speedy abolition," the "thinly disguised aims" of "this new Union" were "extended and perpetual slavery on the one hand, and political and commercial gains on the other."[54]

Smith learned about the use of the war powers during an exchange with Adams in 1839, and it greatly influenced his thinking about the means for ending slavery. He was largely responsible for writing it into the platform at the Syracuse convention in 1855, and used it to justify his militant response to the Slave Power throughout the 1850s. After Adams described the various conditions for abolishing slavery, including the use of war powers, Smith wrote back to say that "your letter has awakened more interest in me than any other production of your pen":

> Though I do not, with yourself, despair of a peaceful and bloodless termination of American slavery; yet my hopes of such an event are faint. Of the speedy overthrow of this measureless iniquity I am confident— but my prevailing apprehension is, that violence will accomplish the overthrow. I feel, nevertheless, that my duty to labor to arrest a vengeful, and to secure a merciful, removal of the great curse of my country, is undiminished.[55]

Smith was confident in the speedy overthrow of slavery, feared that violence would accomplish it, yet labored dutifully to end it peacefully. Eventually he could no longer balance these objectives. He would have to choose between a peaceful approach on the one hand, and an immediate end to the inequity on the other hand, and since he was unwilling to renounce the latter, his abhorrence of violence became, by the 1850s, an acceptance of bloodshed. His "prevailing apprehension" in his letter to Adams was, in fact, that *he* would turn to violence to accomplish the overthrow. But he was unable to acknowledge it at the time, and so wrote "violence" as though it were its own agent.

Their exchange of letters highlights the degree to which their different religious impressions affected their antislavery positions and understandings of the world. Adams agreed with Smith that slavery was "the great curse" of his country, the equivalent of America's original sin. And he, too, despaired of a peaceful end to the evil. But whereas Smith thought that abolition would quickly bring an end to all sin and undo America's original sin, Adams believed that some form of sin would always exist, both in individuals and in the country. Adams viewed slavery as a symbol of America's sin, to be replaced by other symbols; Smith saw it as a synecdoche—abolish the part, and the whole would quickly crumble. And unlike Smith, Adams did not consider himself a prophet announcing a new dispensation and an immediate end to sin, and he told Smith so.[56]

After praising Adams for his efforts in the cause, Smith confronted him for refusing to accept immediate abolition: "You are aware how widespread and deep is the regret, that you cannot subscribe to the doctrine of 'immediate emancipation.' I am for 'immediate emancipation,' because I fully believe that God is for it. He is, and therefore we should be, for the immediate termination of every sin."[57] To which Adams responded:

> You observe that you are for immediate emancipation because you fully believe that God is for it. By this I understand that you hold it as a principle of religious duty. Hence I cannot possibly flatter myself that anything I could say should have any impression upon your mind, to change your opinion; and firmly convinced as I am that the emancipation of slaves . . . is *not* the present will of God, I can only lament that our religious impressions upon these points differ so essentially that I see no prospect of their ever harmonizing in this life.[58]

For Adams, the immediate abolition of slavery was no more the present will of God than the immediate end of all sin. If it were, slavery would be receding rather than spreading. As Adams knew firsthand as a congressman, there was no chance that the federal government would move to emancipate the slaves. He could not see beyond his linear view of history and progress. He did not have the ability, as Smith did, to envision a sharp break that allowed him to transcend the barriers of the past. Smith predicted and prepared for a new dispensation in this life. He interpreted the meaning of "Christian" literally—as messianist— and acted on his interpretation. As a messenger of Christ, he sought to realize this sin-free world.[59]

Adams acknowledged their differences in religious belief: "My religious opinions are dictated by a Monitor within," he told Smith. "I hold none of these because they are held by other men, and least of all from a man who tells me that he comes to me with a message from the Lord." Adams consoled himself that God's reign would occur in the next life, and he adhered to the existing government of his country. For Adams, believing in the abolition of all sin—immediate or otherwise—was a dangerous delusion and a misrepresentation of scripture. One could no more abolish sin than the body. The most one could do was to contain sin, chip away at it, accept compromise, and try to avoid its enticements, whether of wine and women (to which Adams' oldest son, George Washington Adams, had succumbed) or of perfection and prophesy. Even after diligent and righteous behavior, a large gap between this world and the promised land would remain. As Adams put it, the permanence of sin "is too strongly tested by all human experience, as well as by the whole tenor of the Scriptures."[60]

But compromise was precisely what Smith and his comrades so vigorously opposed. The Founding Fathers had compromised their belief in the sinfulness of slavery by seeking gradual abolition, and look where it had got them! Smith thought the doctrine of gradual emancipation was far too "vague," because it advocated an end to the evil "sometime between now and never." His opposition to compromise became increasingly strident over time, fueling his efforts to break down the cultural dichotomies that had long been based on compromise. Without sin, there was no need to maintain the order and hierarchy in society that these dualities imposed.[61]

Adams often indulged in the same idealistic sentiments as Smith, but kept them in the realm of his imagination. In 1819–20, during the crisis over the Missouri Compromise, he wrote in his journal that "the seeds of the Declaration of Independence are yet maturing. The harvest will be what [the painter Benjamin] West calls the terrible sublime." His use of the aesthetic "sublime" perfectly captured his image of emancipation as both glorious and catastrophic, encompassing death and dissolution as well as the rebirth of slaves into men and the Union into a free country. He said as much in his journal a few months later, and again invoked the "sublime": Slavery "is the great and foul stain upon the North American Union, and it is a contemplation worthy of the most exalted soul, whether its total abolition is or is not practicable."

He predicted the dissolution of the Union, its reorganization as a free nation, and concluded that "this object is vast in its compass, awful in its prospects, sublime and beautiful in its issue. A life devoted to it would be nobly spent or sacrificed." But Adams shuddered at the thought of acting on these sublime visions, and would have been horrified (at least publicly) by John Brown's devoting and sacrificing his life to the cause. Adams kept these reform visions in the realm of his imagination and his diary. He heard the sublime callings of his heart, but followed the logic of his head.[62]

Adams' refusal to act on these sublime images paralleled his efforts to seek compromise rather than uproot the existing social order. He untiringly presented abolitionists' petitions, but disapproved of their content. He considered blacks to be an essential part of American society, but not as his social equals and not as an integrated force in society. He championed human rights but opposed equal rights. He believed in a great chain of being, with humans falling somewhere between the worm and the seraph, and dark-skinned peoples occupying the lower end of the hierarchy of humanity. He would never have befriended or confided in Frederick Douglass to the degree he did with Gerrit Smith. While Smith sought to dismantle social hierarchy, Adams clung to it. And while Smith and John Brown lived in biracial societies and endorsed interracial marriage (in theory at least), Adams considered black-and-white intimacy and friendship as "unnatural passion" on the part of whites. His view of blacks in American society resembled that of the lower classes: if the white "rabble" had the right to vote, so should blacks, and he kept his distance from both groups. For him, democracy implied not a new social order, but a sense of duty and discipline correlative to rights.[63] Adams stood poised, in other words, between the Enlightenment worldview of his father, other Founders, and gradual abolitionists on the one hand, and the Romantic worldview of most immediate abolitionists on the other hand.[64]

But at the two Syracuse conventions, Gerrit Smith and his comrades stood apart from other immediate abolitionists. They were more successful than their peers in treating blacks as full and equal members of society, and in their ability to embrace both the terror and exhilaration that would accompany the new dispensation in a world free from sin. Most other immediatists never acted on their violent impulses and tendencies. They focused instead on moral suasion to free others from sin.

Smith and his comrades reversed the psychology of horror and despair that accompanied violent means. They conceived of the project of emancipation as sublime and apocalyptic, much as Adams did, but instead of shunning it, they acted on it, and experienced at Syracuse an ecstasy of liberation and release, as though the oppressive burden of sin and its attendant hierarchies and dualities had been lifted at last.[65] Although Gerrit Smith, McCune Smith, and Douglass were much more ambivalent about their use of violence than Brown, they nevertheless accepted this sublime image.

These men's sublime vision of America, and their efforts to dismantle cultural dichotomies, can be seen as grotesque—an aesthetic mode characterized by the attempt to fuse two incompatible realms. Thomas Mann, the great twentieth-century novelist and critic, described the grotesque as "the only guise in which the sublime may appear," adding that the grotesque is "the genuine anti-bourgeois style." Radical Abolitionists' meetings could also be characterized as antibourgeois and grotesque. One would have a hard time defining their two conventions at Syracuse—with blacks, whites, and Bloomers all freely intermingling; guns and money being exchanged; and speeches advocating revolution—as bourgeois. In fact the mainstream press often referred to their meetings as "promiscuous" because of their diversity and eccentricity. Their conventions were also grotesque in the sense that they sought to realize their perfectionist visions of America.[66] In many respects, their political and social visions resembled the literary and poetic visions of Ralph Waldo Emerson and especially Walt Whitman.

❧ Ralph Waldo Emerson was a prophet of "newness" and was thus a disgrace to himself and his family. So concluded John Quincy Adams in 1840. Adams, who abhorred the fashionable quest for whatever seemed "new," described with regret the "wild and visionary phantasies" that had recently cropped up in New England, and singled out Emerson as a leading perpetrator of these "phantasies." Emerson, he said in his journal, "after failing in the every-day avocations of a Unitarian preacher and school-master, starts a new doctrine of transcendentalism, declares all the old revelations superannuated and worn out, and announces the approach of new revelations and prophecies." Adams grouped Emerson with Garrison, phrenology, animal magnetism, and Jean-Paul Marat, the incendiary French journalist and revolutionary, and said they all acted as ingredients in "the bubbling cauldron of religion and politics."[67]

In 1840 Emerson did not approve of Garrison's or other abolitionists' methods; but by the mid-1850s he was an outspoken opponent of slavery, and greatly admired Gerrit Smith. In 1854 he described Smith as being rooted to a vision of the world that sought "something not selfish, not geographical, but human and divine." Smith "has the respect & tears of gratitude of Mankind." Two years later, Emerson expressed a wish to meet Smith and to hear him speak (there is no record of his doing so), noting that Smith's renown had lately become "more and better than ever."[68]

Smith and his comrades reciprocated this respect. Beginning in the 1850s, they quoted or paraphrased Emerson in their own writings. In a speech in Boston in 1858 Gerrit Smith paraphrased Emerson's introduction to *Nature* (1836) by saying: "The will of the Great Father is that every generation shall enter upon and run the race of life free from the dead weights which a former one might have been tempted to hang upon it." The following year he summarized Emerson's view of nature by proclaiming in a sermon: "Every man is, in an important sense, bound to make up a Bible for himself," adding that it was a mistake to study religion "in books rather than in nature."[69] Smith also owned two *cartes-de-visite* photographs of Emerson, as a way to keep him ever-present at Peterboro.[70] Frederick Douglass referred to Emerson as "the sage of Concord" and "the philosopher of Concord" in his speeches, and he, too, paraphrased Emerson's analysis of nature: people who harbored "bright and glorious visions" were often those who discovered "books in the running brooks," he noted. In many respects, Douglass' understanding of self-reliance and of America's composite racial and ethnic makeup mirrored Emerson's.[71] James McCune Smith was, of the four men, probably the most familiar with Emerson's writings, and he quoted him directly in 1854 in criticizing Garrisonian abolitionists.[72] John Brown was the only one of the four who actually met Emerson (in 1857), and he considered him among his "foremost" New England friends.[73]

Emerson also embraced Smith's and his comrades' use of violence. In 1857, after Brown returned from Kansas as something of a war hero among abolitionists, Emerson heard him speak at the town hall in

Concord and liked what he heard. Brown "gave a good account of him-self." He breathed the air of liberty, the same air that was "breathed by thousands & millions." He is "the rarest of heroes, a pure idealist": "He believes in two articles—two instruments, shall I say?—the Golden Rule and the Declaration of Independence," and was willing to have "a whole generation . . . pass away by a violent death, than that one word of either should be violated in this country." After Brown's capture at Harpers Ferry in October 1859, Emerson echoed the sentiments of Gerrit Smith and Frederick Douglass by saying that slaveholders should be treated "as felons who have disentitled themselves to the protection of the law": "No matter how many [John] Browns and [Gerrit] Smiths" slaveholders might "catch and kill," liberty would still triumph. After Brown was convicted of treason, Emerson borrowed the words of a friend (Mattie Griffith) by calling him "that new saint . . . who, if he shall suffer, will make the gallows like the cross."[74]

Emerson was not always so effusive in his praise of Brown's raid on Harpers Ferry, however. He also said that Brown "lost his head there" by invading the South, and was "precisely what lawyers call crazy, be-ing governed by ideas, & not by external circumstance." In this sense, Brown lived up to Emerson's doctrine of self-reliance and sacred self-sovereignty more fully than Emerson did himself. Like most other white abolitionists, Emerson did not abandon white laws and conven-tions to the degree that Smith and Brown did. He did not identify and empathize with blacks as they did, either in his writings or in his life.[75] For Emerson, John Brown was like a swimmer who enjoyed the water in a turbulent sea of ideas. Emerson remained on the banks, describing the sea at length but fearing the plunge.[76] He was a revolutionary, but his revolution was aesthetic, based on experiments in language and rhetoric rather than on his ability to act on his ideas.[77]

Emerson's aesthetic revolution closely paralleled Radical Abolition-ists' political revolution. Central to both was a subjective notion of the self in a state of continuous flux. While romantics narrowed the gap between the ideal and the real, body and soul, and sacred and profane, and thus allowed "character" a certain degree of fluidity, Radical Aboli-tionists surpassed Emerson's rhetoric and approached Whitman's poetics in their efforts to dismantle not only these dichotomies, but those separating black from white, civilization from savagery, along with the racial divisions associated with these realms. A fluid and subjective conception of the self greatly facilitated these men's efforts to break down racial hierarchies and envision an egalitarian and pluralist society.[78]

Although Radical Abolitionists did not define themselves as literary artists, Smith, Douglass, McCune Smith, and Brown did experiment—in varying degrees—with new forms of language and political and religious expression. One could characterize their understanding of the Constitution as radically avant-garde, for they overturned almost seventy years of interpretive precedent. They foreshadowed William James—whose writings on religion and identity owed a great deal to Emerson and Whitman—in their emphasis on belief itself and the will to believe, rather than on the external basis of their beliefs.[79] This is what allowed them to interpret the Constitution in a way that was radically different from that of the Framers—who created the document—as well as all subsequent rulings from the judiciary and legislative branches of government.[80] In the 1850s Gerrit Smith sculpted a new religion that was devoid of authoritarian doctrines and based solely on emotions and instincts that resided in the "spirit in a heart." He admitted "that there would be a great diversity of religious views" in his religion—much as James later described the many varieties of religious experience. And Smith's acknowledgment that "the religion of all holy hearts would be substantially the same" is something James would have accepted. The concept of pluralism articulated by Radical Abolitionists and James was a far cry from an embrace of complete relativism, however. As the philosopher Isaiah Berlin put it: "Pluralism is not relativism—the multiple values are objective, part of the essence of humanity rather than arbitrary creations of men's subjective fancies."[81]

These aesthetic and political understandings of the self and the nation have close ties with the concept of "religious modernism." The historian William Hutchison describes religious modernism as the adaptation of religious ideas to modern culture, the belief that God is immanent or indwelling, and the idea that the kingdom of God can be realized on Earth. Religious modernists sought to minimize the distinctions between the sacred and secular, this world and the next, the ideal and the real, and religion and science. Hutchison calls Transcendentalists such as Emerson and Whitman important precursors to religious modernists, but one could also include Radical Abolitionists, for their faith in these modernist principles enabled them to seek a heaven on Earth and to elevate "higher law" over legal precedent. Moreover, religious modernists, Radical Abolitionists, Emerson, and Whitman all believed that sin could be abolished through individual and collective regeneration.[82] Without sin, there was no need to elevate one person over the next, a state of affairs that promoted empathy. Empathy greatly facilitated the convergence of black and white identities among these Radical Abolitionists. By contrast, most other abolitionists achieved only sympathy. Not surprisingly, "empathy," equivalent to the German word *Einfühlung*, has aesthetic roots. The term was first used in 1872 to describe abstraction and internal subjectivity in theories of art, whereby the subject (or viewer) identifies so closely with the feelings evoked by the object (or image) that subject and object are fused—the viewer becomes one with the image.[83]

In his 1855 *Leaves of Grass* Whitman articulated an empathic vision of America surpassing even that described by Radical Abolitionists a week earlier at Syracuse. Their respective visions shared many of the same features. Both visions evoked a democracy of inclusion, but without its inherent flaw—dating back to the Greeks—of forging that inclusion by excluding women, slaves, and blacks.[84] Both portrayed a sacred society in which divinity dwelled within all people. Both contained an aesthetic of fluidity and connectedness between one person and another (and between Whitman and the reader), regardless of differences. And both contained elements of the sublime. For Whitman, the sublime appeared in the grotesque images of Southerners and Northerners, prostitutes and saints, blacks and whites, all living together in harmony. But while Radical Abolitionists at Syracuse focused on the means for achieving the new age, Whitman assumed that it had already arrived. For Whitman, his poetry itself created the condition of a pluralist society that was no longer burdened by sin. It was in his poetry, rather than in his prose works or his life, that the new age was possible.[85]

The opening paragraph of the introduction to *Leaves of Grass*—the first words after the title page—orients the reader by describing not a future vision but a nation reborn:

America does not repel the past or what it has produced under its forms or amid other politics or the idea of castes or the old religions . . . accepts the lesson with calmness . . . is not so impatient as has been

supposed that the slough still sticks to opinions and manners and literature while the life which served its requirements has passed into the
new forms.

America does not repel the past because the new dispensation has already arrived; it can therefore accept its past mistakes with calmness.
The country has shed its dead skin, passed into new forms. The next
paragraph similarly stresses a present rather than future vision: "*Here at
last* is something in the doings of man that corresponds with the broad-
cast doings of the day and night." "*Here is*" a "nation of nations." "*Here
is* action untied from strings." "*Here is* the hospitality which forever in-
dicates heroes."[86]

Since the new dispensation has already arrived, the narrator throughout the poems seems unburdened by sin: I "am not the poet of goodness only . . . I do not decline to be the poet of wickedness also," Whitman states in the first untitled poem, which he later called "Song of
Myself." Two lines below he underscores his insouciance about sin:
"Evil propels me, and reform of evil propels me . . . I stand indifferent."
Since the narrator is wholly unfettered by sin, no obstacles impede his
boundlessness, either in form or in content. His is a new "kosmos," and
he can therefore gratify his passions and instincts and not worry about
death: "Walt Whitman, an American, one of the roughs, a kosmos, /
disorderly fleshy and sensual . . . eating drinking and breeding, / No
sentimentalist." And a few lines later: "Copulation is no more rank to
me than death is." In the reborn nation, the concepts of sex and death
no longer carry the weight of sin. In Whitman's poetics, one need not
be concerned with sin or with controlling one's passions. But for Radical Abolitionists and Emerson, the break with the past had not yet occurred, and since evil still ran rampant, they had to vanquish it while
controlling their passions so as to remain free from evil themselves.[87]

Whitman was deeply indebted to Emerson's writings and encouragement, and referred to him in the mid-1850s as "dear Friend and
Master." Yet in his poetry he fulfills rather than echoes his mentor's
prophesy of a new age. John Quincy Adams correctly noted that Emerson "announces the approach of new revelations and prophesies." The
first sentence of Emerson's manifesto, *Nature*, clarifies his vision as
something in the future: "Our age is retrospective."[88] In *Leaves of Grass*,
the "wild and visionary phantasies" that Adams feared have been real-

ized in poetic form. Whitman therefore need not concern himself with the means or methods for achieving his heaven on Earth. This is one reason why he kept his distance from abolitionists. Unlike Emerson and other literary friends, Whitman refused to champion John Brown's militancy. Ironically, Whitman's stance on slavery more closely resembled that of John Quincy Adams, but for vastly different reasons. Both men constructed sublime images of emancipation, were moderates seeking gradual abolition, and refused to act on these visions. They kept them contained to the page, much as they sought to contain slavery, and refused to befriend or identify with blacks. Adams shunned his sublime image because he dreaded the destruction that would accompany it. Whitman realized his ideal of a reborn nation in his poetry, but did not confuse it with the imperfect world in which he lived. Instead of seeking to *fuse* the ideal and the real, he *exchanged* the objective world for a poetic reality in *Leaves of Grass*. His poetic reality stems from and depends upon his book of poems. In his life he kept the two worlds separate.[89]

Despite these differences between Whitman and Radical Abolitionists, a few contemporaries linked them. There is no record that Whitman knew or corresponded with Gerrit Smith, McCune Smith, Douglass, or Brown. Yet a number of other militant abolitionists knew Whitman, liked him, and praised his poetry. They include Franklin Sanborn, Richard Hinton, and James Redpath, who were co-conspirators in Brown's raid on Harpers Ferry; and William Thayer and Charles Eldridge, the publishers of his 1860 edition of *Leaves of Grass*.[90] Sanborn, who was also a friend of Gerrit Smith, directly linked Whitman and Smith: he kept a portrait of Gerrit alongside portraits of Emerson and Whitman. And Sanborn saw a close resemblance between Whitman and Gerrit Smith, particularly in their "broad and loving humanity" and "a little" in their personalities. Whitman himself, when asked in the 1880s by his friend Horace Traubel why he had never associated with abolitionists, replied that it "wasn't because they were too radical. It was because they were not radical enough." He considered his poetry and poetic self more extreme than the politics of Radical Abolitionists. But his self-characterization downplays his writings as a journalist, which opposed slavery but did not embrace immediate abolition, as well as his unwillingness to befriend blacks and to act on the revolutionary ideas in his poetry. Indeed his advice to Traubel on social and political (as opposed to poetic) issues was much different, and here he reveals the separation of poetic and political self: *"Be radical,"* he told Traubel; *"be radical—be not too damned radical."*[91]

ʷ Radical Abolitionists were "madmen," William Lloyd Garrison concluded. Garrison considered the party a threat to his principle of disunion and an adulteration of his belief in nonresistance, and a few months after the 1855 Syracuse convention he denounced them in his newspaper.[92] Radical Abolitionists attacked not only "'the Garrison party' at the North" and "the slaveholders at the South," but the whole nation for misinterpreting the Constitution. "Like the madman who contended that all others were insane but himself," Radical Abolitionists thought they were "the only sane persons in the republic."[93] Though Radical Abolitionists thought they were following Christ's example, Garrison and countless others considered them mad. He did not understand (or chose to ignore) the radical subjectivity with which Gerrit Smith and his comrades interpreted the Constitution.

A year later, in 1856, after learning of the Radical Abolitionists' nominating convention at Syracuse, Garrison again compared them to madmen: "I see . . . Douglass, McCune Smith . . . and Gerrit Smith have called a convention for the purpose of nominating candidates for the Presidency and Vice Presidency of the United States!" he derisively told a friend. "Can any thing more ludicrous than this be found inside or outside of the Utica Insane Asylum? It is really sad to see so good a man as Gerrit Smith befooled in this manner."[94]

That is precisely where Gerrit Smith found himself three years later: the New York State Asylum for the Insane at Utica. Shortly after John Brown was sentenced to die for his incursion into the South, Smith suffered a brief but complete emotional collapse. He was a leading conspirator in the raid, and the only one who—in its aftermath—considered it wrong.

Brown's raid on Harpers Ferry marked the culmination of the violent methods prescribed by these men. It was the end of Smith's and Brown's respective efforts to align themselves with their black comrades and to prepare for a new age. Brown died as a result of the raid. Smith experienced profound guilt over his participation in it, and believed himself culpable for all the lives lost. After becoming delirious and unable to eat or sleep, his family committed him to the Utica Insane Asylum. Following his recovery in early 1860, he began to distance himself from Douglass, McCune Smith, and other black friends. He viewed his close friendship with blacks, as well as his role as a prophet, as the dark sources of his violent proclivities. In his mind he had associated too closely with the wrong crowd; he had been corrupted by his black friends.

Ironically, John Brown was widely considered to be mad but vehemently denied it (as did Frederick Douglass and most other blacks). Gerrit Smith went mad, but was widely accused of faking his madness to avoid being indicted for his complicity in Brown's raid. Douglass and McCune Smith (and other black abolitionists) were seen as insolent, since most whites used a different standard for criticizing blacks. Both Brown and Smith—along with other white abolitionists—were also called "monomaniacs." Monomania clinically meant a form of insanity in which one or more faculties of the brain were "deranged" (as opposed to "mania"—the derangement of all faculties—which Smith was diagnosed with at the asylum). Monomania was characterized by obsessive behavior—as though a person were "possessed" by a certain desire or objective—before the term gave way to the designations of manic-depressive (or "bipolar") illness and schizophrenia, depending on specific conditions. But monomania was also a popular epithet applied to diligent reformers. Southerners, for instance, called John Quincy Adams a monomaniac for his efforts to defend the right of petition. In this society, the boundaries separating madness from sanity depended more on ideological than on psychological distinctions.[95]

Herman Melville understood the nature of monomania in 1850s America. In *Moby-Dick* (1851) he links Captain Ahab's monomaniacal obsession with the white whale to the state of American society. If Ahab (or Adams) was insane, then so was a large part of the population. Like Ahab pursuing the whale, Americans everywhere found in phrenology, photography, Spiritualism, animal magnetism, and other pursuits the means to strike through the pasteboard masks of visible objects and probe the deep recesses of the heart. Those who sought to realize their sublime visions—their "wild and visionary phantasies," as Adams called them—were likely to be labeled insane. So were those who dared to expose the inconsistencies between the exterior and interior realms—as in Ahab's pursuit of the evil but *white* whale, or Smith's and Brown's efforts to become black, or even Adams' sympathy with anyone "as dark as a Mexican," as Southerners accused. They, too, were often thought mad. Frederick Douglass, like Melville, understood the protean nature of insanity in antebellum America: "I believe everybody [is] more or less insane—at times," he privately noted.[96]

The methods of Gerrit Smith, McCune Smith, Douglass, and Brown suggest that the limits to their reform vision were significant. They achieved an extraordinary union. Gerrit Smith and John Brown were virtually unique among white men in their efforts to identify themselves as blacks and to befriend Douglass, McCune Smith, and other blacks. They embraced their black hearts, renounced racist doctrine and ideology, and sought to extend equality throughout the country. But these efforts cost Brown his own life and those of many others. Douglass left the country to avoid arrest and almost certain death in the wake of Brown's raid, and McCune Smith was already beginning to suffer from the weak heart that would eventually kill him. Still, these two black men emerged from Brown's raid comparatively unscathed, thus reversing the usual assumption that blacks were more vulnerable to violence. Gerrit Smith temporarily lost all perspective on present reality, and permanently forfeited his close friendships with blacks, his appreciation of their culture, and his self-conception as a passionate outsider. Despite his remarkable success at remaking himself, he could not overcome the deep recesses of his racism.

CHAPTER TWO

Creating an Image in Black

Poets, prophets, and reformers are all picture makers—and this ability is the secret of their power and of their achievements. They see what ought to be by the reflection of what is, and endeavor to remove the contradiction.

—FREDERICK DOUGLASS, "PICTURES" (CA. 1864)

If we cannot imagine ourselves as different from what we are and as-sume that second self, we cannot impose a discipline upon ourselves, though we may accept one from others. Active virtue as distinguished from the passive acceptance of a current code is therefore theatrical, consciously dramatic, the wearing of a mask. It is the condition of ar-duous full life.

—WILLIAM BUTLER YEATS, "ESTRANGEMENT" (1909)

Two months after the 1855 Syracuse convention Frederick Douglass published his second autobiography, *My Bondage and My Freedom*. The former slave was already the most famous black man in America and one of the most famous in the Western world. His first autobiography, *Narrative of the Life of Frederick Douglass, An American Slave, Written by Himself*, published ten years previously, had sold tens of thousands of copies and had already been translated into French. In addition to his skills as a writer, Douglass was a brilliant public speaker, widely consid-ered by whites and blacks alike to be among America's best, at a time when public speaking was one of the country's most popular forms of entertainment. He had used the power of the word (and of his own voice) to write himself into public existence. He continually revised and redefined himself through language, and with his second autobiog-raphy he was updating his public image.[1]

My Bondage and My Freedom begins not with words, however, but with an image. An engraving of Douglass by John C. Buttre, based on a daguerreotype, appears as the frontispiece (Figure 1). Below the engraving, near the bottom of the page, is Douglass' autograph. Douglass looks directly into the camera lens in a dramatic and crafted pose. The pose sends a message that is repeated throughout the book—one of artful defiance, or "majestic wrath," to paraphrase one of Douglass' female admirers.[2] The texture of the engraving—sharp detail and rich contrast—complements his formal attire and the forthright message to come. The emphasis on physicality—the furrowed brows, the firm lips, the neat but coarse beard, the pugilistic position of his arms—blurs the categories of white and black, for his skin appears very light, and his hair is neither straight (white) nor woolly and tufted (black). Thus a message of physical aggression and defiance by a black man is softened, "whitened," and made publicly palatable through the formal qualities of the picture. Form and content work together to create a darkly romantic—a sublime—image.[3]

Douglass, John Brown, Gerrit Smith, and James McCune Smith all created pictures of themselves to further their abolition cause. These pictures shed enormous light on each man's individual self-conception and respective approach to the cause. At the 1855 Syracuse convention they appear as a unified biracial quartet, sharing similar worldviews and hopes for the future. But as individuals they differed dramatically, even at the height of their alliance in the mid-1850s. Their individual self-definitions crossed racial lines. They defined themselves publicly by constructing authentic, intelligent, and black performative selves—the wearing of a mask, so to speak—that helped them to blur and subvert racial barriers. Their success at constructing public personas depended more heavily on class, education, and religion than it did on skin color. Their public personas were linked to (but did not mirror) their private self-definitions. In other words, how they defined themselves publicly in the mid-1850s differed from who they were privately.

🢡 Douglass photographed as well as wrote himself into public existence, and his visual persona (much like his written self) often stood at odds with his private self. In the frontispiece to *My Bondage*, his arms lose almost all detail in the wrists and hands. The position of his right thumb and the slope of his left hand appear awkward and unnatural. John C. Buttre, the engraver who cut the image from a photograph, apparently altered the daguerreotype by drawing the fists in freehand. Whether or not Douglass requested this transformation, he liked the engraving enough to include it as the frontispiece of his book. Douglass also looks quite young in the image—in fact a bit too young for his thirty-seven years. Although he never knew exactly when he was born, he could estimate his age within a year.[4] Here he presents himself as a younger man by almost a decade. He looks considerably older in an 1852 daguerreotype (Figure 2), which shows him with graying hair and a thinner, more mature face. His features in his frontispiece more closely resemble those of an 1847 daguerreotype (Figure 3), probably

Figure 1. Frederick Douglass. Engraving by J. C. Buttre.
Reproduced in Douglass, *My Bondage and My Freedom*
(New York: Miller, Orton & Milligan, 1855), frontispiece.

the one on which Buttre based his engraving. These incongruities highlight the degree to which Douglass' public self differed from his private self. Far more than John Brown, Gerrit Smith, and James McCune Smith, he succeeded at creating a public persona that collapsed racial hierarchies and boundaries. The more effective he and his comrades were at creating black performative selves, however, the greater disparity there was between an "artistic" public self and a private self that remained largely circumscribed by those aesthetic

Figure 2. Frederick Douglass. Half-plate daguerreotype
by Samuel J. Miller, 1852. Art Institute of Chicago.

boundaries. In Douglass' case, he was (and is) extremely difficult to penetrate and know as a private individual.

Douglass' passion for pictures was far from unique. By the mid-1850s the country was experiencing an explosion of visual imagery, and Americans had their pictures taken at an unprecedented rate. Daguerreotypes, tintypes, ambrotypes, *cartes-de-visite*, mass-produced engravings, and illustrated newspapers infiltrated every town. Visual culture, much like print culture, offered a way to recapture lost com-

Figure 3. Frederick Douglass. Daguerreotype, 1847.
National Portrait Gallery, Washington, D.C.

munities by imagining new ones. Its emergence coincided with the increasing crisis over the slavery controversy, along with a prolonged period of accelerating social change. In the face of these crises, the emergence of visual culture helped people to redefine themselves and their communities. Chronic social change typically involves a new emphasis on the present and future, a replacement of past identities for fragmented, diffused, and changing self-conceptions, and a newfound unwillingness to accept hypocrisy. Visual culture emerged, then, at the very time when people were seeking to probe beneath the surface of things, to root out hypocrisy, and to discover a more stable and enduring reality. The question "Who am I?" loomed large on a national scale, and Americans often answered that question with pictures.[5]

Abolitionists were no different. In fact, based on the abundance of extant abolitionist imagery, they probably had their pictures taken with greater frequency, and distributed them more effectively, than other groups.[6] Their desire to transform themselves and their world fueled their interest in images, which helped to make visible the contrast between their dreams of reform and the sinful present. Gerrit Smith, McCune Smith, Douglass, and Brown stood apart from other abolitionists in their ability to embrace fluid conceptions of the self and to exchange past identities with future ones. They grappled with the question "Who am I?" all their lives. In varying degrees, they believed that remaking themselves through pictures was one step toward achieving their new world. Frederick Douglass in particular sat for his "likeness" whenever he could; he had his portrait taken at least as much as Walt Whitman, who is legendary for having visually created and recreated himself.[7]

Douglass believed that "true" art could transcend racial barriers. A good part of his fame rested on his public-speaking and writing talents. But he also relied heavily on portrait photography and the picture-making process in general to create an authentic and intelligent black persona. After selling some ten thousand copies of *My Bondage* in the first few weeks of publication, he knew that his public persona could spread more quickly through his portraits than through his voice, and he continually sought to control how he appeared in those portraits.[8] For example, in an 1849 review of *A Tribute for the Negro*, by the Quaker abolitionist Wilson Armistead, Douglass praised the prose but attacked the imagery, including the engraving of himself (Figure 4). The engraver had cut the image of Douglass from a painting (Figure 5), but had added a smile, rendering him with "a much more kindly and amiable expression than is generally thought to characterize the face of a fugitive slave," as Douglass accused.[9] Although he was no longer a fugitive, Douglass wanted the look of a defiant but respectable outsider. "Negroes can never have impartial portraits at the hands of white artists," he stated: "It seems to us next to impossible for white men to take likenesses of black men, without most grossly exaggerating their distinctive features. And the reason is obvious. Artists, like all other white persons, have adopted a theory respecting the distinctive features of Negro physiognomy."[10] The vast majority of whites could not create "impartial" likenesses of African Americans (even though they might be able to *write* about them impartially) because of their preconceived notions of what blacks looked like.

Douglass' criticism of white artists helps to explain why he was so taken with photography: he thought that the veracity of the daguerreotype (the most popular form of photography in America from its invention in 1839 through the mid-1850s) prevented the distortions and exaggerations that came from the hands of whites. He also knew that the vast majority of daguerreotypes (about 95 percent) took the form of portraits. He wrote two separate speeches on "pictures," in which he celebrated photography and praised Louis Daguerre, the inventor of the daguerreotype, as "the great discoverer of modern times, to whom coming generations will award special homage."[11] The photograph— and accurate renditions or sympathetic engravings such as the one he used for his frontispiece in *My Bondage*—became his medium of choice for representing himself visually. For Douglass, Daguerre and his invention had turned the world into a gallery of "true pictures," allowing an ex-slave or a "servant girl" to have pictures of themselves "such as the wealth of kings could not purchase fifty years ago." Yet the democratizing aspect of photography was only part of the reason why he thought photographs contributed to the cause of abolition and equal rights. He well knew that most Americans, including slaveholders and proslavery sympathizers, were in love with the photograph.[12]

Douglass believed that the daguerreotype contributed enormously to the picturemaking process in general, and in his mind all humans sought accurate representations both of material reality and of an unseen spiritual world. This affinity for pictures is what distinguished humans from animals: "Man is the only picture-making animal in the world. He alone of all the inhabitants of earth has the capacity and pas-

sion for pictures." Emphasizing the humanity of all humans was central
to Douglass' reform vision, since all but the most radical of Americans
defended inequality and racial hierarchies on the grounds that black
slaves and their descendants were fundamentally different from other
humans.[13]

Most white Americans in the 1850s believed that blacks were innately inferior, incapable of self-government, and thus unable to participate in civil society, and they used pictures—though usually not

Figure 4. Frederick Douglass. Engraving. Reproduced in
Wilson Armistead, *A Tribute for the Negro: Being a Vindication
of the Moral, Intellectual, and Religious Capabilities of the Colored
Portion of Mankind* . . . (Manchester: William Irwin, 1848),
following p. 456.

photographs—to show it.[14] Scientists as well as artists resorted to pictures. In 1854 the respected ethnologists Josiah Nott and George Glidden published an influential and popular book called *Types of Mankind*. In it they included numerous engravings that evoked a strong affinity between blacks and gorillas. The first printing sold out immediately, and the second edition, published the same year as Douglass' *My Bondage*, featured an engraving that compared the heads and skulls of a "creole negro," a "young chimpanzee," and a *statue* of the white

Figure 5. Frederick Douglass. Oil on canvas, ca. 1845.
National Portrait Gallery, Washington, D.C.

Apollo Belvidere (Figure 6). The image was meant to encapsulate their argument: blacks were more akin to apes than to humans. One did not even need to be literate to understand their "scientific" claim.[15]

Douglass attacked these racist arguments by championing the "truthfulness" of the photograph and stressing the picturemaking proclivity of all humans. By doing so he emphasized humanity's common origins, and the superiority of imagination over reason. The "full identity of man with nature," he said, "is our chief distinction from all other beings on earth and the source of our greatest achievements." While "dogs and elephants are said to possess" the capacity for reason, only humans sought to recreate nature and portray both the "inside soul" and the "outside world" through such "artificial means" as the photograph. Making pictures required imagination, and Douglass quoted Ralph Waldo Emerson to argue that the realm of the "imagination" was the "peculiar possession and glory of man." The power of the imagination, he said, was "a sublime, prophetic, and all-creative power." Imagination could be used to create a public persona in the form of a photograph or engraving. It could also be used to articulate a sublime and prophetic vision of a sin-free world, as he and his comrades did at Syracuse in 1855. The power of the imagination linked humans to "the Eternal sources of life and creation." It allowed them to appreciate pictures as accurate representations of some greater reality, and it helped them to realize their sublime ideals in an imperfect world. As Douglass aptly put it: "Poets, prophets, and reformers are all picture makers—and this ability is the secret of their power and of their achievements. They see what ought to be by the reflection of what is, and endeavor to remove the contradiction." He even went so far as to suggest that "the moral and social influence of pictures" was more important in shaping national culture than "the making of its laws."[16]

Douglass also created pictures with words. His 1855 autobiography represents a textual analogue to the frontispiece of the book. The book traces Douglass' life from slavery to freedom, and its structure—in both pictures and words—portrays an intelligent and authentic black performer who is ready and able to resist slavery and oppression. Immediately following the frontispiece is Douglass' elaborate dedication to Gerrit Smith, in which he praises Smith for "ranking slavery with piracy and murder" and denying its legal and constitutional existence. At the outset of the book, then, Douglass suggests that slavery is a state of

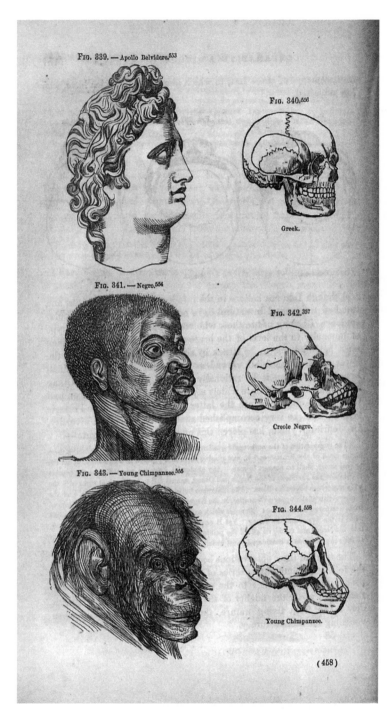

Figure 6. *Apollo Belvidere, Negro, Young Chimpanzee*. Engraving.
Reproduced in J. C. Nott and George R. Gliddon, *Types of Mankind: or,*
Ethnological Researches (Philadelphia: Lippincott, Grambo, 1855).

rebellion (or war), which needs to be dealt with in the same way that pirates and murderers are—through physical force.

The introduction to *My Bondage*, written by James McCune Smith, frames Douglass' narrative. It is a brief biography of Douglass' life that focuses almost exclusively on his accomplishments as a freeman and stresses his importance as a "Representative American man." The "secret" of Douglass' performative power, McCune Smith argues, stems from his success in continually transforming himself: he has "passed through every gradation of rank comprised in our national make-up, and bears upon his person and upon his soul every thing that is American." For McCune Smith, Douglass is a symbol of America, his progress made "visible" by his remarkable "style" of writing and speaking. He recounts how a well-known Whig politician and editor (and no friend of Radical Abolitionists) after hearing one of Douglass' speeches told a white colleague: "I would give twenty thousand dollars if I could deliver that address in that manner."[17]

Douglass acknowledged his success in creating an effective black public persona. During his "life as a freeman," he defines himself primarily as a public speaker: this section of the book is followed by an "Appendix" containing excerpts of six speeches (plus one public letter), which is longer than all the other chapters of his "life as a freeman" combined. In the genre of slave narratives, there was no precedent for representing oneself as a freeman in American society. This is one reason why Douglass begins his "life as a freeman" by saying that "there is no necessity for any extended notice of the incidents of this part of my life." In slave narratives, the author focused on his life in bondage and described the horrors of slavery in the hope of converting readers to abolitionism. In struggling to create a new genre and to find a style that would fit his new life as a freeman, Douglass presented himself as a performer, unadorned as it were, with a narrative framework. He arranged the speeches chronologically so that readers could glimpse the evolution of this public persona. Speaking, writing, and photography worked together in his book to create a powerful picture of an intelligent, authentic, and black performer.[18]

❧ In September 1856 John Brown sat for his portrait (Figure 7). Although he was not yet well known at the national level, he was quickly gaining fame as a freedom fighter in Kansas. As his reputation for militant abolitionism grew, he increasingly sat for his "likeness." He had numerous portraits taken of him while in Kansas, and preferred to have black artists or abolitionists represent him. This daguerreotype was created by John Bowles, a Kentucky slaveowner who had emancipated his slaves and become an abolitionist and comrade of Brown in Kansas. Bowles was quite familiar with Brown's willingness to befriend and identify himself with blacks, and one might argue that he portrays

Figure 7. John Brown. Daguerreotype by John Bowles, 1856.
Boston Athenaeum.

Brown as someone who blurs the line between black and white: the da-guerreotype is slightly underexposed, rendering Brown's tanned skin even darker than it actually was. Brown's face appears tawny, as dark as Douglass' in the frontispiece of *My Bondage*.[19]

There are many other similarities between Bowles's portrait of Brown and Douglass' frontispiece. Brown stares defiantly into the camera lens, with furrowed brow and tight lips. In their portraits throughout the 1850s, Brown and Douglass typically stare into the camera lens, thus disregarding portrait conventions of the time, which called for men to look beyond or away from the camera lens. Brown also looks younger than he actually is. He is fifty-six years old in the portrait, but could easily pass for a man a decade younger. And Brown's pose resembles Douglass': it is dramatic, intense, and self-conscious, with an emphasis on physicality. His arms are forcefully crossed, and his hands grip his elbows in a posture of defiance. And like Douglass, Brown appears to be in extraordinary physical shape, all muscle and sinew, as though he could fight, run, or live in the wilderness for weeks on end.[20]

The aggressive postures of Brown and Douglass convey something of their greater propensity for violence and reliance on God's will, relative to Gerrit Smith and James McCune Smith. Of the four men, Brown had the greatest proclivity for violence, for which he became famous. His quest to vanquish slavery resembled Captain Ahab's resolve to kill the white whale: In *Moby-Dick*, Melville's narrator could have been referring to Brown when he says of Ahab: "There was an infinity of firmest fortitude, a determinate, unsurrenderable wilfulness, in the fixed and fearless, forward dedication of that glance." Brown's "unsurrenderable wilfulness" stemmed not from his own will (in his mind), but from God's. He never wavered in his prophecy, and frequently referred to himself as an instrument in God's hands. His use of violence to end slavery was inseparable from his role as God's prophet seeking to resurrect society from the cesspool of slavery. And like Captain Ahab, he had a profound influence on his men. Douglass, McCune Smith, and Gerrit Smith were influenced by Brown's exhortations to destroy slavery through violence, much as the crew of the *Pequod* was almost bewitched by Ahab's monomaniacal pursuit of the white whale. Brown encouraged Douglass, McCune Smith, and Gerrit Smith to seek vengeance and death against *their* Moby Dick, whatever the cost:

"God hunt us all, if we do not hunt Moby Dick to his death!" Ahab cried to his men. His tocsin might as easily have come from the mouth of John Brown, with "Moby Dick" as metaphor for slavery.[21]

Douglass similarly described the control that God had over him, and he, like Brown, was more prone to violence than McCune Smith and Gerrit Smith. While there is no record of McCune Smith and Gerrit Smith ever actually engaging in physical violence or resistance, Douglass got into fights and shoving matches a number of times. In one sense he built his public persona on his conquest of the "nigger-breaker" Edward Covey, who sought to break him into a docile and pliant slave. In *My Bondage* Douglass characterizes his fight with Covey in deeply symbolic and religious terms: after thrashing Covey, he gains "a glorious resurrection, from the tomb of slavery, to the heaven of freedom."[22] He also notes that the "mere circumstance" of his move from Colonel Lloyd's plantation, on the Eastern Shore of Maryland, to Baltimore represented "the first manifestation of that 'Divinity that shapes our ends, / Rough hew them as we will.'" (Douglass' quotation, from *Hamlet*, is the same that Abraham Lincoln—the other great nineteenth-century "self-made" man—used to account for *his* destiny.)[23] Actually, the first manifestation of God's will over Douglass occurs earlier in his autobiography, and it involves violence. He describes how he received a wound while fighting as a young boy, "which made a cross in my forehead very plainly to be seen now." It was as though God had given his seal of approval to physical resistance. The scar is barely visible in the engraving, though more noticeable in daguerreotypes, and it does not look much like a cross.[24] In Douglass' subtle rendering, God rather than slaveholders had marked (or branded) him as a young boy, and his sovereignty remained imprinted on Douglass' forehead as well as in his nature and destiny through manhood.

These similarities between Douglass and Brown suggest that class, education, and religion mattered more than skin color in their success at constructing public identities. Of the four men, John Brown and Frederick Douglass were the most alike. They achieved the greatest fame, had lower thresholds of violence, and never publicly wavered in their determination to follow God's will. They were also harder to penetrate as private individuals, and were more comfortable and successful in their public roles as abolitionists. They relied on their public images as abolitionists in part because they did not have other careers or identities to fall back on. One was a former slave, the other a bank-rupt artisan, and neither had much education. They *had* to rely on their public personas for their financial well-being and insider status. Their investment in the cause as a *material* vocation reinforced their religious imperative—the most important source of all four men's abolitionism. Brown and Douglass thus *had* to be more concerned with how they presented themselves to their audiences—in pictures and in speaking. From one perspective, they exchanged their private pasts as a slave and a bankrupt for Christlike public personas: Douglass displayed Christ's emblem on his forehead, and Brown finally hung on it at Harpers Ferry (according to Emerson and Thoreau).[25]

  In 1856, after a disastrous term in the U.S. House of Representa-tives in 1853–54, Gerrit Smith published his *Speeches in Congress.* He was fifty-nine years old, the elder statesman of the four men; and his book, like *My Bondage*, includes his portrait as the frontispiece (Figure 8). It is an engraving by Alexander H. Ritchie, based on a da-guerreotype from the late 1840s. Much like Douglass and Brown, Smith chose to recreate himself as a younger man, a practice that con-tinued into the 1860s, for he used this same engraving as the frontis-piece of his 1864 book on religion. Creating a portrait of oneself as a young man seemed appropriate to these agitators. Transforming America evidently required youthful strength and vigor. In one sense, their public image of youthfulness was consistent with their anticipa-tion of a new age, their ability to dispense with linear chronology, and their willingness to dismantle fixed markers of identity (such as race, class, and age) in order to achieve a more fluid self.

Smith's wide collar, perched high on his neck, hints at his efforts to reimagine himself as a young aristocratic rebel. As a college student he had affected the "flowing hair" and "broad 'Byron Collar'" of his poetic hero, and retained the look throughout the 1850s.[26] Byron's life and poetry struck a resonant chord with Smith: when he died at age thirty-six while fighting in a war of liberation in Greece, he was famous throughout Europe and America as a poet, genius, and aristocrat turned rebel who had overcome the deficiency of his club foot to assert his manliness. Moreover, by becoming a martyr of freedom, Byron had shown that he was willing to act on the message of his poetry, much as Gerrit Smith and his comrades sought to realize their political ideals. For Smith (as for McCune Smith, Douglass, and countless other American male reformers), there was something appealing about Byron's tendency in both his life and art to set his face against society and embrace the rebellious qualities of youth, idealism, and unfettered freedom. Byron also resembled these Radical Abolitionists in his quest for continual self-transformation while remaining "constant" in his "strong love of liberty," as the poet put it. It is understandable, then,

Figure 8. Gerrit Smith. Engraving by A. H. Ritchie.
Reproduced in Smith, *Speeches of Gerrit Smith in Congress*
(New York: Mason Brothers, 1856), frontispiece.

that Gerrit Smith, McCune Smith, and Douglass frequently quoted Byron in their correspondence, speeches, and published writings as a source of inspiration, particularly those lines that invoked rebellion and self-transformation.[27]

Gerrit Smith was uncomfortable in his role as a public figure, however. He was much less successful than Douglass and Brown at creating a compelling public persona. He felt entirely out of place in the spotlight in Washington as a dissident congressman, and quit before his term had expired. He ranked himself in the "first class" as a public speaker but acknowledged that Douglass and Brown were more effective. And he did not like to campaign for his elections, preferring instead to have Frederick Douglass stump for him. Even his use of pictures to help him reimagine himself and his world remained at a private and personal level. He owned an extraordinary photo album containing hundreds of *cartes-de-visite* of friends, family, and fellow reformers, along with portrayals of European royalty and marble statues; but the album was meant for private rather than public consumption. And unlike Douglass and Brown, in his frontispiece he looks beyond the camera lens in the customary "visionary gaze" for men of wealth, education, and eminence. His trademark signature below the portrait, "Your friend Gerrit Smith," betrays his preference for personal and private interaction. His book of speeches, which sold few copies, was read primarily by friends, and he had to be persuaded to publish it. And although he wrote an autobiographical sketch in 1856—a genre that by its very nature represents a public construction of the self—he never published it and refused requests from publishers to have his biography written.[28]

Smith's inability to create a compelling public persona stemmed in part from his struggles to resolve the contradiction of a white man seeking to become black. He reveals this dilemma in his autobiography, as does John Brown. Brown wrote a short autobiographical sketch in 1857 at the request of Henry Stearns, a young admirer and son of a Boston abolitionist, and, like Smith, never published it. The most prominent feature of their autobiographies is the distance between narrator and subject: Smith and Brown use third-person narrative voice, a highly unusual vantage point (at the time) from which to characterize oneself. Their choice of perspective underscores the problems they faced trying to define themselves as black men, for the characters they write about are, by virtue of their ancestry and upbringing, white. It was as though they implicitly understood the contradiction of describing their white pasts while seeking to become black, and by writing in the third person they distanced the one self from the other.[29]

Smith had more difficulty than Brown in reconciling his racial identity. On the one hand, he continually publicized his efforts to remake himself into a black man. In an 1854 congressional speech, he emphasized that he was not only "born and bred" among "negroes and Indians as well as whites," but happily recognized "in every man [his] brother—ay, another self," and sought to infuse this racial fluidity into "everyone who is without it." He sought to show by his vote and his actions that he was "a colored man," and worshipped in black churches when not at his integrated church in Peterboro, believing that the segregated pews of white churches were blasphemous. On the other hand, Smith harbored a deep-seated and rarely acknowledged angst about his black identity, even during the high point of his radicalism in the 1850s, as is apparent in some of his unpublished writings. He never entirely rejected white society. For most of his life he lived in the "mansion-house" in the village of Peterboro that his slaveowning father had built, even though he did turn Smithfield into an egalitarian and interracial—but still mostly white—community. He continued to cultivate friendships with eminent (and racist) whites. And there is no record of his ever seeking out black photographers to represent him.[30] As a result, he was less successful than John Brown at cultivating a black performative self. Brown made war on white laws and conventions, lived in the mostly black community at North Elba, and continually quoted Hebrews 13:3, exhorting his audiences to "remember them that are in bonds as bound with them," which for him meant an empathic blending of racial identities.[31]

Despite these differences, Smith and Brown stood apart from the vast majority of their white peers, who thought that all blacks should strive to become "white," and thus accept an inferior rank in the social hierarchy as the way to solve the "problem of race." Many of Douglass' and McCune Smith's peers did in fact seek to become white in their demeanor and physical appearance in the hopes of rising above other blacks. These four men struggled to reverse this trend by blurring the boundaries of black and white. McCune Smith conveyed the idea that a black heart represented the standard of excellence by noting that Gerrit was as "moral, benevolent, [and] good as any black man on the face of the earth."[32]

Gerrit Smith defined himself primarily as a philanthropist, which he conceptualized as a private persona. He responded to solicitors rather than seeking them out, and never went to great lengths to publicize his philanthropy. His signature under his portrait, "Your friend Gerrit Smith," underscores his identity as a friend of humanity, as does the warm and congenial expression on his face in his frontispiece. He always responded to the scores of daily solicitors asking for help (typically twenty-five to thirty-five letters a day), but often at the expense of legibility, and his handwriting in the frontispiece is as good as it got in the 1850s.[33] As a young man, he wrote in a relatively clear and legible hand (although his mother complained about his penmanship when he was in college). But as his reputation for generosity grew, so did the solicitations, and he handled the deluge of requests by writing so quickly that his letters in the 1850s appear at first glance to have been written in a foreign language. His handwriting was legendary among his friends and acquaintances. Frederick Douglass chided him about his "calligraphy," saying it resembled "a straight mark." The abolitionist Sarah Grimké complained of trying to "decypher" his letters. Many beneficiaries could not read his writing when they received money from him; and for years his own son, Greene Smith, had no idea what his father had written. Even mailmen had trouble with it. In 1852 the postmaster of a neighboring town outraged Smith by returning one of his abolitionist circulars with the following words on the envelope: "This writing is as incomprehensible as the cause he advocates—can't read it."[34] It was as though Smith's handwriting was a cryptic code or secret script, and learning how to read it became a rite of passage into a sacred circle of true believers in the cause of humanity. Indeed, his cryptic hand stemmed largely from his determination to respond to all who called upon him, and thus to live up to his self-image as a philanthropist. In his autobiographical sketch he reinforces this self-image: "To use a word which is somewhat trite in these days, Mr. Smith is entitled to be called a philanthropist. For as he shows that he is a lover of Christ because he keeps his commandments, so he proves himself a lover of his fellow men, because he practically endeavors to *relieve* their *woes.*"[35]

🎜 Sometime in the mid-1850s, James McCune Smith walked down Broadway in Manhattan to 23rd Street, opposite the Fifth Avenue Hotel, and at the spacious gallery of Johnson, Williams & Company had his portrait taken (Figure 9). He had it printed as a *carte-de-visite* and sent a copy to Gerrit Smith, who put it in his photo album. The portrait shows McCune Smith in his early forties, formally dressed, and looking beyond the camera lens in a visionary gaze. His pose closely resembles that of Gerrit Smith in his frontispiece, and it fits his upbringing. Of the four men, McCune Smith was unquestionably the most learned and broad-ranging intellectual. He had three degrees from an

Figure 9. James McCune Smith. *Carte-de-visite* by
Johnson, Williams & Co., Photographers, ca.
1855. Madison County Historical Society, Oneida, N.Y.

eminent university, an established interracial medical practice and pharmacy in New York City, and a spacious house in Manhattan. He was highly respected by white physicians for his medical practice and scientific writings, and even more esteemed by black abolitionists for his intellect and knowledge of race and reform. His essays on racial conditions and the state of America and reform were closely read and sometimes incorporated in the speeches and public writings of Gerrit Smith and Douglass. McCune Smith was also a voracious reader of history and literature—particularly Romantic writers—from Robert Burns, Lord Byron, and Emerson, to Washington Irving, George Bancroft, and Herman Melville. In fact he published a brief critique of Melville's *Moby-Dick*, an obscure work in its time.[36]

McCune Smith's interpretation of *Moby-Dick* conveys something of his erudition and aesthetic taste. In a March 1856 essay titled "Horoscope" he likened the *Pequod*, the whaling ship in the novel, to the ship of state in American politics. Horace Greeley, the influential editor and Republican party leader, was a "boatsteerer" much like Stubb, the second mate of the *Pequod*. "On the eve of an election," Greeley "shrieks out" to his party "like Stubb in Moby Dick" after spotting a whale: "'Start her, start her, my men! . . . start her like grim death and grinning devils, and raise the buried dead perpendicular out of their graves, boys—that's all. Start her.'" (McCune Smith was quoting from chapter 61 of *Moby-Dick*, "Stubb Kills a Whale.") For McCune Smith, those in charge of both the *Pequod* and the American ship of state were in pursuit of the wrong thing: the white whale on the one hand, whiteness and respect for white laws on the other hand. They were thus sacrificing "the one thing needful"—"HUMAN BROTHERHOOD"—and the "belief that all men are by nature *free* and equal." Horace Greeley "has avowed, in coarse terms, his belief in the inferiority of the negro to the white man, and his disgust at the idea of social commingling with his black brother." So did every other major political leader in America. As a result, any hopes for "the cause of Human Freedom" "are doomed to be blasted." In McCune Smith's estimation, by ignoring the multiracial makeup of their country American leaders were following the plight of the *Pequod* and heading toward destruction and death. His "horoscope" was more accurate than he knew.[37]

Most of McCune Smith's readers did not understand his obscure references to works such as *Moby-Dick*, however, and his essays were not widely read. Of the four men, he was (and remains) the least known, particularly outside abolitionist circles. He was a thoroughgoing intellectual but never felt comfortable in the role of *public* intellectual. He was more private even than Gerrit Smith. He never published a book, only pamphlets, which typically did not sell as well. And he was the only one of the four who never wrote an autobiography. His *carte-de-visite* portrait conveys something of his relative shyness about constructing a public persona: he displayed it not publicly, as Gerrit Smith did his frontispiece, but sent it privately to his friend; and the features of his profile fade away at the top of his head and below his shoulders, as if to suggest that he did not shine brightly as a public figure. It stands in stark contrast to the portraits of Douglass and Brown. In one sense, McCune Smith was *too* learned in his speech and bearing and *too* experimental and abstruse in his prose to reach a wide audience and create an effective black persona. Additionally, he had light skin; in fact his skin looks lighter than Brown's in their respective portraits. But he was "not ashamed to own, *that through my veins flow, freely flow, dark Afric's proudest blood.*" His style and bearing prevented him from becoming a widely known public performer and writer.[38]

McCune Smith nevertheless believed that a black performative self could be extremely effective in breaking down racial barriers. After seeing a performance by the singer Elizabeth Greenfield, popularly known as the "Black Swan," at the Broadway Tabernacle in March 1855, he concluded that "true art is a social leveler, and thoroughly isocratic," or egalitarian. Greenfield's performance was so powerful that she collapsed racial barriers and created an integrated community in the Tabernacle: "Never was the Tabernacle so thoroughly speckled with mixed complexions; blond gentlemen sat side and side with dark ladies," and "colorblind" white women sat next to black men. Greenfield refused to succumb to "the requirements of American Prejudice," for instead of trying to hide her ancestry, she stood forth "simple and pure a black woman." McCune Smith urged his black readers to see Greenfield perform: "apart from the rich musical treat, they will have an opportunity at looking into their own hearts." A black heart, he felt, could create a fictional reality (in the form of an artistic self) that transcended American prejudice.[39]

McCune Smith went so far as to predict that African Americans would one day triumph over their white oppressors through the power of their art. The "true" art of a black heart would not only break down social barriers; it would redefine American cultural expression:

> we are destined to write the literature of this republic, which is still, in letters, a mere province of Great Britain. We have already, even from the depths of slavery, furnished the only music which the country has yet produced. We are also destined to write the poetry of the nation ... We are destined to produce the oratory of this Republic; for since true oratory can only spring from honest efforts in behalf of the RIGHT, such will of necessity arise amid our struggles.

McCune Smith was rhetorically a century ahead of his time in declaring that American literature, music, and performance would be shaped and defined by black cultural expression. And he did his part to create a new literature for the republic; he published a series of essays in *Frederick Douglass' Paper* that he called "Republic of Letters."[40]

But McCune Smith also recognized the shortcomings of relying solely on a performative self to combat racism. "The colored man must do impracticable things before he is admitted to a place in society," he acknowledged in 1854. "He must speak like a [Frederick] Douglass, write like a[n Alexandre] Dumas, and sing like the Black Swan before he could be recognized as a human being." He well knew that his own medium of choice, the essay, coupled with his experimental style, had limited popular appeal, especially compared with public speaking, photography, and stage performance.[41]

McCune Smith defined himself primarily as a farsighted teacher and intellectual who preferred to work away from the public glare. He hoped for future recognition and acknowledgment of his labors, and said as much in a poignant letter to Gerrit Smith in 1848: "I will fling whatever I have into the cause of colored children, that they may be better and more thoroughly taught than their parents are." His work was "not of today only but of centuries," and it suited him "because it is very hard, and somewhat noiseless": "In the series of metamorphoses I must have had a coral insect for a millio-millio-grandfather, loving to work beneath the tide in a superstructure that some day, when the labourer is long dead and forgotten, may rear itself above the waves, and afford rest and habitation for the creatures of his Good, Good Father and All." By 1855 his vision of social metamorphosis would acquire an urgency that had not existed in 1848, though he still preferred to remain "beneath the tide."[42]

McCune Smith and Gerrit Smith, like Douglass and Brown, crossed racial boundaries to define themselves. They had far more in common with each other than with their comrades. They were less successful as public figures, but more introspective and self-critical—especially Gerrit Smith. They were more reticent about relying on violence and God's will. And both were formally educated, with established and financially successful professions outside of their abolition work. McCune Smith was even accused by some of his black colleagues of being *too* successful: the black abolitionist William Wilson (who wrote under the pseudonym "Ethiop") resented McCune Smith's "back office with cushioned chairs," along with his use of obscure literary references, and "idle time for readings of that sort." Other blacks envied his spacious house and well-tailored clothes, all of which he owed to his education and medical practice.[43] McCune Smith and Gerrit shared one other thing in common: they had lighter skin than Douglass and Brown (at least in their photographs), further blurring racial categories. All in all, they lacked the material urgency as well as the disposition and means to create the kind of public and performative black masks that Douglass and Brown acquired. There was greater fluidity between their private and public identities, and greater consistency between their past and present lives. After college, they went home, and lived in Peterboro and New York City for the rest of their lives. Despite their enormous self-transformations, they retained a core of consistency: they remained, from their early adulthood to their deaths, a land baron and philanthropist on the one hand, and a physician and intellectual on the other.

The public personas of Douglass, Brown, Gerrit Smith, and McCune Smith were, despite varying degrees of effectiveness, important components in their identities as Radical Abolitionists. They orchestrated their identities in visual as well as religious and political terms. Prophets need to see themselves clearly, and these men were no exception; their visual self-definitions provided clear markers of their self-fashioning. Their public personas also helped give them access to the public sphere, which represented a form of power, thus allowing them to define themselves as social outsiders with insider status. Gerrit

Smith's great wealth and James McCune Smith's interracial medical practice gave them immediate access to the public sphere, at least within their communities. Brown and Douglass had to rely more heavily on their public personas as writers, speakers, and militants in order to gain insider status. All four men had to infiltrate white society and become bourgeois in order to effectively attack white bourgeois conventions. To see how that happened, we need to turn to their formative years and their first glimpses of God's world on Earth.

CHAPTER THREE

Glimpsing God's World
on Earth

Come dearest offspring of the art!
Shine out upon this widow'd heart.
And oh! imparadise me for an hour,
In sweet delusion,—that, in thee
Far more than pencil lines I see,
E'en glowing features of a living power.

— GERRIT SMITH (1820)

Between two worlds life hovers like a star
'Twixt night and morn upon the horizon's verge.
How little do we know that which we are!

— LORD BYRON, *Don Juan* (1824)

Gerrit Smith was the only member of this interracial alliance who, as a young man, could afford to have his portrait painted. It was the customary thing to do for a patrician who had recently entered manhood (Figure 10). Smith's portrait bears a striking resemblance to his 1856 frontispiece in *Speeches in Congress* (Figure 8). Both portraits show him as a pleasant and sociable man who would not take himself too seriously. And both show him emulating his hero Lord Byron, wearing a high collar; in the painting he also follows Byron's style (as portrayed in engravings of the poet and described by contemporaries) of letting a few strands of hair break the hairline and fall toward the brow. As young man and old, Smith lived in the "mansion-house" his father had built on the northwest corner of the village green in the remote village of Peterboro. The path from patrician to Radical Abolitionist had more to do with heart and soul than with external appearances. You did not need to change the way you looked to acquire a black heart.[1]

Apart from the effects of time on the body, there are only a few subtle clues to suggest Smith's change of heart: as a young man he has a
slight smile, and looks more congenial than does the older agitator; and
in the painting he appears to be looking down at the viewer, perhaps to
give him a more mature demeanor. Although his signature does not
appear under his painting, he elsewhere betrays his identity as a young
patrician by closing his letters with "Your humble servant," often adding "Esquire" after his name for proper effect. Eventually he would
abandon these flourishes. Not only would "your servant" become

Figure 10. Gerrit Smith. Oil on canvas, ca. 1818.
Syracuse University Library, Special Collections.

"your friend," but the 1855 Radical Abolition convention at Syracuse forbade "Rev's.," "Hon's.," and other titles from the names of those recorded as participants.[2]

The two portraits of Gerrit Smith convey a sense of both the continuity and remarkable change that linked the young patrician to the later revolutionary. Smith's self-image in the mid-1850s provides an excellent frame of reference for understanding the great social, spiritual, and psychological distances he traveled as he remade himself. This mid-1850s reference point is similarly helpful for appreciating the transformations of Frederick Douglass, James McCune Smith, and John Brown. The trajectories of these men, from patrician, artisan, and slave into reformer, were marked by a series of tragic and fortuitous events over which they had little control. Despite their differences, they all experienced chronic social change, upheaval, and instability, which forced (or allowed) them to redefine themselves, to discard old dreams and acquire new ones. As a result of their precarious circumstances they began to search for a more secure and enduring reality. They turned away from the structures and values of their material world, on which they could not depend, and started to give greater weight to their spiritual visions and passions of the heart, thereby initiating the process of self-transformation that would ultimately converge in their identities as Radical Abolitionists.

❧ Even as a young man, Smith thought of himself as something of a romantic rebel. In 1816, as a sophomore at Hamilton College, he received a copy of Lord Byron's *Siege of Corinth* from a college friend, who had parodied Byron's dedication to John Hobhouse by inscribing on the flyleaf his token of esteem for Gerrit, characterizing him in Byronesque terms. Gerrit, the friend said, was both sentimental and superior-minded, ambitious and Epicurean, poetic and partial, sincere and hoaxing, generous and gambling.[3] As a college student Gerrit loved Byron's darkly romantic vision and melancholy lyrics. He also exhibited—especially in later life—the volatile mood swings for which the poet was so well known. "In appearance I do not denote sickness," he wrote his mother in 1815 from college, "while the interior suffers grievously." But he refused to cleanse his soul: "Repentance ne'er has graced my impious lips or heart—it yet remains . . . perhaps to be the duty of a dying bed." Yet he vowed to stand "firm and resolute" and to "meet the rude and venomous obstacles of this world without a murmur."[4] Here were the darkly romantic, irreverent, and rebellious qualities of the Byronic hero.

As an adult Smith revolted against the conventions of white society; as a youth he rebelled against the authority of his father. In the same letter to his mother, he attacked his father for being "but a nominal" parent "for so long a time." He called himself "a friendless son" on account of his father, but declared that "desperation shall never become my property." He deeply loved his mother, considered her a "saint," and frequently wrote her from college. But he rarely corresponded with his father, and when he did, his letters bristled with anger. Throughout college he addressed his father as "Dear Sir" and accused him of trying to interfere with his studies. His father refused to forward even *"paltry money"* for his education, forcing Gerrit to borrow from friends to pay for room, books, and board. But he vowed not to let his father's treatment of him interfere with his studies: "I *will* pursue my studies unless extraordinary interventions occur," he told him in a November 1816 letter. His father had no reason for treating him like a child: "As you well know, I am no fop, no drunkard, not addicted to any kind of profaneness, [and] my only aim is respectability as a scholar and a man worthy of his relatives and friends. Perhaps I am too ambitious! But nothing is more forbidding to me than a man of unconcern, void of motive, energy, and action." Gerrit tried to conciliate his father, often visiting him upon request. But "never, no not once have I met the welcome smile, always cold and repulsive." To make matters worse, his father sometimes passed near Hamilton College in his travels "and did not even notify [him]." At one point while still in college, Gerrit lost almost all hope of achieving any kind of intimacy with his father: "I have visited for the last, perhaps," he told him. "If affection cannot be restored, let at least respectful friendship be maintained."[5]

Gerrit's father, Peter Smith, was a self-made man. He was born in 1768 in Rockland County, New York, to parents of Dutch ancestry. The family had little money, and in 1784, at age sixteen, he moved to New York City to seek his fortune. He briefly pursued his taste for the theater by acting in bit parts on the stage of the Park Theater. But he primarily worked as a clerk in a merchant's office for a few years, and then ran a bookshop for a few more, eking out a meager living. His luck turned when he met John Jacob Astor, another poor but ambitious young man. They formed a fur-trading partnership and established a fur store in the city. During the summer months they sailed up the Hudson River to Albany on a sloop, disappeared into the wilderness to trade with the Mohawks, Oneidas, Cayugas, and Senecas, and transported the furs back to New York to sell. In 1789 Smith moved to the recently formed settlement of Utica, New York, to cultivate further his relations with the Oneidas, while Astor stayed in New York to manage the shop. Their business, though physically grueling, was extremely lucrative, and by 1792 Smith was wealthy enough to marry Elizabeth Livingston, the daughter of James Livingston, a lawyer, Revolutionary War colonel, and member of the eminent Hudson Valley Livingston family.[6]

After his marriage Peter Smith exchanged the rugged life of a fur trader for the genteel career of a land baron. He amassed close to a million acres of land, and in 1806, when Gerrit was nine years old, he moved his family from Utica to the village of Peterboro, in the township of Smithfield, which he had named and founded. Located in the center of Madison County, about midway between Syracuse and Utica, Peterboro was (and is) an isolated community in the hills of central New York. In geography and style, it stood apart from the other settlements in the area, which consisted primarily of transplanted New Englanders and Quakers. Peter Smith's new residence reflected his social status. It was wholly self-contained, accessible only by a narrow winding road, and resembled a landed estate or southern plantation far more than it did a New England or Quaker village. The Smith "mansion-house," as it was called, comfortably slept twenty-two guests—not counting the Indians who often camped in the halls and on the piazza—and was decorated with aristocratic elegance. Peter Smith acquired a chair that had been owned by James Madison, a chest of drawers brought to America by Baron von Steuben, a desk rumored to have belonged to Napoleon, and a rosewood dining table that accommodated twenty people. The estate itself consisted of thirty buildings spread across thirty acres of land, another few hundred acres of farmland, and numerous slaves to maintain the estate. Because of his status in the community, Peter Smith was named the first judge of Madison County, even though he had no legal training, little education, and, until about 1815, difficulty constructing a grammatically correct sentence.[7]

Gerrit was not the only one who found his father cold and repulsive. Many contemporaries considered Peter Smith "a hard sharp, shrewd man, close at a bargain, selfish and grasping." He sought, unsuccessfully, to control his children in the same domineering way he managed his land transactions. He tried to arrange the marriage of Gerrit's older sister Cornelia to John Adams Smith, which he considered a great match for business reasons. Cornelia was eighteen years old at the time, and rebelled by breaking off the engagement and marrying the first man who would have her, all in the space of eight days. She bluntly told her father that it was an act of revenge. He was furious, pitied himself instead of considering her plight, and accused her of trying to destroy his reputation, his family, and his peace of mind. He banished her from the mansion-house, but she ignored his decree, and when Peter found out about one of her visits, he stormed into the dining room, shattered a plate by throwing it to the floor, and stormed back to his land office. He forced Gerrit and his older brother Peter Skenandoah to spend their childhoods until the age of sixteen at manual labor. Gerrit worked side by side with his father's slaves, against his will, feeling sorry for both himself and his "poor" and "friendless" co-workers.[8] It was an experience he never forgot; it made his understanding of slavery not something abstract and conceptual but palpable and real, and it eventually helped him to empathize and identify with slaves and the poor.[9] Gerrit's older brother, perhaps as a partial response to his father's tyranny over him, turned to drink and eventually became a complete inebriate. Gerrit may have realized that the methods employed by his older brother and sister to assert their independence were less than ideal. In any event, he chose a far more effective way to gain autonomy over his father: education.

He entered Hamilton College in nearby Clinton, New York, in 1814, and was ambitious and determined, as he told his father, to pursue his studies. He was eighteen years old, could read, construe, and parse enough of Virgil's *Aeneid*, Cicero's *Select Orations*, and the Greek Testament to pass his entrance exam, and was one of fifteen admitted to the freshman class. He soon became attached to Byron, joined the Phoenix Society, one of Hamilton's literary societies, and decided that he wanted to become a man of letters, seek his literary fame, and per-

haps couple his passion for literature with a career in law. He vowed to
persist in the "laudable pursuit" of literature, as he told his mother in
1815. "I shall never cease while life and feeble action last. Let me
sacrifice my life to a noble purpose, in preference to one which will
tend to disgrace my memory." He was studious and diligent, and
though he indulged his romantic melancholy with a decanter of gin
more than once, he described himself accurately when he told his father that he was no drunkard, dissipater, or profligate. Hamilton College was extremely paternalistic; it had a strict code of conduct that forbade drinking, gambling, absence from the twice-daily chapel services,
and any form of sexual activity, and Gerrit never received a demerit,
reprimand, or fine. Aside from occasional bouts of drinking and a few
innocent letters in which he fantasized about sex, his only vice was
gambling. His propensity for gambling was probably an accommoda-
tion of his father's behavior as much as a form of rebellion, for his father gambled all the time with land (although he would not have described it as such). Conscious or not, Gerrit's diligent pursuit of his
studies and ardent desire for a literary career represented a powerful
act of rebellion against his father.[10]

It was not that Peter Smith was wholly averse to education. He recognized its use value for becoming a gentleman, and briefly served as a
trustee of Hamilton College, which had opened in 1812. But Peter
Smith saw education solely as a means to an end—a way for his son to
become polished and respectable enough to further the family name
and business interests. He did not consider education a prerequisite to
genteel authority. After all, he had little education, no classical training, and although he could speak Oneidan and Jersey Dutch, he was
lost in Latin and Greek. He was no "mushroom gentleman"—one who
sprang up overnight from the dung—but a cultivated gentleman, or so
he thought. He was not only one of the wealthiest men in the country,
but Madison County's first judge, a trustee of a central New York college that patterned itself after Yale, and related by marriage to the eminent Livingston family.[11]

Peter Smith could not understand Gerrit's zealous devotion to his
studies or his romantic inclinations. Given the "cold and repulsive"
looks he gave Gerrit, he probably thought that his son's Byronic collar
and wisps of flowing hair looked ridiculous. Instead of encouraging
Gerrit's studiousness, he tried to undermine it by being miserly with

his allowance, and when he did write his son, he pestered him to get involved with land deals that Gerrit was not the least interested in. When Gerrit requested money, whether to pay for food, books, and firewood (and perhaps gambling), or to go to Montreal to perfect his French, his father balked and got angry. Yet when Peter Smith tried to sell Gerrit a "great property," which required close supervision, "active management," and thus time away from his books, his son did not respond. Father and son lived in different worlds.[12]

Gerrit would undoubtedly have pursued his literary dreams had a series of tragedies not permanently disrupted his life and opened the way to reform and eventual revolution. The first of these occurred at his graduation. He received the top academic honors at Hamilton, and delivered the valedictory address at his commencement on August 26, 1818. His father did not attend the graduation ceremonies, but his mother, though gravely ill, made the half-day trip to Clinton from Peterboro. But she was too sick to see her son graduate, and on August 27, the day after commencement, she died of "cholera morbus." Gerrit was devastated. Forty-one years later he admitted that his mother's death had been one of the most important "epochs" in his life, sparking "the religious element" within him. It was the first indication that he could not rely on the objective and material world for stability and direction.[13]

His mother's death did not immediately alter his plans, however. He still proposed to follow his "most ardent desires" and pursue literature. He was also in love with the daughter of Hamilton's president, the Reverend Azel Backus. Wealtha Backus was her name, and Gerrit sometimes referred to her as "Wealth." President Backus died during Gerrit's junior year in college, and shortly thereafter he and Wealtha got engaged. They were married on January 11, 1819, five months after his mother's death. Gerrit moved out of the mansion-house, away from his father, and lived with Wealtha and her mother and brother. In spite of his mother's recent death, President Backus' death, and his father's seemingly heartless attitude toward him, he was happy. He was deeply attached to Wealtha and her family, and had looked upon President Backus "as a father." "Never was there a family more affectionate nor never one more worthy of the affection of others," he said of the Backuses. He essentially found through them the love that was now missing at the mansion-house.[14]

It did not last long. In October 1819, seven months after their marriage, Wealtha died, from what doctors called "dropsy of the brain." It was the second crushing blow for Gerrit in little over a year, and he was paralyzed with grief. "I absent myself from church," he wrote a few months after her death, "for I am too much occupied with my sorrows to receive either knowledge or consolation."[15]

Instead of going to church he spent the afternoon looking at a portrait of Wealtha, and it was a most enlightening afternoon. The portrait "fills me with recollections, with sorrows, and even with emotions of pleasure which I cannot suppress," he confessed. And then, resorting to a Byronic style of verse, he tried to render her portrait real, to feel again her breath, her touch, her love. "Come dearest offspring of the art," he beseeched the portrait. "Shine out upon this widow'd heart"; "imparadise me for an hour." He searched beneath the "pencil lines" of the image, looking for that "sweet delusion"—the "glowing features of a living power"—desperately seeking a fictional (and sensual) reality that could allay his grief. "Still more dear charm!" he urged the picture, but however hard he tried, his ability to fuse art and life, to replace the objective world for a fictional or spiritual reality, was still many years away. Initially, his picture of Wealth could not fire the passions of his heart, even though it was joyous to his eyes:

> . . . And now my sight,
> Joys in the swells of life and light—
> While my full heart, abandon'd to the strife
> Of its own bitter agony.

The portrait was no more than an "illusive, transient joy."[16]

"Ah Wealth!" he cried as he looked at the portrait, hoping that it would become real. He remembered that "happy hour" "on time's unfriendly shore," when they had last "communed together." Since that fleeting hour,

> . . . Peace has forsook me—
> Of all the chords that string this breast,
> Not one has kindly sounded rest—
> Each strives to swell the note of misery.

He longed to return to the time "when the wide world was brighten'd o'er" with her "every charm and power of happiness." Unlike the charm of the picture, Wealth's charm had brought him a bright, wide world. But "that time's no more!"

> That world, how small it has become!
> Its beauty and its gilding gone—
> Its dark remains yield naught but wretchedness.[17]

Gerrit had lost his Wealth (and his symbol of wealth), but by rendering the portrait poetically and struggling to make it real, he pointed the way to a new world, a new source of wealth, and radical reform: "Man's heritage is not below," he realized. "His home is Heaven." He vowed "to follow thee—when the eternal voice / Wakes me from time's illusive dream." He would indeed be awakened from the illusory dream of linear, chronological time, but instead of following his Wealth to heaven, he would strive to make his home a heaven on Earth. That could not happen, however, until he had a change of heart. As for now, "I have a heart but cold, / Compared with those of happier mold." So "cold and base" was his heart, that he had been unable to shed "one tear for thee." He had not let fall even "one tear to tell the world that he," though "so barren of all good," "had feeling left"—a feeling of "a secret source" that was "dead to" life's grit "force."[18]

After looking so long at his picture of Wealth, and wanting to believe it to be real, he began to unlock that secret source of feeling, and "now" his tears came bursting forth "in one redeeming flood." He even thought that he "could see / that cherub form so dear to me." It was his first glimpse of "the glowing features of a living power" that existed beneath the pencil lines of the portrait—and beyond the precarious world in which he lived.[19]

By glimpsing the living power of the portrait and expressing this power through verse, Gerrit anticipated the "visionary mode" of Walt Whitman and Edgar Allan Poe. Poe thought that "all certainty is in dreams": "All that we see or seem / Is but a dream within a dream," he declares in "A Dream within a Dream" (1849). But for Poe (unlike Whitman), the reality of dreams and visions provoked terror instead of comfort and hope. For Smith, the living power of a portrait would become increasingly vivid as his world became less and less stable.[20]

❧ Peter Smith, meanwhile, had been at least as devastated as Gerrit by his own wife's (Gerrit's mother's) death. He became intrigued by the spiritual fires that had already begun to ignite the "Burned-Over District" of western New York in 1818.[21] He confessed to Gerrit that his mind "was so much confused" that he "could neither think, nor speak, nor write upon business." Although he still complained about the "cruel" treatment from his children, he and Gerrit began to patch up some of their differences and get along. Gerrit started writing "Dear Father" in his letters rather than "Dear Sir," and Peter confided to his son that he still harkened after the treasures of the world, despite his newfound fascination with the spiritual realm: "And what can I expect from the world? Have I not tried it sufficiently to satisfy me [that] there is no happiness in it for me?" He wanted to believe that he had been "cruelly treated," "robbed of the happiness [he] was entitled to." He wanted to reconcile himself to the world as it was rather than "give it up so!" But he could no longer believe these things. "What can I do?" he asked his son. He suddenly realized, perhaps for the first time in his life, that he could do "nothing without a new heart!" In a statement that foreshadowed the religious writings of William James, Peter Smith told his son: "O, for faith, that we might believe in the reality of things not seen!" Like his son, Peter Smith had begun to probe beneath the surface of the visible world in search of a more truthful and meaningful reality. Soon he could be seen roaming the countryside, delivering Bible tracts to settlements, announcing his mission as he approached by blowing on a gospel trumpet of Jubilee, and bearing signs that described the message of "Eternity."[22]

As a result of his newfound faith in the reality of things not seen, Peter Smith lost interest in business. In October 1819, two months after Wealtha died, and in the midst of a financial panic and severe economic recession, he suddenly decided to retire and move to Schenectady, and asked Gerrit to take over his vast property concerns. Gerrit had virtually no experience in business, and later acknowledged to a friend that "the prospect" of managing his father's estate "had no charms for him, for it would defeat the realization of his most cherished aspirations." But his older brother Peter Skenandoah, already on his way to alcoholism, and his younger brother Adolphus, "insane" (or retarded) from birth, were in no position to manage anything. Gerrit decided, "out of filial regard to his father," but "with feelings of great reluctance," to accede to his father's request. He moved back to the mansion-house in November (along with Wealtha's mother and brother), fully aware that the management of his father's estate would engross all his time, require his best energies, and give an entirely new direction to his future.[23] He spent most of his waking hours staring at ledgers in his father's land office—a cramped, eight-by-ten-foot brick building that stood at the front of the estate. The land office, unlike the mansion-house, was dark and crude, lacking all amenities. Its sole purpose was to handle and preserve deeds and titles, notes and correspondence, and it no doubt felt at times to Gerrit like a prison-house of money.[24]

In little more than a year after reaching "manhood," then, Gerrit Smith found himself back home in the mansion-house, assuming responsibilities he disliked for a father he found cold and distant, his literary dreams shattered, and the two people he had loved most in the world, dead.

❧ If Gerrit Smith felt like a captive in his own house, Frederick Douglass was one. Their respective communities were, in some respects, quite similar. The Lloyd plantation on the Eastern Shore of Maryland, where Douglass lived from ages eight to ten, physically resembled the Smith estate. Lloyd's Wye House rivaled the Smith mansion-house in luxury. Douglass described the "immense wealth" and "lavish expenditure" that filled the Wye House, and a recent historian has called it "unquestionably one of the most handsome houses in America." The open porch with Grecian columns that Douglass admired in the Wye House (later replaced by an enclosed verandah) also defined the facade of the Smith mansion-house, and Douglass always felt at home during his visits to Peterboro in the 1850s. By the time Smith took over his father's estate, servants had replaced slaves, but the two communities were nevertheless largely self-sufficient, functioning like small cities unto themselves. Both estates had a milkhouse, a smokehouse, an icehouse, and storage facilities; and they employed or owned numerous artisans and servants along with fieldhands and farmhands. Harriet Tubman used the language of the plantation to describe Smith's mansion-house after visiting him at Peterboro; she called it the "Big House." And Douglass' characterization of the Lloyd plantation in his 1855 autobiography comes close to capturing what Peter Smith sought to replicate when he designed his estate: "In its isolation, seclusion, and self-reliant independence," Douglass said, "Col. Lloyd's plantation resembles what the baronial domains were, during the

middle ages in Europe." Douglass' description of the southern plantation also characterized the Smith estate: it was "a little world of
its own, having its own language, its own rules, regulations, and
customs."[25]

Despite these similarities, the two communities stood worlds apart,
for one was a patriarchal, the other a slave society. The difference was
enormous. Southern masters justified slavery in part by defining themselves as patriarchs and considering their slaves as part of their extended family. Slaves experienced not only the subordination and rigid
hierarchy of a patriarchal system, but they were also treated like domesticated animals, and could be bought, sold, branded, punished, or
slaughtered at any time. However oppressed Smith may have felt, it
would still require a leap of imagination for him to identify and empathize with slaves.[26]

As a slave, Douglass by definition experienced chronic social change,
instability, and upheaval. In theory he was a total outsider on the plantation, wholly alienated from his family. He occupied a liminal state
between life and death, animal and human, person and thing; he had no
name of his own, no identity independent from his master, and his only
autonomy came from work or rebellion. Any dreams and desires were
thwarted by his status as a slave. His sole hope was one of complete
self-transformation.[27]

In practice Douglass was an exceptionally privileged slave, but that
fact did not change his basic condition as a complete outsider. His
story is well known and has been told with great skill, so it can be summarized.[28] He was born Frederick Augustus Bailey in 1818—the same
year Smith graduated from Hamilton College—at Holme Hill Farm at
Tuckahoe Creek, in Talbot County, Maryland. He never knew with
certainty who his white father was, rarely saw his mother, and was
raised by his grandmother, Betsy Bailey. He describes his alienation
from his family by noting that "the practice of separating children from
their mothers, and hiring the latter out at distances too great to admit
of their meeting . . . is a marked feature of the cruelty and barbarity of
the slave system. But it is in harmony with the grand aim of slavery,
which, always and everywhere, is to reduce man to a level with the
brute."[29]

Yet the first six and a half years of Douglass' life were, he admitted,
"about as full of sweet content as those of the most favored and petted
white children," for the slaveholder had nothing to fear from "impotent

childhood." He was thus "freed from all restraint," and indulged in his "boyish nature" by running "wild" in the open air and bright sunshine around the log hut where he lived. He did not yet realize that he was a slave and that his master would attempt to tame his "wildness." But "clouds and shadows" began to "fall upon my path." His grandmother told him that he and the little hut and lot where he played belonged to a mysterious and abstract person called "Old Master," who would eventually take him away. The thought of being separated from his grandmother was "intolerable," haunting him while he played. Even as a young child, he realized that the sorrows and joys gleaned from his external surroundings were but "transient."[30]

In the late summer of 1824, Frederick's grandmother brought him to Wye House. He was six years old, three years younger than Gerrit had been when his father moved him to Peterboro. There he discovered brothers and sisters he had never known. He also lost his grandmother. She deceived him, left him at Wye House without saying a word, and when he discovered her deception, he became senseless, flinging away the fruit his brothers and sisters offered him, ignoring their words of kindness and consolation, and crying himself to sleep. The incident left a deep and lasting impression on his young mind. It was his "first introduction to the realities of slavery," his first realization that as a slave he was wholly dependent on the will of someone he had never seen—an "inexorable demi-god," as he aptly put it, "whose huge image on so many occasions haunted my childhood's imagination."[31]

It would not be long before Frederick began to search beyond the visible and material world for a more lasting and reliable reality. He would soon begin to exchange his dependence on a "demi-god" for a God who offered hope of a new world and self. The transformation began two years later, in 1826, following another move, this time to the Fells Point section of Baltimore; and it coincided with his learning to read and write. Douglass' largely self-taught literacy kindled an imaginative and religious awakening. It gave him the power to revolt against his master and to assert a degree of independence. It also enabled him to "look away to heaven for the rest denied me on earth," and eventually to envision the "sublime scene" of a heaven on Earth.[32]

The *Columbian Orator* enabled Douglass to envision a sublime heaven on Earth. This widely read collection of patriotic speeches designed for young boys was almost revolutionary in its message. It became one of the most important documents in his young life, exhorting him to a higher calling and inspiring him to imagine a better world from the "terrible reality" in which he lived. It also explicitly denounced slavery. Douglass devoted an entire chapter of *My Bondage and My Freedom* to the book, concluding that "my spirit was roused to eternal wakefulness." With knowledge from the book, coupled with his own "human nature" and experiences, he found himself able to contest "the religious advocates of slavery." He literally began to see "liberty" everywhere: "I do not exaggerate, when I say, that [liberty] looked from every star, smiled in every calm, breathed in every wind, and moved in every storm." The *Columbian Orator*—much like Gerrit's portrait of Wealth—gave Douglass the means to probe beneath the surface of his "terrible reality" for a vision of liberty. And the title he chose for his chapter on the *Columbian Orator*—"A Change Came O'er the Spirit of My Dream"—was a line from Lord Byron's poem "The Dream." For Smith and Douglass alike, Byron symbolized a male liberator who could replace a defective world with a poetic and spiritual reality.[33]

In the very next chapter of *My Bondage*, Douglass describes his religious awakening. It started when he heard a white Methodist minister (probably an itinerant evangelist) preach that "all men, great and small, bond and free, were sinners in the sight of God; that they were, by nature, rebels against His government; and that they must repent of their sins." Douglass did not know how to respond to this liberating message of social leveling from a white man, and so he consulted "a good colored man" named Charles Johnson, who told him how to pray and what to pray for. Douglass does not mention what it was he prayed for. He does, however, describe his initial struggle for conversion: "I was, for weeks, a poor, broken-hearted mourner, traveling through the darkness and misery of doubts and fears." He then experienced what William James would later characterize as a conversion by "self-surrender," prompted by the "subconscious": he discovered "that change of heart which comes by 'casting all one's care' upon God, and by having faith in Jesus Christ, as the Redeemer, Friend, and Savior of those who diligently seek Him." He saw the world "in a new light" and "seemed to live in a new world, surrounded by new objects" and "animated by new hopes and desires." He loved everyone, slaveholders not

excepted, but he "abhorred slavery more than ever." "My great concern was, now, to have the world converted." He had purged himself
from sin, and here began his efforts to sacralize the world, to end all sin
and replace the imperfect world with a heaven on Earth. By 1855,
when he wrote *My Bondage*, he reinterpreted earlier events in his life—
such as his move to Baltimore and the sacred scar on his forehead—as
signs that the kingdom of God resided within him and theoretically
within all individuals.[34]

❧ On September 10, 1824, James McCune Smith stood face to face
with one of the most famous men in the Western world and delivered a
short speech. He was eleven years old, and the top student at New
York City's African Free-School No. 2, on Mulberry Street. The man
he faced, the marquis de Lafayette, was a dashing French nobleman
who had served as a major general in George Washington's army, had
helped America attain independence, and was known as "the Hero of
the Worlds." He had been elected an honorary member of McCune
Smith's school in 1788, and was now visiting the school as part of a
tour of the United States. McCune Smith was technically still bonded
to his mother's owner and worked for him as a blacksmith. His father
was a merchant whom he never knew. But his speech disguised his social status as a bastard and bonded child. It was "gracefully delivered,"
according to the *New-York Commercial Advertiser*, and was gratefully
received by General Lafayette, who bowed and said, "I thank you, my
dear child."[35]

McCune Smith's bondage differed substantially from that of Frederick Douglass. He never described his experience working as a blacksmith, which suggests that his master required little labor of him and
probably gave him a kind of de facto freedom. When he delivered his
speech to Lafayette, he could hope for complete freedom from his
master in another three years. He later acknowledged that he owed his
freedom to the "Emancipation Act of the State of New-York."[36] The
state had a begun a process of gradual abolition in 1799 by freeing all
children born to slave mothers after July 4 of that year—as McCune
Smith had been—but only after serving their masters until age twenty-
eight (for men). Another state abolition law of 1817 agreed to free its
remaining slaves on July 4, 1827.[37]

McCune Smith understood that his precarious world depended upon the whims of unknown whites. He revealed as much in his speech to Lafayette:

> In behalf of myself and fellow-school-mates may I be permitted to express our sincere and respectful gratitude to you for the condescension you have manifested this day in visiting this institution, which is one of the noblest specimens of New York philanthropy.

It was a gracious speech for the time, and had probably been prepared for him by his teacher, Charles C. Andrews. He betrays no frustration or disappointment at being so dependent upon whites. It would require legal freedom and many more years of education for McCune Smith to assert his independence.[38]

His freedom came three years later, and he described the event as the beginning of a new epoch. New York City blacks celebrated their freedom on July 5, 1827, to distinguish the event from the national Independence Day.[39] "It was a proud day, never to be forgotten by young lads," he vividly recalled. As a slave he had experienced "perils oft" and "dangers oft," had lived in "the gloom of midnight, dark and seemingly hopeless, dark and seemingly rayless." "But now, through God's blessing," he found himself transformed, facing "the joyful light of day." He marched through the crowded streets and neighborhoods that he could now, for the first time, consider *his* streets, *his* neighborhoods, and part of *his* identity. His feet moved effortlessly, keeping time to the jubilant songs of freedom. He found himself shouting, "full-souled" and "full-voiced," for joy. Although he never described a religious conversion experience, Emancipation Day was the equivalent. It was the first step in his quest to realize a new world. The "joyful light of day" that he experienced with freedom would eventually be transformed into a sublime vision of America.[40]

McCune Smith's formal education would be crucial to that vision. It shaped his identity from an early age, much as Gerrit Smith's education and family wealth defined him. His teacher at the New-York African Free-School, Charles C. Andrews, was an important influence in his life. Andrews, who was white, believed in gradual emancipation through colonization (as did most other early white abolitionists). For Andrews (and many of his peers), blacks' "degraded" condition stemmed from oppression and enslavement rather than from innate behavioral traits. Education, he felt, was the antidote to their plight. As McCune Smith described it, Andrews was not "deeply learned," but was "a good disciplinarian," encouraged and inspired his students, and taught them one of the most important lessons of their lives: to believe themselves as smart and as capable as anyone else, "and to regard the higher walks of life as within their reach." Andrews "regarded his black boys as a little smarter than whites." The results of this lesson were invaluable. Of the hundreds of boys and girls (aged fifteen or less) who were classmates with McCune Smith in the 1820s, an unusually high percentage did indeed reach the higher walks of life. They included Henry Highland Garnet, the famous abolitionist; Ira Aldridge, the preeminent black Shakespearean tragedian; Charles L. Reason, professor of literature and languages at New York Central College; his brother Patrick Reason, an accomplished artisan who was asked to engrave the coffin plate of Daniel Webster; the Reverend Alexander Crummell, an internationally respected minister and intellectual; and Samuel Ringgold Ward, a brilliant public speaker and well-known abolitionist. Few primary or secondary schools—black or white—could boast this kind of success.[41]

McCune Smith was fortunate in other aspects of his education. After graduating with honors from the New-York African Free-School in 1828, he received additional instruction from Peter C. Williams, a black clergyman who presided over St. Philip's Episcopal Church, one of the largest black churches in the city. Williams, who helped hundreds of black students throughout his adult life, taught McCune Smith Latin and encouraged him to apply to medical school. After McCune Smith was denied admission from the Columbia College and Geneva, New York, medical schools on account of his race, Williams encouraged him to apply to the University of Glasgow, in Scotland. McCune Smith was admitted, and Williams raised enough money to pay for his education. In the summer of 1832 he took "a sorrowful leave of his kind, affectionate, and dearly loved mother," said good-bye to a large circle of admiring friends, and set sail for Scotland.[42]

❦ From a very young age, John Brown neither trusted nor liked the world around him. His autobiographical sketch, which is the primary source of knowledge available to critics and historians regarding the first twenty years of Brown's life, emphasizes above all else his trials and tribulations. His very first memory was one of being tempted by the things of his world: he "*stole* . . . three large Brass Pins belonging" to a little girl. When he was five years old his family moved from his birthplace of Torrington, Connecticut, to the village of Hudson in Ohio's Western Reserve. To get there he traversed "a wilderness filled with wild beasts & Indians" and fended off "Rattle Snakes which were very large." His life in Ohio was no more stable or reliable than in Connecticut, even though his father, Owen, established himself as a prominent tanner. At about age six, "he was placed in the School of *adversity*." Even though "his earthly treasures were very few, & small," his "attachments" to them were "strong and earnest," and he suffered "sore trials" because of it. He lost a yellow marble that a poor Indian boy gave him, and the loss "*took years to heal.*" "I *think* he cried at times about it," Brown recalled. He caught and tamed a bobtail squirrel and "almost idolized his pet," but "this too he lost," and he "was *in mourning*" for a year or two. A little ewe lamb that his father gave him "sickened and died," and "this brought another protracted *mourning season.*" He began to consider these trials and tribulations as "part of his early training." He finally realized—while still quite young—that these tragedies represented a "*much needed course* of discipline" for learning how to shun and distrust worldly possessions. The discipline worked, for he eventually "passed through" his reliance on material things, realizing that "the Heavenly Father sees it best to take all the little things out of his hands which he has ever placed in them." By his own reckoning, John Brown learned at an early age to rely on the spiritual passions of his heart and to have faith in the treasures of heaven.[43]

Eventually Brown would seek to make his home and country a heaven on Earth, but doing so would require losses and mournings of a far greater sort than marbles and ewe lambs and squirrels. The first great loss occurred when he was eight years old. His mother died, and he described the feeling of emptiness resulting from her death as "complete and permanent." He "continued to pine after [her] for years." The War of 1812 added to his disenchantment with the world. His father worked as a beef contractor on the Detroit front during the war, and young John helped him by rounding up cattle and driving them to army outposts in Michigan. "The effect of what he saw during the war was to so far disgust him with Military affairs, that he would neither train, or drill; but paid fines; & got along like a Quaker until his age finally . . . cleared him of military duty." He became a member of his father's Congregational church in Hudson in 1816, after making a formal profession of faith. He *acted* like a Quaker, however, seeking perfection but accepting an imperfect world. His formal conversion to Christianity stemmed in large part from his "serious doubt as to his future well being." After his conversion, he "ever after" remained "a firm believer in the divine authenticity of the Bible" and retained "a most unusual memory of its entire contents." As his losses and sufferings increased, his Bible would become more "authentic" and real to him than the world around him, and he would depend upon the one but not the other.[44]

During the War of 1812, Brown became "a most *determined Abolitionist*," though not yet an immediatist. After finishing one of his cattle drives, he stayed with a landlord and saw him severely beat his slave— a badly clothed and poorly fed boy about Brown's age—with an iron shovel for no apparent reason. Brown sympathized with the slave, no doubt linking his own vulnerability with that of the bloodied boy, and concluded that God was the father of them both. He realized that masters acted like demigods, and this made him aware of how evil slavery was. As his own worldly sufferings increased, he would refuse to compromise his impulse to perfection with the world's cruel ways, and his "determined" abolitionism would become "*Eternal war* with slavery."[45]

But Brown was not yet a social outsider. Soon after his formal conversion, he decided to pursue a career as a minister. On the recommendation of his Congregational minister in Hudson, in the summer of 1816 he went to study at Moses Hallock's school in Plainfield, Massachusetts, a preparatory school for ministers, artists, and writers. After a few months there he transferred (for unknown reasons) to the Morris Academy in Litchfield, Connecticut, to continue his studies. Within a year he was back in Ohio, flat broke and suffering from an inflammation of the eyes. He accepted this setback, as he did all others during this period, with the "true resignation" of someone who knew not to place much faith in his worldly surroundings.[46]

When Brown returned to Hudson he set up his own tannery instead of working for his father, and thus established independence from him. Historians have typically described Brown as fiercely ambitious, independent, and wanting to be in charge, but often for the wrong reasons. Given the wholly unpredictable and unstable state of society, he had learned not to place much faith in social status. He sought instead to become independent from society and its vicissitudes. To achieve this he had either to become an outcast from white society—as he did after failing in business—or to attain enough power within its existing structures to gain a degree of independence, which he now sought. In fact Brown, Douglass, Gerrit Smith, and McCune Smith were eventually all self-employed, and thus enabled to stand aloof from social norms and conventions.

For Brown, achieving independence from society meant seeking control over his immediate environment. He exacted strict control over his tannery and his family. "It was Brown's fixed rule," wrote one employee, "that his apprentices and journeymen must always attend church every Sunday, and family worship every morning." He started teaching Sunday school in Hudson, instructing his pupils to have faith in God and not in worldly authority. He was also a rigid domestic patriarch. He married Dianthe Lusk in 1820, and seemed proud that she was a *"remarkably plain"* girl as well as "neat industrious & economical." Evidently, Brown wanted a wife who would not rebel against his rule, and in this he was successful, unless one interprets Dianthe's emotional troubles as a form of rebellion. Brown similarly demanded complete obedience from his children. In 1826, when his three-year-old son Jason (the second oldest) told his father of a dream he had had, and insisted "that it was the reality," Brown "thrashed him severely," but did so with tears in his eyes. He had no qualms about treating visions as reality, for he was already doing that himself. It was the kind of vision that concerned him. He wanted to make sure that his son's visions came from God. He did not recognize that the brute force he employed against his children (and, later, against proslavery advocates) was of the same sort that masters used to control their slaves.[47]

For Brown, seeking independence from worldly concerns meant trying to carve out his own sphere of autonomy, which began with his family and increased dramatically over time. He could not, as Gerrit Smith did, use inherited wealth (and power) to gain independence. He had to exert control over his environment, using brute force if necessary, first as a businessman and later as a militant abolitionist. As more and more tragedies befell him, he became totally fed up with his world, and sought to replace it with the "authentic" and sublime visions in his Bible.

❧ The women in Gerrit Smith's life pointed the way to heaven. If the deaths of his mother and Wealtha Backus sparked his spiritual visions, his marriage to Ann Carroll Fitzhugh set his world aflame with sacred fires. She gave new meaning and direction to his life by fostering his spiritual growth and his desire to make the world sacred. Her influence on him was not unusual, for women represented a leading force in the spiritual fires that transformed western New York into the "Burned-Over District." The men who organized and led the numerous religious revivals, voluntary societies, and reform organizations certainly contributed to the sacralization of society; but conversion often began at home.[48]

Gerrit married Ann Fitzhugh in January 1822, fourteen months after he took over his father's estate. Nancy, as friends and family called her, was a Southerner by birth. Born at Hagerstown, Maryland, she was a cousin of the famous proslavery theorist George Fitzhugh, and was also related to Robert E. Lee and his nephew Fitzhugh Lee. Like Gerrit, she grew up on an estate with plenty of wealth and numerous slaves, and during her childhood her family moved to Rochester, New York. She was seventeen when they married, eight years younger than Gerrit, and, given her aristocratic heritage, she probably felt right at home at the Smith mansion-house.[49]

By all accounts theirs was a match made in heaven. Guests at the mansion-house often remarked on their compatibility. One houseguest recalled Gerrit's declaring one morning: "You have heard of the expression 'Hell has broken loose': well, when my wife comes down to breakfast I feel as if Heaven had broken loose." William Lloyd Garrison summed up their marriage by saying: "If ever two souls were perfectly mated, it was surely so with them."[50]

They started a family immediately, and Gerrit began showing more interest in affairs of the spirit. Their first child, Elizabeth, was born September 20, 1822, and their son Fitzhugh came two years later. Around the time of Elizabeth's birth, Gerrit told his uncle that he wanted to enter the "Gospel Ministry," but his uncle dissuaded him. He did not have that "uninterrupted calmness" necessary for the profession, his uncle said, adding that Peter Smith would probably not release him from the care of the estate. In 1825 Gerrit became the superintendent of his local Sunday school and helped distribute Bibles and religious tracts. Despite these signs of faith, however, he had neither experienced a formal conversion nor cleansed himself of sin by embracing temperance. That same year, while Nancy was away visiting friends, he boasted of "a great feast" he was planning, and said he looked forward to drinking up "all the wine." She would "return to an empty house."[51]

Nancy led her husband to the ways of the Lord. On March 6, 1826, Gerrit's twenty-ninth birthday, she wrote to him from Richfield, New York, where she was recovering from an illness, and expressed her hope that a spiritual birth would accompany his birthday: "I wish you many happy returns of this day, my dear husband, but with how much more joy would I celebrate it if it were the anniversary of your spiritual birth!" Within two weeks, Gerrit and Nancy formally joined the Presbyterian church in Peterboro and made public confessions of their faith in Jesus Christ as their God and savior. By 1827, a shift in Smith's values was apparent. He had quit drinking, sold off properties that distilled or contributed to the manufacture and sale of liquor, and become an ardent temperance reformer. Drinking, he now realized, was a sin that corrupted mind, body, and soul. But he was still a long way from defining himself as a passionate outsider. His membership in the family of Christ was formal and institutional rather than emotional and transformative. And his reform efforts were quite respectable, almost de rigueur, for the temperance, Sunday school, Bible, and tract societies were organized and run by social elites. His identity still depended on social status.[52]

Gerrit's early interest in African Americans similarly reflected his dependence on genteel norms and conventions as the primary source of his values. In 1826, the year of his formal conversion, his "favorite project" was an American seminary "in which to prepare young Africans for the Gospel Ministry," and he explored "the many facts and speculations" that were "unfriendly to such a project." In March 1827 he told Samuel Cornish, the editor of the first black newspaper, *Freedom's Journal*, that he was "both willing and able to do a little for unhappy Africa and the children that have been torn away from her." But he wanted to help blacks according to the conventions of white respectability. *Freedom's Journal* was an ardent foe of the American Colonization Society, which sought to colonize free blacks in Africa and encouraged slaveowners to manumit their slaves. The vast majority of black abolitionists denounced the Colonization Society because they thought it sought to rid the country of free blacks without attacking slavery or advocating black equality within America. Among white reformers, colonization was the only socially acceptable means for ending slavery. It sought gradual and consensual emancipation, and thus did not threaten an existing social order that conceived of America as a white man's country. Gerrit did not want his name associated with Cornish's newspaper, which attacked white supremacy, and he chastised Cornish for publishing an article that announced his intention to establish the black seminary.[53]

The reports of Gerrit's philanthropy attracted the attention of the Reverend Ralph Randolph Gurley, secretary of the American Colonization Society, who advised him to spend his money on schools in the society's African colony of Liberia rather than in America. Smith responded with a contribution to "the great and holy cause of colonization," joined the society, and over the next several years spent tens of thousands of dollars on colonization.[54] In 1830 he told the Reverend Gurley: "For the last four years, the twin evils of intemperance and our black population have engrossed about all my patriotic concern. Not until these evils are conquered, will our dear country be free." In Smith's view, the "twin evils" of intemperance and the black population were stains on the fabric of his society.[55]

In one sense, these "twin evils" affected Gerrit's own sense of freedom. The essence of sin and slavery was a denial of self-sovereignty, a negation of will and of the idea of freedom. Gerrit had witnessed the sins of slavery and drink firsthand and had experienced the loss of personal freedom in his own home. Had his older brother, Peter Skenandoah, not become attached to drink at an early age, Peter Smith might well have asked him to manage the estate, leaving Gerrit to pursue his literary dreams. Gerrit later called slavery "the horror of my childhood." Although he was still a long way from accepting blacks and the poor as his social equals, the sins of slavery and intemperance had interfered with his own freedom and well-being, and he began a lifelong attack against both forms of depravity.[56]

The Panic and the Making
of Abolitionists

I have felt great sympathy with all true hearted Second Advent believers in their great disappointment at the non appearance of their Lord + Master . . . [but] it was not necessary that Christ should be visible to our fleshly eyes, in order that he should reign in the world . . . Who cannot see + feel that we have entered upon a new era.
—ANGELINA GRIMKÉ WELD (1845)

The Passion of Jesus became for him the only reality; the need of his own body was but a part of that conception.
—WILLA CATHER, *DEATH COMES FOR THE ARCHBISHOP* (1927)

Throughout the 1820s Peterboro had been a village of drunkards, Gerrit Smith concluded in 1833; "more than every other man in it was a drunkard." Rum had flowed more readily than water. In Peterboro alone, a village of sixty to seventy families, there were half a dozen taverns, and in the town of Smithfield, seven distilleries served 2,700 people. Not until about 1830, when temperance reform began to exert its influence, did the villagers begin to quit drinking and the taverns and distilleries shut down.[1] Peterboro was not that unusual. During the 1820s Americans consumed more alcohol (on a per-capita basis) than at any time before or since. According to one historian, in the late 1820s the average adult male drank about eight fluid ounces a day of distilled spirits (whiskey, rum, gin, brandy), and one-quarter of adult males twelve ounces or more. The manner of drinking was also telling: people tended to prefer communal binges, and drank to get drunk. In the minds of many of these drinkers, intoxication symbolized freedom, and communal bingeing reflected the spirit of equality. But from Smith's perspective, America was a nation awash in drink and sin.[2]

Smith's attitude toward temperance highlights his evolution as a reformer in the 1830s. He considered drink and slavery to be sins, but tolerated them during the 1820s and early 1830s. After the panic of 1837, however, he experienced a new birth. He internalized God's sovereignty, created a sacred self, and sought to create a heaven on Earth, first in his community of Peterboro, and eventually throughout the country. His reform trajectory parallels that of John Brown and intersects with those of Frederick Douglass and James McCune Smith at the time of the financial panic and subsequent depression. Brown, Douglass, and McCune Smith also embraced sacred self-sovereignty in the late 1830s, and sought to create a heaven on Earth. Once they were able to conceive of God as indwelling, they no longer needed to rely on existing hierarchies as the source of meaning and order.

These four men's spiritual evolution was part of a recurring tradition in Western culture. In some respects they reenacted the experience of various Protestant sectarians during the seventeenth-century English civil wars, who rejected state authority in their quest to purify society. Indeed, Brown and Douglass both claimed as a hero Oliver Cromwell, the famous Puritan "saint" who signed Charles I's death warrant and became "Lord Protector" of the British Commonwealth from 1653 until his death in 1658. Lesser-known religious enthusiasts like John Lilburne and his Levellers, Gerard Winstanley and his Diggers, and James Nayler and his millennialist Quakers also serve as legitimate antecedents for these four abolitionists, for they were much more egalitarian than Cromwell in their vision of a sacred society.[3]

Events surrounding the panic of 1837 and subsequent depression contributed enormously to all four men's transformation into passionate outsiders. Eighteen thirty-seven in particular was a "crucial year" in antebellum reform, and in some respects the panic was as decisive as the 1929 stock-market crash in altering the mood of America.[4] It brought a severe depression—one of the worst in American history—after a period of easy credit, high prices, and general optimism. It also coincided with new methods for abolishing slavery, a sharp decline in anti-abolition mob activity, and heightened tensions in race relations among black and white reformers. It marked a turning point in the values and worldviews of Gerrit Smith, McCune Smith, Douglass, Brown, and reformers in general. For Gerrit Smith and John Brown, the panic shattered their remaining faith in normative social structures.

It was the catalyst that led to their self-conceptions as outsiders and their ability to identify with blacks and the poor rather than with the white mainstream. The panic also coincided with Douglass' escape to freedom and McCune Smith's return to New York City as the country's first certified black physician; and it may have facilitated their ability to achieve insider status.

❧ Given the high degree of drunkenness at Peterboro, it is perhaps understandable why the problem of temperance, coupled with that of slavery, represented the primary focus of Gerrit Smith's spiritual energies. He joined the American Temperance Society in 1826 (the year it was founded), which was also the year he became interested in colonization. Soon he was treating temperance as a sacred ritual that he applied to all facets of his life. He promoted temperance throughout Madison County and the state, and blamed the high incidence of debauchery and death from drunkenness on "sober drinkers"—on those who could drink with impunity: "The selfishness of temperate drinkers—of those who look upon their own things only, and have no compassion for the many who cannot drink without getting drunk," struck him as particularly unchristian. Christian behavior and "natural compassion," he told a friend in 1829, "should induce us to do all we can to prevent the circulation of spirits amongst us." Abstinence was a test of one's inner, spiritual disposition.[5]

Smith eventually became dissatisfied with the American Temperance Society, however. Although the organization advocated total abstinence from distilled spirits, it tolerated the drinking of wine, beer, and hard cider. This distinction was linked to class differences: the lower classes drank distilled spirits, which were cheaper, while the upper classes typically preferred wine. The American Temperance Society was run by men of wealth and distinction, and Smith eventually became aware of the class conflict within it. From 1826 until 1837 he tried to balance his personal belief in total abstinence with the society's approval of fermented wines and ciders. But in late 1837, following the financial panic, he became fed up with its tolerance of fermented liquors and came close to resigning.[6]

Smith's evolution in temperance reform parallels the path he took in antislavery. He joined the American Colonization Society in 1827, one

year after joining the Temperance Society, and totally rejected colonization in 1837, at the very time he repudiated the Temperance Society.
From about 1834 to 1837 he tried to balance the principles of colonization with those of immediate abolition. Because of his wealth, he was
one of the Colonization Society's most important members. But he
also believed in the efficacy of immediate abolition endorsed by the
American Anti-Slavery Society, along with its refusal to compromise
with sin. He read William Lloyd Garrison's *Liberator*, attended numerous Anti-Slavery Society meetings, and cultivated many abolition
friendships long before he became a committed immediate abolitionist.[7]

Smith was highly unusual among white reformers in his efforts to
juggle a gradualist approach to slavery and drink while also seeking the
immediate end of the two evils. Most other prominent white
immediatists had been former colonizationists and temperance reformers, including William Lloyd Garrison, Theodore Dwight Weld,
and Lewis and Arthur Tappan. But unlike Smith, once they accepted
immediate abolition they made a clean break from colonization, and
viewed the Colonization Society as an enemy and an impediment to reform. The shift represented not only a change in strategy, prompted by
the persistence of slavery, but a fundamental reorientation in their vision of society. Immediate abolitionists refused to compromise with
sin. They waged verbal and moral warfare on colonization, calling it a
conspiracy against human rights. Colonizationists countered by arguing that immediatists threatened social order and stability.[8] Smith
hated this warfare and sought to alleviate it. From 1831 until 1837 he
chastised both groups for not working together to end slavery and improve the condition of African Americans. He believed that immediate
abolitionists' emphasis on moral persuasion, coupled with the Colonization Society's efforts to send blacks back to Africa, could serve the
cause of the slave and humanity.[9]

Smith's attempt to balance the gradualist and immediatist approaches to drink and slavery from the late 1820s until 1837 reflected
his dependence on the existing social order while at the same time he
struggled to become free from sin. He kept a pragmatic eye on whatever worked, in the event that all sin could not be abolished immediately. Although he sought emancipation from all evil and tried to inter-
nalize God's sovereignty, he resigned himself to a gradual end of sin

and clung to his elite social status. Sin still dwelled within, and consequently he needed worldly support and guidance.

Gerrit and Nancy Smith's correspondence reveals their battles with sin during this period. In July 1832 Gerrit wrote Nancy from Utica to say that he had attended church and communion the day before, but felt frustrated because his "mind was not in that spiritual frame I had hoped it would be in": "Pray for me, my dear wife, that I may believe, that I may have true faith, that my heart may be made clean, and that after all my professions and privileges, I may not be a castaway . . . In no way can we serve one another so well as by fervent, wrestling, persevering prayer for each other." Three years later Nancy confessed to Gerrit: "I have been so occupied in conflict with Satan and a wicked heart that my mind has not found leisure to think of nor feel its loneliness." They had not yet internalized the kingdom of God, had not yet acquired a spiritual anchor and clean and pure hearts.[10]

In 1834, despite the emergence of the American Anti-Slavery Society and the spread of state abolitionist societies, Smith still hoped for reconciliation between the Anti-Slavery and Colonization Societies. In July 1834 he attended the inaugural meeting of his town's Anti-Slavery Society and noted that "the constitution is good." But he did not join. He could "not join the Anti-Slavery Society as long as the war is kept up between it and the American Colonization Society," a war for which he blamed each organization. A month later he told Elizur Wright, secretary of the American Anti-Slavery Society, that he was familiar with the "wicked prejudice" and "corruption" of many colonization members. But he refused to "believe" or "even to suspect" that its leaders were corrupt. He was close friends with the Reverends Ralph Gurley and Leonard Bacon, two important leaders of the Colonization Society, who held genuine antislavery views. He summarized the current state of the Colonization Society by comparing the relationship between its managers and members to that between the "Savior" and the "reckless faults of His own disciples."[11]

In 1835 a slight shift in Smith's values became apparent. Antiabolition mobs viewed the rapid growth of antislavery societies as a dangerous threat to the social order, and they attacked abolitionists with a vengeance. In August 1835 he noted that "every mail of late brings accounts of the lawless, riotous, murderous spirit which is prevailing over the land," and asked the Lord to defend "the cause of the oppressed." A few days later, after attending what he described as "a great anti-abolition meeting" in Utica, he concluded that the proceedings were not "agreeable" to his "feelings." "Christian morality did not characterize them."[12]

Two months later, Smith experienced an anti-abolition mob firsthand. On October 21, 1835, he and Nancy attended the inaugural state antislavery convention at Utica. They had planned simply to visit the meeting but not to join the society, but their plans changed. Soon after the proceedings began, a well-organized group of about a hundred lawyers, bankers, and merchants—all of them Democrats—forced their way into the Presbyterian church, where the abolitionists were in session, and began a "respectable riot." The mob was organized by Samuel Beardsley, a Democratic congressman from New York and a friend of President Andrew Jackson. Their goal was to break up the meeting, drive the abolitionists out of town, and publicize their opposition to abolition in order to strengthen the Democratic party in Utica. Though outnumbered by four to one, the mobsters marched down the aisle of the church, yelling and heckling, presented the abolitionists with resolutions of protest, and demanded an end to the meeting. In a poignant moment that revealed how the problem of slavery could divide a family as well as a country, one of the mobsters confronted his father—an aged minister and the secretary of the convention—and demanded that he relinquish the minutes of the meeting. The father acquiesced, and the mobsters, after breaking up the meeting, promenaded into the street, cheering and congratulating themselves on their success, while the humbled abolitionists scurried to the Utica Temperance House to decide where and when to reconvene.[13]

Smith was outraged by the riot, and his reaction reveals his willingness to employ violence to defend his "identity" as a "man," as he put it, and to uphold free speech and "fair play." He volunteered his mansion-house as a place to reconvene, and the few hundred abolitionists began the thirty-five-mile trek to Peterboro. Smith was "so much excited with the horrid scenes of the day" that he stayed up all night preparing a speech. In the morning, the abolitionists resumed their meeting at the Presbyterian church of Peterboro. Although the Democratic mobsters were nowhere in sight, Smith boasted to his friend Leonard Bacon, an avid colonizationist: "Our people prepared their fire arms to surround the [Peterboro] Church and to shoot down the Utica Mob, which we learnt [erroneously] was on its way to break up the Meeting. I am a poor peace man you will think, when I tell you, that I was as determined as anyone to employ deadly weapons against the invaders of our rights."[14]

In his speech Smith formulated his first attack against the conspiratorial designs of the Slave Power. Deprive people of their rights, he said, and they ceased "to be MEN." But the South had "tongue-tied" the North in the war that had broken out between the two regions. Moreover, "craven and mercenary spirits at the North" were in concert with the "insolent demands of the South." He urged peaceful measures to end slavery, but emphasized that "we are not willing to be slaves ourselves." The Slave Power was at the root of the actions of the Utica mobsters, he concluded, and it threatened his and other abolitionists' freedom and manhood.[15]

A month after the Peterboro convention, Smith formally resigned from the American Colonization Society and joined the ranks of antislavery members. His new allegiance, however, much like his formal conversion at the Presbyterian church in 1826, signified an external shift in affiliation more than it did a change of heart. His resignation stemmed primarily from his fears that the Colonization Society was now tacitly aligned with the Slave Power. In his letter of resignation to the Reverend Gurley, he accused colonizationists of being "far more interested in the work of [preserving] slavery than in the work of colonization." Colonizationists had condoned in their newspaper the attack on abolitionists at Utica—and a much more menacing attack on William Lloyd Garrison in Boston the very same day. The society had aligned itself with the South in its efforts to stifle free speech. He thus could not remain a member of both societies without subjecting himself to "charges of inconsistency." But Smith also told Gurley that he still believed in the validity of the Colonization Society's original intent to help "the free people of color . . . escape from the unrelenting prejudice and persecution under which they suffer." He included the balance of three thousand dollars on his subscription, and said that if, "at some future period," the society focused on the "remedy" of slavery rather than its "preservation," he would consider rejoining.[16]

Smith's continued sympathies with the Colonization Society from 1835 to 1837 underscore the lack of substantive change in his self-definition as a reformer. In a letter to Lewis Tappan in April 1836, he said he preferred not to speak at the upcoming American Anti-Slavery Society's anniversary meeting: "I admit that at the present time, I do not come up to the standards of some of my anti-slavery brethren. I do not regard the Col[onization] Soc[iety] and colonization itself with the abhorrence which they manifest toward them." He was persuaded to speak at the meeting anyway, and although he condemned slavery, he showed relatively little sympathy for blacks themselves, and referred to slaves as "degraded" and "vile" on account of their bondage. Similarly, he was willing to use "deadly weapons" against the Utica mob to protect himself. But he felt that a slave was not supposed to rebel or revolt. He was still a long way from identifying with black people and trying to make himself "a colored man." As he later noted, his values during this period remained "worldly and aspiring."[17]

Once Smith came to identify with blacks and to see in their oppression his own sufferings and struggles, he not only wholly repudiated colonization but began to condone and eventually encourage slave insurrections and black militancy. This kind of identification, however, required a radical shift in his locus of value, a significant turn inward, away from the authority of white society, toward the passions of the heart. It was precipitated by the panic of 1837, and to a lesser extent by the deaths of three family members (his daughter Ann, his son Fitzhugh, and his father) within a two-year period, from April 1835 to May 1837.[18] These tragedies obliterated worldly markers of status, hierarchy, and identity. They made him realize that wealth, power, even life itself, were fleeting and unreliable. They fractured his self-conception as a patriarch and land baron, and led directly to the formation of his identity as an outsider who believed in the literal coming of a new and perfect age.

During Smith's spiritual evolution from the mid-1820s to 1837, his wealth increased even as he increasingly loathed business. In the mid-1820s he bought property in Oswego County and stock in the Oswego Canal Company. He was soon the majority stockholder, and his Oswego investments became extraordinarily profitable. In 1835 wild speculation drove up his property values by about 30 percent per month, and during the winter of 1835–36 he calculated his holdings in Oswego alone to be worth about one million dollars. But he hated business and sought to free himself from its daily, mundane obligations. "I am still exceedingly desirous to wind up all my landed concerns, and to retire from business," he wrote an associate in October 1835. Eighteen months later, on April 13, 1837, his father died. As one of the executors of the estate, Gerrit tried to convert land to cash to distribute to the other heirs. But in May 1837 banks suspended specie payment. The panic of 1837 was under way, and he decided to pay the heirs cash from his own account at prepanic prices in exchange for their rights to the property. Simultaneously he became liable for an additional $200,000 as a result of his tendency to endorse notes from family and friends.[19]

Such imprudent generosity almost forced Smith into bankruptcy. His land in Oswego County alone plummeted from a value of around $1,000,000 to $120,000 almost overnight. Only a loan for $200,000 from John Jacob Astor, his father's former business partner, saved him from insolvency. Even with the loan, the scarcity of money kept him at the brink of bankruptcy and bound to his office, ledgers, and land he could not sell until the mid-1840s. It was as though the objective, quantifiable structures of society had vanished into thin air. Decimal points shifted, altering values by factors of ten and a hundred. Sevens became twos, eights turned into fours. Suddenly, it seemed, he could no longer rely on stability and direction from the outside world. The rational order and distinct social hierarchies inherent in the principles of the Colonization and Temperance Societies no longer made any sense to him.[20]

In the wake of this financial turmoil, Smith repudiated both the American Colonization Society and the American Temperance Society. He condemned colonizationists for opposing "immediate and unconditional" emancipation and rejecting "the doctrine that slavery is sin." And he denounced the Temperance Society for condoning wine drinking among the "refined and polite" "upper classes" while warring against the ardent spirits of the lower classes. Temperance reform, he announced in a November 1837 broadside, "passed by the rich man's decanters and demijohns . . . to quarrel with the poor man's jugs and bottles." Any form of drinking was a form of bondage and a sin, and in the wake of the panic, he refused to compromise with sin. (He would later embrace the teetotaling, Washingtonian temperance movement that emerged in the 1840s and was led by reformed working-class drunkards.) Smith now affirmed immediate abolitionism as the most direct manifestation of his faith: "The motto of immediate, entire and

universal abstinence from sin is . . . much more appropriately claimed
by the abolitionist than by the subscriber to the principles of the Temperance cause," he concluded in his 1837 broadside.[21]

Smith had, in very short order, become a passionate outsider. He began to define himself as a "fanatic" and an "outlaw," with "no influence" left in society because of his abolitionism and financial woes. In
August 1837 he told his agent, John B. Edwards: "I wait impatiently to
see your good name enrolled amongst the anti-slavery *fanatics*; and I
flatter myself, that your heart, though it should be in opposition to the
prudence of your head, will soon get it there."[22]

Smith also ended what had been a long, rich, and intimate correspondence with Ralph Gurley and Leonard Bacon, two of his closest
colonization friends. Bacon was a staunch foe of the American Anti-Slavery Society, and the last letter he wrote Smith before the Civil War
summarizes in rich imagery his fears of abolitionism. After reading an
1837 report from the New-York State Anti-Slavery Society, he told
Smith—"with the frankness which becomes our friendship"—of the
"great pain" that the report had caused him:

> Throughout the report there *seems* to be something like an attempt to
> excite some of the basest and most dangerous elements of political malignancy. They that take the sword shall perish by the sword; and they
> that attempt to array the poor against the rich, the laborer against the
> employer, the country against the city, may find, too late, that they
> have evoked from the abyss demons whose might and malignity their
> art cannot control.[23]

For Bacon, associating with the lower classes and tampering with the
social order threatened to turn sin loose from the passions of the heart.
As a Congregational minister who taught at Yale, Bacon was anything
but a perfectionist. He believed not only that slavery symbolized
America's original sin, but that blacks embodied sin. Like most other
colonizationists, he thought the only way blacks could be redeemed
and reborn was through African colonization. He could not unburden
himself from the concept of original sin, and thus embraced rigid dualities for rendering order and stability on society. Any attempt to dismantle these dualities "evoked from the abyss" the demons of the poor,
the laborers, the uncivilized wilderness of the country, and blacks—

which needed to be checked by the rich, the employer, the civilized city, and whites, who knew how control their passions and demons. Allowing demons to escape from the abyss of people's hearts, Bacon warned, would unleash dark phantoms of sin that the "art" of abolitionists could not control.[24]

The panic had served to free Gerrit Smith from the fetters of sin. With his external conditions so precarious, he turned to affairs of the spirit with heightened zeal and sought to realize his spiritual visions. He became more exacting in applying his religious passions to worldly affairs, and strove to dismantle the dualities that Bacon affirmed. Both Gerrit and Nancy experienced deliverance from the depravity of original sin, embraced sacred self-sovereignty, and became "members of the family of Jesus on earth."[25]

As a result of their newfound perfectionist vision, Gerrit and Nancy embraced William Miller's prophecy of Christ's advent "about 1843" and, when that year passed without incident, on October 22, 1844. As 1843 approached, the Smiths and thousands of others in the Burned-Over District became increasingly expectant that a literal heaven on Earth would commence with an apocalyptic end to sin followed by Christ's second coming. In February 1843 Gerrit chastised a minister for not having "a clear vision" of "the Second Advent of Our Lord": "The primitive Christians had the Second Coming continually before their eyes. Why should it not be such with modern Christians," especially when "the present year, in the judgment of thousands of holy men and women, is the last year of time"? The Smiths faithfully read the *Midnight Cry*, the Millerite organ, and in January 1843 Gerrit wrote its editor, Joshua Himes, to say that its message "has become the uppermost subject in our thoughts." On October 21, 1844, Gerrit received in the mail four copies of the *Extra Midnight Cry*. "It declares that the world will end at three tomorrow morning," he noted, even though "time may possibly continue until the 23rd or even the 24th." Gerrit, Nancy, their daughter Elizabeth, and their two-year-old son Greene worshipped together, "perhaps for the last time." Gerrit looked forward to a glorious reunion with their deceased son and daughter: "How my eyes have flowed at the welcome thought that we shall meet our dear Fitzhugh and Nanny [Ann]! Oh, the treasures of religion!" Gerrit penned these details in his diary at "half past 8" that evening of Monday, October 21, in the form of a letter to "My Dearly Beloved." It was the apocalyptic equivalent of a suicide note as he awaited his new world.[26]

Historians typically view Millerites as quietists who stood aloof from social-reform institutions. Yet most Millerites were active reformers— even at the height of their millennial expectations—and many of them, like the Smiths, remained committed abolitionists. Millerites can be seen as quietists only in the sense that they tended to distance them-selves from *institutional* reform organizations. Like many other radi-cals, they sought to "come out" from corrupt institutions and churches, and tended to rely on individual and local (rather than national) efforts to reform society. During Gerrit's Millerite phase, he distanced him-self from the national reform organizations and focused his energies on his immediate community. Although he was one of the founders of the Liberty party in 1840, save for his role in its founding he did not be-come an active member until 1844, when William Miller's prophesy of a new world failed to materialize. In fact in his autobiographical sketch he stated that he "was one of the first organizers of the Liberty Party," but said that this occurred in 1844, when he became an active member, even though he knew that the party was founded in 1840. It was in the wake of the Millerite "disappointment" (and the political debate over the annexation of Texas) that Smith wholly embraced the Liberty party and Bible politics.[27]

Smith's emphasis on individual and local efforts in the early 1840s was also a function of his frustration over the breakup of the American Anti-Slavery Society. After the society's annual meeting in 1840, mem-bers fragmented into two additional national societies: the Liberty party, which focused on political action; and the American and Foreign Anti-Slavery Society, a more conservative group of evangelical, church-oriented reformers who opposed equal rights for women. Smith was disgusted with the "disgraceful and injurious wranglings" in the controversies over women's rights (which he supported), obser-vance of the sabbath, and government participation, including voting; and he considered the breakup largely a result of the competitive and ruinous bickering over these issues. He was determined not to get in-volved in members' feuds, yet remained ready and willing to cooperate with abolitionists of all stripes, from heathens and "infidels" to mili-tants, disunionists, and those denying women's equal participation.

"I think it right to stand aloof from our National Anti-Slavery Organizations, until I am convinced that they are not, and are not likely to be, theatres on which my beloved abolition brethren will consume their time and energies in torturing and mangling each other," he told a friend in 1840. A year later he said much the same thing to William Ellery Channing: "I must confess to you that I more and more doubt the expediency of the great Benevolent Associations of this Age. They have done much good. But there is much reason to fear that they will do—if they have not already done—much evil."[28]

Smith did not remain inactive, however. He emphasized "church and individual action" in his community, and founded the nonsectarian and fully integrated Church of Peterboro, in part because his Presbyterian church refused to endorse abolition and racial equality. He established another nonsectarian and integrated church at nearby Oswego. He also corresponded frequently with Southern planters, in the hopes of convincing them to liberate their slaves. And he began to purchase the liberty of slaves. All in all, he felt that these efforts "do more for the cause of the slave than our antislavery organizations have ever done—and they have done much."[29]

It was during this period that Smith began to focus intensely on the cause of slaves and free blacks. He had rejected Bacon's conception of the heart as a demonic abyss, and no longer considered the "black population" as "evil," or slaves as "vile" and odious.[30] In 1838 he again spoke at the anniversary meeting of the American Anti-Slavery Society, and his speech reflected a dramatic change from his views at the same meeting in 1836. He looked back on his association with the Colonization Society as an example of his "ignorance of the colored man's heart":

Had I communed with him [instead of standing] entirely aloof from him, I should not have been the victim of colonization delusions for so long a time; for, as soon as I came to commune with him . . . and in a word to make myself a colored man—I saw how crushing and murderous to all the hopes and happiness of our colored brother is the policy of expelling the colored race from this country.[31]

In an important sense Smith actually did "make" himself "a colored man," and began to view the world as though he were black. In his speech he attacked the pervasive prejudice and oppression against northern blacks and offered a simple definition of "abolition" by way of personal example:

> A year or two since, a little colored girl came to my house. A child in my family [his daughter Elizabeth] asked her if she knew what abolition meant. She promptly replied: "it means kindness to colored people." Kindness to colored people! A beautiful and happy definition! And if there be in our ranks, any whose hearts do not respond to this definition, let them be assured . . . that they are abolitionists in word and in name—not in deed and in truth.[32]

Only "true" abolitionists followed the "happy" and "beautiful" aims of the heart and strove for empathy in thought, word, and deed. From the panic of 1837 until the Civil War, Smith viewed the Golden Rule as an example of empathy, and two of his favorite biblical passages were versions of this creed: "Remember them that are in bonds as bound with them," and Jesus' injunction "to become as little children" in order to create a heaven on Earth, which was also a basic perfectionist creed.[33]

Smith's change of heart coincided with his acceptance of blacks' use of violence to liberate themselves and fight oppression. By the mid-1840s, black abolitionists increasingly rejected the paternalism of most white abolitionists, as well as Garrison's doctrine of nonresistance. Following the Supreme Court's 1842 decision in *Prigg v. Pennsylvania*, which threatened black personal-liberty laws, Samuel Ringgold Ward, himself a fugitive, wrote to Smith to say that blacks could "do nothing but give physical resistance." In 1843 Henry Highland Garnet delivered an "Address to the Slaves" before a national convention of black abolitionists. He advocated a general strike among slaves, and the use of physical resistance in their quest for freedom, though he did not advise them to "attempt a revolution with the sword, because it would be INEXPEDIENT." Those attending the convention, including Frederick Douglass and James McCune Smith, narrowly rejected his militant proposals. Nevertheless, Garnet's speech marked a turning point in the abolition movement: it was vigorously denounced by the vast majority of white abolitionists, and highlighted the rift between blacks' and whites' attitudes about fighting slavery. A year earlier Gerrit Smith had given his own "Address to the Slaves," which was widely endorsed by blacks, condemned by most whites, and probably influenced Garnet's speech. Smith encouraged slaves to engage in what he admiringly called the "black-hearted" measures of "running away" and "yielding to necessity" by stealing. He was not opposed to physical resistance but, like Garnet, stopped short of advocating violent insurrection for reasons of "expediency."[34] In 1843 he accepted the view that a "human government, which takes life," was not necessarily "unchristian." And in 1846 he supported "a plausible argument" for "the righteousness of a defensive war" against slavery.[35]

Smith began to accept violent means to end slavery and sin at the very time he sought to replace his material world with an apocalyptic, sin-free reality. It is no wonder that so many Millerites were also fervent abolitionists (though it is unknown how many Millerites accepted violence). The greatest obstacle separating the status quo from abolitionism was the ability to believe in a heaven on Earth, and Millerites had already crossed that bridge. The Millerite disappointment contributed to Smith's acceptance of violence: when the new dispensation failed to materialize, he felt driven to play a more active role in bringing it about.

Smith's understanding of violent means in relation to the advent of a heaven on Earth is revealed in an 1839 public letter to Henry Clarke Wright, a prominent member of Garrison's Anti-Slavery Society. Smith told Wright that his views on the subject of peaceful versus violent means were "not entirely settled." He acknowledged that many friends thought he was "tending" toward an acceptance of violence, but he clung to the principle of peaceful means. He thought the New Testament offered the primary justification for peace, and he paraphrased Christ by saying: "'My kingdom is not of this world. If my kingdom were of this world, then would my servants fight, that I should not be delivered to the Jews.'" Since "fighting was contrary to the mind of Christ, when He was on the earth, it must be so now," Smith added. His ambivalence about violence in 1839 suggests that he was reconsidering the traditional Christian view of violence: *if* Christ were to appear and say that His kingdom *was* of this world, then Gerrit would fight for Him. By 1844, as he read the *Extra Midnight Cry* and anxiously awaited the end of the world, he had become convinced that Christ's kingdom *was* of this world. From his involvement in the Millerite movement in the early 1840s, through his leadership in the

Radical Abolition party and conspiracy with John Brown, he remained convinced that the new dispensation was eminent, and he accepted violence as a means to realize it.[36]

❧ On September 3, 1838, a new world literally opened up for Frederick Douglass. As Gerrit Smith descended into near bankruptcy, Douglass became a free man. "The dreams of my youth and the hopes of my manhood were completely fulfilled," he recalled. Time seemed to slow down, for he "lived more in [this] one day than in a year of my slave life." Smith, too, no doubt felt that time was being compressed as he watched assets that had been acquired over a lifetime vanish within a few months. For both men it was a moment of profound transformation, joyous and exhilarating for Douglass, hand-wringing and terrifying for Smith. After safely reaching New York, Douglass wrote a friend: "I felt as one might feel upon escape from a den of hungry lions." Smith, after watching his assets vanish, probably felt as though he had been flung from his comparative safety of wealth into a pit of ravenous beasts. From radically different origins, both men experienced new births at almost precisely the same moment. Thereafter they sought to create a world in which lions and lambs, blacks and whites, could live together in harmony.[37]

The panic of 1837 affected Frederick Douglass (and other black abolitionists) much differently than it did Gerrit Smith. While the depression led to Smith's descent into outsider status, it coincided with Douglass' and other blacks' emergence as insiders who wielded cultural capital and varying degrees of autonomy, social status, and power. Following the panic there were increasing tensions between black and white abolitionists, resulting in an upsurge of black political action, conventions, newspapers and journals, an emphasis on self-help, and a greater degree of militancy in fighting the oppressions of white society. Black abolitionists did not need to be awakened to the evils of their society, and one might go so far as to suggest that the panic and depression inspired them to attack white society, which no longer appeared so stable.[38]

Although the panic coincided with Douglass' ascent to insider status, it did not dramatically alter his efforts to replace his world with a sacred vision. In this sense the timing of his spiritual evolution differed from that of Gerrit Smith. Smith had multiple conversion experiences in his evolution toward perfectionism. He underwent a formal conversion in 1826, but only after the panic could he repudiate sin, renounce his material world, and try to effect an alternate reality. By the early 1830s Douglass had already cleansed himself from sin, envisioned a new age, and sought to realize it. Events surrounding the panic and depression merely fueled this desire.

Douglass' faith in a sublime and glorious new age similarly developed in stages. It began in 1826, when he moved to Baltimore, learned how to read and write, and was introduced to the *Columbian Orator*. His vision of a new world became much more vivid in 1833, according to his account in *My Bondage and My Freedom*. In March of that year he moved from Baltimore, where he had lived in comparative comfort as a slave, to St. Michaels, on the Eastern Shore of Maryland, to live with his new master, Thomas Auld. As he arrived at St. Michaels he witnessed the "gorgeous" and "sublime" spectacle of the heavens preparing to part "with its starry train": "The air seemed filled with bright, descending messengers from the sky. It was about daybreak when I saw this sublime scene. I was not without the suggestion, at the moment, that it might be the harbinger of the coming of the Son of Man; and, in my then state of mind, I was prepared to hail Him as my friend and deliverer." He knew from the Bible that when "the stars shall fall from heaven," the advent of Christ was at hand, and they were now falling.[39]

Douglass' faith in the second coming was tested (but not destroyed) by the severity and harshness of his new master. Auld starved and whipped Douglass, and became even more tyrannical after his conversion at a Methodist camp meeting. Douglass saw Auld's newfound evangelical faith as mere formality and show: "The natural wickedness of his heart had not been removed, but only reinforced, by the profession of religion." For Douglass, a true conversion penetrated the heart. Yet very few Southern ministers "*dared* to show" a "warm and philanthropic heart." Despite Auld's brutality, Douglass refused to cower before him—indeed, he refused even to call him "master." Auld thought him bold and insolent, and hired him out as a field hand to Edward Covey, who had established a reputation as an accomplished "nigger breaker." Covey sought to destroy Douglass' hope and faith in a better world, and thus "cure" him of his insolence. He whipped and brutalized Douglass whenever he had the chance. Douglass perceptively likened his plight under Covey to that of oxen who needed "to be broken" or tamed, recalling (perhaps unknowingly) Aristotle's maxim that the ox "is the poor man's slave." Break him Covey did, until Douglass' vision of a new world seemed a fading glimmer. "I was broken in body, soul, and spirit," he admitted, and on Sundays, his only day off, he lay "in a sort of beastlike stupor."[40]

Yet Douglass refused to be permanently broken. One Monday morning in August 1834, he stood up to Covey at the risk of his life. For two long hours, he resisted Covey's attempts to brutalize him, parrying every blow and flinging him on the ground several times. Douglass' legendary fight with Covey clarified his vision of the new dispensation and gave him the confidence to try to realize it. It was, he said, the "turning point in my 'life as a slave.' It rekindled in my breast the smouldering embers of liberty" and "revived a sense of my own manhood." His fight did not so much alter his faith in a new world as bring it back into sharp relief. It made him realize that "a man without force is without the essential dignity of humanity." Thereafter he was determined to gain his freedom by any means possible.[41]

As a result of his fight with Covey, Douglass understood that physical resistance could make him feel free. According to traditional understandings of the master-slave relationship (or "dialectic"), first articulated by the philosopher Georg Hegel, the slave's forced labor provides him with consciousness, humanity, and a degree of autonomy, while making the master dependent upon the slave for his work. Recently, the cultural critic Leonard Cassuto has reinterpreted the master-slave dialectic by cogently analyzing Douglass' fight with Covey. For Cassuto, "doing Covey's work makes Douglass feel *more* like a slave, not less." It is Douglass' physical aggression, rather than his labor, that makes him feel free: he "uses his conscious resistance to create and define himself as a person independent of his master." Cassuto thus revises Hegel's paradigm: "In the world of the American slave, physical resistance is work." As Douglass himself recognized, Covey "had been mastered by a boy of sixteen" and could no longer assert his tyrannical will over him.[42] Gerrit Smith described a similar feeling of independence and resurgence of manhood after he took up arms to defend himself against the anti-abolition mob. Both men found in physical resistance a sense of power and autonomy that, in the short run, helped to bridge their racial differences and unite them. Douglass appropriately ends the chapter in which he describes his fight with Covey by quoting Byron's *Childe Harold's Pilgrimage:* "Hereditary bondmen, know ye not / Who would be free, themselves must strike the blow?" The line became a common refrain for Douglass, Gerrit Smith, and McCune Smith throughout the 1850s. The Byronic ideal of the male liberator and freedom fighter who dispensed with fixed markers of social status—particularly heredity—was central to their sacred vision and interracial bonds.[43]

Covey unwittingly taught Douglass to use physical resistance as a means for sacralizing the world. Following their fight Douglass found "the heaven of comparative freedom." He became "a freeman in *fact*" even though he was "still a slave in form." He had reached the point at which he was *"not afraid to die."* He plotted an escape with other slaves in 1836, which failed, and returned to Baltimore in April of that year to become an apprentice for the shipbuilder Hugh Auld, Thomas Auld's brother, with his vision of a new world still at the forefront of his mind. Auld hired Douglass out as an apprentice caulker, and the eighteen-year-old slave formed numerous friendships with other free blacks in Baltimore. His hopes for a new dispensation, and his desire to help bring it about, can be gleaned from a vow he made during a debate with some friends while still a slave: he said he never intended to stop fighting "until he was a United States senator." It was a breathtaking statement, full of hope and confidence that a new world of interracial equality was at hand.[44]

The panic and depression may have facilitated Douglass' efforts to become free. When he returned to Baltimore in 1836, Hugh Auld's shipbuilding business had failed, and he wanted a stable source of income from Douglass. The inflationary cycle that preceded the panic may have squeezed Auld's profit margins. The swift decline in prices following the panic may also have been a factor in Auld's willingness to accept Douglass' proposal, in the spring of 1838, to guarantee Auld three dollars each week in return for hiring his own time, collecting his own wages, and furnishing his own room, board, and caulking tools. During a period of falling prices, such a "guaranteed" source of fixed income would have been attractive to Auld. Similarly, the money that Douglass and his fiancée Anna Murray were saving for his escape had greater purchasing power after the swift decline in prices. And after Auld's business had failed, Baltimore shipbuilders received a number of lucrative contracts to build slave ships, so that when Douglass hired himself out, skilled caulkers such as himself were in high demand.[45]

The exact degree to which the panic and depression aided Douglass' ability to escape is unknown. In any event, on September 3, 1838, he boarded a train heading north, disguised as a merchant sailor and carrying a seaman's protection pass, and realized his dreams of freedom. He formally changed his identity by changing his name to Frederick Douglass, and found work in the shipyards of New Bedford, Massachusetts. Within three years he was well known as an antislavery lecturer, and William Lloyd Garrison's American Anti-Slavery Society hired him to spread the word of abolitionism. For the rest of his life he would mark his new birth of freedom by celebrating it in place of his unknown birthday.[46]

❧ Gerrit Smith was not the only white man to be profoundly affected by the panic of 1837. Although historians have tended to downplay the depression that followed, its impact shook American culture at its roots, prompting whites throughout the North to reexamine their beliefs, values, and understandings of America.[47] The panic itself followed on the heels of the most prosperous year the United States had ever known, and led to "America's first modern depression." The economic historian Douglass North convincingly argues that in severity it was comparable to that of 1929.[48] Although there were several up-and-down cycles between 1837 and 1843, overall domestic and export prices declined precipitously. Cotton prices plummeted by over 50 percent, wages in New England textile mills fell by as much as half, and over one-third of New York City workers lost their jobs. Northern agriculture fared no better; crop prices fell to an unprecedented low in 1843, at a time when farmers increasingly produced for regional and national markets. After the crash the wealthy abolitionist Arthur Tappan owed over one million dollars, a level of debt that was unfathomable for most of his contemporaries. Not only individuals "but whole communities were involved in the general collapse."[49]

Contemporaries characterized the panic and depression in language that approached the apocalyptic. *Niles' Register* announced that nine-tenths of the country's factories closed in the wake of the panic. The *New-York Knickerbocker* reported "rumor after rumor of riot, insurrection, and tumult." And Albert Brisbane asserted that "scarcely a dozen men" between Albany and Buffalo had escaped bankruptcy. Accounts of shattered hopes and dashed dreams were commonplace, and a number of observers lost faith in the very idea of progress: "The Nation has been drawing on the Future, and the Future dishonors the draft," said one reporter. According to Henry Ward Beecher, "men awoke from gorgeous dreams in the midst of desolation. The harvest of years was swept away in a day." Americans wandered "like bereaved citizens among the ruins of an earthquake, mourning for children, for houses crushed, and property ruined forever." Although Beecher never rejected market capitalism, in the wake of the panic he characterized the very idea of debt—on which commerce so heavily depends—as "an inexhaustible fountain of Dishonesty": "The borrower is the servant to the lender. Debt is a rigorous servitude." For Beecher, debtors were like slaves rebelling against their servitude: "Some men put their property to the flames, assassinate the detested creditor, and end the frantic tragedy by suicide, or the gallows." Horace Greeley echoed these sentiments: "I would rather be a convict in a State prison, a slave in a rice-swamp, than to pass through life under the harrow of debt." Though hyperbolic, these pronouncements show that Northerners thought their material world was disintegrating. They experienced a profound sense of alienation, and reacted by trying to redefine themselves and their society.[50]

The depression years 1837–1844—and especially the "crucial year" 1837—represented not only a period of social change but also a critical moment in antebellum reform.[51] With their world crumbling around them, reform-minded Americans sought to replace it with "higher laws," spiritual visions, and other, more stable, realities. Gerrit Smith's transformation following the panic parallels a much larger shift in values among reformers, away from the material and external, toward the spiritual, idealistic, and internal. In the wake of the panic, the perfectionist John Humphrey Noyes began to put into practice his sacred vision of community. Simultaneously, Garrison developed his doctrine of nonresistance and disunion. Henry Clarke Wright embraced Noyes's perfectionism, became an agent for the New England Non-Resistance Society, and, like Noyes, began to rethink the basic structures of family.[52] Theodore Dwight Weld ended his brilliant career as an antislavery lecturer and began to move away from institution-based reform toward "body-based personal piety." Wendell Phillips came to power as an abolitionist within a year of the panic, and devoted his life to the cause. Joshua Giddings' status plummeted within six months of the panic. He went from "a man of independent means" to a bankrupt, found redemption in the God of nature, and abandoned his respected law career for political abolitionism. The panic and depression "triggered widespread reevaluations" in the American Anti-Slavery Society, according to Robert Abzug: "Latent divisions in the movement came to the fore," and in 1840, as the number of converts to the cause accelerated, the organization splintered.[53]

Although this shift in orientation involved many factors not directly related to the panic and the depression, what is significant is the depth and breadth of ferment that occurred in reform organizations during this period. Mormons significantly expanded their ranks and secretly embraced polygamy as a way to "restore" the traditional marriage practices of biblical patriarchs. Shakers began to exhibit a "rich outpouring" of creative forms of worship and ecstatic dance, including "spiritual manifestations," in which members were "led by angels through heavenly places." Experiments in communal living emerged at Brook Farm, Hopedale, New Harmony, and more than thirty other Fourierist-based associations, which by John Humphrey Noyes's assessment "reached the proportions and acquired many of the characteristics of a religious revival." Temperance reform began to draw widespread support from skilled artisans, clerks, and common laborers.[54] William Miller's predictions of the end of the world began to flourish in the cities, as did millenarianism in general, so much so that the New York State Lunatic Asylum at Utica blamed the "derangement" of roughly one-third of its patients in 1843–44 on "Millerism" and "religious excitement." One psychiatrist went so far as to argue that "thousands who have not yet become deranged [by Millerism] have had their health impaired to such a degree as to unfit them for the duties of life forever."[55] Emerson was "most severely" affected by the panic, and began emphasizing "the practical side of idealism," urging his audiences to embrace the divinity within, act on the reality of the unseen, and follow their subjective consciousness. In late 1837, he gave his first antislavery address, and in 1840 he helped found *The Dial*, the magazine of the Transcendental Club. Whitman was forced to work as a rural schoolteacher as a result of the panic, a job he detested. He became a "dissatisfied" and "gloomy young" man, saw the world as dark and foreboding, and developed a "visionary mode" of writing that described angels and images from the spirit world.[56]

The ferment of reform contributed to the social fragmentation and atomization that were already under way. But most white reformers, in their quest to rebuild their world or to replace it with an alternate reality, saw their plight as separate from that of blacks. They ignored or downplayed the multiethnic nature of their country, defined their utopian communities as white, and left untouched the barriers separating blacks from whites. Indeed the social instability during this period contributed to racial tensions. Most white reformers contained the assault on their society and their sense of freedom by retreating into white, insular spheres. Gerrit Smith was an exception. Although his reform efforts focused primarily on his own community until the mid-1840s, he conceived of that community in interracial terms. And as he became more involved in political abolitionism, his pluralist vision expanded, until he sought to intervene in areas that refused to accept his vision.

It was during this period of ferment in the North that the distinct vision of the Slave Power emerged. Gerrit Smith, Joshua Leavitt, William Goodell, and other men who became political abolitionists gave definition to that image, and were instrumental in deflecting anxieties away from themselves and onto slaveholders.[57] As early as 1836 Smith had warned his fellow Northerners that they must oppose slavery "in self defense." Otherwise, Southern slavery would "supplant the liberty of the North" and reduce Northern laborers "to a herd of slaves." Two years later he castigated laboring men for their willingness "to become tools for 'gentlemen of standing and property'"—a euphemism abolitionists used to describe anti-abolition mobsters. "The same spirit which enslaves" blacks "would as readily . . . brutalize and enslave the poor white man," he said, referring to the Slave Power and its allies. Texas' petition for annexation into the Union as a slave state in August 1837 provided further evidence of the Slave Power's quest to broaden its domain. Joshua Leavitt traced the "hard times . . . more to slavery than to any or all of the other alleged causes." By 1842 even mainstream Northern newspapers were bluntly asserting that "slavery" was the "cause" of "hard times." These arguments, however specious, provided answers to the fear, unrest, and economic volatility that plagued Northerners. As the slave population grew and slave territory expanded, the image of the Slave Power as the ultimate villain became an increasingly important source for explaining the contradiction between the illusion of order and the harsh reality of instability and unrest.[58]

Many abolitionists cited the murder of the abolitionist editor Elijah P. Lovejoy on November 7, 1837, in Alton, Illinois, as a catalyst for their conversion to the cause. After having his press destroyed three times by Alton mobs in little more than a year, Lovejoy purchased a fourth press in October 1837 and defended it and himself with a gun. When anti-abolitionists demanded that he surrender it, he refused and was killed in a shootout. His resistance put the doctrine of nonresistance to its first serious test. Although most abolitionists responded to Lovejoy's use of violence with mixed praise and condemnation, a few hailed him as a martyr, and his death prompted abolitionist sympathies from some important individuals. Emerson's first antislavery speech was a direct response to Lovejoy's death. Wendell Phillips stated that "the gun which was aimed at the breast of Lovejoy brought me to my feet." And Gerrit Smith noted that Lovejoy's death would "lead . . . thousands of professing Christians who have hitherto stood aloof from our cause" to act on their principles and spiritual visions. But as Smith knew from his own experience, this transformation was far more likely to happen if reformers already felt adrift in their material world. Lovejoy's murder represented one more link in a chain of depression, unrest, the rise of the Slave Power, and political destabilization that would ultimately lead to war.[59]

❧ John Brown was among the many reformers who considered Elijah Lovejoy's murder the spark that fired his fervent abolitionism. But Brown's reference to Lovejoy's martyrdom needs to be understood within the context of social and religious forces that transformed him into a militant abolitionist. Soon after Lovejoy's death, Brown and his father attended a memorial prayer meeting, and, according to witnesses, at the close of the service Brown stood up near the back of the room, lifted his right hand, and announced to the assembly: "Here, before God, in the presence of these witnesses, from this time, I consecrate my life to the destruction of slavery!" Lovejoy's death certainly upset Brown, but it was not so much the event itself that led to Brown's oath. Rather, Lovejoy's death signified for Brown all that was wrong in the country, in much the same way that the Slave Power later symbolized for Northerners the source of their fears and anxieties.[60]

Lovejoy's death coincided with a series of tragedies in Brown's life, culminating in the panic of 1837, that made him want to replace his existing world with his millennialist and perfectionist vision. Brown's transformation began in 1826, when he moved his family to the settlement of New Richmond, Pennsylvania, in the Randolph Township near the Ohio border, where he hoped to succeed in business and establish himself as a community leader. He impressed the other settlers with his hard work and righteousness. He served as the postmaster from 1828 to 1835, organized an "Independent Congregational" church that held services in his tannery, and planned to start a school for black children.[61]

It was in New Richmond that Brown's serious troubles began. In 1831 his four-year-old son Frederick died, followed the next year by his wife Dianthe, both from illnesses. He hired a housekeeper named Mary Day to help care for his five remaining children, and within a year married her. By the end of 1834 he had no money to run his tannery (much less start a school for black children) and decided to start fresh. In the winter of 1835–36 he moved his family back to Ohio, this time to a small village near Hudson called Franklin Mills, in the hopes of establishing himself as a successful businessman. Land prices in the area were booming, and Brown got caught up in the speculative frenzy. A new canal had recently been completed that ran from Akron to Franklin Mills, which Brown thought would transform his town into a great manufacturing center. He purchased large blocks of land with borrowed money, plotted out imaginary towns and subdivided lots, and envisioned the day when he would be the town patriarch, leading his community in the ways of righteousness. But money got tight, banks refused to pay specie, and creditors began foreclosing. According to Brown's biographer Stephen Oates, "former friends and business associates dragged him relentlessly into [court], suing him for loans he could not repay, land payments he could not make, contracts he could not fulfill." Brown lost his farm, even though he kept one creditor at bay with a shotgun, and was accused of being dishonest and incompetent. His world seemed to be bringing him almost nothing but death, debt, and business failures.[62]

The panic marked a turning point in Brown's life. His son John Jr. aptly summarized his plight: "The financial crash came in 1837, and down came all of father's castles, and buried the reputation he had achieved of possessing at least good common-sense in respect to business matters." Brown staved off bankruptcy until 1842 only by borrowing new money in other states to pay off old debts. He got expelled from his Congregational church for escorting a group of blacks to his family pew, in protest against its segregation rules. In 1840 he tried to start fresh again by settling on wild lands in the Ohio Valley of western Virginia that had long been owned by Gerrit Smith.[63] Gerrit had inherited the land—about twenty thousand acres—from his father, and donated it to Oberlin College in 1839, after hearing that the school was in need of money. Though mired in debt himself, Gerrit considered the land useless for his own needs. It required surveying, it was a long way from Peterboro, and he felt that he could not "make judicious and profitable sales of it." He admired Oberlin's policy of admitting women and blacks, the land was relatively close to the college (about two hundred miles southeast), and he "rejoiced" in being able to give it away. Brown learned of the gift through his father (a trustee of Oberlin), applied for the job of surveyor, and asked Oberlin officials to allow him to settle his family there. But Oberlin did not hire him, and his plan fell through. Brown would eventually settle on another parcel of Smith land—this one in the largely black community of North Elba, New York. But first he would suffer through eight more years of business failures as a wool merchant, and watch four more children die of disease in the space of ten months.[64]

It is almost impossible to comprehend Brown's militant crusade against slavery outside the context of his business failures and bankruptcy. Following the panic, his beliefs and worldviews underwent a profound transformation. He became an outsider, rejected the values and beliefs of his material world, and revised his understanding of God and the permanence of sin. Brown has almost always been viewed as an orthodox Calvinist whose religious views never changed. But they did change, and dramatically so, after the panic. He sought to replace his world with God's law and dominion, believed that all sin could be abolished, and waited expectantly for a new age to begin.[65]

Although Brown's writings on religion are sparse, it is possible to reconstruct his spiritual evolution. Before the panic he could accurately be described as a Calvinist in the tradition of Jonathan Edwards, the famous colonial New England divine. After settling at Franklin Mills and organizing his Independent Congregational church, he often gave the sermon himself when he could not find a minister, and usually preached from the writings of Edwards, whose beliefs had influenced his own understanding of God and whose sermons were among the few books Brown owned.[66]

Edwards was an important figure in the development of perfectionist and millennialist thought in antebellum America. His doctrines were central to the elaboration of perfection developed in the early 1830s by John Humphrey Noyes, the founder and leader of the utopian community at Oneida, New York. Edwards emphasized the spiritual "affections" of the heart, yet rigorously defended original sin and foreclosed the possibility of antinomianism and free will. For Edwards, "God exercised absolute sovereignty over man not by physical coercion but by arranging the motives which determined his actions." But if one started with Edwards' theology, and either dismantled his Calvinist determinism or embraced antinomianism by removing intermediary institutions that separated God from the self, perfectionism became possible.[67]

This is precisely what happened in the evolution of perfectionist thought. The idea that perfectionism was immediately possible became "one of the nineteenth century's most persistent and socially significant religious themes," according to the historian Timothy Smith, and Edwards was partly responsible for this development. Edwards' successors at Yale, particularly Nathaniel Taylor, believed that he tended to stifle individual effort by denying free agency. Taylor urged individuals to take control over their own actions, asserting that they could perfectly obey the law of God without the aid of God's grace. He thus affirmed individual agency as part of the process of forging a union with God and living righteously. But he refused to take the next step—to consider perfection a possibility—and when Noyes, his former student, declared himself perfect in terms of motivation, attitude, and assurance of salvation from sin, Taylor was outraged. He thought Noyes's beliefs would lead to antinomian excess and turn people loose to do and legitimate anything they wanted to do. He essentially disowned his former student, and was among those ministers responsible for revoking Noyes's license to preach.[68]

John Brown took a different route to perfectionism. While Taylor and Noyes dismantled Edwards' strict determinism, Brown departed from Edwards' theology by embracing his antinomian impulse. He continued to emphasize the absolute sovereignty of God, and defined himself as a Calvinist, but he violated a fundamental tenet of Calvinism. For Calvinists, God alone knew who was among the elect. But after the panic Brown internalized God's sovereignty and felt sure that he had been chosen for eternal salvation. More than that, he came to view himself as God's prophet and instrument, whose purpose was to show the world the path to perfection and righteousness. Internalizing God's sovereignty and conceiving of himself as his instrument paved the way to the possibility of perfection and a new age, obliterating the notion that sin was permanent. It was as though Brown inverted the idea of the Protestant work ethic: his material *failures* (rather than his successes) convinced him of his election and his vocation as a prophet. His unquestioning faith in the latter eventually destroyed all sense of humility and led to extreme forms of self-righteousness.

Brown hints at his spiritual evolution in an 1848 article he published in the black abolitionist newspaper the *Ram's Horn*, in which he posed as a black man and chided himself for tamely submitting to white laws and authority. "I was first a Presbyterian," he notes, and then began to associate with Quakers. But he "could never think of acting with" his Quaker friends because "they were the rankest heretiks," though he does not specify the reason for their heresy. "The Methodists denied the doctrine of election," he continued. But "since becoming enlightened by Garrison, Abby Kelley, & other really benevolent persons, I have been spending all my force on my friends who love the Sabbath & have felt that all was at stake on that point just as it has proved to be of late in France in the abolition of Slavery in their colonies." Brown's statement suggests that after becoming "enlightened" by Garrisonians, he devoted his energies to converting his friends to Garrisonian antinomianism and "come-outerism." He followed Garrison in "coming out" from evil institutions and doctrines, including the clergy's emphasis on the sanctity of the sabbath. For Brown as for Garrison and Gerrit Smith, instead of adhering to the letter of the law, one needed to follow the spirit of Christ. Instead of outwardly observing only the sabbath as sacred, one should inwardly and outwardly serve God at all times. Instead of obeying the sin-ridden earthly government, one must heed the government of God.[69]

Brown's correspondence corroborates the spiritual evolution outlined in the *Ram's Horn* article. It reveals his move away from Jonathan

Edwards' brand of "mystical Calvinism" in the early and mid-1830s, toward prophecy and perfectionism after the panic. In 1838 he told his family to follow the example of "Ezra the prophet," the Israelite scribe who "prayed and afflicted himself before God" when he and his people "were in a strait." Ezra was an apt model for Brown, for he knew the laws of the Lord, demanded that his people obey them, and executed strict judgment upon those who refused. The following year Brown urged his family not to "get discouraged, any of you, but [to] hope in God, and try all to serve him with a perfect heart." Although Jonathan Edwards embraced the spiritual affections of the heart, he conceived of the heart as perfect only within the millennium and an infusion of grace, which for him had not yet happened. In 1852 Brown fully revealed his perfectionist and millennialist leanings: "God grant you *thorough* conversion from sin," he told his children, "& full purpose of heart to continue steadfast in his ways through the *very short* season of trial you will have to pass." Brown's anticipation of the millennium made for a "*very short* season of trial." And a few years later he looked "forward to a time when 'peace on earth and good-will to men' shall everywhere prevail." This is the outlook of a perfectionist and millennialist, not of a mystical Calvinist.[70]

❧ James McCune Smith is the only member of this interracial alliance whose evolution into radical abolitionism did not involve an act of physical resistance. Gerrit Smith and John Brown resorted to firearms to fend off mobs and creditors, and Douglass described his fight with Edward Covey as the turning point in his life. McCune Smith kept his head in his books and his eyes on his studies at the University of Glasgow. He was generally in class from early morning through midafternoon, and then until late in the evening he studied Latin, Greek, Logic, moral philosophy, natural philosophy, mathematics, and eventually medicine and surgery. In Scotland he established himself as an intellectual who believed that the mind and heart together represented the most effective weapons against bondage and oppression.[71]

Soon after his arrival at Glasgow McCune Smith became known and respected among his white peers as a dedicated scholar and ardent abolitionist. His black admirers in America celebrated his accomplishments in higher education by noting that he "entered the arena of intellect to combat with a host of aspirants . . . each striving to excel the other in the intellectual conflict," and graduated first in his class, snatching "the prize from hundreds of competitors." McCune Smith also became a charter member of the Glasgow Emancipation Society in 1833, and his white colleagues were so impressed with his intellect that their belief in innate racial equality became "less a matter of abstraction to us" than "a present living reality." In his work with the Emancipation Society, McCune Smith urged "the physically harmless, but morally omnipotent, weapons of truth and righteousness" in the fight against slavery, adding that if physical means were employed, he "would be among the first to resist them." Moral weapons, he felt, would prevail in ending slavery.[72]

McCune Smith's reluctance to use physical force until the late 1840s reflected not only his identity as an intellectual and his success as a physician, but the absence of a sublime, apocalyptic vision that would usher in the new age. He believed in the millennium as much as Douglass, Brown, and Gerrit Smith, but his anticipation of it lacked the violent imagery that his future comrades associated with it. Additionally, there was a comparative dearth of racial conflict at the University of Glasgow and in Scotland in general, at a time when his black peers in America faced an upsurge of racism and racial oppression. These conditions contributed to his growing self-confidence and faith in peaceful means for ending slavery. The only racial confrontation he experienced while in Scotland occurred while he was preparing to return to New York in 1837. The American ship captain refused to grant him cabin passage because of his race, which not only infuriated him but "also insulted those with whom I have had the delight of associating, during the last five years." No native of Scotland "would deny the social board to any man on account of the color of his skin." His white colleagues in the Glasgow Emancipation Society confronted the captain and persuaded him to allow McCune Smith to sail home as a cabin rather than steerage passenger.[73]

Upon his return to New York McCune Smith was treated as a celebrity among his black friends. By any standards, his credentials were impressive. He was only twenty-five years old, and in the space of five years had received his bachelor's, master's, and medical degrees at a prestigious university. An article in the *Colored American* shaved two years off his age to make his credentials seem even more impressive, and his professional accomplishments were frequently cited to inspire the free black community. Virtually every speech he gave in the first year after his return was covered by the black press and reprinted in its entirety. His speeches reveal his self-definition as an intellectual; they were well researched and densely argued but lacked oratorical and performative power. His 1837 speech on "the fallacy of phrenology," for example, resembled a classroom lecture to science students. He used as props skulls and extemporaneous drawings and spoke the language of a scientist to refute the phrenological claim, promoted by racist whites, that the size, shape, and capacities of the brain could be apprehended by measuring the external contours of the skull. He noted that the "dogmas of phrenology" focused exclusively on the realms of the material and physical, and thus threatened to incite a crisis of faith in the "doctrines of Christianity" and the reality of the unseen.[74]

After the initial flurry of renown in New York City's black community, McCune Smith settled into a relatively comfortable middle-class lifestyle. He married Malvina Barnet, the daughter of one of the most esteemed black families in the city, who shared McCune Smith's passion for scholarship, teaching, and abolitionism. Despite the adverse effects of the panic and depression, he established an interracial medical practice and pharmacy in the respectable neighborhood of West Broadway, and started a family. Although it is difficult to determine the degree to which the panic affected his medical practice, since his profession was relatively immune to economic downturns he probably began his career at a comparative advantage over most other businessmen.[75]

McCune Smith joined the American Anti-Slavery Society shortly after his return to New York, and he probably met Gerrit Smith at the 1838 annual meeting, for both were keynote speakers. His speech preceded Gerrit's, and their different emphases reveal their different self-conceptions and approaches to abolitionism. Gerrit's speech was provincial in focus. Aside from a trip to Montreal as a college student, he had never left his country or the Northeast (and he would never set foot on another continent). He dwelled on the prejudice of Northern whites, and urged his mostly white audience to make themselves into colored men. McCune Smith, on the other hand, analyzed slavery from a global perspective. He argued that contrary to white abolitionist perceptions, black revolutionaries in the French colony of St. Domingue were the first group to advocate immediate emancipation. Although he did not discuss the issue of violent means, his praise for Haiti as the leader in immediate and entire emancipation and as the first self-governing black state in the New World foreshadowed his later acceptance of rebellion and revolution.[76]

Three years later McCune Smith elaborated on the significance of the St. Domingue revolution in a brilliant lecture at the Stuyvesant Institute in Manhattan. After summarizing the revolution in rich and accurate detail, he concluded that the bloodshed and violence on the island were not, as most white Americans believed, the "fruit of emancipation," but rather the product of slavery and caste. White Americans frequently pointed to the St. Domingue revolution to justify their racist views of emancipated blacks as bloodthirsty creatures seeking vengeance against their former masters. McCune Smith correctly noted that whites had caused far more bloodshed and deaths on the island than blacks: only 2,000 whites had been killed by blacks, whereas 10,000 of the 40,000 black insurgents had been slain by whites. Though acknowledging that slave revolutions "have generally proved the most fierce and sanguinary of all wars," he stressed that the St. Domingue revolution was relatively mild by comparison. In the servile war in Italy in 71 B.C.E., Spartacus and his slaves—who were not black—had killed far more people than had the St. Domingue slaves. He portrayed Toussaint L'Ouverture, the leader of the St. Domingue revolt, as a Christlike figure, seeking "equal rights to all men" and avenging the injuries of whites not through bloodshed, but "by forgiveness." Slavery itself was far "more destructive of human life than the wars, insurrections, and massacres to which it gave birth," for before the revolution, slaveowners in St. Domingue "destroyed no less than 5,000 human beings per annum" by working them to death. The "horrors of St. Domingue" that whites so often referred to stemmed from slavery and white oppression. The casualties of the revolution were mild by comparison. McCune Smith revealed in the speech an understanding of slavery and racial attitudes surpassing that of just about all his contemporaries.[77]

McCune Smith and Gerrit Smith established a cordial but distant relationship in the late 1830s and early 1840s. McCune Smith wrote Gerrit in 1839 to solicit money to help Alexander Crummell complete his theological training. Crummell, a recent graduate of Oneida Institute, a manual-labor school that accepted both blacks and whites, was having difficulty obtaining a license to preach as an Episcopal minister "on account of his complexion." McCune Smith hoped Gerrit would help Crummell complete his studies in the British West Indies or Canada. Although Gerrit contributed twenty dollars, their relationship waned until the mid-1840s. Not until Gerrit decided to establish the black community of North Elba, and asked McCune Smith to act as trustee and select the beneficiaries, did their relationship grow into an intimate and rich friendship.[78]

❧ Gerrit Smith faced a mountain of debt. In 1842 he owed creditors over $600,000 and became delinquent on part of it. He was forced to pay from 10 to 20 percent interest, was threatened with lawsuits, and faced possible bankruptcy. He responded by selling property "in all directions as fast" as he could, as he told one friend. He put the mansion-house up for sale, and although he never sold it, he and his family moved a mile away, to a modest, twelve-hundred-square-foot, wood-framed split-level house in Smithfield. They called it "The Grove" and lived there off and on throughout the 1850s, even after Gerrit had recovered financially. He dismissed most of his assistants and clerks, and Nancy and his daughter Elizabeth helped him manage his properties, negotiate debts, and stay out of bankruptcy. He relied entirely on his wife's estate for his abolitionist expenses, and pared his living expenses to about six hundred dollars per year, little more than a skilled laborer's annual wage. Although he was a long way from being poor or impoverished, he often referred to his "threatened bankruptcy" and "pecuniary embarrassments," which was another way of acknowledging that he had become a social outsider.[79]

By late 1846 Smith was again financially solvent, and he began giving away enormous amounts of money and property. He considered poverty a virtue as long as its source stemmed from efforts to create a sacred society. Through his philanthropy he effectively transformed Peterboro and Madison County into a multiracial community. He and Nancy spent tens of thousands of dollars purchasing the liberty of slaves, including those formerly owned by Nancy's family. They paid for their transportation north; encouraged them to settle in Peterboro and Madison County; gave them food, clothing, and shelter; helped

them find employment; and dined, attended church, and socialized
with them. They also opened their home to fugitives, and either paid
their way to Canada or attempted to purchase their liberty at discounts
from prevailing market prices.[80] "I trust that when [my debts] are paid,"
Gerrit told a friend in 1846, "I shall have a heart to reduce myself, if
not to a poor man—yet well nigh to a poor man—by purchasing the
liberty of the enslaved poor."[81] Despite his rhetoric, Smith remained
extremely wealthy. He retained his most valuable property as a source
for his philanthropy, and was probably a millionaire on paper. Still,
over the course of their reform careers, Gerrit and Nancy spent as
much as eight million dollars on sacralizing the world, which was "perhaps eight times" greater than the estate Gerrit left at his death.[82] In
one five-year period, from 1846 to 1850, he gave away an astonishing
200,000 acres of land to poor blacks and whites in one of the largest
acts of philanthropy by an American to date. Most of the Smiths' philanthropy was targeted directly to individuals: slaves; poor free blacks,
whites, and women; members of their community; and those willing to
devote their lives to vanquishing the Slave Power.[83] In 1990s currency,
they gave away between $600 million and $1.1 billion.[84]

Smith's generosity became well known, and Peterboro became a haven for beggars, tramps, wandering drunks, and the disabled. "Beggars
infested the county," one contemporary complained. A lot of poor people did come and go from the mansion-house. Smith's diary is filled
with accounts detailing the arrivals and departures not only of fugitive
slaves but also of a "deaf child," a "beggar woman," a "wandering pil-
grim," a "colored, illiterate man, calling himself a missionary," a "poor
old Dutch woman," a "begging blind man," an "insane literary colored
man," a doctor with "five deaf mutes and a blind child," and an Indian
and his "drunk friend." They stayed a night or so, dined at the Smith
table, and left with money, a few days' worth of provisions, and instructions to avoid alcohol and tobacco and to serve God, the slave, and all
humanity. Those who could not make it to Peterboro often received a
check from Gerrit or Nancy to help relieve their woes. Solicitors appealed to the Smiths for everything from money to "factory cotton
enough for a nightgown" to protection against an abusive husband.
One man, having lost his "digestive apparatus," implored Gerrit "for
its recovery."[85]

Dinners at the mansion-house were legendary for their eccentric
makeup. One frequent guest recalled that they often included "wealthy

and refined visitors from the metropolitan cities," "at least one or two fugitive slaves," "a crazy Millerite or two," Indians, and "some enthusiastic adventurer."[86] The Smiths made little distinction between deserving or undeserving poor or on the basis of skin color or occupation, either in their own home or in the community. "Does not Christ pity the sufferings of the vilest man on earth?" Gerrit publicly asked his townspeople in 1842. "Then must not his disciples do likewise?" "The good Samaritan" should not "inquire into the moral character of the wounded man."[87] Through their example, the Smiths sought to create a diverse, utopian community whose organizing principles were love, empathy, and tolerance rather than power, patriarchy, and wealth.

Gerrit saw himself as the leader of his utopian society at Peterboro and Madison County. In this sense he was similar to John Brown, who, no matter where he lived, always sought to be the leader of his community. Smith's and Brown's conceptions of themselves as community leaders were closely linked to their roles as prophets preparing for a new age. But unlike John Brown, Smith was extremely tolerant, and thus deviated from the tendency of utopian leaders to exert despotic control over their communities. Smith asserted control over his villagers at Peterboro through philanthropy rather than through patriarchy or bourgeois authority. He anointed his community, as it were, with wealth. He used his great wealth to encourage neighbors to avoid drink and tobacco, to become fervent abolitionists, and to accept blacks as full and equal members of his community. Instead of threatening their well-being, he enticed them with gifts, and they responded with enormous enthusiasm. Virtually every African American who visited Peterboro considered it a model interracial community. And when Smith ran for Congress in 1852, he received every vote but two in Smithfield and an overwhelming majority of the votes in Madison County. From the mid-1840s until the Civil War, Madison County was one of the largest (per capita) abolition communities in the country. Even the rum drinkers and tavern owners who rejected his money respected him. There is no record of any protest against his efforts to transform Peterboro into an abolitionist and interracial community.[88]

Smith believed that transforming Smithfield into a utopian community would have a centrifugal effect; it would be the first stage toward establishing a sin-free country. In March 1845 he expressed this belief to two neighbors. He had recently begun devoting more energy to the Liberty party, and sought to impress upon them the importance of voting for Liberty candidates. The country had "just robbed" Mexico "of territory enough for five or six of our states, to the end that American slavery may be perpetuated." But slavery was "so glaring an absurdity" that if only one little town stood "unanimously, or nearly so," against it, this "righteous" example would quickly spread and the "slavery of this nation would speedily fall." He beseeched his neighbors to act on their beliefs by voting for Liberty men and to help make their little town of Smithfield an "honored and immortal town." "Do your duty and others will follow," he said. "Life is short," since the new age was at hand, "and we have no time to lose in doing good."[89]

Partly as a result of Smith's community work, Madison County remained a remarkably stable but diverse community from 1840 to 1860; at a time when neighboring counties were growing dramatically, Smithfield's population declined slightly from 1830 to 1860 and ranged from 1,600 to 1,700 people.[90] The population of the county increased at a snail's pace, from 39,000 in 1830 to 43,000 in 1860. By contrast, the county's population of blacks and immigrants both doubled over the same period, and by 1850 Peterboro had become a diverse and multiethnic community. Although there was a large net natural increase of births over deaths in Madison County, outmigration to growing cities like Utica and Rome helped keep the population of the county stable. The vast majority of Madison County residents—many of whom became Millerites as well as abolitionists—were farmers, and the community remained extremely self-contained. These conditions contrasted sharply with those in neighboring counties like Oneida, where most people lived in Utica and Whitestown and depended almost entirely on external markets for basic levels of subsistence. Smith had the requisite wealth to connect Madison County to the burgeoning national market economy, and thereby transform his community into a growing industrial center. But he sought to preserve its rural and communitarian makeup.[91]

The village of Peterboro seemed especially resistant to modern times, and its physical layout reflected its utopian sensibility. The village green was rimmed with homes that from a distance resembled a series of rowhouses. Interspersed among them were two drugstores, two groceries, a tailor's shop, the post office, and two inns—the Fay House for drinkers, and Smith's temperance house. The green itself was fenced, and served as a pasture for the communal livestock. The village geography remained virtually unchanged from 1834 until 1859. Residents of Smithfield produced enough barley, wheat, corn, oats, butter, cheese, wool, and fabric for local consumption. The average home had three hogs and two horses, and there were sawmills, gristmills, a carding machine, an ashery, and a tannery to facilitate household production. As a result of this local production and exchange, the community remained relatively independent from the combative and oppressive snares of the national market revolution.[92]

In its perfectionist sensibility, Peterboro was in some ways similar to John Humphrey Noyes's Oneida community, which was only about twenty miles away. Noyes carried perfectionism to a far greater extreme than Smith did, however, and, in stark contrast to Smith's tolerance, he demanded total authority and control. The Oneida community abhorred slavery in every form, from black bondage and drink to marriage and private property. It was also an entirely white community, and sought to insulate itself from worldly affairs, whereas Peterboro residents were racially and ethnically diverse and active political abolitionists. Since the Oneida community considered marriage to be a form of female bondage, members practiced "complex marriage," which in theory was a sacred expression of "free love" but in practice exposed most of the women to Noyes's own sexual urges. Oneida members also raised children as well as their livestock communally. Gerrit and Nancy Smith never championed Noyes's notion of complex marriage, but neither did they publicly condemn it (they were unfamiliar with the details).[93]

Gerrit and Nancy Smith were friends with John Humphrey Noyes, and they shared many beliefs. In the spring and summer of 1837, shortly before Noyes began experimenting with communal living and complex marriage, he proposed, "on certain conditions, to join hands with [the Smiths] in pushing antislavery," according to his nephew George Wallingford Noyes. Noyes was living at home in Putney, Vermont, at the time (he settled the Oneida community in 1847), and although the details of the arrangement are not known, Gerrit and especially Nancy "expressed lively interest" in Noyes's perfectionism. But the proposal fell through, and they shaped their communities according to their respective perfectionist visions.[94]

Their different visions of perfection led to different approaches for dealing with slavery and their sin-filled world. Both Smith and Noyes believed in sacred self-sovereignty, and thought that humans, by becoming born again in Christ and following his example, could become perfect. They believed in "coming out" from the evils of society and defining themselves as outsiders. And they agreed that a perfectionist must declare war on the current government of the United States, and wage it with the weapons of Christ. But they differed as to the means. As a political abolitionist, Smith declared war on the government through intervention. His understanding of the new dispensation—which began with the apocalypse—accommodated his violent means and created a sense of urgency to end sin through blood atonement if necessary.[95]

Noyes had a different conception of the millennium and perfection, and thus responded differently to his society at large. Whereas Gerrit pieced together his perfectionist and millennialist vision in a makeshift and informal fashion, Noyes's path was calculated and academic. He had studied at Andover and Yale, and was profoundly influenced by the theologians Moses Stuart and Nathaniel Taylor. He reinterpreted Stuart's writings to argue that Christ's second coming had occurred in 70 c.e. and that the "final resurrection and judgment of mankind" would occur in 1880 (the same year, ironically, that the Oneida community would come to an end). For Noyes, the final resurrection and judgment were near at hand, and he was confident "that perfection was now attainable." But instead of fighting to preserve Christ's kingdom, he advocated "renunciation and repudiation" of the world, and sought to stand aloof from its sins.[96]

Noyes essentially advocated disunion from society, and his disunionism was similar to but smaller in scale than that urged by William Lloyd Garrison. In fact Noyes was directly responsible for Garrison's doctrine of disunion.[97] Garrison's doctrine, which replaced the existing government with the government of God, first appeared in 1838 in the form of nonresistance. In March 1837 Noyes awakened Garrison to nonresistance with a powerful letter: "I am willing that all men should know that I have subscribed my name to an instrument similar to the Declaration of '76, renouncing all allegiance to the government of the United States, and asserting the title of Jesus Christ to the throne of the world." The only solution, for Noyes, lay in "coming out" from society by repudiating its government. "It was as though Noyes had explained and simplified all of Garrison's longings and de-

sires," the historian John L. Thomas observes, and Garrison succumbed immediately to Noyes's logic.[98]

There was "an inherent paradox" in Noyes's and Garrison's version
of perfectionism that they failed to understand, which Gerrit Smith
and his fellow political abolitionists avoided. As Thomas shrewdly
notes, their perfectionism "pointed out the good society and then refused permission to advance toward it. Agreeing on the nature of evil,
[Noyes and Garrison] were unwilling to employ the political power
needed to wipe it out. As to both means and ends [their] perfectionism
postulated anarchy by reducing social wrongs to a question of personal
sin and appealing not to community interest but to individual anxieties."[99]

As a political abolitionist, Gerrit Smith expressly used the institution
of government to fulfill his goals, and employed political power to wipe
out evil. Instead of postulating anarchy, he appealed directly to community interest and national welfare through his philanthropy,
speeches, and Bible politics. In contrast to Noyes and Garrison, Smith
and his allies retained a dynamic balance between their impulse to perfection and their sin-filled world through political action, intervention,
and violence, beginning in the mid-1840s. And while Noyes's and Garrison's brand of perfectionism contributed to the social fragmentation
wrought by the panic and depression, which led in turn to the fragmentation of the national antislavery movement, Smith and his comrades sought to shore up the social chaos by embracing a kind of mystical nationalism—similar to that described in Whitman's *Leaves of
Grass*—that was free from sin and extremely diverse in its body politic.
For Smith, the black community of North Elba would become the
clearest manifestation of his sacred and pluralist vision.[100]

CHAPTER FIVE

Bible Politics and the Creation
of the Alliance

There seems something weird and forbidding in this utter blackness
... Now the woods . . . are displaced by the iron wall, almost touching
the roadside; against its steep abruptness scarcely a shrub can cling,
scarcely a fern flutter; it takes your breath away; but . . . beyond this
stern passway, this cave of iron, lie the lovely lakes and mountains of
the Adirondacks, and the homestead of John Brown. [It] seems beyond the world.

—THOMAS WENTWORTH HIGGINSON, "JOHN BROWN" (1860)

[John Brown's hope] was to build a true American city on a hill that
would give the lie to every skeptic in the land. There were many such
utopian schemes and projects afoot in those years, a hundred cities on
a hundred little hills, but [Timbucto] may have been the only one that
aimed at setting an example of racial harmony. This would be our er-
rand into the wilderness, he said.

—RUSSELL BANKS, *CLOUDSPLITTER* (1998)

In January 1846, one month after Texas entered the Union as a slave
state, Gerrit Smith began to implement reform measures that were
grander in scale than anything he had yet done, and he had already
done quite a bit. Over the past decade he had helped build the American Anti-Slavery Society into a nationally prominent organization
through speeches, petitions, and donations amounting to some fifty
thousand dollars. He had purchased the freedom of scores of slaves,
financed their resettlement to Madison County and other parts north,
and had transformed Peterboro into one of the most abolitionist
and interracial communities in the country. He had helped to found
the Liberty party, and in 1844, when he actively began to bear witness
to it and promote its growth, the party's presidential candidate, James

G. Birney (Smith's brother-in-law), received over sixty thousand votes.[1]

But in the face of an increasingly belligerent Slave Power, these accomplishments now seemed insignificant. The votes for Birney had contributed to James K. Polk's 1844 presidential victory over Henry Clay, and President Polk was now looking for an excuse to begin war with Mexico in order to enlarge the country's southern (and slave) boundaries. Smith's hopes that the interracial and abolitionist makeup of Peterboro and Madison County would "naturally" spread throughout the country were not being realized. And the slaves Smith had emancipated amounted to little more than one thousandth of one percent of the country's slave population. Since 1837 his principal aim had been to "abolitionize the public mind."[2] But the number of slaves kept increasing, and Northern oppression of blacks continued unabated. Smith had long recognized that empowering poor Northern blacks could be a potent weapon against both proslavery Northerners and the slave system. He now sought to do that by giving them land.

It was this land that brought the four men together. Smith embarked on a plan to give away 120,000 acres of wilderness land in the Adirondacks to three thousand poor New York blacks, and his gift was the catalyst that united him with James McCune Smith, Frederick Douglass, and John Brown. Through his gift Smith hoped to establish an independent and self-sustaining black community that would serve many purposes: it would protect settlers against antiblack prejudice and enable them to obtain suffrage, and it would serve as a model for compensated emancipation throughout the country, whereby slaves would receive free land and slaveholders money. With his gift of land, Smith was seeking to realize his ideal of a pluralist and egalitarian country.

Smith conceived of his gift as part of his broad understanding of Bible politics, and it led directly to his alliance and friendship with Douglass, McCune Smith, and Brown. No other white man had the willingness and wherewithal to grant blacks such independence. Giving land to three thousand poor blacks offered them the vote, for by cultivating their plots they could meet the New York state black suffrage requirement. The land also represented an alternative to black emigration; it allowed recipients to become self-sufficient and to resist antiblack prejudice *within* America. Partly as a result of Smith's gift,

McCune Smith and Douglass abandoned Garrisonian nonresistance for political action and Bible politics. Douglass campaigned for Smith's congressional election in 1852, and saw in his victory a new era that would bring freedom, land, and suffrage to blacks. McCune Smith encouraged blacks to settle on their new land, and viewed the community as an important step toward achieving a pluralist country. John Brown, after hearing of Smith's gift, decided to settle there permanently; and it was here, in his new home in the Adirondacks, that he conceived of and planned his incursion into the South. Smith's ideal of a thriving wilderness community was designed as an alternative to violence, but it ended up contributing to these four men's acceptance of it.

❧ The inspiration for Smith's gift stemmed in part from his acquaintance in 1844 with George Henry Evans, the well-known labor leader and editor of *Working Man's Advocate* and *People's Rights*. Evans considered "land monopoly"—by which he meant the ownership of private land by a few wealthy elites—the primary cause of poverty. He advocated the free distribution of all public land to the "landless"—those who owned no property—coupled with severe restrictions on the amount of land any individual could own. In July 1844 Evans vilified Smith in his newspapers for his vast property holdings, calling him "one of the largest Slaveholders in the United States." Every acre Smith owned was an acre denied to each "enslaved" Northern worker who had no land, accused Evans. Smith was thus denying hundreds of thousands of Northern whites their freedom, and keeping them "in a worse state of ignorance, degradation, misery, and vice" than slavery. Evans wanted to provoke Smith and convert him to the cause of land reform, and he sent Smith a copy of his newspaper containing the diatribe.[3]

Smith responded immediately, pleading ignorance to Evans' reform views: "So secluded is my life—so far from the world's track—that I never before heard of yourself, nor of these newspapers" that had carried the attack. Smith sympathized with the plight of the worker, said the government "would do well" to distribute public land to the landless, and believed that large landowners should likewise give away lots to the laboring poor. But he emphasized his priority to the cause of the slave and blacks in general—whom he called "the poorest of the poor":

> When you tell abolitionists that the order of doing good is, first, to those near you, and then to those afar off; they will . . . tell you, that an infinitely more important order of benevolence is, first, to labor for the total repudiation of the Heaven-forbidden idea of property in man, and for the establishment of man's right to himself; and then, for the establishment of his right to that which by Heaven's ordination, is the subject of property.[4]

Smith's response, which also represented the position of Douglass, McCune Smith, and John Brown toward the laboring poor, shows that he was not indifferent to poor white workers, but rather established preferences according to the degree of evil.[5] He hoped that "Agrarians" (labor reformers) and "Abolitionists" could work together: "You can enlighten abolitionists by inculcating upon them the great truth that men have a natural right to the soil," he told Evans. And abolitionists could enlighten labor leaders by telling them to include slaves and blacks in their vision of land reform. Smith sent Evans money to help unite the two groups. It was "a present," he said, from his wife Nancy, who was especially "interested in your alliance."[6]

Evans was so impressed with Smith that in 1846 he asked him to run for New York civil office under the National Reform Association (NRA), the labor party he had organized and led. The NRA had recently acquired the slogan "Vote Yourself a Farm," and sought to create republican townships of 160-acre plots for poor laborers that would be funded by reserves of government land. The NRA also encouraged union activity to combat the influence of big business, and proposed a ten-hour day for factory workers. Smith was flattered by Evans' offer and said he felt "a deep interest in the objects of the 'National Reformers.'" But he could not consent. He had no "relish for public life." Even if he had wanted to run for office as an NRA candidate, he considered himself "quite too odious to get it." He urged Evans to choose NRA candidates who "pitied the poor" and whose motto would be "that no man be poor, and no man be rich—that no man be overworked, and that no man be underworked." It was a refrain Gerrit would repeat until the Civil War.[7]

Evans prompted Smith to act on his vision of land reform; but the vision itself was not new to Smith. He had "cherished for years" the belief that wealthy individuals should divide their lots into, "forty or fifty acres" and give them to poor workers who wished to reside on them, as he told Evans. But "in many cases" wealthy land barons had inherited their property laden with debt, and "these debts have been greatly increased by liabilities for friends." The debts must be paid "before the owners can have either a legal or moral right to give away the land." Smith was in effect describing his own circumstances and his reasons for inaction.[8]

In February 1846 Smith began to act on his and Evans' vision. He embarked on a plan to reduce his debt, still hovering around $500,000, so that he could begin giving away large amounts of land. He announced a series of public auctions to sell 750,000 acres, constituting the bulk of his holdings, which were scattered throughout almost every county in the state. Although much of the land went unsold, he cut his debt in half within six months. He continued selling unwanted assets, and by 1849 his debt stood at a very manageable $100,000. He even considered selling his valuable canal and waterfront property in Oswego, but decided to keep it as a source of revenue for his philanthropy. He realized that his wealth, if invested properly, could generate more income and property for the poor than if he were to give it all away.[9]

On August 1, 1846, Smith announced his intent to give away 120,000 acres of land to three thousand poor New York blacks. The land was located in the wilds of the Adirondacks, near Lake Placid, New York, primarily in Essex and Franklin Counties. He appointed trustees in different regions of the state to supply him with the names of eligible recipients. James McCune Smith and two black ministers, Charles Ray and Theodore Wright, served as his principal trustees and were responsible for the New York City region, which had the largest concentration of blacks (about eighteen thousand) in the North. "For years I have indulged the thought that when I had sold enough land to pay my debts, I would give away the remainder to the poor," Smith told them. He acknowledged Evans' influence by declaring: "I am an Agrarian. I would that every man who desires a farm, might have one; and I would, that no man . . . covet the possession of more farms than one." He drafted deeds to assign to two thousand recipients, and planned to convey the remaining thousand deeds within a year or two, after selling more land.[10]

Smith gave enormous discretion to McCune Smith, Ray, and Wright in selecting beneficiaries, and imposed only a few eligibility requirements. Since both his home and his land were in New York, he thought it suitable to select recipients from his state. They had to be between the ages of twenty-one and sixty. They had to be landless (although he separately gave plots to McCune Smith, Douglass, Brown, and a few other black abolitionists who already owned land). They could not be "drunkards," although he tolerated occasional drinkers. And they had to be black, for although he did not want to put "a bounty on color," he concluded that blacks were "the poorest of the poor, and the most deeply wronged class of our citizens."[11]

Smith limited his gift to blacks mainly as a response to antiblack prejudice in general and New York state suffrage laws in particular, which required blacks to own $250 in freehold property to vote. "I confess that this mean and wicked exclusion has had no little effect in producing my preference," he said in his initial letter to the trustees. He admitted that the land was of poor quality and would not automatically grant suffrage to the recipients—that would have required farmland worth $750,000, which he did not have. But his gift brought the recipients within reach of the vote, for their forty-acre plots would be worth $250 after they had cultivated the land.[12] Improving the condition of free blacks would ultimately help loosen the bonds of slavery. His gift would empower blacks by allowing them to become self-sufficient, enfranchised, and thus able to fight slavery more effectively. The absurdity of enslaving and oppressing people on the basis of skin color would be exposed when thousands of blacks lived and worked like whites.[13]

Smith announced his gift on August 1, the anniversary of emancipation in the British West Indies. Both he and McCune Smith saw resemblances between the condition of free blacks in the United States and freedmen in the West Indies. Implicit in Smith's gift was a type of freedom much different from that pursued by the architects of British emancipation. British policymakers sought to transform slaves into wage earners who continued to work for their former masters. Wage labor, they thought, would prevent former slaves from "regressing to the imagined barbarous life of their African ancestors." But most slaves defined freedom differently; on the whole, they preferred to work small plots of land on which they could earn their subsistence and resist the authority of former masters. Smith's plan was based on the preference of West Indian slaves rather than British policymakers; it presented a model of freedom that allowed poor blacks to become self-sufficient and relatively insulated from white oppression. It allowed them to become "respectable."[14]

Smith recognized that his plan threatened a market-based capitalist economy, which depended on large cash crops and economies of scale. He was fully aware of the sharp decrease in productivity and profitability in the British West Indies following emancipation, because of blacks' preference for subsistence farming. He was virtually unique among white abolitionists in distinguishing between moral and material progress. What mattered was neither the productivity of the freedmen and women, nor the economic effects of emancipation, but obedience to God and the moral state of the individual and society. He said as much in an 1840 letter to the Tennessee slaveowner and planter John Cooke, in an effort to convince him to liberate his eleven hundred slaves. He cited the example of the British West Indies as a case in point. After emancipation the moral condition of the islands had dramatically improved even as their economy had suffered a steep decline. On the one hand, there was "far less crime on these islands than there was during slavery," despite widespread predictions that with freedom the islands "would run blood." On the other hand, "the exports of the islands are less. This is true—and the inference is, that the people labor less than when in a state of slavery. Perhaps they do—and if any people have a right to be lazy, it is they who have through life been subject to compulsory toil." From Smith's perspective, the two main reasons for the decline in exports were "inadequate wages offered" to the former slaves, and their "reasonable" desire "to consume and enjoy a larger share of the products of their toil than was allowed them before emancipation." He assumed that Northern blacks would also prefer to consume the fruits of their own labor, and now, six years later, he was giving them a chance to do that with his gift.[15]

Smith felt that blacks would quickly rise to the condition of whites if they could receive the fruits of their labor. "What people of color, with all their rights accorded to them, are capable of becoming in this nation," he told Cooke, "is an experiment yet to be tried. Hitherto we have seen how far and how rapidly they can rise under all the dead weights we attach to them." He cited numerous examples of these achievements: A large number of free blacks could read and write. They had built good schools and impressive houses of worship. In some Northern communities, blacks and whites freely intermingled. He cited his own village, in which "colored persons sit where they please in our sanctuaries—and I know not the family in our village that would reject a decent colored person from their table." There was an integrated female school twenty miles from Peterboro—"one of the best schools in the country," Smith noted—and at nearby Oneida Institute the top student, William G. Allen, though a slave eighteen months ago, was now "unsurpassed by any member of the school." One of Smith's neighbors, Samuel Ringgold Ward, was "black as ink" and the most "eloquent and logical debater" of anyone his age that Smith had ever witnessed. All blacks needed was a chance, and he hoped his gift would offer them that chance. But nowhere did he link black success with profitability, productivity, or the capitalist marketplace.[16]

In many respects Smith's gift represented an experiment in black emigration (or colonization) *within* the country. As he told Cooke, he vehemently opposed the American Colonization Society for rejecting immediate emancipation and denying that slavery was a sin. But at the same time, neither he nor other abolitionists objected to blacks' efforts to colonize themselves, since a black colony provided protection against antiblack prejudice. In fact he referred to his gift as "the colored colony," or "North Elba." The settlers themselves (including John Brown) called it "Timbucto," after the fabled city in West Africa, which was legendary for its racial and ethnic diversity, its tradition of scholarship and learning, and its "primitive" economy but "cosmopolitan" makeup. The settlers on Smith's land even designed and erected a red flag with the word "Timbucto" emblazoned on it.[17]

Black abolitionists themselves considered Smith's gift a viable alternative to black emigration. In March 1849 Henry Highland Garnet, one of the trustees of Smith's land, began embracing the idea of "colonization in any part of the United States, Mexico or California, or in the West Indies, or Africa, wherever it promises freedom and enfranchisement." He cited the African Republic of Liberia (which was founded by the American Colonization Society) as an example, but also mentioned "the Smith Lands in Franklin, Essex, and Hamilton Counties" as "a home and a field of labor for colored men." Garnet added that Frederick Douglass and other "men of thought" shared his favorable views of Timbucto. He therefore could not understand why Douglass opposed Liberia as an alternative location. Amos G. Beman, a black clergyman from New Haven, noted that "there is quite a fever in this city among the colored people . . . to procure homesteads in some part of the country." He wanted to know if a thousand acres at Timbucto could be purchased from Smith for New Haven settlers, preferably near a parcel that Smith had given to James McCune Smith.[18]

McCune Smith had understood the importance of a settlement like Timbucto even before Gerrit Smith conceived of his gift. In 1841 he had argued that black migration was one way for an oppressed minority to escape slavery, and he cited the example of the Jews. "The Jews, held in slavery by the Egyptians, after suffering dreadful oppression, at length gathered themselves under a leader raised up by God, and migrated from the House of Bondage." He also noted that the Jews "differed in complexion from their Masters." Some blacks had followed the example of the Jews by migrating to Canada, Liberia, and the West Indies. But McCune Smith emphasized that "we are not a migrating people. The soil of our birth is dear to our hearts, and we cling to it with a tenacity which no force can unhinge, no contumely sever." More important, by remaining in America to battle and overcome slavery, blacks "will do more for human Liberty than could be accomplished by emigration. By the latter course we might escape from, but would leave untouched an evil institution, which, by our present course we are destined to overthrow." In one sense, Timbucto would become for McCune Smith a kind of Zion in America, with Gerrit Smith, himself, and eventually John Brown its leaders, "raised up by God." It would offer a way for poor New York blacks to find liberty without leaving the nation of their birth.[19]

Gerrit Smith's conception of Timbucto as a form of protection for blacks ultimately led to his advocacy of compensated emancipation. In 1846, shortly after announcing his gift, he told McCune Smith, Ray, and Wright: "I wish you to understand that there is one use of property far more delightful to my heart than giving it away to the poor. It is expending it in the purchase of my fellow-men from under the yoke of slavery." He was "utterly insensible" to the arguments made by many abolitionists (particularly Garrison and his followers) that purchasing a slave's freedom legitimated the idea of human property and thus participated in the sin of slavery. Smith likened compensated emancipation to ransom money: paying slaveholders for their slaves' freedom was like paying a murderer "the sum which, with his dagger at the throat of his victim, he demands for the release of that victim." It was ransom money, but it also saved lives and made men free.[20]

Smith first proposed compensated emancipation during his congressional term in 1854, as an alternative to the Kansas-Nebraska bill that was then being debated. Three years later, while helping John Brown plan his incursion into the South, he proposed a more detailed plan as a last-ditch effort to end slavery without bloodshed. At a National Compensation Convention in Cleveland in 1857, organized by the pacifist Elihu Burritt, he suggested a formula whereby each master would receive for each slave $150 from the national treasury and $75 from the emancipating state. Each slave would receive $25 plus a plot of land. He assumed that the $525 million needed for his scheme to work could be raised by having the federal government sell off its remaining public lands. And he attacked Burritt's plan (drawn from earlier proposals by Rufus King and Daniel Webster), which appropriated public land to pay off slaveholders but provided no remuneration to slaves. Sounding more like an Agrarian than an abolitionist, Smith asserted: "I am a land-reformer, and I hold that to the landless belongs the vacant land. Slavery is a great evil; but land monopoly, because it has manifold more victims, is a far greater evil. Moreover, there could have been no Slavery but for land monopoly." Smith's scheme of compensated emancipation made little economic sense, for it would have required the federal government to borrow enormous sums until it sold the public land that was left after the landless had received their plots. He also had no conception of economic growth, and assumed that a nation of independent landowners would be content as self-sufficient entrepreneurs and would not want to increase their holdings. But he remained adamant in his belief that ending land monopoly was "the only sure way to abolish and prevent the return of" slavery. In one respect, his plan for compensated emancipation was analogous to his 1846 gift of land, extended throughout the country. In each case, he sought to secure blacks' freedom with small plots of land.[21]

Smith's gift of land can also be seen as an important precedent in the debates about land distribution during the Civil War and Reconstruction. The questions of how to dispose of confiscated Southern land and how to organize black labor became major points of conflict in the transition to free labor. Most American abolitionists and policymakers, much like their British counterparts, understood the term "free labor" for blacks to mean working for wages on plantations. But to blacks themselves, "free labor" meant farming their own land—"reaping the fruit of our own labor," as one former slave put it—and living largely apart from the marketplace. A few radicals, such as Wendell Phillips, George Julian, and Thaddeus Stevens, insisted on land grants for freedmen and sought sweeping agrarian reform. Gerrit Smith, having suffered considerable backsliding after John Brown's raid, no longer advocated land redistribution. But long before the war, his gift of land had been a kind of dress rehearsal for the project of distributing land during Reconstruction.[22]

❧ When James McCune Smith heard of Gerrit Smith's gift, he could scarcely believe it. Why would any white man, of his own accord, go to such extremes on behalf of blacks? He concluded that Gerrit must have been inspired by God. He assumed that the duties suddenly thrust upon him as trustee must also have been a signal from God, and he devoted himself to them with the zeal of a recent convert. He diligently sought out eligible recipients, served as the principal trustee, and within a month of Smith's announcement he and his co-trustees presented Gerrit with a list of two thousand recipients and a preliminary roster of the remaining thousand names. On September 1, 1846, he, Ray, and Wright addressed the recipients, informed them of Gerrit's reasons for the gift, and told them how they might make the most of it. God was responsible for the gift, they said, and to him should go the glory and thanks: "To God be the glory, Who, through this human instrument [Gerrit Smith] has been pleased to open to us a 'land of promise' in the midst of the land of oppression." No words could "express [their] gratitude," for they believed that "the approval of a satisfied conscience" was sweeter to Gerrit "than the voice of praise."[23]

McCune Smith, Wright, and Ray urged the recipients to assume the burdens and responsibilities of owning land. Antiblack prejudice had for too long "consigned to us dependent employments at reduced wages," thereby creating "the feeling of dependence and uncertainty" that "ever crushes the energies and deadens the faculties of men":

> Now, however, once in possession of, once *upon our own land*, we will be our own masters, free to think, free to act; and, if we toil hard, that toil will be sweetened by the reflection, that it is all, by God's will and help, for ourselves, our wives and our children. Thus placed in an independent condition, we will not only be independent, in ourselves, but will overcome that *prejudice against condition*, which has so long been as a mill stone about our necks.

The gift was an experiment, they concluded, echoing Gerrit Smith's words to General John Cooke, an "experiment in behalf of long suffering, long crushed, down-trodden, and bleeding humanity." For Gerrit, his gift was in part an experiment to see "what people of color" were "capable of becoming." But for McCune Smith, Ray, and Wright, it was "an experiment for the RACE! not of Africa, nor of Cush, but for the race of mankind! The cause of our common race, is, in a manner, entrusted to our hands."[24]

McCune Smith, Ray, and Wright outlined the ways in which the recipients could make full use of their gift, and thereby "strike a blow for liberty, as you alone can strike." They urged them to retain their lands against the designs of whites, who sought to deny them their gift. They warned them against numerous newspaper reports that maligned both blacks and Gerrit and asserted that the land was worthless. They entreated them to cultivate the land, noting that it lay in clusters so that they could, "by mutual aid," overcome difficulties and create an independent black community. "You will have to cut down timber, erect dwellings therefrom, till the land, and undergo the labour and privations incident to pioneer cultivators." But this work, "though formidable in appearance," would not be "half so hard as the difficulties and privations cheerfully undertaken and surmounted by thousands of men in this republic." They cited the example of countless white men, women, and children who were at this very moment heading west in wagon trains toward Oregon, traveling thousands of miles over "an almost trackless wilderness, crossing streams, passing over high and precipitous mountain paths . . . to begin the labour of pioneer cultivators." They told the recipients to save, save, save, and to use their money to purchase the oxen, wagons, plows, and other necessities needed to begin their new life in the wilderness. They reminded them that the land had been given to them free from debt and encumbrances. "Keep it free, if you would preserve your own independence—*keep it free.*" They exhorted them to avoid all alcohol and tobacco. And they drew on the language and spirit of Emerson in urging them to practice "SELF-RELIANCE," adding that it must be accompanied by "MUTUAL-RELIANCE": "Away with this false mistrustful spirit, born of slavery! Away with mutual distrust. Let us—regardless of complexion—trust one another."[25]

McCune Smith heeded his own advice: he began to trust and befriend Gerrit Smith as he had never before done with a white man. His openness first became apparent in a December 1846 letter, after he had returned to New York City from a visit at Peterboro with his wife Malvina. For the first time with Gerrit, he abandoned his deferential and formal tone and lowered his guard. It was a long, rambling, emotional letter that conveyed his innermost thoughts. Formally, it resembled a self-reflective journal entry rather than a letter to a social superior. It was even written in the form of a journal, over the course of two days, with the date of the second day, "Dec. 18," scribbled in the margin to designate a new day and a new thought. It included medical advice (Gerrit had been suffering from digestive problems, particularly constipation, which he called his "local ailments"), the trials of his own medical practice, a combination of awe and skepticism regarding his friend's gift, and a warning to Gerrit that his philanthropy would make him look like a fool in the eyes of society. "Look inward, severely and closely," he told Gerrit; "question your soul of its motives, its hopes in relation to its designs":

> Have you, now surrounded with all the appliances of wealth, all the commanding influences which wealth gives, have you carefully surveyed the long chasm which intervenes between your present and your contemplated position in society? You have borne much and well for the truth's sake and for the sake of your fellow man, but what you contemplate doing [giving your land to blacks] will, in the present state of society, subject you to trials more painful than anything you have endured. You have borne the taint of fanaticism; you must prepare to be branded as a foolish man.

Blacks would also regard Gerrit as a foolish man, McCune Smith warned. "You are accustomed to the scorn and hate of white men; can you bear the cold ingratitude of colored men?" Blacks were borne along the tide of "wealth-worship" as much as whites: "we are but men," and there will be those "so base as [to] laugh at the poverty of the man who made us rich!"[26]

In addition to praise and warning, McCune Smith expressed amazement at Gerrit's pure motives. "There is something even to my mind incomprehensible in your contemplated abandonment of your landed possessions." Although he understood on one level that Gerrit was "truly and simply" obeying "one of the teachings of our Lord and Saviour," he could not fully comprehend why a white man would renounce his wealth and give it to blacks. "How bad must the world be," he concluded, how steeped in it "must my soul be, when so simple an *act*, in accordance with one of His principles, appears strange to me and incomprehensible."[27]

McCune Smith's amazement stemmed in part from the spiritual disconnectedness he was feeling at the time. A few years later he admitted that he had been drawn to worldly values during this period, particularly the enticements of wealth. In 1852 he recalled how he had been involved in a "wealth pursuit association of colored men" from the mid to late 1840s as a means for achieving independence from whites. Frederick Douglass, also a member, had voiced his disenchantment with the group, arguing that "organizations for liberty" would be far more effective than wealth associations. "I laughed at him [Douglass] then, but agree with him now," McCune Smith said in 1852. He realized that "the Keystone of American morals and religion is gold: hence, American society is a poor, dumb, blind dog to whom the sun in the heavens and the sweet harmonies of nature" and humanity "are as a closed book."[28]

By the early 1850s McCune Smith had come to believe that "wealth and caste" were inextricably joined, fueling the swell of hate "in the great American Heart!" He was quite original and far ahead of his time in linking the pursuit of wealth with an embrace of whiteness. He realized that although the virtues of "thrift, punctuality, enterprise, and persistent energy" were admirable, they led all too easily to the pursuit of wealth for its own sake and thus to racial hatred. Consequently, blacks must learn to embrace these virtues without worshipping the god Mammon. Wealth caused men to flee from their black identities and to embrace whiteness and the values of white society "like a dog

with a tin kettle tied to his tail." By contrast, the pursuit of "manhood"—by which McCune Smith meant freedom and independence—
led to the affirmation of one's black identity. McCune Smith's emphasis on "manhood" over "money" marked the shift toward his
antibourgeois attack on white society.[29]

But in December 1846 McCune Smith did not fully understand the
linkage between the pursuit of wealth and the embrace of whiteness.
Nor did he feel particularly close to God. A few days after Christmas
he wrote Gerrit Smith another letter, and again employed the form of
a journal entry that spanned four days. It was even more personal than
his letter of December 17, and the tone was confessional. He confessed
that he envied Gerrit's wealth and his ability to use it to emancipate
slaves and give away land. He even suggested that coveting wealth
might be acceptable if it were used for noble purposes. He was thoroughly discouraged over the defeat of the referendum for equal black
suffrage, and admitted that he felt disconnected from God: "I must
strive humbly to draw near unto God, for renewed faith and hope and
encouragement." He told Gerrit that the heart of the whites must be
changed, and implied that whites must learn how to acquire a black
heart in order for equality and freedom to occur. But he did not know
how this could be achieved. He would soon learn that the transformation must come from affirming "thrift, punctuality, enterprise, and
persistent energy" without succumbing to the trappings of wealth and
greed. Blacks must become bourgeois in order to attack bourgeois values at their root. "Of course it is mind-work," he added in his letter to
Gerrit. "Physical force has no place in" the attainment of black suffrage
and "manhood."[30]

If there was no place for "physical force" in the attainment of manhood, there was a place for physicality. It began with the strenuous life
in the wilderness required of settlers who emigrated to Timbucto;
eventually it would evolve into physical aggression against slavery itself. After meeting with some of the grantees, McCune Smith described them to Gerrit in terms that were entirely physical: "Tall, stal-
wart, hard-fisted, they embody a Hope of the Race."[31] A few years later,
after visiting Timbucto and walking about the plot that Gerrit had
given him, he found himself being regenerated by the rugged wilderness: "I felt myself a 'lord indeed' beneath the lofty spruce and maple
and birch and by the trawling brook, which your Deed made mine," he

told Gerrit, "and would gladly exchange this bustling anxious [city] life for the repose of that majestic country, could I see the way clear for a livelihood for myself and family." Though asserting that he was "not afraid of physical labor," he did not think it prudent to abandon his medical practice for farming, believing that the sparse population at Timbucto would not support a physician.[32]

Gerrit Smith expressed similar sentiments about the regenerative powers of the wilderness. As he told McCune Smith in 1846, he urged all poor blacks (even those who did not receive land from him) to quit "their city life, their servile life, their self-indulgent life" for remote tracts in the state. "On these tracts of land they will begin a new life. There they will brave the rigors of the wilderness, and make for themselves a hardy and honorable character." While he "regretted" that his gift was mostly in "colder and less fertile" parts of the state, he was "becoming reconciled to what, at first thought," was "so great a disadvantage." "The chances are ten to one that the settlers . . . will work out a far better character than they would, were they to choose their homes on fat lands and under genial suns [conditions]."[33]

By embracing the regenerative powers of the wilderness, McCune Smith and Gerrit Smith reveal their extraordinary bond with Romantic ideology, which was central to their understanding of themselves and each other. In their adherence to physical labor in the wilderness, they combined two aspects of the American Romantic tradition: the perfectionist doctrine of individual salvation; and the conservative formula of the frontier as a safety valve for servile life in the city. For them, the primitive conditions of the frontier wilderness regenerated the spirit and self and flowed outward, from the individual to society. It was in the Adirondacks, where Timbucto was located, "that masses of (non-Native) Americans first learned to cherish the wilds as a place of solace" and spiritual regeneration. Gerrit Smith's and McCune Smith's celebration of the restorative powers of the wilderness and of nature in general stemmed from the Romantic conviction that "the perfected individual—the truly free American—could be created only by the reunification of mental and physical labor," to quote the historian John Thomas. This quest to fuse mind and body was widespread in nineteenth-century America, embraced by Romantic reformers ranging from Transcendentalists and Fourierists to advocates of manual labor. Entering the wilderness, it was thought, maximized the attainment of moral perfection and of "knowing God," and it spawned freedom. The wilderness regenerated the individual by uniting body and soul, thus effecting salvation and freedom. And the Adirondack wilderness, which was far from urban centers and at the periphery of American civilization, was a location that fueled the utopian thinking of McCune Smith, Gerrit Smith, Douglass, and Brown. It was here in particular that these four men could envision a multicultural heaven on Earth. Everything seemed possible in this raw wilderness land.[34]

Gerrit Smith and McCune Smith carried this fusion of body and soul to its logical conclusion—into the realm of race. Most reformers believed that the soul of every individual was equal in the eyes of God, but they distinguished body from soul when the body was black. Yet if God viewed all souls as equal, then the wilderness, which helped unite body and soul, was the logical place to achieve black freedom. Gerrit Smith and McCune Smith linked the primitive conditions of the Adirondacks to the quest for black freedom. The Adirondacks—and particularly Timbucto—could unleash the bonds of domestication associated with slave and servile conditions, allowing body and soul to run wild and become free.[35]

The correspondence between Gerrit Smith and McCune Smith—in both form and content—highlights their efforts to bridge racial barriers. In a November 1846 letter, for instance, in which Gerrit shared with McCune Smith his hopes for the "colored colony," he repeated his empathic plea for Americans to "look on every other man as a brother—as, indeed another self"—instead of "trampling upon and crushing each other." Immediately following this entreaty he quoted a stanza of Robert Burns's song "Is There, for Honest Poverty," which attacked the great gulfs separating rich from poor, slave from free:

> For a'that, and a'that,
> It's comin yet for a that,
> That man to man, the world a'oer,
> Shall brothers be for a'that.

That Gerrit expressed his emotions by quoting the famous Scottish bard's song is not in itself remarkable. What is significant is that McCune Smith, Gerrit Smith, and Frederick Douglass all quoted the same stanzas by Burns in their letters to one another and in their speeches, much as they exchanged the same quote from Lord Byron:

"Hereditary bondsmen! know ye not / Who would be free themselves must strike the blow?" Sharing passages from these Romantic poets helped tighten their alliance and friendship. It signified a kind of code or dialect confirming that they were of the same mind in the matter of slavery and race, part of a unified group that affirmed blackness and opposed white conventions.[36]

What is particularly fascinating about their choice of Burns—and especially this stanza—is the formalist similarities it shares with African-American spirituals and secular songs: both styles employ a vernacular wholly separate from the language of elites; and both repeat lines and phrases, and use short words and relatively simple metering, so that the songs can be easily remembered and passed on to others. Perhaps it is not surprising, then, that numerous other blacks also quoted liberally from Burns in their letters and addresses. That Gerrit Smith quoted Burns immediately after his entreaty to empathize and identify with blacks and the poor suggests that he was rendering in poetic terms his efforts to become a black man.

Frederick Douglass expressly acknowledged the link between his own voice and that of Burns. At the 1849 Robert Burns Anniversary Festival in Rochester, he told the crowd of mostly native Scotsmen that he felt both pleased and privileged "to mingle my humble voice" with that of Burns. He felt such kinship with Burns that while lecturing in Scotland in 1846 he made a special "pilgrimage" to Burns's home and met Burns's sister. Douglass recognized in Burns's life and poetry parallels with his own plight and that of other blacks. Both were oppressed by elite whites and were treated like brutes: "Burns lived in the midst of a bigoted and besotted clergy . . . who . . . looked upon the plowman, such as was the noble Burns, as being little better than a brute."[37] Douglass was so moved at the Burns celebration that he kept his speech quite short and said that "this is not a time for long speeches." He did not consider a speech the appropriate form for expressing such intense emotions. (He said much the same thing speaking on the eve of Lincoln's Emancipation Proclamation: "This is scarcely a day for prose. It is a day for poetry and song, a new song.") For Douglass, Burns's songs and not a speech constituted the appropriate language for expressing the emotions of the moment. He told the crowd that if anyone took offense to his kinship with Burns on account of his skin color, the poet himself was to blame, for he had taught Douglass that "a man's a man for a'that." Douglass' identification with Burns and Gerrit Smith's use of Burns's song to give poetic voice to his own black identification highlights the interconnectedness with "others" and the protean nature of identity politics that these men were able to achieve.[38]

⚋ The regenerative power of the wilderness not only helped McCune Smith and Gerrit Smith blur racial identities; it contributed to their acceptance of violence. They linked Timbucto—especially its regenerative spirit and physical vigor—to their broad conception of Bible politics; and this coupling of Romantic ideology with political action resulted in their efforts to intervene against the slave system with physical force. Although neither of them moved to Timbucto, they embraced the physicality of its frontier spirit as they worked together to found the community. At the very time that Gerrit Smith conceived of his gift, he began to describe his abolitionism in physical terms: "Evening before last," he told a friend, "I walked miles in mud and in the dark to plead for the slaves . . . I would cheerfully walk this evening five miles could I persuade one proslavery voter of his sin." By 1849 he had become "reluctant to help any person attend school" other than a manual-labor school: "I have for many years felt that I am called to do for the *bodies* rather than the *minds* of my fellow men." McCune Smith visited Timbucto several times and found the rigorous exercise and harsh climate refreshing. When he needed a respite from the city, he visited Gerrit in Peterboro, where the two friends took longs walks each day in the isolated hills of Madison County.[39]

McCune Smith and Gerrit Smith viewed the founding of Timbucto as a direct manifestation of their Bible politics. It was a way for them to create a small-scale model of society that was based on the sacred ideals of equality and liberty, and it allowed them to work around the perversions of civil government, which neglected its duty to protect the people. Over time McCune Smith and Gerrit Smith would bypass the statutes of civil government in other ways as well: they would distinguish political action from legal action, rely on "higher" laws as their judge, and endorse extralegal means to fight slavery. In an important sense, Timbucto—and Bible politics more generally—was a way for them to achieve a dynamic balance between their impulse to perfection and the sinful present reality. Timbucto was tangible evidence of their efforts to realize an American heaven on Earth.

Gerrit Smith's gift of land played a central role in McCune Smith's conversion to the Liberty party and eventually to his acceptance of violence. McCune Smith had been a member of Garrison's American Anti-Slavery Society since his return from Scotland in 1837, but by 1840 he had become skeptical of white abolitionists and their societies. White abolitionists defined freedom, equality, and independence differently from blacks, he argued, and the American Anti-Slavery Society had done nothing to seek "Social Equality either of Slaves or Free Blacks." He also opposed the Liberty party in its early years, though not on the grounds that the Constitution was a proslavery document, as Garrison and his cohorts argued. In 1841 he wrote that the Constitution, despite its proslavery clauses, was based on the "general principles" of the Declaration of Independence, "which declares 'all men to have certain inalienable rights.'" But he was not yet ready to become a convert to political abolitionism. In 1844 he called the Liberty party an "irreverent admixture of blasphemy and demogoguism" for fusing politics and religion and spreading false hopes and expectations about American government. He also distrusted the motives of many leading Liberty party men, especially Alvan Stewart and James G. Birney, and chastised the party for ignoring the black press and the plight of Northern blacks in general.[40]

After working with Gerrit Smith to distribute land, McCune Smith realized that not all whites were untrustworthy—not this one, anyway. As a result of his friendship with Gerrit, combined with his frustration over Garrison's Anti-Slavery Society, its exclusionary policy of disunion, and the persistence and spread of slavery, his attitude toward the Liberty party and political abolitionism changed. "I believe that I am fully up to the doctrine of 'No vote for the slaveholders, nor for any who will vote for a slaveholder to occupy a civil or religious office,'" he told Gerrit in 1848. "I am a late convert" to political abolitionism, "but none the less a firm one." He accepted the antislavery character of the Constitution on the basis of faith rather than legal analysis. He had followed his heart and not his head. The heart, not reasoning, could spot a kindred spirit.[41]

As McCune Smith immersed himself in the National Liberty party (and later the Radical Abolition party) he became increasingly critical of Garrisonians. He accurately described how blacks had been responsible for the American Anti-Slavery Society's emergence and survival in its early years; yet once the society could stand on its own without black patronage, it had abandoned blacks. In the early years of the organization, Garrison had hired blacks as agents for his mostly black subscribers, advised and attended black conventions, "and gave some good advice and received some." But as soon as Garrison could support his organization without black patronage, he had replaced the forty black agents with white ones, and treated blacks as subordinates. McCune Smith coined the word "Garrisonism" for this kind of white paternalism.[42]

While Garrison considered himself the founder of immediate abolitionism in America, McCune Smith noted (also accurately) that blacks "almost began the present movement" of immediatism and "certainly antedated many of its principles." When New York was still a slave state, blacks had marched through streets declaring their humanity and brotherhood despite the remonstrances of white abolitionists. Twenty years before the American Anti-Slavery Society promoted the ideal of political equality, the black Pennsylvanian James Forten had protested a bill that would have required blacks to register and carry certificates at all times or else risk being sold into slavery. Forten had also presided over the famous Anti-Colonization Meeting in Philadelphia in 1817, which demanded that blacks be treated as citizens of their *"birth land."* And *Freedom's Journal*, the first black newspaper, attacked colonization and championed immediatism in 1827, four years before *The Liberator* issued its first number.[43]

McCune Smith concluded that blacks were "already a *'power on the earth'*" when Garrison came onto the scene, and that Garrison had borrowed many if not most of his black predecessors' ideas and principles. But instead of feeling "grateful" to blacks, Garrison expected blacks to feel "grateful" to him. It was another "Garrisonism," which left blacks "poor and blind and bleeding." Instead of championing black rights, the American Anti-Slavery Society embraced ideas like "anti-Sabbath" or "the Phantom of Disunion" that ignored the conditions of both Northern blacks and slaves. Becoming a truehearted immediatist required "a new birth," McCune Smith asserted, which meant both a newfound awareness of the sin of slavery and the acquisition of a black heart. Blacks and whites "ought to be allied and bound together by hooks of steel." The twain "ought to be, but are not, one flesh." This state of affairs existed because white Garrisonians refused to accept black standards and perspectives; they refused to try to understand what it was like to be black.[44]

McCune Smith's embrace of Bible politics eventually moved beyond the legal measures of voting for abolition candidates, seeking black suffrage, and proposing land redistribution. His leadership in the Radical Abolition party was only one political forum in which he sought violent redress against oppressive conditions. In 1855, the same year he chaired the Radical Abolition convention at Syracuse and helped develop its platform of violence, he told Gerrit that he had organized "a new 'Abolition Society'" in New York City (called the New-York City Abolition Society), designed to abolish slavery "by means of the Constitution; *or otherwise.*" These last two words, which he underlined in his letter to Gerrit, were also included in the articles of the society: "Should there be any quarrel in the future as to the meaning of them, I mean fight," he told Gerrit. Political action had come to mean something entirely different from legal action.[45]

❧ In December 1847 Frederick Douglass received from Gerrit Smith a deed for forty acres of land at Timbucto. He had just moved to Rochester, New York, from Massachusetts to start his newspaper, the *North Star*, and the first issue had just come out. He was still affiliated with William Lloyd Garrison's American Anti-Slavery Society, had never met Smith, and Smith's letter accompanying the deed—plus a check for a two-year subscription to the *North Star*—was his introduction to handwriting that looked at first glance like a "straight mark." After deciphering the letter, Douglass realized that his plot of land came from a much larger parcel that Gerrit had divided among seven other black leaders—William Wells Brown, William Nell, Charles Remond, Henry Bibb, and the three Clarke brothers, Lewis, Milton, and Cyrus. (It would have been a formidable community of black writers and activists had they chosen to settle on the land, but none of them did, in part because Douglass, Nell, Remond, and the Clarke brothers were all Garrisonians at the time, and Garrison treated Gerrit Smith and other political abolitionists as traitors to his cause.) Smith's gift was meant as a kind of housewarming present from a resident of the state and an ally in the cause: "I welcome you to the State of New York," Gerrit said. "In this, your new home, may you and yours, and your labors of love for your oppressed race, be all greatly blessed of God." Douglass had no idea how to respond to this greeting. After thinking it over for a month, he published Smith's letter in his newspaper. Thus began their correspondence and their practice of making public their letters and their friendship—a practice that would continue throughout the 1850s.[46]

After this strange beginning, Douglass' relationship with Smith followed a path closely resembling that of McCune Smith and Gerrit. He befriended Gerrit, embraced Timbucto as an exemplary community, and combined Bible politics with the ideology of the frontier. The results were revolutionary. Within two years of receiving Smith's gift, Douglass became a political abolitionist and abandoned his loyalty to Garrison and the doctrine of nonresistance. He turned his newspaper into an organ of the National Liberty party in 1851, and endorsed armed rebellion to fight slavery.

Like McCune Smith, Douglass saw in "the Smith Land" (as he called it) the potential for blacks to combine physical vigor with spiritual faith, become self-sufficient, and advance the race. Two months after receiving Smith's letter of introduction, he urged the grantees to take advantage of Smith's "generous and magnificent donation" and cultivate their land:

> The sharp ax of the sable-armed pioneer should be at once uplifted over the soil of Franklin and Essex counties [where Timbucto was located], and the noise of falling trees proclaim the glorious dawn of civilization throughout their borders . . . Come, brethren, let it not be said, that a people who, under the lash, could level the forests of Virginia, Maryland, and the whole Southern States, that their oppressors might reap the reward, lack the energy and manly ambition to clear lands for themselves. Let us make those who declare us incapable of taking care of ourselves, slanderers before all the people.

One year later Douglass publicly urged slaves to display a similar kind of "energy and manly ambition" by rebelling, and thus make slanderers of whites who said that slaves were incapable of taking care of themselves. At an antislavery meeting in Boston in 1849, he alarmed his Garrisonian audience by saying he would rejoice if he heard that "the slaves had risen in the South, and that the sable arms which had been engaged in beautifying and adorning the South, were engaged in spreading death and devastation." For Douglass, the physical vigor of wilderness life inspired people to strike for their freedom, whether by felling trees or by killing their oppressors.[47]

But a thriving black community of "sable-armed" pioneers at Timbucto never came into being. By 1848 only about twenty or thirty families had settled on the land. The would-be pioneers, in order to move and settle on their new land, needed wagons, horses or oxen, tools, and enough staples and supplies to survive until the first harvest, and all this cost money. (These start-up costs proved to be one of the major obstacles to using the frontier as a safety valve for white unemployment and low wages in the cities; the pioneers who migrated west came primarily from the middle classes.) McCune Smith acknowledged these barriers, and estimated that each settler would need about $100 for the move, which constituted roughly one-third of the annual earnings of the working poor. He hoped the recipients of Gerrit's gift would be able to raise the money themselves through thrift and industry, and he and Gerrit never discussed alternative sources of funding. For his part, Gerrit simply did not have an extra $300,000 in cash to give settlers for start-up costs.[48]

About a hundred people managed to make the move to Timbucto, but they faced additional problems once they arrived. As Gerrit had acknowledged from the outset, the land was of poor quality and the climate extremely harsh, though McCune Smith and Jermain Loguen considered the plots "as good land as any man can need." The settlers not only needed to raise enough crops to survive; they had to generate some surplus in order to pay yearly taxes. By the mid-1850s many of them faced foreclosure by the New York State Treasury. More problematic still were the designs of whites living in the region who sought to cheat the grantees out of their money. Some posed as guides or "pilots" when grantees came to examine their land, and showed them lots that were not theirs—often on a mountain peak or a swamp—and then demanded outrageous sums for their services. At least one unscrupulous land surveyor convinced some of the recipients to settle on land that did not correspond to their deeds. Consequently, a number of settlers sold their land for a song to swindlers, gave it away as remuneration for bogus fees, or found that they had been trying to cultivate inferior land that was not theirs. Understandably, they became discouraged and returned to the city.[49]

Gerrit was frustrated at the low turnout of settlers, and although he blamed antiblack prejudice, at times he also lashed out at blacks themselves for internalizing this prejudice and remaining servile to white institutions. He said as much in an 1848 letter to Charles Ray that was published in the *North Star*. Although "friendly whites" could help diminish the obstacles of prejudice and oppression, "the colored people must themselves work out their own redemption." This could not happen so long as they "remained servants of another race." The only way for blacks to avoid positions of servility was to leave their cities and villages, "scatter themselves over the country," and become independent farmers and mechanics. The greatest obstacle blacks faced—and Gerrit acknowledged that he suffered from it as well—was "the contempt of others for us," which led to "self-contempt in us," thereby draining one's spirit and energy. "The free colored people of this country have lost their self-respect" by associating with political and religious institutions that held them in contempt, he said out of frustration. Even men of such "rare talents" as McCune Smith and Douglass had at times "degraded themselves" by endorsing political candidates who "detested" blacks.[50]

❧ Although Douglass did not completely break with William Lloyd Garrison until May 1851, his move to Rochester to establish the *North Star* was itself an assertion of independence from his former employer. The move was made possible by a highly acclaimed eighteen-month British tour from August 1845 to April 1847, in which admirers raised enough money for him to purchase his freedom and start his own newspaper. The trip was a milestone in his life, as important in many respects as his fight with Covey and his escape from bondage. As he told Garrison while there: "I seem to have undergone a transformation. I live a new life." He left for Great Britain as a brilliant author and orator, but subservient to the white paternalism of the American Anti-Slavery Society. He returned as a proud and self-reliant black man determined to strike out on his own and fulfill a dream of becoming an editor.[51]

Even before the trip to England and Scotland, Douglass had been frustrated with the American Anti-Slavery Society. As early as 1843, during a lecture tour in upstate New York, Ohio, and Indiana, he found himself at odds with the society's white leadership. He was touring with his black colleague Charles Remond and the white agent John Collins, who was also a Fourierist opponent of private property; and during a stop at Syracuse, Collins tried to deflect the focus away from slavery and onto the evils of private property. Douglass and Remond were outraged; they publicly confronted Collins, and Douglass threatened to quit the tour if Collins persisted in trying to divert attention from slavery. The society's headquarters in Boston, even while admitting that Collins had been out of line, reprimanded Douglass and Remond for publicly challenging a white colleague, and considered docking their pay. One white member characterized Douglass' and Remond's behavior as "monkeyism," adding that the two black leaders were "a disgrace to abolition" for their insubordination to the society's white leadership. "As near as I can find," he went on, "Remond and Douglass choose to be the lions of the party and are unwilling to be directed by others." To make matters worse, Douglass was already receiving less pay than white agents, even though he drew the largest crowds and brought more attention to Garrison's society than any other member except perhaps Garrison himself. Most white Garrisonians were unable to treat Douglass (and other blacks) as social equals, and when he asserted his rightful role as a leader, they became incensed.[52]

Given such attempts to constrain him, Douglass' transformation from slave to independent editor in less than a decade was truly remarkable. In fact it provoked a severe crisis of identity. He conveys something of the terror and alienation that accompanied his rapid self-transformation in an 1846 letter to his sister Harriet Bailey. While touring Scotland he became extremely "low in spirits," and reverted to the language of a slave as a way to gain a sense of perspective on the distance he had traveled:

> I felt worse than get out! My under lip hung like that of a motherless colt. I looked so ugly that I hated to see myself in a glass. There was no living for me. I was snappish[.] I would have kicked my grand "dadda"! I was in a terrible mood—'dats a fact! Ole missus—is you got any ting for poor nigger to eat!!!

He told Harriet that seeing her would have relieved this "Horrible feeling." Since that was impossible, he purchased a fiddle, which he had loved to play as a slave, went to his hotel, and struck up "Camels a coming," an old favorite. Within minutes he began to feel better: "Gradually I came to myself again and was as lively as a cricket and as loving as a lamb." The music of his youth (and the plantation dialect) connected his present self to his slave past, providing a marker for measuring the path of his self-making and offering an antidote to feelings of rootlessness. For the rest of his life he would turn to the fiddle for solace, and though he never publicly invoked the plantation dialect, he continually reminded his audiences (and himself) of his former slave status as a way to establish a vantage point from which to view his present self.[53]

His move to Rochester represented another important phase of self-evolution, away from the white paternalism of Garrison and his organization, toward an affirmation of his black self and an emphasis on self-reliance fostered by Gerrit Smith and McCune Smith. The move itself reflected a physical, emotional, and intellectual distancing from Garrisonians. Whereas Garrison had been a "father figure" to Douglass, Gerrit Smith "became his mentor," as the historian David Blight aptly noted. McCune Smith served as a mentor as well, and was thrilled that Douglass had broken with Garrison to start his own paper and affirm his black identity. "I love Frederick Douglass for his whole souled *outness,*" McCune Smith wrote Gerrit in July 1848, in response to Douglass' move to Rochester and founding of the *North Star,* adding: "you will be surprised to hear me say that only since [Douglass'] Editorial career has he begun to become a *colored man.*"[54]

In 1855 McCune Smith acknowledged the extent of Douglass' breathtaking self-transformation. Douglass, he said, had changed more in his eight years at Rochester (in alliance with himself and Gerrit Smith) than he had in his eight-year rise from slavery to internationally acclaimed writer and speaker as a Garrisonian. It was an extraordinary yet accurate assessment. After moving to Rochester, Douglass not only abandoned Garrison's paternalism and nonresistance for political and revolutionary means to end slavery; he added great depth and subtlety to his art of oratory and writing, and became a confident and independent editor and intellectual. Douglass himself was quick to note that his evolution from Garrisonian employee to self-employed editor and publisher could not have occurred without the advice and friendship of Gerrit Smith and McCune Smith. Throughout the 1850s he drew on these men's writings in his speeches, and relied on them for emotional as well as intellectual support. He considered McCune Smith "without rivals" among American blacks for his "talents and learning" and for his "known devotion to the cause of the oppressed people." And he thought Gerrit Smith unique among whites in his generosity and kindness to blacks.[55]

From the beginning Douglass sought to make the *North Star* an independent black newspaper. The black abolitionist Martin Delany began as a co-editor before abandoning the job for other interests. William Nell, another Garrisonian, moved to Rochester with Douglass and served as publisher for two years before returning to Boston after Garrison demanded that he choose between nonresistance and Douglass' growing political sentiments. Douglass hired an all-black staff of local correspondents and writers: McCune Smith covered New York City; William Wilson wrote on Brooklyn under the pseudonym "Ethiop"; and Samuel Ringgold Ward, William Wells Brown, William G. Allen, Jermain Loguen, and George Downing made frequent contributions. Initially Douglass avoided party or organizational affiliation. As he told Gerrit Smith in March 1849: "It is not a party paper, and looks with grateful friendship upon all classes of abolitionists and is not disposed to denounce as knaves those who believe that voting is a duty." Few Garrisonians supported it, yet it was "too strongly Garrisonian to be looked upon with much favor by Liberty Party men." The problem was that few blacks supported it; in 1848 white subscribers outnumbered blacks by a five-to-one margin, and within a year he had spent the two thousand dollars his British friends had given him, and was two hundred dollars in debt. Nevertheless, he vowed that "the paper shall be sustained if any effort of mine can sustain it." His identity as editor resembled his public speaking self: he offered himself to the public as a representative of his race, but spoke primarily to white audiences.[56]

Douglass soon realized that Gerrit Smith was, like himself, struggling to come to grips with his racial identity. Here was a white man who gave away his land to blacks with few strings attached. He appointed blacks to distribute his assets. He welcomed blacks to the state with forty-acre plots. And he supported a black-owned and -operated newspaper with crucial and timely donations. Here was a man who listened to blacks, trusted them, and respected what they had to say. By the end of 1849 Douglass—like McCune Smith before him—began to trust and befriend Gerrit as he had no other white. He found he could argue with and oppose Gerrit on important issues without fearing the loss of a friend, mentor, and benefactor. In March 1849, for example, he publicly opposed Gerrit's address on the unconstitutionality of slavery by calling it "quite unsatisfactory and unsound." While Smith's argument was "worthy of his noble heart, we cannot think such of his head," for it lacked logic, common sense, and analytic rigor. How did Gerrit respond to this criticism? He invited Douglass to Peterboro for a week to debate the matter more thoroughly, and made it clear that whatever the outcome, the mansion-house would always be open to him.[57]

Gerrit's wife Nancy also helped to bring Douglass and Gerrit closer together. Unlike Gerrit, Nancy liked to travel, and visited the Douglass home in Rochester more often than her husband. She befriended Douglass' wife Anna, forged a bond through their common love of gardening, and sent her seeds and cuttings. Nancy also sought to quell scandalous rumors from Garrisonians and other whites about Douglass' relationship with Julia Griffiths, a British white woman who lived in Rochester from 1849 to 1855 and helped manage the newspaper. Both Gerrit and Nancy became close friends with Julia, welcomed her to Peterboro, and remained supportive of her close interracial friendship with Douglass. As the historian John McKivigan astutely notes, "the emotional bond between the Douglass and Smith families in these years was a remarkable occurrence and goes far to explain the strength of the political alliance between the two men" during the 1850s.[58]

Smith made every effort to show Douglass that although he was rich and white, he was in his heart a black man. In May 1850, after learning that Douglass had been punched in the face for accompanying Julia Griffiths and her sister on a walk in New York City, Smith expressed his outrage and empathy: "Think not, my dear Douglass, that it is you colored men alone who suffer from this insane and rampant prejudice. The wound it inflicts on you, it inflicts on us who sympathize with you, and who have identified ourselves and made ourselves colored men with you. In your sufferings, we suffer. In your afflictions, we are afflicted." Smith considered it Douglass' mission "to break down the walls of separation between the two races," as he told him. He contributed to that mission by making himself "a colored man" in his heart, and shedding his emotional and social whiteness as a sign of superiority.[59]

An important moment in Smith's and Douglass' growing friendship and revolutionary alliance occurred at an anti–fugitive slave bill convention in August 1850, which both attended. The convention, which took place in Cazenovia (about ten miles from Peterboro), began on August 21, two days after the Senate passed the Fugitive Slave Act and one month before President Fillmore signed it into law. Smith organized the affair, which drew about two thousand participants and included many prominent New York State blacks (McCune Smith could not attend despite Gerrit's plea). Douglass presided as president, and the convention received national exposure for its revolutionary message. The centerpiece of the meeting was "a Letter to the American Slaves from those who have fled from American Slavery," written by Gerrit Smith posing as a fugitive. The document advocated a massive slave rebellion: it urged all slaves to revenge themselves against their masters; to resist them "unto death" and kill them if necessary; and to confiscate their money, horses, and other property. "You are prisoners of war in an enemy's country" that was "unrivaled for its injustice, cruelty, meanness," Smith proclaimed in his black voice, "and therefore, by all the rules of war, you have the fullest liberty to plunder, burn [and] kill."[60]

Douglass applauded the letter's contents but wanted the fugitives in attendance to be given the opportunity to speak out, and either endorse or reject the letter. After all, the letter purported to be written by fugitives, and however much Smith sought to become a colored man, he was a wealthy white landowner, not a fugitive. Smith agreed with Douglass' point, and said that from the outset he had wanted the fugitives in attendance to endorse and amend it as needed. After a lengthy debate on the letter's contents, it was approved. Douglass publicized the letter in his newspaper, said that it came "from the fugitive slaves in attendance," and noted that it would "cause a howl to go up from all the bloodhounds of our land." It caused a howl from more than proslavery bloodhounds. Garrison's *Liberator* denounced the convention as an assembly of "violent men" who delighted in blasphemy, a move that further distanced Douglass from Garrisonians and their policy of nonresistance. A Madison County newspaper summarized the convention by calling Gerrit Smith "crazy," prompting Smith to write in the margin of the article: "Even in my own county I am regarded as crazy." In the minds of most whites, to identify oneself as a black man and promote slave insurrections was sheer madness.[61]

On the second day of the convention, a Cazenovia daguerreotypist by the name of Ezra Greenleaf Weld, the brother of the famous abolitionist Theodore Dwight Weld, obtained a likeness of the convention in process (Figure 11). The whole-plate image shows Douglass sitting at the edge of the table next to Theodosia Gilbert, who is wearing a day bonnet and bloomers. Gilbert was the fiancée of William Chaplin, who was then in prison for aiding fugitives owned by the Georgia congressmen Robert Toombs and Alexander Stephens. Next to Gilbert sits Joseph Hathaway, one of the vice presidents of the convention. Behind Gilbert and Douglass stands Gerrit Smith in midspeech, his arms gesticulating wildly and his Byronic collar prominently displayed. On either side of Smith, in checkered shawls and day bonnets, are the sisters Mary and Emily Edmonson, former slaves whose freedom had been arranged and consummated by Chaplin. In its extraordinary diversity, revolutionary message, and antibourgeois decorum, the convention was a harbinger of the 1855 Radical Abolition convention at Syracuse. It was at Cazenovia that Douglass fully understood the efficacy and extralegal implications of Bible politics, for it was here he realized that if the Constitution was viewed as an antislavery document, then any law protecting slavery would become null and void.[62]

Five months after the convention, in January 1851, Douglass embraced the Constitution as an antislavery document. As early as 1849 he had acknowledged that the Constitution, if "strictly construed according to its reading," was antislavery. But he continued to believe that the framers of the document had intended to protect slavery. Now he was ready to follow Smith's example and "fling to the winds" those intentions. He was "sick and tired of arguing on the slaveholders' side" of the Constitution, he told Smith, even though he still thought slaveholders were "doubtless right so far as the intentions of the framers" were concerned. He wondered about the morality of creating one's own legal rules and definitions to "defeat the wicked intentions of our Constitution makers." "Is it good morality," he asked Smith, to "put a meaning upon a legal instrument the very opposite of what we have good reason to believe was the intention of the men who framed it"? Was it right simply to ignore "American legal authority"? But he also

Figure 11. Cazenovia Fugitive Slave Law Convention, August 22, 1850.
Whole-plate daguerreotype by Ezra Greenleaf Weld. Madison County
Historical Society, Oneida, N.Y. Gerrit Smith is standing in center;
Frederick Douglass is seated in front of him.

understood the sense of freedom implicit in such antiauthoritarian views, and like Gerrit Smith and McCune Smith before him, he relied on his own radically subjective interpretation of legal doctrine, much as he had long been doing with religious doctrine.[63]

A few months after Douglass' conversion to Bible politics, Smith proposed a merger between Douglass' *North Star* and the *Liberty Party Paper*, then being edited by John Thomas. Smith was unhappy with Thomas at the helm, assured Douglass that he would retain editorial control of the new paper, and agreed to assume the debts of the *North Star* and provide a monthly subsidy of a hundred dollars for two years. Douglass responded enthusiastically: "You want a good looking—as well as a good paper, established in western N.Y. & have a plan to accomplish that object. *I like the plan.*" He wanted to keep the paper in Rochester, and requested that Smith keep his financial support a secret for fear that if word got out, people would not support it. He assured Smith of his allegiance to political action, but emphasized that the merger was incumbent upon "you making me morally, intellectually, and mechanically responsible for the character of the paper." Smith agreed to all these points, and gave Douglass autonomy in arranging the merger and running the paper. He liked Douglass' idea of the new name—*Frederick Douglass' Paper*—and Douglass liked Smith's suggestion for the motto—"All Rights for All!"—which he adopted.[64]

Douglass projected himself into his new paper to an even greater degree than he had with the *North Star*. The very name—*Frederick Douglass' Paper*—conveys that projection, as if to say: "this 'good-looking—as well as good paper' is me." Two weeks before the first issue came out he told Smith: "The paper must be clean, white and strong. The ink pure, black and glossy." In one sense, the new paper united black and white, for it brought together the talented black editor with the wealthy white philanthropist. As financier, Smith provided the "white and strong" background, while the high-profile young editor supplied the "pure, black and glossy ink." Douglass told Smith in the same letter that "your own highly valued name must not be wanting on the first sheet." Smith's name did appear on the first page, but in the background, as it were, to the black and glossy masthead featuring Douglass' own name. Douglass even characterized his new paper as a kind of romantic "coming out" affair between the black editor and white philanthropist: "It should come forth with all the marks of strength," he told Smith, and "there must be nothing clumsy, hasty or awkward in our debut." He was not unhappy with the marriage. A year later he told his partner: "You not only keep life in my paper but keep spirit in me."[65]

In the first issue Douglass told his readers that henceforth he would assume the identity of editor without having to qualify that identity. He was abandoning the custom of signing his editorials "F.D.," which he had done in the *North Star* to remove doubts about his authorship. After three years as an editor he felt he had successfully refuted claims by whites that "an uneducated fugitive slave" could not write with "propriety and correctness." His initials were no longer needed. "We shall now, therefore . . . assume fully the right and dignity of an *Editor*—a Mr. Editor if you please!" It was a name and identity that defined the former slave as a gentleman with a profession who occupied a notable position in society and public affairs. He knew that to fight white bourgeois society effectively, he had to become bourgeois himself.[66]

Douglass made visual the bourgeois respectability of his newspaper (and himself as editor) when he changed the font of his name on the masthead. On May 25, 1855, he got rid of the bold, angular black lines with white trim—signifying the black-on-white identity and collaboration of the paper—that had characterized the old font (Figure 12, top). The new font consisted of solid black lines that were curved and tapered and ended in flourishes of genteel curls and swirls (Figure 12, bottom). The solid black lines were appropriate: Julia Griffiths, who had worked closely with Douglass to launch and sustain his paper, had just returned to London. And although Gerrit Smith still had a strong presence in his paper (and life), he was no longer formally connected with the paper. According to their original agreement, Smith had ended his monthly subsidies, and Douglass at times supported non–Liberty party candidates. Moreover, he and Smith were in the process of organizing the Radical Abolition party to replace the National Liberty party. The solid black font thus reflected the black genteel independence of the paper and editor.[67]

Douglass explained his new look in an editorial that appeared with the new masthead. Another economic depression was plaguing Northern workers, and he told his readers that although the times were hard, money scarce, and the demands upon him "unusually pressing, the respectability and dignity of colored Americans must be upheld." Moreover, "so far as our paper [and Douglass' public persona] is concerned, we are bound that they shall be upheld to the extent of our ability." Appearance should correspond to ability, he said. But he emphasized the importance of the image: "We think a man is wanting in the upper story who invites attention to his fine clothes; but a man is wanting both in the upper and lower story when he pays no attention to his dress." Instead of accepting the current code of inferiority that white society sought to impose upon him, Douglass projected the image of a dignified self. His authentic mask of respectability established an alternative code of conduct that demanded self-discipline, enabled self-transformation, and anticipated social revolution, for it gave the lie to prevailing notions of a self that was fixed and unchanging. Douglass' image of himself and his newspaper provided a potent weapon against white bourgeois values.[68]

❧ Two months before Gerrit Smith announced his land grant to three thousand blacks, John Brown moved to Springfield, Massachusetts, from Akron, Ohio, to embark on the final capitalist venture of his life. The company he established there, Perkins and Brown, consisted of an empty warehouse that Brown planned to fill with wool from western

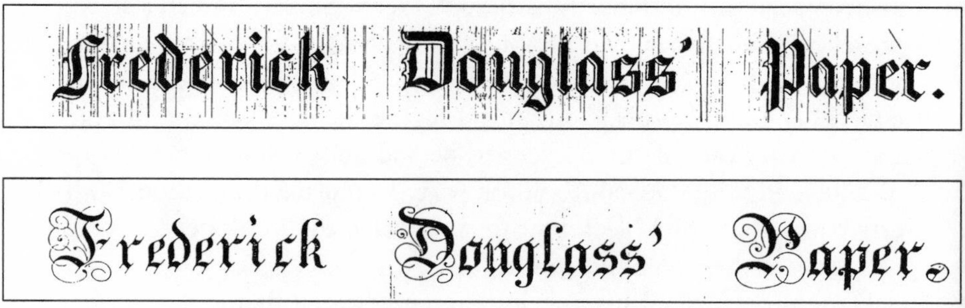

Figure 12. Mastheads, *Frederick Douglass' Paper,*
May 11, 1855, and May 25, 1855.

growers and then sort, grade, and sell to manufacturers. His partner, Simon Perkins, a wealthy businessman from Akron, financed the venture while Brown managed it and brokered the wool. For his work he received a commission of two cents for every pound of wool he sold. Brown's two oldest sons moved with him to Springfield to help. His wife Mary, pregnant for the tenth time, remained in Akron along with his seven surviving children. The venture would fail on a grand scale, but at the time Brown had visions of great success.[69]

Brown's optimism soon turned to despair. In October 1846, four months after moving to Springfield, he learned that his one-year-old daughter had been scalded to death when an older daughter accidentally dropped a pot of boiling water. "If I had a right sence of my habitual neglect of my familys Eternal interests; I should probably go crazy," he told his wife when he heard the news. In Springfield things were no better. The recently passed Walker tariff, which drastically reduced import duties (in part to appease Southern planters), and the declaration of war with Mexico caused wool prices to plummet. Brown refused to adjust his prices to manufacturers, and soon found himself with a warehouse filled with wool he could not sell and a ledger filled with debt he could not erase. He had entered a world of American desperation best understood by slaves.[70]

By 1848 Brown wanted to escape the toils of business and white society. He had heard of Timbucto, and though he had never met Smith nor seen the land, he decided to settle his family there. On April 8, 1848, he visited Smith at Peterboro and made a proposal. "I am something of a pioneer," he told Smith. "I grew up among the woods and wild Indians of Ohio, and am used to the climate and the way of life that your colony find so trying. I will take one of your farms myself, clear it up and plant it, and show my colored neighbors how such work should be done." Smith liked Brown and his plan, and agreed to sell him 244 acres for a dollar an acre on extended credit. In the fall of that year Brown visited Timbucto and was excited by what he saw. "There are a number of good colored families on the ground; most of whom I visited," he wrote his son Owen. "I can think of no place where I think I would sooner go; *all things considered* than to live with those poor despised Africans to try, and encourage them; and to show them a little so far as I am capable how to manage." He moved part of his family there in the spring of 1849.[71]

Brown hoped to transform Timbucto into a self-sufficient and independent black community. He now loathed the competitive, capitalist marketplace, advocated sweeping land reform, and endorsed the motto—frequently expressed by his comrades—that "the right to the soil is as natural, absolute, and equal, as the right to the light and the air." One of the first things he did after moving was to survey the settlers' land in order to protect it against white encroachment. In October 1848, before he moved, he bought five barrels of pork, five barrels of flour, a wagon, and a team of oxen (probably with Gerrit Smith's money) and arranged to have them distributed among the settlers. He arrived with a small herd of Devon cattle, which he also shared with them. He ate with the settlers and literally lived with some of them. When the well-known author Richard Henry Dana, himself an abolitionist, chanced upon the settlement in 1849, he was surprised to find Brown and his family not only eating and living among the settlers, but addressing them "by their surnames, with the prefixes of Mr. and Mrs." McCune Smith and Willis Hodges, a settler of Timbucto and editor of the *Ram's Horn*, similarly acknowledged Brown's efforts (and Gerrit's continued donations) to help sustain Timbucto during its first few years of settlement.[72]

Brown, however, wanted to do more than simply make Timbucto an independent black community. He hoped the settlement would serve as the base of operations for his "Subterranean Pass Way," a militant alternative to the Underground Railroad and the seed of his scheme to invade the South and liberate the slaves. The scheme entailed an elaborate network of armed men in the Allegheny Mountains that extended into the Adirondacks and Timbucto for the purpose of raiding slaveholders' property and running fugitives north to Canada. Brown thought God had created the mountains as the "hills to freedom," and the Alleghenies in particular as "a refuge for fugitive slaves." While still living in Springfield he even had a "Subterranean Pass Way" flag made, presumably for identifying members and depots. Augustus Washington, a black daguerreotypist living in Hartford, Connecticut, photographed Brown apparently holding the flag and pledging allegiance to his future plan (Figure 13). According to Brown's daughter Ruth, he knew when he visited Gerrit Smith at Peterboro in 1848 that moving to Timbucto would offer a way for him to "carry out his cherished scheme" of invading the South. It is not known whether Brown told

Figure 13. John Brown. Quarter-plate daguerreotype by Augustus Washington,
1847. National Portrait Gallery, Washington, D.C.

Smith of his scheme during that meeting, but if it was anything like his meeting with Frederick Douglass a few months later, Smith knew all about the plan when he sold him the land.[73]

Douglass considered his meeting with Brown in late 1848 to be an important moment in the development of his revolutionary thought. He had never before met a white man who appeared so fierce and bitter in his opposition to slavery nor so eager to shed blood. Brown "thought that slaveholders had forfeited their right to live," Douglass recalled. He had studied guerrilla warfare, knew the Alleghenies well, and proposed "to take at first about twenty-five picked men," "supply them with arms and ammunition, and post them in squads of fives on a line of twenty-five miles." His immediate object was to induce enough slaves to join his band so as to "destroy the money value of slave property" by "rendering such property insecure": "If we could drive slavery out of *one county*," Brown told Douglass, "it would be a great gain" and would "weaken the system throughout" Virginia. Douglass was skeptical but thought Brown's plan had "much to commend it." He was immediately drawn to Brown, and from that meeting forward, while continuing to write and speak against slavery, he was "less hopeful of its peaceful abolition."[74]

There can be no doubt that Brown contributed to both Douglass' and Gerrit Smith's willingness to embrace violence. After the passage of the fugitive slave law in 1850, they became far less reticent in promoting violence. Douglass even began to sound like Brown in his endorsement of righteous violence. During a speech at Salem, Ohio, Douglass expressed his "apprehension that slavery could only be destroyed by bloodshed." The ex-slave and abolitionist Sojourner Truth was in the audience, and interrupted Douglass to ask: "Frederick, is God dead?" "No," Douglass responded, "and because God is not dead slavery can only end in blood." It was a powerful rebuttal to Truth's question, for despite his "apprehension," Douglass implied that he knew God's thoughts, and thus knew that slavery would end in blood.[75]

Douglass immediately recognized in Brown someone who not only identified closely with blacks and their cause, but sought to shed his white identity and become a black man. After meeting Brown for the first time in late 1847, he described him in the *North Star* as someone who, "though a white gentleman, is in sympathy a black man, and as deeply interested in our cause, as though his own soul had been pierced with the iron of slavery." A few months later, Douglass probably knew that Brown had sent his essay "Sambo's Mistakes" to Willis Hodges, the editor of the *Ram's Horn*, for publication. In the essay Brown affects the voice and tone of an urban Northern black and criticizes his black self and other blacks for "tamely submitting" to whites instead of "nobly resisting their brutal aggressions" and affirming their black manhood. Hodges, who was already a friend of Brown (and soon a neighbor at Timbucto), knew him to be white but preserved Brown's assumed black identity by publishing the essay anonymously. Since Douglass was also a friend of Hodges, and contributed frequent editorials to his newspaper, he too was probably familiar with "Sambo's Mistakes" and its source. Douglass and Hodges endorsed Brown's (and Gerrit Smith's) black personas because they knew them to be "authentic" masks rather than parodies or caricatures such as blackface minstrelsy. Indeed, Hodges had been the one to declare in his newspaper that "Gerrit Smith is a colored man!" over a year before publishing Brown's essay.[76]

Brown felt entirely at home at Timbucto. He established intimate friendships with many of the settlers, and despite almost freezing to death during a snowstorm one winter, he loved the mountainous terrain, the climate, the clear streams, and the fragrant air from the spruce and balsam. "Every thing you see reminds one of Omnipotence," he said of the region. But a number of things kept him away from Timbucto from 1851 to 1857, including a series of lawsuits associated with his wool business, and then his efforts to "save" Kansas from slavery—for which he acquired the title "Captain." Nevertheless, from the time he moved there he considered the black settlement his permanent home and final resting place. On his return to Timbucto in 1857, he stopped at Canton, Connecticut, in order to take home a highly prized family relic: the tombstone of his grandfather (and now his namesake), Captain John Brown, the Revolutionary War soldier who had died defending his country. The face of the tombstone bore the inscription: "In Memory of Captn John Brown, who died at New York, Sept. ye 3, 1776, in the 48 year of his Age." On the reverse side Brown inscribed an epitaph for his son Frederick, who had recently died in Kansas: "In memory of Frederick, son of John and Dianthe Brown, born Dec. 21 1830 and murdered at Osawatomie Kansas August 30, 1856 for his adherence to the cause of freedom." Brown placed the tombstone where he wanted his own grave to be, about twenty yards from his house, facing the front door, near a large granite boulder. For the next three years, whenever family members left the house, they were reminded of the significance of their name: Browns were willing to die for the cause of freedom. In December 1859, three more names would be added to the tombstone.[77]

❷ "The election of Gerrit Smith—What an era!" Frederick Douglass proclaimed. It was wholly unexpected, considered impossible by some, but Mr. Smith was going to Washington. The voters of Madison and Oswego had elected him to Congress by a large majority, and Gerrit himself could hardly believe it. He was simply "too far in advance of the people and of the age" to get elected, as Douglass put it. Although Madison County was staunchly abolitionist, Oswego, a bustling industrial town, was not. And people knew that Smith was a revolutionary. Recently he had broken into the Syracuse police station to free William "Jerry" Henry, a fugitive awaiting extradition to the South who had lived in Syracuse for years as a carpenter. The event became a national sensation, and although no one got hurt, Smith would have gone to jail instead of to Congress had he been convicted under the terms of the fugitive slave law.[78] Douglass campaigned heavily for Smith, giving at least eighty speeches, and contributed to his victory (according to Gerrit). On the eve of the election, Douglass continued to express reservations about Smith's chances for victory: "The people say they are going to vote for Gerrit Smith—and say he shall be elected. This however, I deem unreasonable. How could such a thing be? Oh! if it could only be so, the cup of my joy would be full." After the election he put the metaphor into the indicative mood, telling his friend: "The cup of my joy is full." Even William Lloyd Garrison was elated; he considered Smith's victory "among the most extraordinary political events of this most extraordinary age." Smith's election seemed to bear witness to Christ's presence in an age (and in Douglass' cup) that did not follow linear notions of time and progress.[79]

Smith was lucky to get elected, and he owed his victory in large part to a local issue that had nothing directly to do with slavery. Particularly in Oswego County, businessmen wanted lower tariffs and a reciprocity treaty with Canada. Smith supported free trade, and his wealthiest property was in Oswego. He was nominated on an independent ticket by a coalition of antislavery Whigs, Democrats, Free Democrats, and Liberty men, and reluctantly accepted the nomination. He considered his nomination the "evil wish" of unprincipled businessmen who only wanted free trade with Canada. But he also recognized an opportunity to disseminate his doctrine of Bible politics in Congress, which he reduced to seven "creeds": immediate abolition (there was "no law for slavery"); sweeping land redistribution (people had as much right to the soil as to "the light and the air"); full suffrage regardless of race, class, gender, or religion; free trade; the abolition of national wars (though he said nothing about righteous violence); severe restrictions on internal improvements (the province of the government was simply to protect persons and property); and direct elections of the president and all other political positions. Able advisers did most of the campaigning for him, and they urged him to focus on free trade while speaking in Oswego.[80]

Smith was terrified about going to Washington. The mansion-house at Peterboro had been his home for forty-five of his fifty-five years, and he had traveled very little outside the state. He worried about leaving the "extensive private business" that he still conducted out of the land office his father had built. His preparations for the move betray his fears about living in a commercial, slaveowning city. He sought to create a space for himself that resembled his patrician identity and heritage. Whereas most congressmen boarded in lodginghouses, Smith bought a spacious house and had extensive repairs done. He sent his best horses to Washington under the care of an employee, and traded in his old "six seat square Rockaway" coach for a "Fine Closed Coach." If he could not live in Peterboro, he would try to retain his patrician status in Washington.[81]

Douglass helped alleviate Smith's fears. He featured glowing articles on Smith in virtually every issue of his newspaper during the months that elapsed from election to taking office. And he wisely urged Smith to become acquainted with parliamentary procedures:

Do get yourself the best manual of Parliamentary rules which the country affords—forget, for a little while, subjects of greater weight—shut yourself up—place me in the chair of the H[ouse]—surround yourself with a company of the most watchful and skillful parliamentary tacticians—and make yourself such a master of the rules of Congress, as to defy all the mantraps which they will surely set for your feet.

After this stern advice (which Smith unfortunately did not follow) Douglass suddenly caught himself: "Now just hear the impertinence of this runaway slave!!" But he knew Smith was no ordinary aristocrat. "Ah! but he knows who he is talking to." In fact Smith would have preferred Douglass rather than himself in the House, and said as much. He knew his friend had a far more compelling public voice and persona.[82]

With encouragement from Douglass and other friends, Smith kept "divinely busy" trying to change the country. In his first congressional session he gave more speeches than any other member of the House (by his own reckoning), and hosted lavish dinners for virtually every member of the House and many from the Senate. His hospitality in Washington was no less eccentric than in Peterboro. Among those who dined at his temperate "cold water table" and listened to his "Bible politics" were the proslavery Southerners Preston Brooks, Alexander Stephens, and Robert Toombs; the architect of the Kansas-Nebraska Act Stephen Douglas; and the former prizefighter William "Boss" Tweed. Amidst this group were abolitionist colleagues such as Charles Sumner and Joshua Giddings. He thought he performed well in Washington, and so did many abolition comrades. "You have realized the fondest hopes of your friends," Douglass wrote Smith early in the session; and he reprinted all Smith's congressional speeches in his paper. Joshua Giddings thought Smith exhibited enormous courage. A few black friends compared him favorably with John Quincy Adams, who had been known as "old man eloquent." Angelina Grimké Weld assured Gerrit that he stood "panoptic in the armor of truth and ready for the shock of battle at any moment." And in a moment of private self-affirmation, Smith likened himself to "Jupiter" while speaking in Congress, "thundering and shaking with his thunderbolts his throne itself."[83]

But Smith felt entirely out of place in Washington. His "panoptic" vision and "thunderbolts" lacked power. He was laughed at for being "a sentimentalist and not a statesman" who followed his "heart" and not his "head," as one congressman said of him. He was ridiculed for following his own principles instead of those of a party or faction. And he regarded most congressmen as hard drinkers or drunkards who swore profusely and squirted their tobacco juice "upon the carpet." He was astounded at the amount and frequency of drinking that went on in Congress. Indeed, two years later, when Preston Brooks bludgeoned Charles Sumner, Smith felt sure that alcohol was behind the deed: "But for liquor" Brooks "would never have committed his enormous crime," he sadly noted. Smith had got to know Brooks; the young Southerner had sorrowfully confessed to him his drinking problem and had expressed his desire "to subscribe to a Congressional Temperance pledge," but never did. Congress, Smith concluded in a letter to Douglass, "preeminently needs to witness the achievements of the Temperance reformation, the Tobacco reformation, and the religion of Jesus Christ." He became so frustrated and disgusted with the culture of Congress that halfway through his term he resigned his seat.[84]

The passage of the Kansas-Nebraska Act was the immediate impetus for Smith's resignation, and the debate over it coincided almost precisely with his stay in Congress. The bill, which repealed the Missouri Compromise and opened the territories of Kansas and Nebraska to slavery through the doctrine of popular sovereignty, was introduced in the Senate on December 14, 1853, one day after Smith took his seat in the House. At the end of May 1854, when President Pierce signed the bill into law, he told his attorney he wanted to resign and needed to know what legal formalities he had to follow in order to do so. In June he announced his intention of resigning to his constituents, and tendered his resignation on August 7. The only public explanation he gave was the "pressure of my far too extensive business" and his "deeply secluded life." But the main reason was his loss of hope in abolishing slavery through legal and peaceful means. The antislavery cause had "nothing to hope for from the present Congress," he told Douglass in a public letter, adding that his hope for "a bloodless termination of American slavery is less now than it was when I went to Congress." He had warned congressmen in his speech on the Nebraska bill that slavery would "go out in blood" unless immediate action were taken, and he offered a plan of compensated emancipation, drawn from England's example, in the hope of averting bloodshed. He suggested $400 million to compensate masters, four times what England had paid to liberate

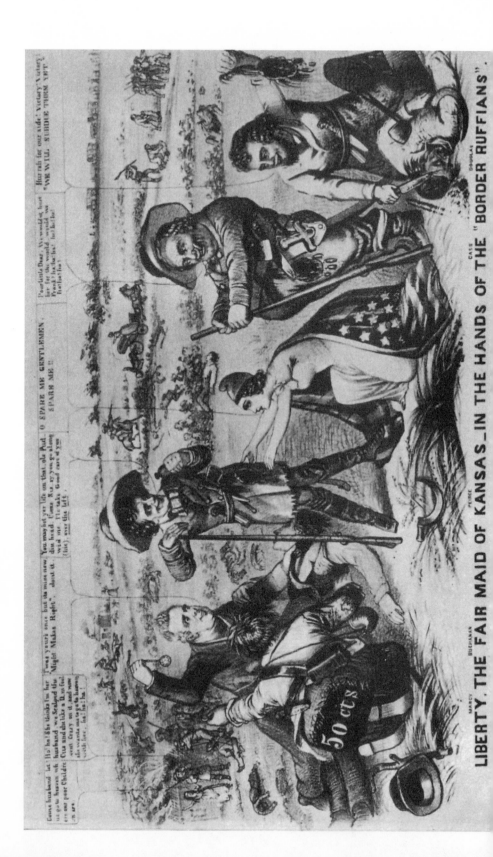

LIBERTY, THE FAIR MAID OF KANSAS—IN THE HANDS OF THE "BORDER RUFFIANS".

one-fourth the number of slaves, along with "liberal" provisions for slaves (though he gave no details). The Kansas-Nebraska Act made clear to him that Congress would not abolish slavery—indeed, it sought to extend it—and he felt powerless to effect any kind of change. As he later put it: "Having done what I could for" the cause of freedom while in Congress, "I came home to do much more" by organizing and financing guerrilla warfare.[85]

Smith did very little when he first returned to Peterboro, however. He was discouraged not only by his ineffectiveness (the reciprocity treaty with Canada was the only bill he had supported that passed) but also by the vicious attacks on him that stemmed primarily from Horace Greeley's influential *New-York Tribune*. The paper accused him of siding with slaveholders on free trade and lower tariffs and of pandering to them by inviting them to dinner. And it excoriated him for supporting the annexation of Cuba, without explaining his reasons for doing so. Annexation would end the African slave trade with Cuba, Smith argued, and it would remove Spanish troops from the island, leaving it under the control of Spanish creoles, who he felt would quickly abolish slavery. If the Slave Power took control of the island, hostile free blacks—many of them "men of genius and education"—would revolt, and a revolution on the order of St. Domingue's would ensue. Moreover, Smith endorsed annexation only if the Cuban slaves themselves agreed to it, and until freedom came he assumed they would prefer the less brutal form of American slavery.[86]

These criticisms were minor compared with the *Tribune's* slander regarding Smith's stance on the Kansas-Nebraska bill. Smith outraged Greeley and other nonextensionists by refusing to participate in a plan by a group of Northern congressmen to table the Nebraska bill and prevent it from being voted on; the plan violated Smith's understanding of free speech and the democratic process. He was the first to admit that his principles of democracy were conflicted, for his violation of the fugitive slave law and his call for slave insurrections also violated the democratic process. But on these matters he took his stand "outside the

Figure 14. LIBERTY, THE FAIR MAID OF KANSAS—IN THE HANDS OF THE "BORDER RUFFIANS."
Political cartoon, 1856. New York Public Library.

government" and became a "confessed revolutionist." As a congressman, he wanted to uphold the principle of free speech. Because of his
refusal to participate in the plan, the *Tribune* published numerous articles saying first that Smith had voted for the Nebraska bill, then that he
had not voted on it at all. The vote occurred at a night session, "amidst
gross drunkenness," according to Smith, and the paper accused him of
sleeping instead of voting. Smith did vote against the Nebraska bill,
however, and although the *Tribune* eventually retracted and apologized, the slander had a powerful effect. He felt the paper had "ruined
my abolition character," and when he returned to Peterboro, many
close friends were surprised to learn that he had indeed voted against
the legislation. His most humiliating moment occurred when a National Convention of Colored People at Cleveland, believing the *Tribune's* slander, said of Smith: "We heartily regret the refusal of our recent ardent friend, Hon. Gerrit Smith, to serve the cause of the
oppressed."[87]

After recovering from these insults Smith once again took his stand
"outside the government" and became a "confessed revolutionist." He,
Douglass, and McCune Smith moved much closer to the militant position of John Brown. Douglass and McCune Smith, trusting neither
Greeley nor his newspaper, refused to believe that Gerrit had not
voted on the Nebraska bill, and understood his frustrations and reasons
for resigning. Douglass wished that Smith had "had a little more vine-
gar in his constitution" while in Congress, but he too, was ready for
war: "In the name of God, let the battle come," he publicly proclaimed
at the same time Smith decided to resign. He agreed with "every step"
of Smith's congressional decisions save his position on Cuba, and on
that he respected his purpose. He also agreed with Smith that "the
movement to abolish American slavery is a failure," meaning that
peaceful measures had failed. By early 1855 Gerrit, McCune Smith,
and Douglass were organizing the Radical Abolition party as a militant
alternative to the perversions of civil government.[88]

The passage of the Kansas-Nebraska Act convinced these men of the
savagery employed by the Slave Power to preserve slavery. Many other
Northerners would soon agree. An 1856 political cartoon depicts the
nature of the political elites who allowed slavery to enter the Kansas
territory (Figure 14). At the far right, Stephen Douglas, knife in hand
and tomahawk at his side, scalps a free-soiler in Kansas. On the left,

William Marcy and James Buchanan rob a free-soiler. And in the middle, a drunken Franklin Pierce leers at the "fair maid" of liberty while Lewis Cass stands behind her, gripping his phallic rifle as he prepares to rape her. For Gerrit Smith, McCune Smith, Douglass, and Brown, this kind of savagery needed to be fought with savage means.

CHAPTER SIX

Learning from Indians

❧

It is very painful to a good man to use any other weapons than those of love and truth; but it is idle to "cast your pearls before swine," or cata-mounts . . . here, where there is no law, if a man does not defend him-self, he must die.

—CHARLES STEARNS, "LETTER FROM KANSAS" (1856)

He must master or be mastered; while to show mercy was a weakness. Mercy did not exist in the primordial life. It was misunderstood for fear, and such misunderstanding made for death.

—JACK LONDON, *THE CALL OF THE WILD* (1903)

On Monday night, March 14, 1859, James McCune Smith attended a "stirring" literary event: a public festival in New York City honoring Martin Delany for his recently serialized novel, *Blake; or, the Huts of America*. Covering the festival for *Frederick Douglass' Paper*, McCune Smith told his readers that the blacks in attendance used language in ways that greatly facilitated the fight against racial oppression. They called each other "black" rather than "colored," and for McCune Smith, the term "black" (or "negro") instead of "colored" was like a "lion" forging "the pathway of our progress," since it promoted black pride. The festival's organizers appropriated words for their own pur-poses and felt free to create new terms: "Have not we blacks as good a right as the whites to invent words?" McCune Smith asked his readers. He also had high praise for Delany's novel, which was then being seri-alized in the *Anglo-African Magazine*, a black abolitionist monthly that McCune Smith himself contributed to and helped to edit. The high point of the evening occurred when Delany read from his novel, to a rapt and enthusiastic crowd.[1]

Delany may well have recited the dramatic moment in which Henry Blake, the fugitive slave and hero of the novel, becomes a revolutionary following his "advent among the Indians." Blake's visit to the Choctaw nation represents a turning point in the novel, for he learns from Indians the virtues of violence in resisting white oppression and authority. Mr. Culver, the "intelligent old Chief" of the Choctaw nation, accepts Blake as a friend and brother, offering him the "pipe of peace" and "olive-branch of hope" to symbolize the union between the two races. Culver then shares with Blake his wisdom about using violence to resist white oppression: "If you want white man to love you, you must fight im!" he says, and urges Blake on to violent rebellion: "Go on young man, go on! may the Great Spirit make you brave!" The young black rebel heeds the chief's advice. He prepares to incite a slave rebellion in Arkansas, and begins to associate himself and other black insurrectionists with the "patriots" and "soldier[s] of the American Revolution."[2]

Blake learns from the Indians to combine violence, manly courage, and divine inspiration as a formula for ending slavery and oppression and purifying the country of sin. Gerrit Smith, McCune Smith, Douglass, and Brown shared a similar revolutionary ethos during the peak of their militancy in the 1850s.[3] They identified with the Indian as a symbol of the savage fighter par excellence, who rejected white laws and civilization and found hope, strength, and courage from the wilderness and the Great Spirit in Nature. Their revolutionary ethos was closely linked to their embrace of the symbolic Indian, their understanding of manhood, their sacred visions of America, and their acceptance of savage means to fight slavery.

While these men had little or nothing to do with actual Indians, identifying with the symbol of the savage warrior revealed central components in their worldviews and reform visions during the height of their alliance. Their embrace of the noble savage grew directly out of their Romantic ideology. In one sense, they applied the Byronic ideal of a courageous rebel and freedom fighter to an American context. Romantic heroes were nothing if not men of action, and the noble savage was, for them, an American variation of the Byronic hero. Additionally, their symbolic link with Indians reflected their efforts to dismantle the almost unquestioned cultural dichotomy of savagery and civilization. They justified and accepted savagery as a means of vanquishing slavery and thus advancing civilization. They found in the symbol of the Indian grounds for violently attacking a corrupt civilization.[4]

Identifying with Indians reflected these men's revolutionary ethos in three specific ways. First, by linking their self-conceptions to Indians and by embracing the regenerative power of nature and the frontier wilderness, they redefined one of the structuring metaphors of the American experience, what the cultural historian Richard Slotkin calls "regeneration through violence." Most white Americans entered the wilderness to tame it. They became like dark-skinned savages in order to conquer dark-skinned peoples, and emerged from their regression reaffirming their whiteness and "virtuous" characters. Gerrit Smith, McCune Smith, Douglass, and Brown inverted the mythic ideal of re-generation through violence: they completed the transformation into dark-skinned savages in order to vanquish the Slave Power, which they viewed as a demonic, racial Other. They symbolically united with Indi-ans and used savage means to conquer slavery and the white establish-ment. Like their white friends, Douglass and McCune Smith believed that by employing savagery to conquer slavery, they would emerge from their regression purified, their virtuous characters clarified and regenerated.[5]

Second, identifying with Indians revealed their understandings of manhood in the context of fighting slavery. In this context manhood was defined by a battlefield code that required physical resistance and fighting prowess to defeat the enemy. Gerrit Smith, McCune Smith, Douglass, and Brown affirmed an aggressive form of manhood that linked physical force to one's savage instincts and animal passions. The historian Anthony Rotundo describes this form of manhood as a "primitive masculine" ideal, which stressed dominance and conquest through harnessing the energy of primitive male instincts and sav-agery—exemplified in the symbol of the Indian—that lurked beneath the veneer of civilization. For these four men, savagery was not some-thing to be shunned; rather, it needed to be controlled and harnessed. As Douglass put it, "To know man civilized we must study him as a savage . . . We are all savages in childhood . . . And men . . . are only children of a larger growth."[6]

Finally, the revolutionary ethos of Gerrit Smith, McCune Smith, Douglass, and Brown reflected their efforts to redefine America as an egalitarian and pluralist society. Like many of their Romantic prede-cessors and contemporaries—from James Fenimore Cooper and Washington Irving to Walt Whitman and Henry David Thoreau—

they linked the symbol of the Indian to American national identity. By including Indians in their self-conceptions they not only emphasized their American rather than European or African roots; they also underscored the need to change existing laws and customs to accommodate the diversity they saw inherent in the origins of America.[7] They constructed a mythic vision of American history that accorded with their hopes for a sin-free future. Patriots of the Revolution had based *their* conception of the new nation on freedom and equality, and these men sought to fulfill the ideals their forefathers had left hanging in the balance. They saw themselves as thoroughly American, linked by ancestry to the country's pluralist origins. John Brown and Gerrit Smith boasted of grandfathers who had fought as patriots in the Revolution, and Brown claimed that a family member had landed at Plymouth on the *Mayflower*. McCune Smith traced his ancestry to one of the earliest colonial settlements, consisting, he said, of Indians, whites, and blacks who lived together in harmony. Douglass connected himself and all African Americans to the nation's origins by referring to the simultaneous landing of Pilgrims and slaves on a continent inhabited by Indians, noting that "we are, some of us, descendants of those who fought for our country, who bled for it, and died for it. Let us be treated as well as the sons of those who fought against it."[8]

Identifying with the symbol of the Indian was part of a recurring trend among reformers throughout American history, one that was "dedicated to the establishment of a new social order consonant with the liberal ideals of the age," according to the historian Robert Berkhofer. In the minds of these men, the persistence and spread of slavery perverted the meaning of America and stood in the way of their faith in a new age. Identifying with Indians, who were symbolically free and untrammeled by the outworn institutions of the Old World, paved the road to revolution, reform, and a regenerated country. Berkhofer notes that visions of a future Christian millennium and a "primitivist" past of a "paradise on earth" represented flip sides "of the same coin of human aspiration" for a way of life that was radically different from the one in the present.[9]

There were limits in their efforts to create a heaven on Earth, however. Even as they rejected old boundaries and hierarchies, they constructed new ones. They placed their vision of America at the top of their new moral framework. In the absence of traditional structures they clung to the *idea* of America and considered it the best hope for humanity. Moreover, they distinguished redeemed individuals from the unrepentant defenders of slavery, and retained the Christian doctrine of blood atonement for the remission of sin. Finally, while they were remarkably successful at collapsing the dichotomies of sacred and profane, body and soul, and black and white, they were less successful in dismantling the dualities of savagery and civilization, which is why their Indian identification (especially that of Gerrit Smith) sometimes appears tentative or speculative. They identified only with the symbol of the Indian, and were quick to dissociate themselves from the vast majority of actual Indians who were thought to be dying out. In fact the Indians of the West were on the defensive in the 1840s and 1850s and had little chance of effective resistance. Nevertheless, attacking the dichotomy separating civilization from savagery represented an important breakthrough among antebellum reformers in their quest to dismantle social hierarchies and envision a new world.[10]

❧ James McCune Smith publicly defined himself as an Indian, even though there is no record of his being part Native American. Throughout the 1850s he authored articles and essays for *Frederick Douglass' Paper* under the pseudonym "Communipaw." His new name derived from a colonial Indian settlement in what is now Jersey City, New Jersey. Communipaw had become legendary—in large part because of Washington Irving's writings on New York—as an interracial community of blacks, Indians, and Dutch settlers who successfully resisted an invasion of Virginians demanding submission to the English crown. He called himself a "descendent" of Communipaw, and many of his "Communipaw" articles expressly invoke savagery as the appropriate means to fight slavery.[11]

McCune Smith was careful to distinguish real Indians from symbolic savages, however. One of his few recorded references to actual Indians occurred in 1844, and it is highly revealing. In a letter to Horace Greeley, he attacked the assumption—prevalent among Northern whites as well as Southerners—that free blacks in the North died out more quickly than did slaves in the South. He cited the 1840 census to refute the claim, and then argued that because of prejudice, free blacks were "taught to believe themselves naturally inferior." They were "shut out from the temples of higher literature" yet "taunted with ignorance," "driven from what are called churches, yet branded with impiety." This, he added, "has been no trifling conflict. The Indian race have perished in a like encounter." Here was one of the primary fears of identifying with real Indians: they died out, and free blacks in particular, who continually struggled to retain the few rights they had, felt justly skeptical about affirming an association with a group that was excluded from the body politic and widely assumed to be perishing.[12]

During the 1850s, when he went by the name of Communipaw, McCune Smith downplayed or ignored Indians who were dying out, and focused instead on Indian savagery as an effective means for fighting one's oppressor. The most notable instance occurred in an 1851 article on Louis Kossuth, in which McCune Smith, writing as Communipaw, fondly refers to Frederick Douglass as "an outside barbarian," and eventually says as much of Kossuth. Kossuth, a Magyar nationalist who led the 1848 revolution for Hungarian independence, had just completed a triumphal seven-month tour of the United States. Although many abolitionists would eventually denounce him, during his tour he was championed as a freedom fighter. Most contemporaries characterized Kossuth as "white," but McCune Smith portrays him as a dark-skinned noble savage after describing him as a Byronic hero of "mesmeric power" whose "leadership is as much philosophical as physical." "There is some divinity 'stirs within him,'" McCune Smith says (echoing the language Douglass used to describe himself). There is "grandeur in the very conception of him." He urges his readers to follow Kossuth's example of violent rebellion to cleanse America of sin: "Our case needs the baptism of blood, before it can be placed upon the level of his sympathy." He refers to Kossuth as a Byronic hero by having him quote the line from Byron's *Childe Harold's Pilgrimage* that he, Gerrit Smith, and Douglass repeated throughout the 1850s: Kossuth "had scarcely touched our shores when he thundered in *our* ears, 'Hereditary bondsmen! know ye not / Who would be free, themselves must strike the blow.'" For McCune Smith, Kossuth was, like Lord Byron before him, "the idol of the American nation."[13]

Following these accolades, McCune Smith turns Kossuth into a dark-skinned warrior, as if to emphasize the need to become dark-skinned and savage in order to vanquish slavery and regenerate America: "The fun of it is, that Kossuth . . . is *not a white man*. He is not a

Caucasian, and, thank God, he is not an Anglo Saxon. Put that in your pipe and smoke it. Confessedly the greatest man in Christendom is not a white man! His complexion is swarthy, between a mulatto and a quadroon." Kossuth's head had none of the features that phrenologists and ethnologists associated with great white men: "His forehead is neither high, nor perpendicular." "The greatest height of skull is just before the ear: he has not what Phrenologists call concentration or self-esteem." Kossuth "is by blood a Mongol; and therefore according to Ethnography belongs to the second best race of mankind." "Moreover, he is a Sclave, not a Magyar. And Sclaves are the race from whose condition the word Slave has been Anglicised."[14]

In McCune Smith's rendering, Kossuth becomes an "outside barbarian," the same term he greets Douglass with at the beginning of his essay. The "greatest man in Christendom" is a dark-skinned Mongol with a low and slanted brow. As McCune Smith well knew, ethnologists associated these cranial features with small brains, lack of intelligence, and a tendency toward barbarism. These same scientists would have Kossuth belonging to an inferior race. In effect, McCune Smith sought to collapse the dichotomy of civilization and savagery and to overturn ethnographic assumptions that placed whites at the pinnacle of creation.[15]

McCune Smith defined civilization itself as the commingling of races. He believed that the seed of America's greatness lay in its composite racial origins. "The essential condition of civilization is expressed in the etymology of the word," McCune Smith proclaims in an essay called "Civilization," "which is derived from civis, co-ivis, 'coming together.'" Whatever prevented the different races from coming together "constitute[s] barriers against civilization; and in proportion as these barriers have been broken down, mankind have advanced." Frederick Douglass cited McCune Smith's essay in his 1854 attack on the pseudo-scientific claims of racial inferiority: "our great nation," Douglass states, "so distinguished for industry and enterprise, is largely indebted to its composite character." For both men in the 1850s, the notion of "white civilization" was a virtual contradiction in terms.[16]

❧ Frederick Douglass similarly defined himself as an Indian in the 1850s. In fact, during Douglass' childhood, rumors floated about that he was descended from Native Americans. And in 1865 his son Lewis, while visiting relatives on the Eastern Shore of Maryland, wrote his father to say: "Your cousin Tom Bailey . . . told me that your grandmother [Betsy Bailey] was of Indian descent." Douglass never publicly acknowledged any Indian ancestors, however, and his literal genealogy is not as important as how he defined himself.[17] Throughout the 1850s he identified with symbolic Indians and savagery to help him fight the Slave Power. In his 1855 autobiography he describes how his old master Captain Anthony often referred to him as his "little Indian boy." It is an association absent from his 1845 autobiography—at a time when he was still allied with Garrison and nonresistance. In an 1850 speech he linked all slaves with Indians: "The slave finds more of the milk of human kindness in the bosom of the savage Indian, than in the heart of his *Christian* master." In the late 1850s he found strength and courage from the "Great Spirit" in nature. And in an essay written during the Civil War he conflated savage and civilized life and invoked the Indian weapon of the bow as a metaphor for explaining the violent tactics needed to conquer slavery: "The bow must be unbent occasionally, in order to retain its elastic spring and effective power, and the same is true of mankind; a brief excursion in the woods," "a transient communion with the silent and recuperative forces of nature," "constitute an elementary worship" and "impart tone and vigor to the mind and heart."[18]

Douglass, like McCune Smith, acknowledged that real Indians were dying out. "The plundering of the Indian," he wrote in 1847, "is a crime to which no honest man can look with any degree of satisfaction." Douglass favorably compared real blacks to real Indians at the same time that he identified himself and other freedom fighters with the symbol of the noble savage. "The Indian dies, under the flashing glance of the Anglo-Saxon," he stated in an 1854 speech. "*Not* so the negro; civilization cannot kill him. He accepts it—becomes a part of it." He resolved the paradox by distinguishing symbolic Indians from real ones. Symbolic Indians knew how to fight and did so, and therefore remained untrammeled by white encroachment. Actual Indians often chose not to fight the white establishment; they negotiated with them, accepted their treaties, and compromised their freedom. They died as a result.[19]

In the 1850s Douglass downplayed or ignored Indians who were dying out. He preferred instead the symbol of a brave, American warrior. This symbol provided a source of hope in his vision of a future America, and it reflected and reinforced his posture of militancy toward a Slave Power that was becoming increasingly belligerent. He embraced the idea of American civilization and united himself and his race with "America and Americans," whereas many of his black counterparts (such as Martin Delany) became black nationalists and advocated black emigration to other countries. Douglass qualified his acceptance of America by viewing assimilation as inseparable from his millennialist and sublime vision of a free and equal country. He sided with symbolic Indians in order to destroy slavery and bring about an imagined community that was egalitarian and interracial but devoid of real Indians. In an 1850 speech he proudly proclaimed that the slave "leaves the man of the *Bible*, and takes refuge with the man of the *tomahawk*. He rushes from the praying slaveholder into the paws of the bear. He quits the home of men for the haunts of wolves." Here Douglass parted company with a *slave* civilization, uniting instead with the "man of the *tomahawk*," bears, and wolves—with the great fighters in the American imagination—in order to effect the right kind of civilization. The real Indians who died out were nowhere to be found in this vignette.[20]

In identifying with the symbol of the Indian, Douglass subverted racial stereotyping that viewed America and civilization in general as "white" and antithetical to dark-skinned savagery. By allying himself with the "man of the tomahawk" against "the flashing glance of the Anglo-Saxon," he was effectively saying that he and other African Americans knew how to fight efforts to enslave, colonize, and kill them. He would either fight for his free and equal place in America or die trying, and he would employ the same means as the enemy. His response to the Fugitive Slave Act, which he frequently repeated, was: "The only way to make the Fugitive Slave Law a dead letter, is to make a few dead slave-catchers."[21]

Douglass brilliantly attacked the dichotomy of white civilization and dark-skinned savagery in "The Heroic Slave," his only work of fiction. Published in 1853 in his newspaper and in *Autographs for Freedom*, a book of antislavery testimonies, Douglass' novella fictionalizes the historical character Madison Washington, a Virginia slave who escaped to Canada, returned to free his wife, and was reenslaved in the attempt. After being sold to a trader, Washington was sent south to New Orleans on the slave ship *Creole*, where he led a successful mutiny in 1841. Although Douglass knew little about Madison Washington, "The

Heroic Slave" wonderfully reveals the virtues of violence in his imagination. In fact Douglass' subversion of white civilization and dark-skinned savagery is a central motif in the novella.[22]

Throughout "The Heroic Slave" Douglass associates Madison Washington with wild animals. He combines in Washington's character the savagery of wild animals with the intelligence, eloquence, and religious faith of civilized men and favorably compares him to powerful gods and brave men as well as to wild beasts. "Madison was of manly form," but his movements resembled "the strength" and "elasticity" of "the lion." His face, like Solomon's, was "black but comely," and his eyes were "lit with emotion," but they "kept guard under a brow as dark and as glossy as the raven's wing." His voice was an "index of the soul"; it was "full and melodious" and could "charm," but it could "terrify as well." He was "intelligent and brave," having the "head to conceive, and the hand to execute." "His whole appearance betokened Herculean strength; yet there was nothing savage or forbidding in his aspect."[23]

There were, however, savage and forbidding aspects to Washington's character. While Washington "was one to be sought as a friend," he was also "dreaded as an enemy." His lionlike strength and elasticity, his dark brow that looked like a raven's wing, and the terror that could sometimes be heard in his voice were reserved for his enemies. But in relation to his friends these savage and forbidding traits were controlled by his intelligence, beauty, and eloquence.[24]

Washington attained his freedom by drawing on his savage instincts and seeking refuge and regeneration in the untamed wilderness. He ran away from his master and lived nearby in the "dismal swamps" for "five long years," in order to be near his wife. The "wild beasts" of the wilderness offered him and other fugitives "the mercy denied by our fellow men." With "a cave for [his] home during the day" and the freedom to "wander about at night with the wolf and the bear," he became "partly contented" with "his mode of life" in the "wilderness that sheltered him," and decided to reside there permanently.[25]

Washington did not long remain in the wilderness, however, for a conflagration destroyed it, prompting him to flee to Canada. Washington describes the fire in sublime, apocalyptic terms: "It was horribly and indescribably grand. The whole world seemed on fire, and it appeared to me that the day of judgment had come; that the burning bowels of the earth had burst forth, and that the end of all things was at hand . . . The very heavens seemed to rain down fire through the towering trees; it was by the merest chance that I escaped the devouring element." Captivated by the sublimity of the scene, Washington "looked back to behold its frightful ravages, and to drink in its savage magnificence." Even God, it seemed, was, like Madison Washington (and Douglass), fighting savagery with savage means: the conflagration symbolized "the day of judgment" and was prescribed by "the very heavens." In Douglass' imagination, God planned to scorch the bowels of the Earth until blacks could live as free men with equal rights in a new dispensation, and not as wild animals—or, even worse, as slaves.[26]

Washington's successful mutiny offers a source of regeneration for the country as well as deliverance for himself and the other slaves. He and the other slaves take command of the ship by controlling their violent impulses and killing only two men, the captain and the slaves' owner. He associates the mutiny and the men he kills with the spirit of the nation's founding ideals. "LIBERTY, not malice, is the motive for this night's work," he tells Tom Grant, a white sailor from Virginia who accuses him of murder. "We have struck for our freedom, and if a true man's heart be in you, you will honor us for the deed." "We have done that which you applaud your fathers for doing, and if we are murderers, *so were they.*" Tom Grant is stunned by these words: "I forgot his blackness in the dignity of his manner, and the eloquence of his speech," the sailor says. "It seemed as if the souls of both the great dead (whose names he bore) had entered him." Grant suddenly realizes the truth of Washington's statement. He acknowledges the slaves' courage and willingness to fight, in contrast to his fellow white sailors, who respond to the mutiny by clinging "terror-stricken" to the rigging, "like so many frightened monkeys." And he vows never again to endanger his life by setting foot on a slave ship.[27]

In Douglass' imagination, violence accomplishes several objectives. It frees Washington and the slaves on board the *Creole* and subverts racial stereotypes. As a result of the mutiny, blacks are viewed as courageous fighters, and Washington as an eloquent, intelligent, and "superior man," whereas the "terror-stricken" whites resemble "frightened monkeys." Tom Grant, the white Southern sailor, realizes that Washington's mutiny is consistent with the nation's ideals. Douglass also collapses the cultural dichotomy separating civilization from savagery.

Virginia suffers profound decay, while Washington's kinship with wild animals becomes a source of regeneration and deliverance through violence. Even God uses violence as a source of regeneration. There is a "savage magnificence" in the apocalyptic fire. In the final scene, Douglass suggests an association between Madison Washington and a heroic Indian chief, further symbolizing the need for regeneration through violence. The mutineers sail to Nassau, where they attain permanent freedom. As they disembark, they "utter the wildest shouts of exultation," and march to free soil "under the triumphant leadership of their heroic chief and deliverer, MADISON WASHINGTON."[28]

Perhaps most significantly, Douglass reveals in his story how the use of violence can facilitate (at least temporarily) the breakdown of black and white barriers. Tom Grant, the white sailor from Virginia, becomes wholly transformed after Madison Washington and the other slaves take over the *Creole*. Grant cannot comprehend how a black can control his violence, defeat his white enemy, and emerge morally and physically superior. He initially associates the slaves' mutinous actions with their savage behavior, and calls Washington "a *black murderer*" and a "murderous villain." But Washington eloquently links his actions to American ideals, and thus "disarms" Grant: Washington "loomed up before me," the white sailor says. "I forgot his blackness in the dignity of his manner, and the eloquence of his speech." Washington had to do two things for Grant to forget his blackness: he had to kill the ship's captain and the slaveowner before he could "loom up before" Grant; and he had to emerge from his violent actions dignified and eloquent. "I felt myself in the presence of a superior man," Grant concludes. In fiction, at least, Douglass' use of violence is successful; it transforms Grant into "something of an abolitionist" who despises slavery.[29]

Through Tom Grant, Douglass also reveals some of the problems Gerrit Smith, John Brown, and other white abolitionists faced in their efforts to break down racial barriers. Despite Tom Grant's transformation, he still harbors resentment against blacks. He learns to hate slavery, forget Washington's "blackness in the dignity of his manner," and even considers him "a superior man; one who, had he been a white man, I would have followed willingly and gladly in any honorable enterprise." But Tom Grant cannot overcome his own "whiteness" as a sign of superiority—he cannot recognize Washington's virtuous character in "one whom I deemed my inferior." Douglass realized that for racial barriers to be removed, whites had to overcome their own whiteness; they had to "forget" their own "Orthodox and Constitutional" skin color, as he later put it, as well as his own "despised and hated" color.[30]

❧ Gerrit Smith's identification with Indians occurred much less frequently and was rhetorically less persuasive than that of his comrades. This is because he was, of the four men, the most ambivalent in his willingness to take up arms and shed blood. Nevertheless, he did identify with Indians, and his acceptance of savage means to end slavery facilitated—in the short run—his ability to shed his whiteness as a sign of superiority. Shortly before resigning from Congress in 1854, he warned congressmen that slavery would "go out in blood" unless immediate action were taken. Following this warning, he identified himself with blacks and Indians: "Born and bred, as I was, among negroes and Indians as well as whites," he said, "and respecting and loving all equally well, this insane prejudice is well-nigh incomprehensible to me." Soon after his speech, Congress passed the Kansas-Nebraska Act, and Smith quit Congress to help found the Radical Abolition party and fund guerrilla warfare in Kansas. "When [slavery] begins to march its conquering bands into the Free States, I and ten thousand other peace men are not only ready to have it repulsed with violence, but pursued even unto death, with violence," he declared in 1856. He apologized for being "too old, and too ignorant of arms, to fight," even though he was only three years older than John Brown. Nevertheless, he vowed to do what he could "for the good cause": "Some can give to [the cause] brave hearts and strong arms, and military skill . . . others can give money to it,—the cheapest indeed, and least meritorious of all the gifts—nevertheless [an] indispensable [gift]. I am among those who can help the cause with this poorest of gifts." For spiritual strength, he sometimes invoked the Great Spirit of the Indians to help make him brave.[31]

Smith had indeed been "born and bred" among Indians and blacks, but he never acknowledged it in his abolitionist rhetoric before the 1850s. From his boyhood in Peterboro until he was about twenty, Indians and slaves outnumbered whites around the mansion-house. Gerrit's father, who spoke fluent Oneidan, remained on excellent terms with Indians even after he abandoned his fur-trading business. He named his first-born son, Peter Skenandoah, after himself and Skenandoah, the famous Oneida chief. And the mansion-house became a kind of hospice for Indians; they were frequent and welcome guests, according to one contemporary, camping in the halls and congregating around the piazza.[32]

Smith continually strove to overcome his whiteness as a sign of superiority, and often attacked the almost universally held belief among white Americans that blacks were innately inferior to whites. His most vehement attack against "whiteness" and a white America occurred in an 1852 public letter to Washington Hunt, the governor of New York, which Douglass reprinted in his newspaper. He acknowledged that whites were "found guilty of hating our fellow man, not for what he believes, nor for what he does," but "for what he can, in no wise, help." In other words, "we hate him for peculiarities, which are purely natural, and for which therefore his Maker is alone responsible." "Our quarrel," then, was "really with God." It was "a fearful quarrel," he added. "Among all the promptings of Satan," nothing was "more horrible." But whites refused to repent; they continued to flirt with the devil by trying to rid the country of blacks through colonization. Smith had his own remedy: "It is we the whites, and not they the blacks, who need 'treatment.'" Instead of "getting up an 'Ebony' line of steamers for expatriating the colored people," he suggested that "an *Ivory* line" for colonizing the white establishment would be an "infinitely better" solution. If whites were "as persecuted, oppressed, and outraged" as blacks, he added, they would be in precisely the same condition. John Brown's views were virtually the same, although he was much more succinct in attacking antiblack prejudice. "Human nature is the same everywhere," he told one abolitionist who claimed that blacks were "a peaceful, domestic, inoffensive race."[33]

❧ John Brown linked his background, upbringing, and self-conception to the symbol of the savage Indian. When he introduced himself to Gerrit Smith in 1848, in the hopes of settling at Timbucto, he said that he was used to the untamed wilderness and "grew up among the woods and wild Indians of Ohio." In his 1857 autobiography, he emphasized that his formative years had been largely shaped by his association with Indians. As a boy he "used to hang about" with them whenever he could; he "learned a trifle of their talk," dressed like them, and learned to hunt like them. He emerged from the guerrilla warfare in Kansas referring to himself by the Indian name Osawatomie Brown, and became widely known as a brave warrior. His fighting prowess in Kansas was based in part, he said, on his association with Kansas Indians, often "whooping and yelling" in their "war-paint," and on his reliance on their fighting tactics.[34]

Brown fashioned himself as a western hero in the tradition of Cooper's Leatherstocking, in which a virtuous white man blurs the boundaries between savagery and civilization in his quest for justice. But from one perspective his self-fashioning misfired, for in the eyes of proslavery Northerners, he became more savage than Indians, and thus not a hero but a devil in disguise. Fifteen days after Brown, four sons, and a son-in-law entered the proslavery settlement with the Indian name of Pottawatomie in Kansas, and hacked to death five unsuspecting and mostly unarmed settlers, the *New York Herald*, an antiabolitionist newspaper, described the incident as follows:

> These devils in human form dragged their captives just outside [their homes, amid the] groans [and] cries [of their wives and children, and left them] cold and dead upon the ground, gashed, torn, hacked and disfigured *to a degree at which even Indian barbarity would shudder.* The windpipe of the old man, for instance, was entirely cut out, his throat cut from ear to ear. The body of one young man has the face and head sacrificed, and the hands are cut and chopped up with a bowie knife.

"These brutes—I cannot call them men," the *Herald* continued, *"would disgrace the brutal Indian."* Two days later, on June 10, the *Herald* identified "the murderers." They were hiding out "in a cave" and "receiving reinforcements from Lawrence and elsewhere": "The leader of this party showed the bloody dagger, and boasted that it did the bloody deed; his name is Brown, two of whose sons are arrested."[35]

Brown's friends and sympathizers also characterized him as a savage, but they saw him as a hero. William Phillips, a friend and comrade of Brown in Kansas, did not ignore Brown's role as the leader of the Pottawatomie murders. Yet Phillips had enormous respect for Brown. In his *Conquest of Kansas* (1856), which was one of the most widely read accounts of Bleeding Kansas from a free-soil perspective, he describes Brown in terms that resemble Douglass' portrayal of Madison Washington. Brown was sought out by friends but "dreaded" by his enemies. Lurking beneath the "stern-looking, hard-featured and resolute" countenance of this pious Christian was a wild animal, ruthlessly pursuing slavery. "Like a wolf," Brown "stealthily, but resolutely, watched" and waited "for his foes." Slaveholders "hate him as they would a snake, but their hatred is composed nine tenths of fear." "He stands like a solitary rock," Phillips concludes, using sublime imagery, with "a fiery nature, and a cold temper, and a cool head—a volcano beneath a covering of snow."[36]

Even if Gerrit Smith, McCune Smith, and Douglass did not read these accounts of Brown's savagery, they were most likely aware of his role at Pottawatomie and definitely knew that Brown employed savage means to preserve freedom in Kansas. Both Gerrit Smith and McCune Smith read the *New York Herald* regularly, and Gerrit, after investing sixteen thousand dollars to send men, munitions, and money to Kansas, closely followed the warfare there. Although they might have chosen to ignore the details involving the massacre, they (and many other abolitionists) viewed Brown's savagery within the context of war, believing that in a brutal environment one must become brutal or die.[37]

The times were rather brutal. Kansas had erupted into full-scale guerrilla warfare before the Pottawatomie massacre, and there were numerous reports of murder, rape, and plunder. On Wednesday, May 21, 1856, three days before Brown's Pottawatomie raid, proslavery settlers burned and pillaged the nearby town of Lawrence, Kansas. The very next day, Preston Brooks bludgeoned Charles Sumner in the nation's capital. Abolitionists and free-soilers of the North felt they were living under a "régime of terror": "Violence reigns in the streets of Washington," wrote William Cullen Bryant, editor of the *New York Evening Post*, following the attack on Sumner. "Violence has now found its way into the Senate chamber. Violence overhangs the frontiers of [Kansas] Territory like a stormcloud charged with hail and lightning . . . In short, violence is the order of the day." Bryant warned that "this plot" of the Slave Power "will succeed if the people of the free States are as apathetic as the slaveholders are insolent." Brown's actions epitomized to Douglass, McCune Smith, and Gerrit Smith the horrible realities needed to end slavery and pave the way to the millennium. Although their writings and speeches suggest their awareness of Brown's role at Pottawatomie, none of them ever uttered a disparaging word about what Brown did there.[38]

Frederick Douglass specifically acknowledged the Pottawatomie murders in his third and final autobiography of 1892. But he continued to justify them: "The horrors wrought by [Brown's] iron hand cannot be comprehended without a shudder, but it is the shudder which one feels at the execution of a murderer." "To call out a murderer at midnight"—which is when the Pottawatomie massacres were committed—"and without note or warning, judge or jury, run him through with a sword, was a terrible remedy for a terrible malady." Gerrit Smith used almost the same words—"a terrible remedy for a terrible wrong"—to describe the vengeance he hoped Brown would wreak on the South by invading Harpers Ferry. To these men, slaveowners had only themselves to blame for Brown's actions: "they had compelled [Brown] to adopt desperate measures," Douglass said in an 1860 speech.[39]

Gerrit Smith, McCune Smith, and Douglass not only embraced Brown's "terrible remedies" in Kansas; they were instrumental in his decision to join the "holy crusade for freedom" there. Brown considered going to Kansas as early as September 1854, but could not make up his mind. The Kansas-Nebraska Act had become law four months earlier, leaving the fate of slavery in the territory to the vote of settlers. He knew that both proslavery and free-soil troops were migrating to Kansas in large numbers to vote slavery up or down. But he was not yet sure if he should join the fight, and decided to seek the advice of his family, his black neighbors at North Elba, and his three close friends. "I have consented to ask your *advice & feeling* in the matter," he told his family, and requested that they find out how his neighbors wished him "to act in the case." He added that he had first sought counsel elsewhere: "I have written Gerrit Smith, Fredk Douglas[s], & Dr. McCune Smith for their advice." Gerrit initially wanted Brown to stay at North Elba (for reasons unknown), and McCune Smith's and Douglass' responses to Brown's letter are not known. But by early 1855 they all encouraged him to go, and were exceedingly glad he did.[40]

These men's involvement in the Kansas warfare strengthened their alliance. As they became more militant, they relied on one another for advice, comfort, and encouragement as never before. After McCune Smith's four young children died from illnesses within a seven-month period during 1855, he reached out to Gerrit in his grief: "My heart yearned to you in the midst of our deep affliction," he said, "and now, when the first sharp bitterness is past, there is no one I would rather commune with among men than you." A year later, while Gerrit was suffering a crisis of fortitude over his frustrating term in Congress and the false accusations that he had voted for the Kansas-Nebraska bill, Douglass offered encouragement and sympathy: "No Mr. Smith, you are not down. Lies cannot put you down. Why, small as I am, it will take something bigger than big lies to put me down. With the smiles of God and the approval of my own conscience, even I can stand—and I have more faith in your ability to stand, than in my own."[41]

Gerrit Smith in particular treated Brown as a hero for his actions in Kansas. After the Pottawatomie massacre, Brown defeated and captured a larger proslavery party led by Henry Clay Pate at the Battle of Black Jack. At Osawatomie, where he acquired his Indian name "Osawatomie Brown," he and a company of roughly forty men defended themselves against a force that was six times larger and better equipped. Gerrit Smith believed that Brown and a few other brave warriors could vanquish the thousands of border ruffians by wielding broadswords and bayonets. "No man in Kansas," he repeatedly said, has done "so much as John Brown—Old John Brown the fighter."[42]

Smith financed and politicized the Kansas crusade through donations and speeches. One month after the Pottawatomie massacre he submitted a resolution at a Buffalo convention, stipulating "that armed men must be sent to Kansas to conquer the armed men, who came against her." He had given up hope that legal means could save Kansas: "You are looking to ballots, when you should be looking to bayonets; counting up voters when you should be mustering armed and none but armed emigrants." Two years later, while running for governor of New York, he rejoiced "that Kansas is safe from slavery" and attributed its "salvation" to a few "brave spirits and strong arms"—particularly John Brown, whom he singled out as being primarily responsible for "saving" Kansas from the talons of slavery. Smith also acknowledged his own efforts to employ his money and organize men for the cause of freedom: "My use of men and money to keep slavery out of that Territory has been limited only by my ability." Frederick Douglass echoed Smith's views, adding that the "important point" about Kansas warfare was "the effect" it had on the abolition movement: "it made abolition-

ists of people before they themselves became aware of it," and "it rekindled the zeal, stimulated the activity, and strengthened the faith of
our old antislavery forces."[43]

Given the savagery in Kansas, it is perhaps fitting that Horace
Greeley's *New-York Tribune*—a Republican paper and the largest-cir-
culation newspaper in the country—explicitly linked the crusade for
freedom there with Indians. John Henri Kagi, who fought with Brown
in Kansas and died while fighting with him at Harpers Ferry, was a correspondent for the *Tribune* during the Kansas warfare, and published
his articles under the name "Mohawk." Kagi's choice of the pseudonym had deep cultural resonance, for eighty years earlier, American
patriots had assumed the identity of Mohawks during the Boston Tea
Party. They had demanded liberty from the British crown by self-con-
sciously dressing as Mohawks and dumping tea in the Boston Harbor,
and they had signed their editorials denouncing British laws "Mohawk." In both instances, revolutionaries sought to establish a new social order consonant with their ideals of liberty and equality.[44]

❦ Frederick Douglass' portrayal of Madison Washington as one who
was sought out by his friends but dreaded by his enemies conveys two
important aspects of his and his comrades' understandings of manhood. Among their friends, they expressed their masculinity in the language of "fraternal love." They were unabashed and effusive in their
respect, praise, and affection for one another, as well as for like-minded
abolitionists who shared their sacred vision of America. Douglass' dedication of *My Bondage and My Freedom* to Gerrit Smith illuminates this
expression of fraternal love (Figure 15). Spread out over an entire page
in lavish and elaborate script, the dedication attempts to make visual
Douglass' "Esteem for [Smith's] character, Admiration for his Genius
and Benevolence, Affection for his Person, and Gratitude for his
Friendship," among many other attributes.[45]

John Brown, who was often viewed as "rigid and stern," could also
be unrestrained in his expressions of fraternal love. William Phillips
described an intimate evening he spent with Brown while in Kansas.
The two men lay on the wet grass under an open sky, their bodies nes-
tled together and sandwiched between their two blankets. They gazed
at the constellations and, like lovers talking, shared their thoughts and

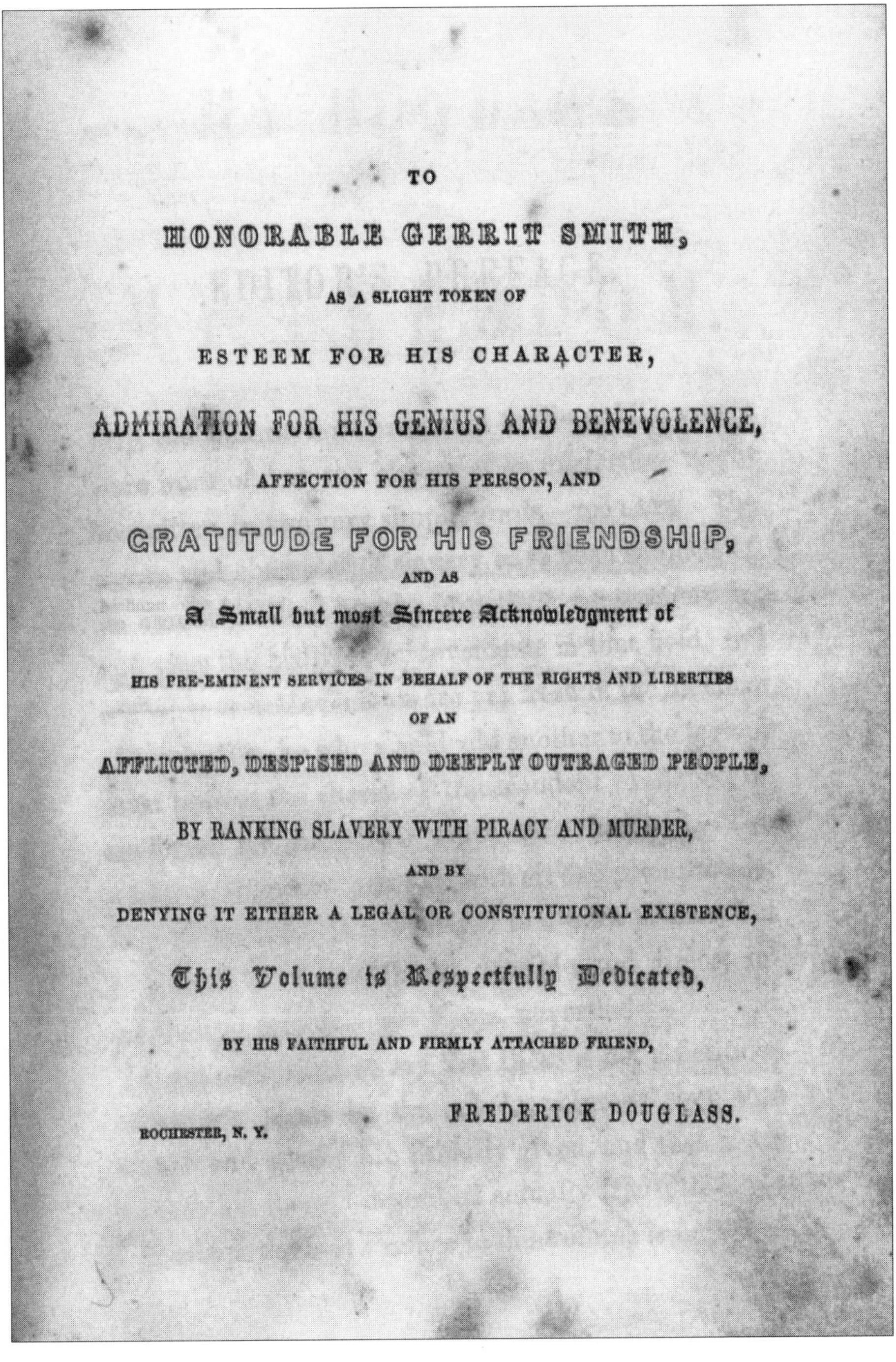

TO

HONORABLE GERRIT SMITH,

AS A SLIGHT TOKEN OF

ESTEEM FOR HIS CHARACTER,

ADMIRATION FOR HIS GENIUS AND BENEVOLENCE,

AFFECTION FOR HIS PERSON, AND

GRATITUDE FOR HIS FRIENDSHIP,

AND AS

A Small but most Sincere Acknowledgment of

HIS PRE-EMINENT SERVICES IN BEHALF OF THE RIGHTS AND LIBERTIES

OF AN

AFFLICTED, DESPISED AND DEEPLY OUTRAGED PEOPLE,

BY RANKING SLAVERY WITH PIRACY AND MURDER,

AND BY

DENYING IT EITHER A LEGAL OR CONSTITUTIONAL EXISTENCE,

This Volume is Respectfully Dedicated,

BY HIS FAITHFUL AND FIRMLY ATTACHED FRIEND,

ROCHESTER, N. Y.   FREDERICK DOUGLASS.

Figure 15. Dedication page of *My Bondage and My Freedom.*
Douglass used elaborate typefaces in his 1855 autobiography to highlight
his friendship and respect for Gerrit Smith.

dreams. In a soft and poetic voice, Brown told Phillips that "the whispering of the wind on the prairie was full of voices" and that "the stars as they shone in the firmament of God" inspired him. "How admirable is the symmetry of the heavens; how grand and beautiful," he murmured as he watched the lights in the sky flicker and flame. "Everything moves in sublime harmony in the government of God." When the two men finally parted, Brown held Phillips "in his stern, hard hands, leaned forward and kissed [him] on the cheek," as Phillips recalled. He never saw Brown again.[46]

To their unrepentant enemies, these men defined manhood as "a battlefield code," to use David Leverenz' expression, a code that combined the fear of humiliation with a determination not to be undone by rivals. Their acceptance of a battlefield code made them think twice before turning and running from the Slave Power. Gerrit Smith revealed his understanding of manhood as a battlefield code in his 1856 call for "armed men" and "bayonets" to save Kansas: "If all manhood has not departed from us, we will not consent to leave our Kansas brethren to be butchered." Fighting the Slave Power in the 1850s was a life-or-death struggle, a series of battles in a sacred war. After passage of the Kansas-Nebraska Act, Frederick Douglass defined the battle lines by asking rhetorically, "Who is on the Lord's side?" James McCune Smith defined manhood according to a sacred battlefield code as well: "The time is come when our people must assume the rank of a first-rate power in the battle against caste and slavery," he said in 1855. "With God's help, we must fight it ourselves . . . The recognition of our manhood throughout this land is the abolition of slavery throughout this land."[47]

Their belief in primitive masculinity pointed to their acceptance of savage instincts and savage means to survive the battle against slavery. Anthony Rotundo documents how men during the 1850s increasingly looked at "'primitive' sources of manhood with new regard." Gerrit Smith, McCune Smith, Douglass, and Brown were part of this emerging trend. They no longer shunned physical passions and savage instincts; they considered them a virtue as long as they controlled them and did not waste them on sinful indulgences such as lust and sex and drink and greed. Their rhetoric and actions are filled with examples of primitive masculinity. The very choice of weapons John Brown used to slay his victims at Pottawatomie underscores his embrace of primitive masculinity during combat. The murder weapons were broadswords ("odd-shaped cutlasses," as one contemporary described them) that dated back to the medieval era and required physical strength, rather than the guns that Brown also carried with him.[48] McCune Smith argued that the source of intellectual power sprang not from the separation between the body and mind but from the fusion of these two realms. Contrary to the "prevalent opinion that physical strength" was wholly "distinct from and independent of intellectual power," body and mind actually worked together, gaining "strength" from one another: "the intellectual keep parallel with the physical strength." Gerrit Smith embraced "the rigors of the wilderness" and similarly emphasized the realm of the body. Survival increasingly depended upon tapping into one's savage instincts and placing muscles at the service of mind and soul.[49]

Embracing primitive masculinity facilitated the efforts of Radical Abolitionists to dismantle the distinctions between body and soul (and body and mind), and between civilized peoples and dark-skinned savages. Primitive masculinity did not always lead to the collapse of these cultural dichotomies. But it did for Gerrit Smith, McCune Smith, Douglass, and Brown; they controlled their instincts and tried to unite the energies of body, mind, and soul against slavery and prejudice.

These four men were not the only abolitionists to attack these dualisms. Thomas Wentworth Higginson, a former Unitarian minister and a friend and compatriot of Brown and Gerrit Smith, wrote a kind of manifesto in which he set out to destroy the "delusion" that body and mind, civilization and savagery, were separate realms. In a series of essays published in the *Atlantic Monthly* from 1858 to 1861 and collected in *Out-Door Papers* in 1863, he issued a full-fledged attack on these dualisms. In his first essay, "Saints, and Their Bodies" (March 1858), Higginson argues that throughout Western history the most revered religious figures had defined sanctity by "a strong soul in a weak body." It was a "foolish delusion." With the "new exigencies of peril" in modern times, "physical courage" and fighting prowess were becoming increasingly important. In the fifth essay of the series, "Barbarism and Civilization" (January 1861), he declares that the persistent elevation of the mind and soul at the expense of the body has led to a "latent distrust of civilization": If civilization "hopelessly" sacrifices the "physical to the mental," "and barbarism merely sacrifices the mental to the physical, then barbarism is unquestionably the better thing, so far as it goes, because it provides the essential preliminary conditions." Given a choice between the two ways of life, barbarism and not civilization provided the essential means for survival.[50]

Higginson did not suggest a return to barbarism. His whole point was to combine civilization and savagery and avoid having to choose between the two realms. Embodied in his idea of civilization was the control rather than the suppression of one's savage instincts. He expressed this idea most succinctly in "Gymnastics" (March 1861), in which he instructs men of all ages, sizes, and proportions to abandon sedentary activities for gymnastics. "Don't go to the Chess-Club," he exhorts; "come with me to the Gymnasium." Higginson is so enthusiastic about the merits of the gymnasium that he not only urges daily use, but guides his readers through an introductory workout.[51]

Why has this militant abolitionist become so obsessed with gymnastics on the eve of civil war? Because "there is, or ought to be, in all of us a touch of untamed gypsy nature, which should be trained, not crushed. *We need, in the very midst of civilization, something which gives a little of the zest of savage life.*" Athletic exercises—and gymnastics in particular—"furnish the means" for developing and controlling one's savage nature. "The animal energy cannot and ought not to be suppressed; if debarred from its natural channel, it will force for itself unnatural ones." Gymnastics, more than any other form of physical training, requires the use of savage instincts for performing noble feats and regenerating mind, body, and soul. Why? Because the trained gymnast must manipulate, control, and master some rather savage-sounding equipment: he must whirl "Indian clubs, or sceptres, as they are sometimes called"; swing on "the *trapèze*"; crawl up a vertical pole "on all-fours in Fiji fashion"; cling to the rings with "arms and legs flying in all manner of unexpected directions"; rebound off a springboard and leaping-cord "like an India-rubber ball"; lift dumbbells; and vault over "a wooden horse." Gymnastics was the perfect training ground for tapping into one's savage instincts.[52] Evidently, the benefits of gymnastics did not entirely escape Gerrit Smith and Frederick Douglass. In 1859 a "gymnastic circus" was set up at the Smith mansion-house at Peterboro, where men and boys in "athletic suits" "show[ed] off their figures" as they "climbed the poles like acrobats, dangled from their feet, and then rode their horses with the style of skilled horsemen." Frederick Douglass used dumb-bells as part of his daily workout.[53]

Higginson is often seen as harboring white paternalist attitudes toward blacks, and in many of his other writings he describes them as docile, inoffensive, and poorly equipped to face the white enemy. But in the context of attacking the dichotomies of savagery and civilization, body and mind, he appears to close the gap separating blacks from whites. In "Physical Courage" (March 1858), the second essay of *Out-Door Papers*, he largely overcomes the stereotype of black submissiveness by portraying blacks who resist their white enemies with extraordinary skill and courage. "Suppled by long slavery, softened by mixture of blood, the black man seems to pass at one bound, as women do, from cowering pusillanimity to the topmost height of daring." Although slavery and racial mixing have "tamed" and "feminized" blacks, they quickly become models of manly courage by tapping into their savage instincts. "Nothing in history surpasses the bravery of the Maroons of Surinam" or "those of Jamaica," he notes. "Agents of the 'Underground Railroad'" reported acts of bravery and self-reliance that "are beyond all Greek, all Roman fame." Countless numbers of African-American men and women "have tested their courage in the lonely swamp against the alligator and the bloodhound," "have starved on prairies, hidden in holds, clung to locomotives, ridden hundreds of miles cramped in boxes," only to repeat these feats "for the sake of wife or child." Who "are we pale faces," he wonders, "that we should claim a rival capacity with theirs for heroic deeds?" Like Douglass' Madison Washington and the idealized image of John Brown, fugitive slaves resisted their "pale-faced" enemies by communing with the wild beasts of the wilderness.[54]

Communing with wild animals, blending the realms of body, mind, and soul, and embracing one's savage instincts overturned one of the defining aspects of slavery—the "*beastializing* aspect," according to David Brion Davis. Throughout history proslavery advocates sought to transform slaves into domesticated animals through the process of neotony, or "progressive 'juvenilization,'" by treating them in the same manner as livestock and other domesticated animals. By using chains, collars, branding irons, whips, and other forms of control and punishment, masters sought to "tame" both wild animals and slaves, and make them submissive, childlike, and less aggressive. The desire to transform slaves into domesticated animals was at the root of Aristotle's natural slave ideal, "which would help shape virtually all subsequent proslavery thought," Davis notes. Aristotle called the ox "the poor man's slave," and his model of the natural slave effectively describes a human who has been "tamed" by neotony. "Tame animals are naturally better than wild animals," Aristotle says, "yet for all tame animals there is an advantage in being under human control, as this secures their survival." Communing with wild animals and using one's savage instincts to conquer slavery and gain freedom undermined slaveholders' efforts to "tame" humans—at least on the all-important level of racist ideology. It also subverted one of the most important psychological foundations on which black prejudice was based: the natural slave ideal.[55]

Perhaps it is understandable that when John Brown invaded the federal arsenal at Harpers Ferry, Virginia, Southern authorities initially thought that he had united with the Pamunkey Indians as well as blacks. Southerners were overcome with fear not only because of Brown's attempt to abolish slavery, but because of what they perceived to be his savagery, highlighted by his alliance with dark-skinned people and his quest to incite a race war. In fact some Southern newspapers reported that Brown and his men brought tomahawks with them for weapons, along with rifles, revolvers, and spears. And one reporter thought that Brown had, like Henry Blake in Delany's novel, been inspired by Indians in his scheme to liberate the slaves; according to this account, Brown remembered the bloody Indian resistance of the Second Seminole War, and "resolved to make the Alleghany and Cumberland Mountains and the Dismal Swamp his everglades." Not only Southerners but the vast majority of Americans were terrified at the thought of an interracial group of Radical Abolitionists rejecting white society and believing that "if you want white man to love you, you must fight im!"[56]

The embrace of savage means to vanquish slavery—in both rhetoric and action—ultimately convinced Americans that the problem of slavery could not be solved by negotiation and rational discourse. The victims of savagery in Kansas and at Harpers Ferry were a prelude to 620,000 deaths during the Civil War, the cost of freeing four million slaves. There was another, lingering cost of freedom. Savage violence regenerated neither the country nor the lives of Gerrit Smith, McCune Smith, Douglass, Brown, and the mass of freedmen and women. Far from it. After losing the fight to end slavery, most proslavery advocates and sympathizers hated blacks even more. Emancipation had been imposed upon defeated Southerners; in response, they "redeemed" themselves by retaliating against blacks. The century of horrible racism and racial oppression following the war stemmed in part from the savage violence that brought slavery to an end.[57]

CHAPTER SEVEN

Man Is Woman and
Woman Is Man

Have you ever loved the body of a woman?
Have you ever loved the body of a man?
Do you not see that these are exactly the same to all in all nations and
  times all over the earth?
— WALT WHITMAN, *I SING THE BODY ELECTRIC* (1867)

[E]ach of us, helplessly and forever, contains the other—male in female, female in male, white in black and black in white. We are a part
of each other.
—JAMES BALDWIN, "HERE BE DRAGONS" (1985)

In December 1855, six months after the inaugural convention of Radical Political Abolitionists at Syracuse, Gerrit Smith redefined the relationship between men and women. "What woman needs to believe and
man also," he announced in a public letter, "is that with the exception
of that physical difference, which is for the multiplication and perpetu-
ity of the race, man is woman and woman is man." Not only blacks and
whites but men and women were exactly the same in every respect,
identical save for the fact that women gave birth and men did not.
Their gender and racial "identities," as he put it, were interchangeable
and independent of physical differences. If men and women could only
believe this, there would be no "sex in the mind," he added playfully,
meaning "an original sexual difference in intellect." But unfortunately,
almost everyone, including "the great majority of the women, who
plead the cause of woman," believed that women lacked the intellectual
capabilities of men. They thought women were inferior to men in the
powers of logic, reasoning, and analysis, while superior to them in the
habits of the heart: passions and emotions (particularly spiritual),
childrearing, and keeping a virtuous house. It was because of these

"foolish" beliefs that men indulged in chivalrous behavior and women responded to their behavior "in the bewitching character of a plaything, a doll, an idol," or "the degraded character of [a] servant." Once people realized that there were no essential differences between the sexes, "they would necessarily believe that man and woman are one in their rights, in their responsibilities, in their duties, dignity, and destiny." Only then would women be able to recover from men their natural rights and independence. Only then would the "Woman's rights movement" be a success.[1]

Smith and his comrades viewed women's rights as part of their broader efforts to dismantle social hierarchies and collapse cultural dichotomies. The spiritual nature of their radicalism forced them to confront the problem of equality across the board, and this included equality of women. Treating men as indistinguishable from women paralleled their attempts to break down the distinctions between blacks and whites, civilization and savagery, bodies and souls, and the sacred and profane, and prepare for a heaven on Earth. In their writings and rhetoric, Gerrit Smith, McCune Smith, Douglass, and Brown all embraced feminism.

Yet in comparison with their quest to end slavery and racial oppression, they devoted little time or energy to the women's movement. This was not for lack of understanding the plight of women. As they well knew, women could not vote, own property if married, attend most colleges, and work in most professions (particularly prestigious and high-paying ones). Legally, they were considered perpetual minors, with few civil rights, little say in divorce laws, and no recourse to husbands who physically and sexually abused them. Gerrit Smith, McCune Smith, Douglass, and Brown chose to focus their energies on what they considered to be the greater evils of slavery, racial oppression, and economic inequality. Ending slavery in particular was their most immediate goal. Slavery represented a state of war, and they assumed that in the process of ending the war, the structures supporting other sins would weaken and crumble as well. Thus, although equality for women was not at the center of their reform efforts, it was part of their millennialist vision, and they did seek, indirectly at least, to improve the condition of women.

It began with their willingness to blur distinctions between men and women, and in this they were not alone. A few months before Gerrit Smith announced that "man is woman and woman is man," Walt

Whitman poetically destroyed men's and women's separate spheres. In the first edition of *Leaves of Grass*, he affirms "the perfect equality of the female with the male" within his new, poetic dispensation. "In all people I see myself, none more and not one a barleycorn less," he sings in the first poem (later titled "Song of Myself"). Race, class, gender, sexuality, and religious doctrine pose no barriers for empathizing and identifying with others. "The wife—and she is not one jot less than the husband," he chants in the poem later titled "A Song for Occupations." As though to drive home his point, the remaining two lines of this three-line stanza speak to the same theme of gender equality and interchangeability:

> The daughter—and she is just as good as the son,
> The mother—and she is every bit as much as the father.

Despite his radical poetics, however, Whitman stood aloof from the women's movement in his life, much as he distanced himself from immediate abolitionism. It was as a poet and through his poetry that he was able to collapse the structures of the evangelical Christian tradition and imagine a heaven on Earth.[2]

Gerrit Smith, like Whitman, had little faith in the prospects for success of the women's movement. Although he supported the idea of female suffrage and women's rights, he also felt that the movement was too far ahead of its time. He knew that reform in the sphere of women's rights would affect every household in the country. He also knew that most Americans—women as well as men—believed that women were neither oppressed nor lacked rights correlative with their natures. Mainstream newspapers relentlessly attacked the idea of women's rights, much as they did abolitionism. "Women's offices are those of wife, mother, daughter, sister, friend," asserted the *New York Mirror* in 1850. "Good God can they not be content with these?" Two years later the *New York Herald* put it this way: "How did woman become subject to man, as she now is all over the world[?] By her nature, just as the negro is and always will be, to the end of the time, inferior to the white race." This widespread belief in the natural inferiority of certain groups of people over other groups was symptomatic of the problem with reforming America. As Smith noted, "there was not enough compass of mind and nobility of soul" among the American people to overcome these prejudices and vanquish temperance, land monopoly,

racial oppression, and slavery. Yet the success of women's rights involved "more comprehensive, and radical, and difficult changes, than
the success of all those other reforms put together." Although Smith
donated money and a little time to the women's movement, he had
more faith in abolishing the greater evil of slavery, and this is where he
focused his energies.[3]

Smith's proclamation declaring men and women as equal and almost
interchangeable was part of a public debate with Elizabeth Cady
Stanton, the prominent women's rights leader. Stanton wanted Smith
to be actively involved in the movement and had asked him to explain
why he had such little faith in it. She knew that Smith's money and energies could greatly advance the cause of women's rights, and she had
enormous respect and admiration for him. She was his cousin (on
Gerrit's mother's side), a close friend of the family, and had named her
third son, Gerrit Smith Stanton, after him. As a child she had regularly
visited Peterboro, and thought so highly of the Smith home that years
later she exclaimed: "there never was such an atmosphere of love and
peace, of freedom and good cheer, in any other home I visited." She
met her husband, Henry Stanton, during one of her visits to Peterboro,
and became a close friend of Elizabeth Smith Miller, the Smiths'
daughter, whom she affectionately called "Julius." But despite their enduring friendship, Smith and Stanton disagreed on many issues.[4]

The nature of the sexes was one such issue. While Stanton argued
for the "sameness of humanity," she made clear distinctions between
men and women, and believed that there was indeed sex in the mind:
"When philosophers come to see that there is sex in the mind and
spirit, as well as in body, then they will appreciate the necessity of a full
recognition of womanhood in every department of life." Not surprisingly, Stanton similarly believed that blacks and whites were innately
different. In an address to the New York legislature in 1854 she
grouped blacks with "idiots" and "lunatics": "We [women] are moral,
virtuous, and intelligent, and in all respects quite equal to the proud
white man himself; and yet by your laws, we are classed with idiots, lunatics, and negroes." Smith's letter announcing the essential sameness
of men and women was in part a response to Stanton. Two months earlier Stanton had expressed to Gerrit's daughter Elizabeth her belief in
innate gender differences: "The joy a mother feels on seeing her baby
after a short absence is a bliss that no man's soul can ever know. There

we have something that they have not!" She made clear that her re-
mark was meant for Gerrit's eyes as well, thus prompting him to
respond.[5]

Smith's public letter was widely reprinted and caused considerable
stir in the reform press. It even created some friction among the female
leaders of women's rights. Susan B. Anthony, another champion of the
movement and a close friend of Stanton and Smith, was much more
sympathetic to Smith's view "of the oneness of the sexes," as she
phrased it: "I thank you for having written that letter," she wrote him
privately, "if for no other reason, [than] that it has roused our women
from the seeming lethargy, and will make them put forth new efforts to
prove that they can accomplish great things in long skirts even." Frederick Douglass worried that his newspaper would be inundated with
submissions from women responding to Smith's letter, and decided to
"draw the curtain" after publishing Stanton's reply, which affirmed the
view that women were equal to but different from men. Douglass entirely agreed with Smith's position, though he felt his friend was "a little hard on" women's rights reformers: "Your letter has made quite a
flutter among the long skirts," he said; "I cannot say more against it,
than that it was the truth overstrongly stated."[6]

Long skirts were part of the problem, according to Smith and
Douglass. Dresses and long skirts, which "imprisoned and crippled"
women, were but "the outgrowth and symbol" of their "helplessness
and degradation." Smith rejected the "characteristic delicacy of
woman" and the "characteristic coarseness of man" in both looks and
substance. Woman needed to attire herself "for the whole battle of
life—that great and often rough battle, which she is as much bound to
fight as man is." To fight effectively, women needed to change their attire. Smith considered the "Bloomer dress"—originally a gymnastic
uniform consisting of a simple skirt and pantaloons—as "unspeakably
better than the common dress." Women who wore them felt themselves emancipated from the bondage of long trailing skirts, petticoats,
and tight corsets. But even the Bloomer outfit did not afford "half that
freedom" that women were "entitled [to] and bound to enjoy." In their
clothing the sexes should resemble each other, he argued, though he
qualified his advocacy of cross-dressing by adding that "decency and
virtue" would require women's attire to be somewhat different from

men's. In an important sense, Smith preached the moral equivalent of war for both men and women: the spirit of war should infuse all aspects of life in the battle against sin, including the domestic sphere, and he wanted women as well as men to be prepared to do battle with the enemy.[7]

A few years later, when the country was consumed with civil war, Elizabeth Cady Stanton articulated a similar war spirit but limited it to the realm of men: "The war spirit has a certain indirect, perhaps direct, influence on my domestic system just now," she wrote Elizabeth Smith Miller. Her boys were drilling every evening in the gymnasium, and Stanton considered the gymnasium "above the 'meeting house' for boys on the threshold of manhood." But her girls skated, danced, and played "much of the time." She had great respect for "saints with good strong bodies," as long as they were male saints.[8]

If Whitman's poetic rendering of women resembled that of Gerrit Smith, Ralph Waldo Emerson's view of women corresponded more closely to that of Elizabeth Cady Stanton. He, too, attacked women's attire and embraced women's rights, but desired an equal but different status between the sexes. In 1849 Emerson bemoaned the tragedy of women's fashions. His source of outrage was their day bonnets: "The tragedy of our women begins with the bonnet," he confided to his journal. "Only think of the whole Caucasian race damning the women to cover themselves with this frippery of rye straw & tags, that they may be at the mercy of every shower of rain." He much preferred the liberating example set by "the Indian Squaw," whose "decisive hat has saved" her from "a world of vexation." In his view of woman's essential nature, however, Emerson stood far from Gerrit Smith. In September 1855, at the very moment Smith was preparing his public letter to Stanton, he spoke at a women's rights convention at Boston and argued for the position of equal but different spheres for women. On the one hand, he embraced women's suffrage, and thought his doctrine of sacred self-sovereignty (or self-reliance) "would be sooner carried in the state if women voted." On the other hand, he accommodated prevailing beliefs about women: they "are more delicate than men," he told his female audience, "delicate as iodine to light,—and thus more impressionable." Women were fundamentally different from men, but complemented them in their strengths: "Man is the will, and Woman the sentiment." Their two natures worked together, facilitating an orderly and symbiotic society. "In this ship of humanity, Will is the rudder, and Sentiment the sail: when Woman affects to steer, the rudder is only a masked sail." His proclivity for order and hierarchy similarly affected his view of blacks. Even as he championed abolition and black rights in the fall of 1855, he felt that "the negro" should be ranked with "the lowest man."[9]

The Bible exacerbated the problem of women's rights. Smith acknowledged that his views of women incurred the "reproach of infidelity." He had no sympathy for mainstream ministers, who argued that women were made to be helpmates of men, forever subordinate to them because of having eaten the apple. He considered Paul's teachings "insane" for treating women as inferior to men, and thought any man who accepted those teachings unfit to "have a wife or a daughter." But the vast majority of Americans accepted these teachings and used the Bible as a way to justify their view of women as "an inferior order of being." This was no different from slaveowners who used the Bible to defend slavery and to treat blacks as chattels, or from voters and politicians who interpreted the Constitution as a proslavery document. People "run to the Bible, not to learn the truth, but to make the Bible the minister of folly and sin," he lamented. "They run from themselves to the Bible." They ignored the Bible's greatest message: that of repentance and salvation, represented by "the fact that Jesus Christ died to save us from our sins." As a result of these practices, "the Bible is, this day, a hindrance rather than a help to civilization," much as the Constitution, as it was generally interpreted, proved a hindrance rather than a help to America. Frederick Douglass echoed these sentiments in his famous speech "What to the Slave is the Fourth of July?" in 1852: "For my part, I would say, welcome infidelity! welcome atheism! welcome anything! in preference to the gospel, *as preached by those Divines* [of mainstream churches]!"[10]

Smith's rhetorical views of women extended into practice both in his personal life and in the village of Peterboro. Elizabeth Cady Stanton did not exaggerate when she characterized the Smith home as possessing a unique atmosphere of love and peace and freedom and good cheer. Gerrit's wife Nancy and his daughter Elizabeth were extremely active in women's rights and abolition and never once hinted that Gerrit encroached on their efforts to work, dress, and live in the same way men did. Nancy had been primarily responsible for leading him to a life of reform in the first place. And his daughter was the first woman in America to publicly wear the "Bloomer dress," before Amelia Bloomer popularized the outfit and gave it its name. On a spring day in 1851 she appeared on the streets of Seneca Falls, New York, wearing a pair of trousers gathered at the ankles under a loose-fitting skirt that reached below the knees.[11]

Gerrit's granddaughter Nannie Miller (Elizabeth's daughter) was the captain of the very first women's "base-ball" club in America. Nannie and her teammates played "bare-ball" in knee-breeches and shockingly short skirts. Virtually everyone in the village of Peterboro showed up for their games, along with scores of men, women, and children from the surrounding area. The team's popularity led to a feature article in one of the regional newspapers, complete with a wood engraving of a game in progress (Figure 16). The image shows a group of strong and competent athletes who stand with their knees bent and weight forward, ready to shag a grounder, spring for a fly, or hit a fast ball. Their focus is on the game and the ball rather than on the impropriety of crouching forward and baring their buttocks to the spectators (and the viewer). The male spectators in the foreground look weak and effeminate by comparison. There was even talk of a match against the Hamilton College men's team, but nothing came of it. The popularity of the Peterboro women's baseball club highlights the radical reconception of women's roles that occurred in Peterboro. These athletes played not only for fun and exercise, but as a manifestation of their rights in the public sphere and their belief in "muscular Christianity," as the feature article on them said. Through baseball, they redefined scripture and their rights in society. And the fans—both men and women—provided faithful support.[12]

An extraordinary equality of love defined Gerrit's and Nancy's marriage. They were best friends as well as lovers, often playful and teasing (even late in life), and in the massive correspondence between them, there is no evidence of any lasting friction. They shared a fervent faith in a new age, and were able to pursue their own interests without growing apart. In many respects, they inverted traditional gender roles: Nancy loved to travel; unlike Gerrit, she toured Europe and made frequent visits to friends throughout New York state. Gerrit preferred to stay at home, working in his land office, entertaining at the mansion-house, and worshipping at his church just across the village green. Nancy was probably away from home more than Gerrit was, and he encouraged her to pursue her love of travel. But they were happiest while together, savored their morning and evening prayers and "nice talks," and wrote to each other almost daily when apart. "My darling, there is a void [when] you are not here," Nancy wrote him from New York City in 1853, after thirty-one years of marriage. It was a common refrain when they were apart. They wrote love poems to each other throughout their fifty-two years together, and their playful show of affection betokened a passion that never waned. On their thirty-second wedding anniversary in 1854, Gerrit wrote Nancy two poems, a playful piece saying he preferred a "single bed," coupled with "The Retraction":

Figure 16. The Last Illustration of Women's Rights—A Female Base-Ball Club at Peterboro, N.Y. Engraving. Courtesy of the National Baseball Hall of Fame and Museum, Cooperstown, N.Y.

Forgive me, my sweet precious wife,
For having written, though in fun,
That I've not found my married life
As happy as my single one.

If ever man was blessed with wife,
I surely am that happy man.
The joy, the charm, of all my life,
Is she, whom first I now call Ann [Nancy's Christian name].

Nancy appreciated his humor and his poems: "Thank you for your sweet verses. I cannot say they were unexpected, for somehow I seem to know by intuition every thing that you are about." Her husband reciprocated this intuitive and empathic understanding.[13]

Nancy was herself a women's rights reformer. In the early 1850s she became an avid Spiritualist, believing that she could communicate with the spirits of the dead. Spiritualism was initiated in America by the Quaker sisters Kate and Margaret Fox, who heard spirit rappings in their home near Rochester in 1848. It quickly became a phenomenon and achieved a widespread following among reformers. As the historian Ann Braude has shown, while not all feminists were Spiritualists, all Spiritualists embraced women's rights and opposed slavery. Nancy's Spiritualism was an extension of her belief in sacred self-sovereignty; it underscored her reliance on inner spiritual instincts rather than on worldly conventions that subjugated women to men. Spiritualism offered a way for her to reunite with her family. She often communicated with her deceased son Fitzhugh, who had died in 1836 at age fourteen from an illness, and in 1852 she began a diary of her correspondence with Fitzhugh's spirit. During one séance in June 1852, Fitzhugh "patted" Nancy repeatedly, spelled several sentences of love to her, and expressed his desire to reconnect with Gerrit as well: "Dear Mother I will be present and [will] listen when you narrate this to our dear Father," Nancy recorded in her diary. Three months later she had another conversation with her dead son and again recorded it in her diary. "These words were rapped out to me: 'Dear mother, I listened attentively to your narrative when you met our dear father after our conversation here.'" On another occasion the dead son told his mother: "I would love to send a message to my father if I could control the medium. Tell him I love him much more than [is possible in] this

world of yours and that I would like to communicate with him."
Fitzhugh wanted to "convince" Gerrit "of the truthful reality of the
spirits and how much love I feel for him." For his part, Gerrit defined
himself as "half a Spiritualist," and liked to "make fun of the earnest
Spiritualism of my dear wife."[14]

However earnest Nancy's Spiritualism, she, like her husband, sometimes questioned the authenticity of the raps and knocks and pats that
purportedly came from the spirit world. During one séance Nancy
asked Fitzhugh to recall some incident in his life as proof of his identity. "The past has nothing interesting to me now," Fitzhugh responded in his raps, "save the love and affection I felt to you, my angel
mother." During another séance, when Nancy feared deception from
the medium, Fitzhugh placated her by rapping: "Dear mother, do
you think I would deceive you, whom I have never ceased to love?"
Nancy overcame her doubts by concluding that "celestial opportunities
avail us nothing unless we have ourselves been elevated up to their
level. If an angel comes to converse with us from on the mountaintop,
he must find our tent already pitched in that upper air." In the Smith
home, the distance between heaven and Earth could be very short
indeed.[15]

❧ In the spring of 1852 James McCune Smith began to create a "Republic of Letters." His new "republic" consisted of a series of
sketches—ten in all, the last one completed in late 1854—depicting
working-class black men and women as heroic and dignified Americans
in a retrograde society that had rejected them. His sketches are word
paintings, really—impressionistic and at times abstract portraits done
in an experimental style. In both form and content they are, like so
many of his other writings, far ahead of their time. He employs a rich
array of wordplay and parody, irony and humor. And he creates a narrator who subjectively participates in the consciousness of his characters while objectively analyzing the culture in which they live. The portraits range in type from a news-vendor, bootblack, washerwoman, and
sexton, to a steward, inventor, whitewasher, and schoolmaster. Their
work is the key to their character; it is what defines them, rather than
their race, class, or gender. In McCune Smith's "Republic of Letters,"

there is no essential difference between men and women, black and white, rich and poor.[16]

The title of his sketches, "Heads of the Colored People," suggests his purpose and betrays his ironic and experimental style. The title parodies the language of phrenology. McCune Smith's "Heads" refer to noble and dedicated workers who have none of the physical and mental attributes phrenologists associated with blacks. His black news-vendor, for instance, has "a fine long hooked nose, evidently from the first families" of Virginia, along with a "sharpish face, clean cut hazel eyes . . . and prominent perceptive faculties." The news-vendor could well be one of the many "incontestable descendent[s] of Thomas Jefferson," who, McCune Smith informs his readers, "contradicted his philosophy of negro hate by seeking the dalliance of black women" and siring a large family of "mixed blood" offspring.[17]

McCune Smith draws on other writers to help him create his "Republic of Letters." He acknowledges his debt to Anacreon, the classical lyric poet who similarly lived in a slave society that called itself a republic, and used wit and wordplay to help establish a republic of letters in sixth-century B.C.E. Greece. With inspiration from Anacreon, McCune Smith "endeavors to win the post of doorkeeper . . . to the Republic of Letters." His new literature will build upon the poetry of Anacreon. It will lead to a "glorious commonwealth, perpetually progressive, free from *caste*," and smiling "upon all her citizens." It will "hold triumphant sway" for future generations, and will be "crowned with perennial laurel in the *coming ages!*"[18]

McCune Smith's "Republic of Letters" may also have been influenced by Herman Melville's *Moby-Dick*. His narrator and characters contain many of the same features as Ishmael and Queequeg, who form an intimate friendship by working, praying, and sleeping together despite their cultural and racial differences. Both Melville's and McCune Smith's characters undermine the cultural dichotomies on which the social order depended. As Ishmael says, he and Queequeg stand above the jeering glances of mainstream Americans—"a lubberlike assembly, who marvelled that two fellow beings should be so companionable; as though a white man were anything more dignified than a white-washed negro."[19] McCune Smith uses almost identical language to convey the incongruity of his noble characters who are maligned by lubberlike whites: His "Heads of the Colored People" are "done with a whitewash brush."[20]

As a cultural gatekeeper to this new republic, McCune Smith links his identity as an intellectual and writer to the working classes he portrays. In his sketch on the whitewasher, he becomes interchangeable with his subject. His whitewasher exploits the racism of whites by charging high fees to whitewash their homes, much as he exposes through parody the ignorance of whites (and some blacks) who celebrate whiteness and ignore the fungible nature of their multiracial society. Both he and his whitewasher are painters, and he admits that his subject is more accomplished at his art: the whitewasher avoids drops and spattering, while McCune Smith "cannot do these clumsy portraits without spattering some people, as I learn by their squealing." Many readers did not appreciate his irony and humor (much as they did not appreciate *Moby-Dick* at the time); and they attacked his efforts to blur racial, class, and gender boundaries. They did not understand that although McCune Smith defined himself as a whitewasher in his art, he apprehended the intricacies of color and acknowledged that people were never white nor black but both. He was also like his whitewasher in knowing "secrets about lime [whites] and lamp black [blacks], and sizing and mixing colors, any of which are worth a patent . . . I know painters who would pay well for a knowledge of this white and color mixing, but money cannot buy it." Money cannot buy an understanding of America's multiracial makeup; nor can it break down the color barriers in society. The "secret" of McCune Smith's whitewasher (and his sketches) is that he knows whites and blacks, men and women, and realizes that each one contains the other.[21]

His sketch of the news-vendor is also self-referential. The news-vendor is a fugitive slave who has been "razed to the knees" and "*kneels* about four feet ten," but "noiselessly does his mission" from the street corner. McCune Smith's own profession as a writer and intellectual was similarly "somewhat noiseless," as he admitted to Gerrit Smith. He acknowledged that he worked "beneath the tide" of popular writers. He identifies with the news-vendor's crippled condition, which resulted from a shipwreck. The ship was lost, the news-vendor went overboard, and his legs were so badly frozen that he had to have them amputated. The tears rush from McCune Smith's eyes when he hears this, and he cries out: "*Christmas Eve, two years ago! 1849!*" On that same night his firstborn child had died, taken from him by a "Shadow feared of man" who "dulled the murmur on her lip." He offers to build a shop for the vendor, using the money he had saved to educate his little girl. She "found rest in heaven," while the news-vendor "manfully met and battled with [his] severest ill on earth." The story of the news-vendor, as with all his letters for a new republic, has a moral: "There is hope in it for all who, like him, are battling against slavery and caste." In one sense, both men have been razed to the knees by a shipwrecked state, their words noiseless, lost beneath the tide in a sea of oppression. But they nevertheless retain their hope for a glorious new republic.[22]

McCune Smith similarly identifies with his bootblack. Both he and his subject were born in New York State; educated and inspired by the Reverend Peter Williams, the well-known black philanthropist; and owed their freedom to Emancipation Day in 1827. And both now owned a "fine property" and were able to command worthy prices for their services. Moreover, the crafts of bootblacking and writing were actually quite similar:

> The boot-polisher, like the word-polisher, has a life with few incidents: stormy and muddy weather rile him, by impeding the polishing process; alterations in the shape of the boot put him to the expense of changing his trees a little, and when patent leather first came into fashion, he had a world of anxiety, which wore away with the cracks and scales which defaced the new article.

Both boot-polishing and word-polishing can be arduous, with few incidents. Weather can disrupt the bootblack's exercise of his craft, much as a stormy climate of opinion can rile the writer and impede the process of composition. Changes in the shape of the boot and in the subject matter of the writer affect the materials available for polishing boots and words. And while patent leather initially posed a threat to the bootblack, the slick style of writing that followed the rise of the penny press threatened the craftsman who carefully constructed each sentence to create nuanced stories and subtle arguments. But patent leather resulted in cracked and scaled shoes that did not last, much as the slick style of writing produced gaps and cracks in logic and analysis, to be discarded after a quick glance. There was a certain durability to the crafts of boot-polishing and word-polishing that could not be replaced by the glitter of patent leather and popular writing.[23]

The most experimental (and powerful) of McCune Smith's portraits is "The Washerwoman," the third in the series. It emphasizes above all the physical strength and endurance needed to accomplish the task at hand:

> Saturday night! *Dunk!* goes the smoothing-iron, then a swift gliding sound as it passes smoothly over starched bosom and collar, and wrist-bands, of one of the many dozen shirts that hang round the room on horses, chairs, lines and every other thing capable of being hanged on. *Dunk! dunk!* goes the iron, sadly, wearily, but steadily, as if the very heart of toil were throbbing its penultimate beats! *Dunk! dunk!* and that small and delicately formed hand and wrist swell up with knotted muscles and bursting veins!

"*Dunk! Dunk!*" becomes the musical refrain, repeated five times in the essay. It serves as a familiar marker in an improvisational piece, returning the reader again and again to the sound and feel of the woman's work. The subject's gender and appearance belie her manly strength and fortitude. Beneath her "delicately formed hand and wrist" are "knotted muscles and bursting veins." Her "eye and brow, chiselled out for stern resolve and high thought," gather "great drops of sweat wrung out by over toil."[24]

In his portrait of the washerwoman, McCune Smith undermines the gender stereotypes that cast women as physically weak, lacking intellectual rigor and emotional fortitude, and unable to do a "man's job." All his heroines aspire to the same standards of primitive masculinity as Radical Abolitionists: loving and loyal to their friends, fierce and determined against their enemies. His washerwoman had been born and raised a slave, until her master, whip in hand, called her upstairs for punishment. As he raised his arm to strike, she "fiercely exclaimed": "'if you dare touch me with that lash, I will tear you to pieces.' The whipper, whipped, dropt his uplifted arm, and quietly slunk down stairs." The washerwoman becomes a "man" by standing up to her master, much as Frederick Douglass had become a man by standing up to Covey. After settling in the free states, she continues to sweat and toil for freedom: "the great impulse of progressive humanity has touched her heart as with flame, and her tired muscles forget all weariness." She seeks freedom from white society for both herself and her son. The father of her son had been her former master, but he was replaced by "the universal, 'our Father, which art in Heaven!'"[25]

McCune Smith's portrait of the washerwoman was too abstract for most readers to appreciate. Even Frederick Douglass, no stranger to an experimental style, did not understand this noble woman. He thought her less than attractive, and warned McCune Smith that washerwomen throughout New York City might dunk him in hot suds for his "faithful pictures of contented degradation." He did not see the dignity in her work or the irony of working for whites as a way to become independent of them.[26]

Women are the greatest heroes in McCune Smith's "Republic of Letters." While his men are dignified, honorable, and diligent, his women are the most courageous, the strongest—both physically and emotionally—and the most patient and hopeful about the dawn of a new age. He ends his series on an appropriately tragic yet hopeful note. His heroine, a stewardess, is an unsung black woman who is as worthy of fame as the white men whose monuments dot the nation's capital. Her name, Anna Downer, suggests her plight. Raised in Connecticut by a virtuous family and well educated, she married while still young and soon found herself single and penniless, with an aged mother to support. She secured a berth as understewardess on the *Arctic* and because of her energy was promoted to chief stewardess of the transatlantic ship. Just when her dream of providing comfort and happiness to her mother seemed close at hand, her ship sank. Before her last and final voyage, McCune Smith "playfully" asked her what she—with her small body and tiny muscles—would do if her big ship went down. "Work at the pumps as hard as I could!" she replied energetically.[27]

Her spirited response, McCune Smith informs his readers, is "worth remembering by all, and especially by those with whom oppression identified her." As the *Arctic* slowly sank, the "strong men" on board gave up to despair, and stood paralyzed, frantic with fear, while Anna Downer "ran from pump to pump cheering the workers and lending a hand." Before long, everyone on board except Anna Downer had given up the ship as lost. The captain found her below deck, all alone at the pumps, steadily laboring. When told to desist, she exclaimed: *"Captain, I am willing to pump as long as I can work my arms!"*[28]

McCune Smith urges his readers to follow his heroine's example. "This great ship of state in which we [live], is no fairer to look at, nor of better material, nor statelier mould, than the ill-starred *Arctic*." The country, like the ship, was storming full speed ahead, without signal or direction, blinded by sunshine and fog, its sides bursting at the seams as the "wild tide of oppression" rushed in. Most abolitionists—particularly Garrisonians—were but "quarter boats"—they had "sheered off" from the ship of state by advocating disunion, and had "no room for black men." A "raft" from the ship was heading toward Kansas, which also refused to accept blacks (a reference to Northern Kansas emigrants who sought to exclude blacks from the territory). "And yet it is our duty to work, work as dying Anna Downer did, as long *as we can move our arms!* We may not save the ship, but like that noble woman, we may leave a deathless name."[29]

McCune Smith's portrait of Anna Downer bears a striking resemblance to the motifs and structures of *Moby-Dick*. Like Melville's narrator, McCune Smith boards a symbolic ship to warn his readers about their ill-fated republic. Both narrators sign onto their ship in the "damp, drizzly November" of their souls, as Ishmael phrased it. In McCune Smith's case, it is November 1854, and slaveowners are invading Kansas. He begins his sketch of Anna Downer in much the same tone as Melville begins *Moby-Dick:* "The leaves are falling in our lane; and the trees, stripped and gaunt, seem prepared to wrestle with the coming storms; and the blossoms are withered, and . . . 'Oh, I am aweary, aweary!'" However weary he was, though, McCune Smith, unlike Ishmael (and Melville), retained a sense of hope for his country and faith in a new age.[30]

McCune Smith's "Republic of Letters" suggests that in life as well as in art, women should be treated as equals of men. Because of the lack of records, there is no way of knowing precisely how far he extended his artistic rendition of women in his life. The little information that exists suggests that there was no tension in his marriage to Malvina Smith. She often traveled with him, visited Peterboro with him to see the Smiths, and was herself an accomplished educator and reformer. Like Gerrit Smith, McCune Smith sometimes made fun of Spiritualism but nevertheless believed in the ability to communicate with the spiritual world. His faith in sacred self-sovereignty—the "warm, spiritual, heart worship" of blacks, as he called it—led him to treat women as indistinguishable from men, in his art certainly, and to some degree in his life.[31]

❧ Frederick Douglass was the foremost male advocate of women's rights in the country. Elizabeth Cady Stanton called him the only man who really understood what it felt like to be disenfranchised. His newspapers overtly linked women's rights with abolition. The *North Star* contained the slogan "Right is of no sex," and the motto of *Frederick Douglass' Paper* was "All Rights for All!" He spoke at more women's rights conventions than any other man of his day, and viewed his participation in their movement as his most noble and selfless achievement. Fighting against slavery and caste "was for my people," as he said; but he stood up for the rights of women even though he was not one. When the world's first women's rights convention met at Seneca Falls on July 19, 1848, Douglass was one of thirty-two men—"hermaphrodites," as the popular press labeled them—to attend. And he was the only one who played a prominent role. The convention's "Declaration of Sentiments" built on the language of the Declaration of Independence, asserting: "We hold these truths to be self-evident; that all men *and women* are created equal." It followed the basic structure of the Declaration as well, listing eighteen grievances and twelve resolutions. Eleven resolutions were adopted unanimously, but the twelfth, which called for women's "sacred right to the elective franchise," was considered too radical by many of the participants. Douglass spoke eloquently on behalf of women's suffrage, and saved the resolution from defeat. He remained so closely linked to women's rights that in 1919 a member of the Georgia legislature opposed ratification of the Nineteenth Amendment (granting women suffrage) on the grounds that "Frederick Douglass is the father and Susan B. Anthony, who received the Negro in her home, is the mother of this amendment."[32]

Douglass' ability to collapse gender differences developed only after he had forged close friendships with Gerrit Smith and McCune Smith. In 1848, shortly after moving to Rochester and while still attached to Garrison's organization, he considered women and men fundamentally different. He called women "the almoners of the race of men," adding that they were superior to men in "the offices of benevolence and kindness." But by 1851, after establishing close ties with Gerrit Smith and McCune Smith and sharing a sublime vision of America, he came to believe that "the well-being and happiness of man" were "precisely the same" for woman: "We advocate woman's rights, not because she is an angel, but because she is a woman, having the same wants, and being exposed to the same evils as man." Nature gave men and women the same powers in all categories, whether "physical, moral, mental" or "spiritual," he said in 1853; they were subjected to the same air, food, water, and light. Women should therefore have the same right as men "to obtain and maintain a perfect existence." He urged women to resist their oppressors physically, much as he told blacks and slaves to do so, by paraphrasing the line from Lord Byron that he, Gerrit Smith, and McCune Smith used so often: "What she desires, she must fight for. With her as with us, 'Who would be free themselves must strike the blow.'" Douglass agreed with Gerrit Smith that "man is woman and woman is man," much as he felt that blacks and whites were essentially the same. Consequently he had little sympathy with those reformers who spoke in segregated halls or compromised their ideals by separating women's rights from abolition.[33]

In his writings Douglass conveys something of the close ideological links between women and slaves in America, and often characterizes the black woman as a kind of archetypal slave. In his 1845 and 1855 autobiographies, he graphically describes female slaves being tortured by white men to expose the power a white master has over a bondwoman. Early in both books his beautiful Aunt Hester ("Esther" in *My Bondage and My Freedom*) becomes a symbol of helplessness when she receives a savage beating for disobeying her master by courting another slave. After stripping Hester from neck to waist and tying her hands to a hook so that she stands extended on a stool, the master snarls, "Now, you d[amne]d b[itc]h, I'll learn you how to disobey my orders!" and then rolls up his sleeves and lays on the heavy cowskin. Young Frederick watches as the "warm red blood (amid heart-rending shrieks from her, and horrid oaths from him) came dripping to the floor." The scene was a "revelation" to Douglass, and in the telling and understanding of it he transforms the symbol of patriarchy into a vignette of gothic horror and helplessness.[34]

Douglass links women with slaves in his journalism as well, and reveals a person doubly damned on account of her race and gender. In 1859 he publicly rebuked the women's rights leader Lucy Stone for inviting Senator Stephen Douglas of Illinois—a rabid racist—to attend a women's rights convention at Chicago: "We hear much about the wrongs of married women, the wrongs of single women, and about the inadequate wages paid to women," he informed Stone in his newspaper. Yet all those wrongs are "trifling," "small dust" in the balance of things, "when compared with the stupendous and ghastly wrongs perpetrated upon the defenseless slave woman": "Other women suffer certain wrongs, but the wrongs peculiar to woman out of slavery, great and terrible as they are, are endured as well by the slave woman, who has also to bear the ten thousand wrongs of slavery in addition to those common wrongs of woman." The symbol of the victimized slave woman challenged the hierarchies of race and gender. Slavery, he knew, was a not only a war between master and slave but another aspect of patriarchy.[35]

Douglass also realized that women had played a vital role in his transformation from slave to famous reformer. His mistress Sophia Auld had taught him to read, thereby empowering him to imagine a better world and try to realize it. It was Hugh Auld, Sophia's husband, who had demanded that she stop: "If you give a nigger an inch, he will take an ell," Douglass quotes Auld as saying. "Learning would spoil the best nigger in the world." Douglass could not have found his way north to freedom without help from Anna Murray, whom he married a few weeks after escaping. She had given him money to purchase his train fare north and clothes to disguise himself as a free seaman on the train. Women had also been responsible for his legal freedom. During his antislavery tour of England and Scotland in 1846, a group of British women had raised over seven hundred dollars to purchase his freedom from his master in Baltimore. And Julia Griffiths provided much-needed help in the business affairs of his newspaper, provoking scandalous reports about the nature of their relationship.[36]

Douglass rarely mentions these women in his public writings. Sophia Auld plays a bit part in his three autobiographies as a way to highlight the destructive effects of slavery on mistresses and to show how slaves were kept ignorant and degraded. It is understandable that he did not dwell on his friendship with Julia Griffiths, for doing so would have fueled the fires of scandalmongers. Part of his silence about the women in his life stemmed from the antebellum tradition that kept men from talking about women other than relatives. Women were all too often viewed as the objects of male lust, and detailed descriptions of them would have led to doubts about chastity. Even public discussions of marriage were bounded by rules of rigid propriety.[37]

But Douglass also played into the romantic label of "representative" American that Gerrit Smith, James McCune Smith, and John Brown helped to foster. In this conceptualization he was nothing if not self-reliant, and to admit that women had facilitated his self-transformation would have made him seem less of a man, less able to rely on spiritual instincts and emotions in remaking himself. In his three autobiographies Douglass never mentions that his wife Anna was largely responsible for his flight to freedom, or that she supported the family by working as a domestic while he lectured abroad for almost two years. Instead, she is referred to almost as an afterthought. In his 1845 *Narrative*, he casually notes that "Anna, my intended wife, came on" after he arrived safely at New York City. Aside from this and a brief mention of his marriage, his only description of her takes the form of an asterisked footnote: "She was free." There is even less space devoted to her in *My Bondage and My Freedom* (1855). In this 462-page autobiography, one sentence is all she receives: "In the meantime," he says, after describing his escape north, "my intended wife, Anna, came on from Baltimore— to whom I had written, informing her of my safe arrival at New York— and . . . we were married." In these first two autobiographies Douglass understandably conceals the details of his escape to protect his accomplices (who faced stiff fines, imprisonment, or enslavement if caught) and to prevent slaveowners from knowing the details of successful escape routes.[38] But in 1892, when Douglass wrote the final edition of his *Life and Times*, there was no need to hide anything. He says he will tell all, but again neglects to mention his wife's aid. About all he says of her is this 640-page book is: "my intended wife came on from Baltimore at my call, to share the burdens of life with me."[39]

Anna Douglass did indeed share the "burdens of life" with her husband. By all accounts theirs was not a happy marriage, which is perhaps another reason why she receives such little space in his autobiographies. She, too, was a child of the Eastern Shore of Maryland, five years his senior. She was the eighth child in a family of twelve, and was born free, her parents having been manumitted one year before her birth. At seventeen she began work as a domestic servant for a family in Baltimore. Keeping house was a job she did well and took pride in. That, coupled with raising five children, was how she shared the burdens of life with her husband for forty-four years. About the only thing they had in common outside of home and children was a love of the violin. When Anna married Frederick she was virtually illiterate and remained so her entire life. Immediately after Douglass escaped slavery, they grew further apart and no longer shared a common set of friends and surroundings. She remained a domestic, while Douglass quickly evolved from a day laborer into an orator, writer, entrepreneur and newspaperman.[40]

As their lives continued to diverge, Anna began to feel the burdens of marriage. She was frequently sick, Frederick was constantly away, and when he was home there always seemed to be white women around. He described Anna to a friend after returning home from a speaking tour in 1857. It is not a pretty portrait:

> I am sad to say that she is by no means well—and if I should write down all her complaints there could be no room to put my name at the bottom, although the world will have it that I am actually at the bottom of it all . . . She still seems able to use with great ease and fluency her powers of speech, and by the time I am at home a week or two longer, I shall have pretty fully learned how many points there is need of improvement in my temper and disposition as a husband and father, the head of a family!

Not only did Douglass feel estranged in his own house, but the woman who ran things was, in his eyes, something of a shrew as well as ignorant and degraded.[41]

With Anna remaining much the same and Frederick constantly changing, love and affection got left behind. In the American tradition, love all too often gets sacrificed as a cost of making oneself anew. This is what made Gerrit and Nancy Smith's marriage so remarkable: they remained intimate and in love for over fifty years because they were able to transform themselves without growing apart. Their radical shifts in identities—from patriarch and wealthy white woman into self-described outsiders, revolutionaries, and aspiring "black man"—did not alter their intimacy. But Gerrit and Nancy had much in common from the start: they both came from wealthy, white, privileged backgrounds, whereas Frederick was a literate slave while Anna was free and illiterate. More importantly, the Smiths shared a faith in a spiritual world that did not die or grow old or become stale. For them, internalizing the kingdom of God and relying on sacred self-sovereignty happened together; for Frederick, it happened without his wife. Although Anna was deeply religious, she depended on a mediator for her faith and could not rely on sacred self-sovereignty. She did not share her husband's faith in a heaven on Earth.[42] As a result, they grew worlds apart.

Although Douglass could embrace women's rights in the abstract, he did little to resolve the unequal status of his wife. Indeed he resorted to extramarital romance to fill the void of love, thus marginalizing his wife even further. Perhaps in part because it was illicit, Douglass did achieve an equality of love in his affair with Ottilie Assing; he treated her as his equal in every respect. Assing was a radical German intellectual who was part Jewish, associated herself with eccentric and exotic artists, and, like Douglass and his comrades, defined herself as an outsider. Born in 1819, she was a year younger than Douglass, and after a tumultuous youth and young adulthood—including the deaths of both parents, a suicide attempt, and a scandalous affair with a famous German actor and director—she came to America in 1852 to start fresh. She was thirty-three years old, had a bit of money left from an inheritance she had mostly squandered, and started writing articles for the liberal German paper *Morgenblatt für gebildete Leser* (Morning Journal for Educated Readers) to support herself. She established herself in abolition circles, and in the summer of 1856 she traveled to Rochester to meet Douglass and propose a German translation of *My Bondage and My Freedom*. The two became close friends, and for the next few years she spent her summers in Rochester, working on her translation of *My Bondage*, which was published in 1860. In the German translation she replaced James McCune Smith's introduction with her own glowing portrait, in which she attributes to Douglass "much of the change in public opinion in favor of the colored population that has occurred in the North for a number of years."[43]

How much time Assing and Douglass actually spent together and how intimate they became is unknown, for they destroyed their correspondence with each other. The only extant source suggesting a sexual liaison is a cache of ninety-one letters that Ottilie wrote her sister Ludmilla between 1865 and 1877. The sisters' relationship was based on rivalry, tension, and downright hatred at times, and Assing's descriptions of her affair with Douglass may have combined a bit of wishful boasting along with truthful reporting. According to her biographer Maria Diedrich, Assing and Douglass began an open sexual liaison soon after they met. That is certainly what Assing wanted: "When you are so intimately connected with one man as I am with Douglass, you will get to know men . . . from a perspective that would never be revealed to you otherwise," she tells her sister in one letter. She adds that she and Douglass were "united in a deeper love than many who were married, without the slightest perspective that it will ever be different."[44]

Assing does not reveal explicitly whether this "deeper love" was sexual, intellectual, or based on something else. But there were three things that kept her separated from Douglass and got in the way of a lasting, intimate, and possibly a sexual union. The first was Douglass' wife Anna. Assing hated Anna, and told her sister that she and Douglass were "separated from each other by a true monster, who herself can neither give love nor appreciate it; what a terrible fate."[45]

Their respective faiths also kept them spiritually apart during the 1850s. Whereas Douglass embraced sacred self-sovereignty, thought "all things are possible with God," and unabashedly declared, "I believe in the millennium," Assing was an outright atheist and had little compassion for anyone else's faith. She acknowledged the spiritual chasm that separated them: "Personal sympathy and concordance in many central issues brought [us] together," she wrote in 1871; "but there was one obstacle to a loving and lasting friendship—namely, the personal Christian God."[46]

Douglass' prudence was the third thing that kept him and Assing apart. He considered his abolition role as part of "a priesthood, occupying the highest moral eminence." He knew that the scandal of an affair (or a bastard child) would destroy his reputation and source of livelihood, and weaken the abolition ranks. In all his relationships he was nothing if not prudent, and was extremely hesitant to expose himself emotionally or otherwise. However Douglass and Assing chose to express their love for each other, it was almost certainly done with discretion and caution.[47]

Gerrit and Nancy Smith never raised an eyebrow about Douglass' relationship with Assing. They treated both Assing and Anna Douglass with kindness and respect, and welcomed both women to Peterboro. (The Smiths also defended Douglass against the scandalmongers in his relationship with Julia Griffiths.) Assing met Gerrit in the summer of 1859 at the Douglass home in Rochester, and at Gerrit's invitation she visited Peterboro a few months later. Assing was much impressed with Gerrit and wrote about him in an essay for her German audience. Her characterization of Gerrit was perceptive and accurate. One of the first things she noticed was his "warm friendship" with Douglass and the high esteem they had for each other. She loved his militancy and unwillingness to "brook any compromise with slavery." And she considered both Gerrit and Nancy delightful to be around. The Smith home was energized with "an agreeable sense of enjoying life," she concludes. The only thing that bothered her was "a certain aura of religious orthodoxy that unfortunately infects even the best of men over here [in America]." The Smiths more than reciprocated this praise: they saw nothing wrong with Assing's presence in their comrade's life.[48]

🥨 John Brown is almost never associated with the women's rights movement. He is too often viewed as a warrior-patriarch, which seems a far cry from feminism. But according to his daughter Annie, "John Brown was strong for women's rights and women's suffrage. He always went to hear Lucretia Mott and Abby Kelley Foster, even though it cost him considerable effort to reach the place where they spoke." Apparently, this was no idle boast on Annie's part. Although there are no extant records of Brown's speaking or writing on behalf of women, most of the women who headed the movement knew him, corresponded with him, and had enormous respect for him. Lucretia Mott, Abby Kelley Foster, Julia Ward Howe, and Susan B. Anthony counted Brown as a friend of both abolition and feminism. Elizabeth Cady Stanton was another admirer. In November 1856, just six months after Brown and his men murdered five men at Pottawatomie Creek, she referred approvingly to Brown in a letter to Elizabeth Smith Miller:

> Our fair republic must be the victim of the monster, slavery, unless we speedily rise in our might and boldly shout freedom. I am sure cousin Gerrit [Smith] holds this view. I know old John Brown does, for a letter from him passed through my hands the other day. Perhaps I may see him after all, for he is expected at Rochester next month, on a visit to Frederick Douglass.

Her letter points to the common cause of freedom that brought together these Radical Abolitionists and feminists in the 1850s.[49]

Brown included women as well as men in his militant efforts to end slavery. In his "Provisional Constitution" he established equal rights for women, including voting, officeholding, and the right to bear arms. Numerous women came to his aid and support. Harriet Tubman helped plan his raid on Harpers Ferry. Brown's own family was privy to the raid as well, and dinner conversation often centered upon his plan to invade the South and arm and liberate the slaves. Brown drew diagrams and maps for his family's benefit, and sought the advice and help of his daughters and wife along with his sons. He asked his daughters Martha and Anne and his wife Mary to join him in Virginia to help with the final preparations: "I find it will be indispensable to have some women of our own family with us for a short time," he wrote his wife from Virginia in July 1859. "I don't see how we can get along without [you], & on that account have sent Oliver [Brown] at a good deal of expense to come back with you; if you cannot come, I would be glad to have Martha and Anne come on." Mary had a five-year-old child to care for, and though she supported Brown's actions, she thought it best to stay at North Elba and look after the rest of the family.[50]

There is also evidence to suggest that Brown was, like Gerrit Smith, at least "half a Spiritualist" himself and sympathetic to this profeminist religion. In the mid-1850s James Redpath became "a devoted believer in Spiritualism," and in the summer of 1857 he returned to Kansas from the East, having recently married a Boston woman who was an ardent Spiritualist. Brown followed Redpath back to Kansas from Boston in November of the same year, and met Redpath, Richard J. Hinton, and a few other comrades at a farm near Lawrence. While there they not only planned their assault on the South but engaged in "a series of remarkable séances," according to Hinton, with Redpath acting as "the chief medium." Although Hinton does not say whether Brown participated in these séances, he uses the first-person plural, and his language suggests that everyone at the farmhouse was involved and that the séances occurred on a regular basis. Even if Brown did not participate, he almost certainly supported his men's communications with the spirit world. Two years later, while in prison waiting to die, he received two sympathetic letters from Spiritualists, one from a man who wanted Brown to continue communicating with the world after ascending to his "new and elevated position" in "the Spirit Realm," in order to share his newfound knowledge of human nature.[51]

If Brown was a Spiritualist and a women's rights reformer in the abstract, he was also a rigid patriarch in practice. As a patriarch, however, he treated men and women, blacks and whites in much the same way.

He ruled the men and women in his home with an iron will, but expected the same duties and obligations of his sons and daughters. Similarly, he governed his company of men with firm resolve, and did not distinguish between white and black comrades. He was away from home more often than not, leaving his wife to manage the burdens of childcare and the homestead by herself. In his absence she acted as matriarch. He expected her to endure the same hardships and loneliness as he did, and refused to place her (or any woman) on the pedestal of feminine virtue and physical weakness. In one sense, Brown lived in a world of premodern household production at North Elba. It was a world in which women worked as hard and had as much responsibility as men in the survival and maintenance of the household. It was a patriarchal world, to be sure, but for Brown it was patriarchal primarily in the sense that he always wanted to be in charge and happened to be a man.

The disjuncture between Brown's and Douglass' feminism in the abstract and their inability in practice to treat their wives as equals points to a larger problem with these four men's reform efforts. They wanted to end all sin and prepare for the millennium, but they focused their energies on slavery as the crucible from which their new world would emerge, rather than risk spreading themselves too thin by giving equal attention to the multitude of evils. As it turned out, by the time slavery was legally abolished, they were no longer capable of redirecting their energies to women's rights (or other evils) with the same fervor as they had with slavery. Brown's apocalyptic raid on Harpers Ferry destroyed his comrades' ability to blur distinctions between men and women, much as it disintegrated their interracial friendship. By 1870 Brown and McCune Smith were dead, and Frederick Douglass and Gerrit Smith had experienced profound reversals in their beliefs that men and women were essentially the same. Now Douglass considered a woman to be "sympathetic in her nature" and "instinctively gentle, tender, peaceful, and orderly." He no longer thought women should embrace the moral equivalent of war to fight the battles of life. Indeed, he considered their greatest virtue to be their instinctive opposition to war: a woman would "naturally shudder at the thought of subjecting her loved ones to the perils and horrors of war," he declared. Gerrit Smith experienced a similar declension toward the mainstream: "Superior physical strength is on the side of men," he said in a public letter to

Susan B. Anthony in 1873. Gone was his belief that "man is woman and woman is man." Now he considered men naturally strong, rough, at times barbaric, and women weak and gentle. And now he felt that men should act in a "full, generous [and] chivalrous" manner toward women. It was a stark reversal from his 1855 public letter to Elizabeth Cady Stanton, in which he lambasted chivalrous behavior and the belief in innate differences between the sexes. The bloodletting needed to achieve a tenuous freedom for black men forced Smith and Douglass (and many other radicals) to consider the costs of ending all sin. It pushed them toward the mainstream and away from their vision of a heaven on Earth.[52]

CHAPTER EIGHT

The Alliance Ends and
the War Begins

❧

The reforms which have swept over this land, have been, after all their
noise and fury, mere acts of intellection; there has been no heart blood
in them, they were brain work all; and intellect does nothing, intellect
can do nothing—is a thinker not an actor, and herein lies the secret—
why all these reforms ended in talk. They lacked heart and will.

—JAMES MCCUNE SMITH, IN *FREDERICK DOUGLASS' PAPER* (1858)

This led me to the idea that the ones who had survived had made
some sort of clean break . . . A clean break is something you cannot
come back from; that is irretrievable because it makes the past cease to
exist.

—F. SCOTT FITZGERALD, "THE CRACK-UP" (1936)

On October 29, 1859, a *New York Herald* reporter traveled to Peterboro, New York, to obtain information about Gerrit Smith's role in
John Brown's raid on the federal arsenal at Harpers Ferry. He took the
New York Central Railroad from New York City to the Oneida depot,
on the border of Madison and Oneida Counties, and stayed overnight
at the depot hotel. The next morning, a Sunday, he traveled the remaining eleven miles by horse and buggy, winding his way through the
hills of Madison County to its summit of Peterboro. He stopped at a
roadside tavern along the way, warmed himself by the log fire, and ordered a three-cent glass of the locally distilled rye whiskey—the only
beverage offered. The other occupants were three old men; one was
lame, another partially blind, and the third almost deaf. The reporter
invited them to the wooden bench by the fire where he sat, and bought
them a round in the hopes of obtaining information about Smith's rumored complicity in the plot for a "negro insurrection." His questions
were met with blank stares, for although his drinking companions were

quite familiar with Gerrit Smith, they knew nothing about "Mr. Harper or his ferry."[1]

The scores of other residents the reporter interviewed were quite familiar with Brown's raid, however. It was front-page news in every major newspaper in New York and around the country. On Sunday evening, October 16, 1859, Brown and twenty-one men—sixteen whites and five blacks—invaded the federal arsenal at Harpers Ferry, Virginia. They had been in the area since July and were renting a farmhouse, known as the Kennedy Farm, which they used as their base of operations. Their plan was to gain control of the arsenal, distribute the cache of weapons to the large population of slaves and free blacks in the area, whom Brown expected to be ready and waiting for him, and incite an insurrection that would spread through the South and result in black freedom.

It was a breathtakingly ambitious plan, and it was doomed to fail. Brown and his men took possession of the arsenal without difficulty, but by Monday afternoon they were surrounded by troops of militiamen. Brown and six survivors took refuge in the engine house of the armory, along with eleven prisoners they had captured. Two of his sons were with him; they were mortally wounded and would soon die at his side. With him also was an emblem of America's revolutionary spirit: a sword that had been owned by George Washington, which Brown kept at hand for moral support. He had confiscated it from one of the prisoners, a distant relative of the first president, and like his ancestor a slaveowner and planter. On Tuesday morning, as two thousand spectators looked on, two soon-to-be rebels, Robert E. Lee and J. E. B. Stuart, led a company of United States Marines in the final assault on Brown's small band. They battered down the doors of the engine house and captured the insurgents, severely injuring Brown in the process.[2]

Peterboro residents had closely followed this news. They knew that Brown was now in the midst of his trial for treason, murder, and conspiring with slaves to rebel. And they knew that Gerrit Smith had been a lead conspirator in the affair. Yet no matter how they felt about Brown or his raid, they remained intensely loyal to Gerrit Smith. Indeed, the most striking aspect of the reporter's investigation was that even though the *New York Herald* was an anti-abolitionist newspaper and considered the Harpers Ferry attack an outrage, the reporter could find no one willing to vilify Smith. Everyone he interviewed expressed

unwavering respect, admiration, and fondness for Gerrit, and the entire community vowed to resist, with force if necessary, any attempt to
arrest him for his role in Brown's raid. Peterboro, the reporter realized, was not only isolated from the bustle of commerce and the din of
public opinion; it stood like a beacon on a stormy sea, where people
lived and worked according to a different set of values.[3]

But the light of the new world that Peterboro (and Timbucto) symbolized was fading. The Harpers Ferry raid destroyed the interracial
alliance that Gerrit Smith, James McCune Smith, and Frederick
Douglass had so courageously developed. It was the climax of their relationship and the culmination of their quest to realize a heaven on
Earth. Not only did John Brown die as a result of the raid, but something died in Gerrit Smith. Smith's attempt to "abolitionize the public
mind" was, like Brown's raid, doomed to fail, and he lost himself along
with his hope for a new world.[4] He suffered a mental collapse from
which he never wholly recovered. In the wake of the raid, he experienced a profound crisis of faith and identity, and felt enormous guilt
over the bloodshed for which he had been in part responsible. He
abandoned his belief in a sacred and pluralist society and doubted that
God could enter into and affect the affairs of the world. He concluded
that his black identification, his close interracial friendships, and his
belief in prophecy represented the dark sources of his violent proclivities. In his mind, he had aligned himself with the wrong crowd by befriending blacks and viewing himself as one. He began to distance himself from Douglass and McCune Smith as well as other blacks. For the
first time in his life he openly embraced the widespread beliefs in innate black inferiority and difference. He could not forgive himself for
his sins, and racism became a way for him to exorcise his feelings of
guilt. He lost his black heart and, with it, his ability to dismantle the
barriers separating black from white, this world from the next, the ideal
from the real, body from soul, sacred from profane, and men from
women. After Harpers Ferry, Gerrit Smith, McCune Smith, and
Douglass all recognized that violence could be as much a barrier as a
bridge in achieving a pluralist society.

❧ The *New York Herald* reporter found that Peterboro residents' defense of Smith went far beyond sectional, abolitionist, and ideological
loyalties. Mr. Farrell, an anti-abolitionist, rum-selling landlord of the

Oneida depot hotel, did not sympathize with Smith's abolition, temperance, and egalitarian sentiments; but he respected Smith and liked him. "Aside from politics," Farrell said, "he's every man's friend, and when that's so, it is difficult to make people consent to let such a man be arrested and taken off to another State." Almost everyone in Madison County had asked a favor of Smith at one time or another, Farrell noted, "and no one ever came away unsatisfied . . . He's a noble old fellow . . . Why, it would take a regiment of soldiers to get him away." Mr. Fay, another anti-abolitionist who owned an inn and tavern (the Fay House) a few doors down from Smith's temperance hotel, expressed similar sentiments, even though his attitudes and vocation flew in the face of Smith's reform vision. Fay noted that "almost all the people" liked Smith, even if they disagreed with his social and political views. Although some of Smith's "best friends" would "never support" him politically, Fay added, everyone recognized that he "does a vast deal of good here, and so plain and so simple in his way of living for a man of his means." Sam Russell, a fifteen-year-old employee of Gerrit, and a former slave whose freedom the Smiths had purchased, declared that all the blacks in the community would *"lose their lives before their benefactor should be taken from his home."*[5]

Although the community remained loyal, their leader was falling apart. Smith's health and safety had become the central concern of the villagers. Mr. Farrell told the *Herald* reporter that Gerrit was "a good deal uneasy," and though he was fearless "where his principles [were] involved," he was "agitated" about the failure of Brown's raid and "very much cut up about Old Brown." A "constant flood of visitors" came and went from the mansion-house, the reporter learned, from "lawyers, relatives, [and] advisors" to "well-wishers." Neighbors kept watch over the property every night, "for fear that a Southern mob might carry [Smith] off in the night." More than a few residents worried that Gerrit might be shot, "assassinated by some emissary of [Virginia] Governor Henry Wise." The reporter himself was viewed suspiciously, even though he had interviewed Smith twelve months earlier and was known by a number of people in the community. As he passed Gerrit's wife and daughter on the piazza, he could see fear and apprehension in their faces. It was a stark change from their cordial welcome a year ago.[6]

The villagers had good reason to be concerned about Smith's health and safety. The reporter was struck by the profound change in Gerrit's countenance over the past twelve months. "His calm, dignified, impressive bearing has given place to a hasty, nervous agitation, as though some great fear was constantly before his imagination." Smith's eyes were as "bloodshot and restless" as those of a "startled horse." He had lost flesh, and his skin, chafed and red, sagged on his face. "He appears an altered man," the reporter concluded. When he inquired about Brown's invasion, Smith started "like a frightened deer." "I can't speak a word with you on that matter," he replied, his deep sonorous voice cracking. "Not a syllable, even to my most intimate friends." The reporter tried to reassure Gerrit that he sought not to implicate or injure anyone. "*I can't speak about it at all,*" Gerrit repeated, this time with higher pitch and frequency. "*I am going to be indicted. If any man in the Union is taken, it will be me.*" He struggled to control himself and, in a calmer voice, said: "I am advised not to approach this subject at all." Then the wild look returned to his eyes, and with desperation in his voice he said: "*I am going to be indicted sir, indicted. You must not talk to me about it.*"[7]

Smith understandably feared an indictment, for on numerous occasions he had publicly betrayed his complicity through thinly veiled references to Brown's raid. In early March 1858 he and five other white abolitionists had formed a secret "committee of six" to advise Brown and raise the money needed for the Harpers Ferry expedition. Almost immediately thereafter, Gerrit began foretelling an incursion into the South and forecasting its salutary effects. On March 25, 1858, for instance, he wrote the Ohio congressman Joshua Giddings to say that "the slave will be delivered by the shedding of blood—and the signs are multiplying that his deliverance is at hand."[8]

Over the next seventeen months Smith became more explicit (and imprudent) in prophesying the raid. On May 24, 1858, two months after forming the "secret six," he met with his co-conspirators at the Revere House in Boston to discuss details of the raid. That same day he conveyed the nature, purpose, and design of the raid to a large and dignified audience that included a handful of U.S. congressmen. The occasion was the thirtieth anniversary meeting of the American Peace Society. Gerrit was a vice president, and he delivered the keynote address at the Park Street (Unitarian) Church in Boston.[9] After outlining his vision of the "millennium," he said the country's persistent "wickedness" had prevented the millennium from occurring, and the crisis had reached a "culminating point." Consequently, "the presence of an armed police is justifiable, nay indispensable." Smith provided examples of this armed police force. When "Border Ruffians" made "forays into Kansas," a government needed to be "extemporized in case the existing one fails of its duty" to end slavery. As Smith well knew, John Brown had extemporized a government of "John Brown's Regulars" while fighting in Kansas. More recently (two weeks before his speech), in Chatham, Canada, Brown and a group of mostly black men had extemporized a government by approving a "Provisional Constitution" and selecting officers to lead his armed police force and govern those areas in the South that he hoped to liberate from slavery. Smith also told his audience that "Sharpe's rifles" might be needed for this armed police force, but neglected to add that he and the other conspirators had purchased those very rifles for Brown's raid. He admitted that his "police force" would be a "brute force," but felt that brutality was needed to vanquish a brutal enemy. It "would be a moral force" as well, however. "The taking of human life," he told the Peace Society, "when necessary to take it, is to be classed not with the most degraded, but with the most honored callings." For Smith, the "power to take life" deterred people from committing murderous crimes. His police force thus had the "power to save" many more lives than it took. Despite some criticism that Smith's speech was "lacking in unity, or logical continuity of thought," the American Peace Society distributed 280,000 printed copies and 20,000 abstracts.[10]

Smith's most outspoken prophecy of Brown's raid came in the form of a public letter to the abolitionist John Thomas on August 27, 1859. He told Thomas and the country that the time had passed for bringing slavery to an end by peaceable means. For years he had published his fears that slavery would go out in blood, and now "these fears have grown into belief." "So debauched are the white people by slavery that there is not virtue enough left in them to put it down." Intelligent and noble black men "have come to despair of the accomplishment of" peaceful abolition "by the white people." "The feeling among the blacks that they must deliver themselves gains strength with fearful rapidity." As a result, an apocalyptic insurrection was at hand: "Intelligent black men in the States and Canada . . . are brought to the conclusion that no resource is left to them but in God and insurrections. For insurrections then we may look any year, any month, any day. A terrible remedy for a terrible wrong! But come it must unless anticipated by repentance and the putting away of the terrible wrong." Smith noted that although the insurgents would be outnumbered, they were acting out God's plan and would therefore be successful. He predicted a day of calamity that included "fire and rape and slaughter." He spoke as one of God's prophets, as a "black" insurgent, and as a principal agent in the scheme. He was warning the country of what was to come unless it repented immediately of its sins.[11]

But his plan—and God's—had gone horribly wrong. The first reports of the raid appeared in the New York newspapers on Sunday, October 18, the same day Brown was captured. The *New York Herald*, which Gerrit read regularly, provided the most-detailed coverage. It quoted liberally from his August letter to John Thomas and suggested that the raiders were "emissaries of the peaceful Gerrit Smith." On October 20 Smith read his name in the headlines, for the *Herald* had reprinted his letter to John Thomas in its entirety, calling it "Gerrit Smith's Manifesto," under a caption that boldly proclaimed: "GERRIT SMITH SUPPLIES THE SINEWS OF WAR." The next day, October 21, the *Herald* reprinted one of Smith's letters to Brown, dated June 4, 1859, that had been found in Brown's possession when captured. "I have done what I could thus far for Kansas, and what I could to keep you at your Kansas work"—"Kansas work" being the conspirators' euphemism for the raid on Harpers Ferry. "You live in our hearts, and our prayer to God is that you may have strength to continue in your Kansas work . . . My wife joins me in affectionate regard to you, dear John, whom we both hold in very high esteem." Smith had enclosed a draft for two hundred dollars with his letter, to keep Brown at his "Kansas work." Although Brown refused to name any of his fellow conspirators, Smith's letters to John Thomas and Brown, along with the draft of his payment to Brown, were enough evidence for the *Herald* to assert that Smith was an "accessory before the fact" and should therefore be arrested and sent to Virginia for trial.[12]

When Smith read the news of the raid and the actual results of his prophecy, he suffered a blow from which he never recovered. Seventeen men had been killed in battle, and Brown and four surviving comrades had been captured and were almost certain to hang. And Smith's own name was intimately linked to these deaths. He was far more sensitive and uncomfortable about the use (and sight) of bloodshed than were his co-conspirators, and more self-critical and introspective. To be sure, he had advocated violence in Kansas and had helped to fund it. But in that instance his violent means had yielded noble ends, for in his mind Kansas had been "saved" from slavery. Now violent action had brought failure, destruction, and death. And as he looked at what he had wrought, something snapped within him. The break affected him both outwardly and inwardly. The outward signs of the blow were noticeable immediately but subsided over time. The internal effects accrued slowly, almost without Gerrit's knowing it; they did not show themselves for some time, but when they did, the change was profound.

To appreciate this transformation fully, it is important to understand Smith's condition leading up to the raid. During the twelve preceding months he had been unusually productive, was wholly absorbed in the scheme, and joyously anticipated the millennium that he felt certain would result from it. An "exaltation of mind" had come over him, according to his doctor: "he never read, studied or wrote with more pleasure. He never had, so he said himself, such confidence in his powers." During this period his son-in-law claimed that he was often "excitable, egotistical, and fond of alluding to his increased intellectual powers," and even "dictatorial, whereas he had heretofore been the opposite." One of Brown's sons who participated in the raid stayed with Gerrit in 1859, and noted that "Smith has his whole soul absorbed in this matter."[13]

During this highly productive period Gerrit wrote his *Religion of Reason,* a series of three published sermons drawn from ideas he had developed during the 1850s. His "new religion" was based solely on individual emotions and instincts, void of all authoritarian doctrines, and represented "the spirit in a heart." He denied that the Bible was the supreme authority and said that individual volition and "reason"—by which he meant instincts and emotions—were one and the same with God's sovereignty. Since "the Bible is the work of man," he argued, it should be used as "the servant of reason . . . Reason must sit in judgment upon the Bible." In other words, one's *instincts* were the sole means of judging and interpreting scripture, much as violence had become the means for making the world sacred. Yet violence was also the hinge on which slavery swung. Perhaps it is no wonder that Smith's religious justification for violence also served as an argument for other Christians' support of slavery.[14]

Smith's new religion accommodated his prophetic inclinations, for if one relied solely on instincts to understand God and interpret scripture, it was easy to confuse one's instinctual urges as messages from God. Smith viewed John Brown as the most pious of men, in large part because Brown was the most vocal and steadfast in his prophecy. He acknowledged as much in April 1859, when he saw Brown for the last time. He was moved to tears by Brown's display of faith and eloquence. Brown and his black comrade Osborne Anderson were at Peterboro finalizing plans for the raid, and at a public meeting in the village Smith stood up and declared: "If I were asked to point out—I will say it in his [Brown's] presence—to point out the man in all this world I think most truly a Christian, I would point to John Brown." The willingness to shed blood in the name of God and his millennium had become the criterion for piety.[15]

But when Smith confronted the detailed accounts of the lives sacrificed at Harpers Ferry, without freeing one slave or coming one step closer to the millennium, his faith began to crumble. The contradiction between his "religion of reason"—which emphasized instincts, embraced prophecy, and justified violence—and his instinctual revulsion against bloodshed produced profound and lasting feelings of guilt. In all his earlier endorsements of violence, he had been spared culpability for actual deaths. In fact he generally preferred not to know about the precise details of the conspiracy, but only wanted to discuss the grand design and intended effects. Now, he could not avoid accounts of the lives lost through a plan for which he was partly responsible. As a close friend put it, Smith became "haunted with the idea that he was culpably responsible for all the lives that have been and will be sacrificed."[16]

Upon realizing that the raid had failed and cost so many lives, Smith began to break down. His crisis of faith collided with his daily rituals and habits. He destroyed all the evidence he could find connecting him to the affair. This alone was a radical departure from his ritual of saving, documenting, and filing every letter he received, and making copies of most of the ones he sent. And it diverged from his tendency to "pour out his whole mind" rather than keep his thoughts and emotions to himself. He became "unceasingly restless" and increasingly erratic in his sleep and eating habits, and expressed great misgivings and worries about his property. The very core of his being, which had always been partly linked to his property, was being jolted as he grappled with the question "Am I a murderer?" Soon he was not eating or sleeping at all, and could not focus his thoughts long enough to pray. When the *New York Herald* reporter interviewed him on October 30, he had not eaten or slept for almost a week. By November 3 his feet were so bloated from lack of sleep that he had to wear moccasins. He could be seen wandering aimlessly about the mansion-house as if in a trance. "At length he became rambling and then incoherent in conversation."[17]

Smith began to hallucinate: he "suspect[ed] his friends" and family "of an intention to betray him"; he was going to be "arrested and carried to Virginia"; "Governor Wise" had "issued a requisition upon Governor Morgan" of New York "for him as a fugitive from justice"; people wanted to "carry him about the country in a cage and submit him to horrible tortures"; demons possessed him and bloated his body; he was going to hell.[18]

On November 7 Gerrit's family, fearing he would take his own life, committed him to the state Asylum for the Insane at Utica. He refused to leave the house, and they had to lie and tell him that a requisition from Governor Wise of Virginia had indeed arrived, and that he must proceed to Virginia. As the carriage traveled the thirty miles northeast to Utica, Gerrit thought he was heading south, to Virginia, to be arrested and tried for his complicity in Brown's raid. The thought was strangely comforting to him.[19]

❧ Governor Henry Wise of Virginia found Gerrit Smith's collapse "very touching." In fact Wise was so moved by Smith's ordeal that after receiving a letter from Smith's nephew describing his breakdown, he wrote back to say that amidst all the "detestable and horrible" aspects of "this Harper's Ferry affair," nothing was "more appealing to our sober senses and reverence for duty as it is defined by law, than the case of Mr. G. Smith." The effects of "these crimes upon [Smith's] mind" went a long way "to prove that he was horrified at the idea that they might—even indirectly—have been ascribed to his influence, action, and intercourse with Brown." Smith's "mental derangement" was itself "most touching" evidence of his innocence. His "earnest and honest" enthusiasm for reform easily led, in the hands of extremists like John Brown, to violence and death. But for Smith, the unintended effects of such zeal had "weighed upon [his] enlightened reason and conscience" and had brought him to his present state. Wise hoped that Smith's breakdown would serve as "a warning to every over-zealous philanthropist, however pure and peaceable" his "motives and means." "Conservatism" must become the "*active* element" in both North and South. Otherwise, the Union would follow the example of Gerrit Smith, and become "a Union of madness."[20]

Ironically, Wise also had great respect for John Brown, despite his assessment of the man as an overzealous extremist. Exercising his authority as governor of Virginia, he chose to prosecute Brown in a Virginia court instead of turning him over to federal authorities (even though Brown had attacked federal property), because he wanted to ensure a speedy trial and prevent Brown and the other prisoners from being lynched.[21] Brown was not "a madman," he said after interviewing him, but "a man of clear head, of courage, fortitude and simple ingenuousness." He had remained "cool, collected and indomitable" throughout his struggle to gain control of the arsenal, and had been humane to his prisoners. True, Brown was "a fanatic, vain and garrulous," but he was also "firm, truthful and intelligent." Wise was particularly impressed by the fact that during the fighting, Brown, "with one son dead by his side, and another shot through, felt the pulse of his dying son with one hand, held his rifle with the other, and commanded his men with the utmost composure."[22]

Wise respected Smith and Brown because they appeared honest, intelligent, and courageous and because they exhibited "simple ingenuousness." But for Wise—and the vast majority of Americans—a prerequisite of respectability was white skin. Wise did not understand the degree to which Brown and Smith had shed their whiteness, and adhered to an understanding of humanity that was based on a black point of view. He and everyone else who defended or apologized for slavery could not conceive of a black man or woman as respectable and honorable. If they had, their own sense of honor and self-respect would have been destroyed, because of their lifelong treatment of respectable people as subhuman beasts. Wise considered Brown's comrades similarly respectable in their fortitude, veracity, and intelligence, "except the free negroes." He had no basis for singling out Brown's black comrades. He had not interviewed them or spent time with them as he had with Brown; he judged them solely on the color of their skin.[23]

Whereas Wise sympathized with Gerrit Smith and refused to indict him—despite glaring evidence of his complicity—he did everything he could to capture and hang Frederick Douglass. Yet the only hard evidence he had linking Douglass to the raid was a brief note, found with Brown's papers, that Douglass had written Brown. It was dated December 7, 1857, two years before the raid, and said simply: "My dear Cpt. Brown, I am very busy at home. Will you Please come up with my son Fred and take a mouthful with me?" For this Douglass was charged with "murder, robbery, and inciting servile insurrection in the State of Virginia." Wise issued requisitions to deliver Douglass to Virginia, and wrote President James Buchanan and the postmaster general for assistance in capturing him. Anti-abolitionist newspapers reprinted Douglass' letter to Brown but omitted the date to make Douglass appear complicit in Brown's raid. The *New York Herald* demanded that Frederick Douglass be arrested with Gerrit Smith as "accessories before the fact."[24]

What Wise and the authorities did not know was that Douglass *had* been actively involved in Brown's scheme. Brown wrote his "Provisional Constitution" during a two-week stay at Douglass' home in Rochester, and Douglass thought so highly of it that he kept an original copy until the end of his life. Brown wanted Douglass to attend the meeting at Chatham, Canada, that approved his "Provisional Constitution," but Douglass, like Smith, chose not to go. They considered themselves more effective in the cause as writers, speakers, and (in Smith's case) philanthropists than as warriors.[25]

Douglass and Smith nevertheless had enormous praise for Brown's plan to invade the South and liberate the slaves. When Brown visited Rochester in April 1859, Douglass was ashamed at the poor reception given him by his fellow Rochester abolitionists. Brown had recently returned from the Kansas territory (again), where he and some of his men had ransacked the homes of two Missouri planters, killed one of them, and liberated their slaves along with other property. When Douglass and Smith heard the news they were elated: "Do you hear the news from Kansas?" Gerrit wrote his wife Nancy. "Our dear John Brown is invading Kansas and pursuing the policy which he intended to pursue *elsewhere*"—meaning Virginia. Douglass responded with similar praise in his newspaper: "A man who will forsake home, family, ease, and security, and in the cause of liberty go forth to spill his blood, if need be, is a man who can look down upon a large part of this world of ours." Brown stood above the mass of humanity, and although his actions "raised a question both of his honesty and his sanity in some quarters," Douglass saw things differently. He "mostly agreed" with Brown's "idea of duty," which bound all humans to interfere with slavery in any way possible and made them complicit "in the guilt of the original crime" if they refused.[26]

Brown desperately wanted Douglass to join him in the raid. Douglass refused only after a lengthy debate with his friend, and primarily because he thought the plan would not work. He learned of the details of Brown's raid on August 20, 1859, shortly before Gerrit Smith foretold the rape, fire, and slaughter that would result from it. Brown had previously "hinted" to Douglass of his idea to attack Harpers Ferry. He had said he could, "with a few resolute men," capture the arsenal and supply himself with arms. "But he never announced his intention to do so," Douglass recalled. He learned of Brown's intentions at an old stone quarry near Chambersburg, Pennsylvania. Douglass had brought with him a black comrade (Shields Green) and some money to aid Brown in what he assumed was the old plan of running slaves north through the Alleghenies. They met with Brown and his white comrade John Kagi, and for the next two days the four men debated Brown's decision to attack Harpers Ferry.[27] "I at once opposed the measure with all the arguments at my command," Douglass recollected. "To me [it] would be fatal to running off slaves . . . and fatal to all engaged." He fully supported Brown in running slaves north, and was prepared to join him in that endeavor. But with this new scheme, Douglass thought his friend "was going into a perfect steel trap, and that once in he would never get out alive." Whether through "discretion" or "cowardice," as Douglass later put it, he refused to participate. Yet at no time did he criticize Brown's motives or militant means: "I am ever ready to write, speak, publish, organize, combine, and even to conspire against Slavery, when there is a reasonable hope for success," he said in defending his decision not to join Brown. "Men who live by robbing their fellow men of their labor and liberty . . . have voluntarily placed themselves beyond the laws of justice and honor, and have become only fitted for companionship with thieves and pirates—the common enemies of God and of all mankind."[28] For Douglass, slaveholders, not the slaves and their allies, were the ones who lacked honor and stood beyond the pale of justice.[29]

Both Brown and Douglass understood the import of their quarry meeting. As Douglass turned to leave, Brown embraced him in a manner "more than friendly" and urged his friend to reconsider: "Come with me, Douglass; I will defend you with my life. I want you for a special purpose. When I strike, the bees will begin to swarm, and I shall want you to help hive them." Brown's trope (as Douglass remembered it) probably referred to "The Beekeeper" in Aesop's fables, which were written from the perspective of slaves, widely read in America, and which Brown knew almost as well as the Bible. The bees in the fable attack and sting their beekeeper after an invader steals some honey and honeycombs. Brown hoped that the slaves would attack their slavekeepers after his own invasion, and he wanted Douglass there to help. But Douglass could not be swayed. Before leaving he asked Shields Green what he had decided to do, and was surprised by his friend's answer: "I b'leve I'll go wid de ole man," Green responded. The four men's parting offers a touching reminder of the colorblind but precarious nature of Brown's small army. Green remained with his two white-skinned comrades, while Douglass began the long trip back to Rochester alone.[30]

When Douglass heard the news of Brown's raid, he was in Philadelphia giving a speech on "Self-Made Men." Given the fact that two of his closest friends had, in one sense, been *too* successful at remaking themselves into black men, his speech was perfectly timed: John Brown had just entered a "perfect steel trap" and was sure to die, and Gerrit Smith was losing his mind. In each case, the loss of health and life stemmed from their ability to empathize with blacks, to see themselves as blacks, and to face the world as though they were black.[31]

In characterizing self-made men, Douglass provided ample justification for his and his comrades' actions, and was cheered after he said: "It is good to think that in Heaven, all injustice, all wrong, all wars, all ignorance, and all vice, will be at an end; but how incomparably better is it, to wage a vigorous war upon these blighting evils and drive them from the present, so that the will of God may be done on earth as in heaven." The Lord's Prayer justified the war on white society. For Douglass, the hallmark of a self-made man was someone like himself—someone who knew the will of God, acted on that prayer, and worked tirelessly to realize a heaven on Earth.[32]

Shortly after his speech Douglass once again found himself a fugitive from justice. Governor Wise requested the sheriff of Philadelphia to arrest him, and he fled to Canada. From there he traveled to England and Scotland for a lecture tour he had planned and organized before Brown's raid. Fourteen years earlier he had also embarked for England and Scotland as a fugitive from justice, and had returned as a free man. This time he would also return to the United States as a free man. The Senate committee inquiring into the Harpers Ferry raid decided to end its investigation without pursuing other accomplices or creating more martyrs, in the hope of assuaging sectional divisiveness, and Governor Wise dropped the charges against Douglass.[33]

Here the parallels between Douglass' two trips to England end. Whereas the earlier trip had laid the foundation for his close alliance and friendship with Gerrit Smith, his acceptance of political abolitionism, and his revolutionary ethos, his second trip in late 1859 was the beginning of the end of his close alliance with Gerrit Smith. Unlike Smith, he never felt remorse over his words or actions during the 1850s, and remained intensely loyal to John Brown. Although many whites considered Brown insane, Douglass (and most other blacks) defended his clarity of thought, calling him one of the greatest of American patriots and heroes: "Are heroism and insanity synonyms in our American dictionary?" Douglass sniped in November 1859. "Heaven help us! when our loftiest types of patriotism, our sublimest historic ideals of philanthropy, come to be treated as evidence of moon-struck madness." People called Brown mad because his actions posed a threat to the barriers separating white supremacy from black degradation. Brown's interracial army struck at the "heart" of those abolitionists who refused to countenance warfare. As Douglass put it, "Brown has attacked slavery with the weapons precisely adapted to bring it to the death. Moral considerations have long since been exhausted upon slaveholders. It is vain to reason with them. One might as well hunt bears with ethics and political economy for weapons . . . Slavery is a system of brute force. It shields itself behind might, rather than right. It must be met with its own weapons." For Douglass, moral laws were written by whites to preserve the order of things. Brown and his comrades sought to undermine that order.[34]

Douglass had even higher praise for Brown in June 1860. He called him "THE man of this nineteenth century," whose life was one of "spotless integrity" and whose name was "covered with a glory so bright and enduring, as to require nothing at our hands to increase or perpetuate it . . . To have been acquainted with John Brown, shared his counsels, enjoyed his confidence, and sympathized with the great objects of his life and death, I esteem as among the highest privileges of my life." For the rest of his life Douglass believed that John Brown's actions were noble and good in the context of the 1850s. But as Brown's war gave way to civil war, Douglass would, like Smith, gradually abandon his revolutionary rhetoric and endorsement of extralegal violence as the means to reform.[35]

❧ James McCune Smith needed no asylum in the wake of Brown's raid, for he exercised more caution than did Frederick Douglass and Gerrit Smith. He was not implicated as a conspirator, and in the months leading up to the raid he betrayed no knowledge of the affair to Gerrit Smith. Like most black Americans, McCune Smith was unwilling to participate actively in the insurrection attempt and thereby suffer the lethal vengeance of white society.[36]

McCune Smith's prudence did not mean that he kept entirely aloof from Brown's raid, however. Indeed, at almost precisely the moment that Gerrit Smith published his letter to John Thomas predicting a massive slave rebellion, McCune Smith issued his own prophetic statement of an impending insurrection. But his announcement was for black eyes only: he published it in the *Weekly Anglo-African*, a small New York City newspaper he had started, which was read almost exclusively by blacks; and the white press never picked up on it. In the July 30, 1859, issue he predicted that a slave insurrection was unavoidable and at hand: "The glorious approach of this triumphal state [a successful insurrection] here in our own land and elsewhere, no power of the tyrant, no chain of the oppressor, no skill or craft of the diplomatist, can stay," he said. "Come it will, and come it must."[37]

Although there is very little evidence pointing to McCune Smith's involvement in Brown's raid, we know that he supported Brown's armed police force long before the attack on Harpers Ferry. He encouraged Brown's style of "collision and bloodshed" in Kansas as well as in "all the slave States" as the most effective way to attain freedom and overturn statutes that barred blacks from settling in free states such as Illinois, Indiana, and Iowa.[38] Like Brown, Douglass, and Gerrit Smith during the 1850s, McCune Smith had little faith in legal action for improving black conditions. Laws were "powerless over the corrupted heart and unbent will of the unpersuaded multitude." In an 1856 essay that appeared in *Frederick Douglass' Paper* a few months after Brown's Pottawatomie massacre, McCune Smith urged blacks to seize their freedom themselves rather than wait for whites to intervene. For inspiration he drew on previous moments in American history when black rebels had taken liberty into their own hands. Denmark Vesey had "suffered gloriously in Charleston," South Carolina, after heading a failed insurrection in 1822. Nat Turner had "turned all Virginia pale with fright" after leading some seventy slaves on a bloody rampage through Southampton County, Virginia, in 1831 that left almost sixty whites and a hundred blacks dead. And in 1851 a few "brave" fugitives at Christiana, Pennsylvania, had defended their freedom against slavecatchers trying to reenslave them by killing one and seriously wounding another. "There is an electric feel about those days" and those men, McCune Smith noted. "The blood stirs, as it ought to stir." The stirring and spilling of blood was the spark that cast a "glorious light on our future":

> Our white brethren cannot understand us unless we speak to them in their own language; they recognize only the philosophy of force. They will never recognize our manhood until we knock them down a time or two; they will then hug us as men and brethren. That holy love of human brotherhood, which fills our hearts and fires our imagination, cannot get through the . . . thick skulls of the Caucasians, unless beaten into them.

Equality and human brotherhood would ultimately be achieved by battling and beating one's enemies. This was the answer to faith in America for McCune Smith, the means for achieving his heaven on Earth.[39]

McCune Smith felt that John Brown's method of violence provided a much-needed antidote to the "inertia" and "apathy" plaguing the abolition movement. Even the slaves in the South were more "vocal and efficient" in shaping white speech and thought, he noted in an April 1858 essay. Southern orators in Congress were being "taunted with their 'African style of oratory,' a style stamped upon them by the negro." A white judge in the South had ruled that a slave had the right to defend himself while being punished if the punishment imperiled his life, and the judge had sentenced an overseer to seven years in prison for murdering a slave who tried to resist punishment. By contrast, judges and juries in New York were letting "white men kill white [and black] men in pastime" with no consequence. If *slaves* were making their mark in Congress and on the bench, "what are we free blacks doing?" McCune Smith wondered. They were too constrained by their adherence to the morality of white society. A white or black man "can no more succeed in politics by cultivating good morals, then he can succeed in oratory by studying algebra." He cited the example of Gerrit Smith, who was as "moral, benevolent," and "good as any black man on the face of the earth—and yet he, a white man though he may be, must fail as a politician." Gerrit Smith and other "black-hearted" men could never succeed in a political arena governed by white laws. Northern reform had moved in the wrong direction: "The reforms which have swept over this land, have been, after all their noise and fury, mere acts of intellection; there has been no heart blood in them, they were brain work all; and intellect does nothing, intellect can do nothing—is a thinker not an actor, and herein lies the secret—why all these reforms ended in talk. They lacked heart and will."[40]

This anti-intellectual stance from one of the foremost intellectuals of the era may seem extraordinary. But it was not unique. Ralph Waldo Emerson, Henry David Thoreau, Thomas Wentworth Higginson, and many other Northern white intellectuals shared similar sentiments. McCune Smith distinguished himself from these other men (with the possible exception of Higginson) in his belief that Northern reformers lacked the black hearts of men like Denmark Vesey, Nat Turner, and John Brown, who acted with their hands and their hearts and their bodies. As Brown himself put it, "Talk was a national institution, but it did not help the slave."[41]

Immediately after Brown's raid, the *Anglo-African Magazine* opened with an anonymous article—which McCune Smith possibly wrote and almost certainly endorsed—that favorably compared John Brown with Nat Turner. Following a brief introduction, the article reprinted Turner's public confession, so that readers could compare "the two methods of Nat Turner and of John Brown." Both Brown and Turner "felt themselves swayed as by some divine, or at least spiritual, impulse." Turner searched "in the air, the earth and the heavens, for [divine] signs which came at last." Brown obeyed spiritual "impulses which he believes to have been fore-ordained" messages from God. Both Brown and Turner acted "cool, calm and heroic in prison and in the prospect of inevitable death." Both "confessed with childlike frankness and simplicity the object they had in view"—emancipation of the slaves. And both provoked "expressions of deep sympathy" from the judges who sentenced them. The main difference between the two men, according to the article, was that Nat Turner's "terrible logic" sought to enfranchise one race by extirpating the other; thus, he and his men murdered every white in their path. Brown believed in the equality of races and was "moved with compassion for tyrants as well as slaves." His object was the immediate end of slavery with as little bloodshed as possible, coupled with the dismantling of racial and social hierarchies. In comparing the two men, the article virtually ignored the fact that Brown was a free white man and Turner a slave. Instead, it emphasized that both men viewed the world from the perspective of oppressed black eyes and hearts. But while one man had sought to invert the color hierarchy, the other had hoped to collapse it.[42]

McCune Smith expressed similar praise and esteem for Brown in an article he wrote for *Frederick Douglass' Paper* following Brown's raid. Most Americans, from Virginians and Republicans to "our abolition friends," dreaded Captain Brown, but with the passage of time this "hero-dread" would become "hero-worship." He knew that Brown's actions struck "the deep chords within us which thrill and yearn towards the old hero!": "So brave and yet so gentle! Such iron nerves surrounding such tender heart! What manner of man is this who suffers his own sons to be shot down by his side without a murmur, and spares the lives of his captives out of regard to their wives and children?" The reason so many people dreaded Brown was the interracial makeup of Brown's insurrection, and this constituted "the most marked instance of hero-dread" of all. Brown and his comrades were no respecters of skin color; they had abolished their whiteness and, from the perspective of white society, threatened the distinction between white and black, good and evil, superior and inferior. How, then, could one tell friend from enemy, American from foreigner, black heart from white?

"Well done John Brown!" McCune Smith cheered. "Well done, seventeen white men and five black men!"[43]

❧ In John Brown's mind the decision to raid Harpers Ferry was a natural extension of his plan to run slaves north through his "Subterranean Pass Way" in the Alleghenies. Despite his failure, he had done his homework and knew the area. He knew that the mountains of Virginia surrounding Harpers Ferry had for years been used as a comparatively safe route to freedom. His friend Harriet Tubman, who helped him plan the raid, frequently used these mountains, which she called the "Great Black Way," to aid escaping slaves in their flight to freedom. He had studied census returns in Jefferson County, where Harpers Ferry was, and had learned a number of important details about the area: the free black population equaled the slave population; slave escapes were so common that an insurance company had been incorporated in the county to insure against slave losses; and a town ordinance had passed a ten o'clock curfew for slaves and free blacks to help curb runaways. Martin Delany, a friend of Brown who had arranged Brown's convention at Chatham, Canada, to approve his "Provisional Constitution," had been born in Jefferson County, knew the area, and encouraged Brown to strike there. Brown also knew that Harpers Ferry bordered Maryland and was about thirty miles south of Pennsylvania, where agitators had achieved notoriety for helping fugitives find their way to freedom. He had read everything he could find on Toussaint L'Ouverture and the Haitian revolution, and treated the accounts of this great revolt as a sort of personal guidebook. As a result of this research, he became convinced that Harpers Ferry was the ideal location for launching his own revolution.[44]

Although the outcome of the raid would undoubtedly have been the same, more blacks might have come to his aid had Brown's timing been better. Almost every analysis of the raid asserts that slaves and free blacks ignored Brown's efforts on their behalf, but some evidence—much of it stemming from oral tradition—suggests that free blacks in Jefferson County and throughout the North and Canada knew of Brown's plans and were prepared to join him. Brown originally scheduled the raid for July 4, 1858 (reflecting his fondness for symbolic value), but the date was postponed when one of his comrades, Hugh Forbes, turned traitor and threatened to expose the raid unless he received money. Harriet Tubman then suggested July 4, 1859, to both Brown and Gerrit Smith "as a good time to 'raise the mill,'" which was the very day that Brown rented the Kennedy Farm to use as his base of operations. According to Franklin Sanborn, Brown planned to strike "about" October 25, 1859, which was nine days after he actually began the attack. He moved up the date by a week because a local woman had spotted black men at the Kennedy Farm, and he thought his intentions might be exposed. Evidently, his attack caught a number of his allies by surprise: Richard Hinton was in nearby Chambersburg "at a black-operated underground railroad post," awaiting word to join Brown. Harriet Tubman was trying to recruit followers. And a group of blacks from Ontario, Canada, were near Detroit, and supposedly on their way to join Brown.[45]

The response of slaves and free blacks in and around Harpers Ferry suggests that they knew of Brown's plan and at least contemplated helping him. Osborne Anderson, one of Brown's black comrades who avoided capture and survived the attack, had felt that a number of free blacks in the area "could . . . be depended upon," and estimated that "there were at least one hundred and fifty actively informed slaves." Anderson said he distributed pikes to roughly thirty of these slaves who came with Brown's men from the plantations, and some early reports of the raid claimed that the "leader, or 'ringleader'" was a man named "Anderson." Eyewitnesses told of blacks in the early hours of the fight being in and around the arsenal with John Brown, and of slaves with spears near the engine house. One of Brown's white hostages recalled that Harpers Ferry "looked like war—negroes armed with pikes, and sentinels with muskets all around." A dozen or so blacks transported arms from the Kennedy Farm to a schoolhouse less than a mile from Harpers Ferry. Other blacks served as messengers for Brown's men and spread the news of the raid to the local community. Still other blacks tore up the local railroad tracks of the Winchester and Potomac Railroad. And A. R. H. Ranson, a local slaveowner and later a Confederate staff officer, recalled that at the time of the raid, his slaves "often turned their eyes on me as I followed behind them in their work—a thing I had never observed before. Their glances made me feel uncomfortable and doubtful—an entirely new sensation in my experience as a slave owner." Brown himself told Governor Wise that he had "promises of ample assistance, and would have received it too" if he had only "put the ball in motion" before federal troops arrived. Although some of these reports may have been exaggerated, they suggest that Brown did try to recruit slaves and free blacks and that these allies did not ignore what was happening. They probably weighed their chances (as Frederick Douglass and Shields Green did) before deciding whether to risk participating.[46]

Slaves throughout the region responded to Brown's capture by burning and destroying property. A local newspaper in Richmond, about a hundred miles south of Jefferson County, reported that "the heavens are illuminated by the lurid glare of burning property." In Jefferson County crops, stockyards, stables, haystacks, tools, and barns were set on fire. One slaveholder in Jefferson County told Governor Wise that Brown's men had instructed the slaves to set fire to stockyards and to destroy property. "They are now carrying it out," he said. "Three stockyards have been burnt in this county alone since their [Brown and his men's] capture and their trial—last night one of mine was burned destroying not less than $2,000 worth of property." Wise sent five hundred more troops to Jefferson County to contain the unrest, but the fires persisted.[47]

Virginia authorities and Northern defenders of slavery sought to assure the country that blacks—both free and slave—ignored Brown and his men. Jefferson County tried to restrict the abolition press from reporting the raid. The Virginian David Strother ("Porte Crayon") covered the raid and trial for *Harper's Weekly*, one of the most popular illustrated weeklies of the day. In both his sketches and writings he assured whites that blacks were incapable of fighting with Brown. Neither threats nor promises could induce "this good-humored, good-fornothing, half-monkey race to join John Brown," Strother wrote in the November 5 issue of *Harper's Weekly*, and his sketches of the raid depicted blacks cowering and shaking with fear. Southerners publicly denied that slaves participated in the raid in any way, and instead spoke of terrified blacks hiding in barns, stables, and hayricks as Brown's men approached. Frederick Douglass, writing from his refuge in Canada, told readers of his newspaper that the South was trying to give the impression that slaves were indifferent to Brown's effort to emancipate them. "This is grossly aside from the truth," Douglass said, and he cited "a prominent actor in the transactions at Harpers Ferry, now at my side," to support his claim. Nevertheless, the Southern perspective held sway, and most accounts of Brown's raid—then and now— ignored blacks' reaction.[48]

Frederick Douglass was right when he said that Brown and his men entered "a perfect steel trap" by attacking Harpers Ferry. But they knew of the risks and were prepared to suffer the consequences of their actions. Douglass, the former slave, knew better than Brown the likelihood of slaves' coming to Brown's aid. Brown knew his success hinged on a coordinated effort between his men and local blacks, but he also had far more confidence and daring than Douglass: "I knew, of course, that the negroes would rally to my standard," he told a jailer after he was captured. "If I had only got the thing fairly started, you Virginians would have seen sights that would have opened your eyes; and I tell you if I was free this moment, and had five hundred negroes around me, I would put these irons on Wise himself."[49]

Unlike Douglass, Brown and his men were prepared to die in their attempt. Harpers Ferry was their Armageddon. John Kagi, Brown's "adjutant-general" in the raid, acknowledged that they would all probably be killed, *"but the result will be worth the sacrifice,"* he emphasized in 1858. They believed their sacrifices would eventually expiate the sins of the nation. Brown likened himself to Samson, who became a martyr by bringing down the Philistines' temple upon himself and his foes: "God has honored but comparatively a very small part of mankind with any possible chance for such mighty & soul satisfying rewards," he wrote Franklin Sanborn in 1858. "I expect to effect a mighty conquest even though it be like the last victory of Sampson." It was an apt comparison: Brown aimed to topple the pillars of slavery upon which the South rested, even if it crushed him in the process. Death was a great social leveler for Brown; it dismantled hierarchies and worldly authority, and it fused this world with the next, the sacred with profane, and black with white. He rejoiced in the face of death, for he believed that he had earned his death by confronting the major problem in his life— slavery.[50]

The prospect of death helped unite Brown's sundry band of seventeen white men and five black men. There is no evidence of any racial conflict among them during the planning or execution of the raid. Osborne Anderson characterized the group this way: "men from widely different parts of the continent met and united into one company, wherein no hateful prejudice dared intrude its ugly self—no ghost of a distinction found space to enter." Shields Green, the fugitive who abandoned Douglass to join Brown, highlights the group's ability to overcome racial barriers. During the battle, he was given a choice between fleeing for safety with his black comrade Osborne Anderson, or following John Brown into the engine house and an almost certain death. Once again Green ignored racial boundaries: he told Anderson almost the same thing he had told Douglass at Chambersburg: "I b'l'eve I'll go down wid de old man." In facing death together, Brown and his men shared a sacred reality that was totally different from the world in which they lived. For them, the new world was literally at hand. Although McCune Smith, Gerrit Smith, and Douglass also shared a vision of a heaven on Earth, their advent did not depend on the likelihood of death in the way it did for Brown and his men.[51]

The happiest moments of Brown's life occurred while he was in prison waiting to die. It was not until October 31, two weeks after his capture, that he wrote his wife and family to apprise them of what had happened, and he emphasized not his woes but his good cheer. He had fought for his life, he said, and then mentioned the deaths of his sons, sons-in-law, and neighbors without remorse or grief. He had several sabre cuts on his head and bayonet stabs in his kidney and sides. He could not hear distinctly, his vision was blurred, he could barely walk, and his white hair was still streaked red from the blood of his wounds. Nevertheless, "under all these terrible calamities, I feel quite cheerful in the assurance that God reigns and will overrule all for his glory and the best possible good. I feel no consciousness of guilt in the matter, nor even mortification on account of my imprisonment and irons; and I feel perfectly sure that very soon no member of my family will feel any possible disposition to 'blush on my account.'" His calamities were but for a moment compared to the "exceeding and eternal weight of glory" that was dawning.[52]

A week later, after being sentenced to hang on December 2, Brown's optimism increased. He was "quite cheerful," he told his wife and family, believing as he did that the "peace of God, which passeth all understanding," ruled in his heart, that his conscience was clear, and that he had not lived "altogether in vain." He felt confident that his violent actions would bring the peace of God; in fact he looked forward to a time when peace on Earth and goodwill toward men would everywhere prevail. He associated his own death with the coming millennium, but stopped short of comparing himself with Christ. Instead, he compared himself with the apostle Paul and felt as happy as Paul had when "*he* lay in prison." Paul thought his own martyred death would advance the cause of Christ, and Brown felt the same way. His entire life had not provided him with one-half the opportunity that this past month had for advancing Christ's message of empathy, and Brown took comfort in his present condition and relished the little time he had left in this world. "I may be very insane," he told a friend four days before his death, in response to the numerous accusations of his insanity. "But if that be so, insanity is like a very pleasant dream to me. I am not in the least degree conscious of my ravings, of my fears, or of any terrible visions whatever; but fancy myself entirely composed, and that my sleep . . . is as sweet as that of a healthy, joyous little infant."[53]

How differently from Gerrit Smith did John Brown handle his afflictions! Unlike his friend, he felt no guilt, and awaited the hour of his death with "great composure of mind & cheerfulness," as he told his family two days before it. None of his family's sacrifices and sufferings were in vain, he assured them. God ruled not only the affairs of "*this* world" but of all worlds, providing a rock under which to set one's feet for all time. "Our *seeming* disaster," Brown wrote his family, would ultimately result in "the most *glorious success*": "So my dear shattered and broken family; be of good cheer and believe and trust in God 'with all your heart and with all your soul.'"[54]

To the moment of his death John Brown—like, apparently, Nat Turner—never wavered in his belief that he had acted out God's will in redeeming the country of sin through bloodshed. At eleven in the morning on December 2 he began his procession to the gallows. As he left his cell, he handed a note to a guard, filled with his idiosyncratic punctuation, that read: "I John Brown am now quite *certain* that the crimes of this *guilty, land: will* never be purged *away*; but with Blood. I had *as I now think: vainly* flattered myself that without *verry much* bloodshed; it might be done." He then said good-bye to his fellow captives. Aaron Stevens, who lay in agony from rifle balls still lodged in his head and neck, bade Brown farewell despite his suffering, adding: "I know you are going to a better land." "I know I am," Brown responded. He climbed onto the open wagon, sat on his oak coffin, and, as the wagon started toward the field where the gallows had been built, looked about him and exclaimed: "This is a beautiful country. I never had the pleasure of seeing it before." An undertaker was with him in the wagon, but no minister, for he wanted nothing to do with a Southern minister who almost certainly endorsed slavery. Only the Virginia militia was allowed in the field, and he now looked intently at its display but said nothing. Upon reaching the gallows he noticed the mayor of Charles Town and the prosecutor who had tried him. "Gentlemen, good-bye," he said without faltering. He stepped firmly onto the gallows, received the hood and noose willingly, and during his ten-minute wait in the dark asked only that he not be detained any longer than was absolutely necessary. His gravestone was ready for him at North Elba, and his God awaited him in heaven.[55]

❦ "I protest," Gerrit Smith screamed into the hall of his ward at the Utica insane asylum. He did not want to be at the hospital, refused to take the marijuana that Dr. John P. Gray, the superintendent of the asylum, had prescribed for him, and would not undress and get into bed as ordered. "Murder," he cried, and accused his servant, who lived with the Smiths at the mansion-house, of trying to kill him. He demanded to be released and "ran about the ward vociferating incoherently." More aides were summoned to contain him. They brought him to Dr. Gray, and he began to calm down. Dr. Gray quietly told him that he was sick, feeble, and insane, and that he must undress and go to bed, at which point Gerrit became furious, shouted "murder" again, and denied his insanity. He finally had to be strapped into bed, and was force-fed a mixture of marijuana and brandy. That first night at the asylum, the medicine did not calm him, and he remained sleepless and incoherent.[56]

Smith suffered from "acute mania" caused by "ill health" and "excessive labor," according to Dr. Gray. Gray was one of the most prominent psychiatrists in the country. As the superintendent at Utica, he instituted such progressive practices as narrative case histories, mind-altering substances, and postmortem examinations. Gray considered mania to be one of the most common forms of insanity. He also believed that insanity was curable; it was a physical ailment rather than a moral or spiritual one, and needed to be treated as such. It was caused

primarily by "physical disturbances" of the body, though it could be
aggravated by "inherited predispositions to disease and by environ-
mental stresses." As an antidote to mania, he typically prescribed
nightly doses of marijuana and brandy, adding small quantities of morphine if the patient remained excited and incoherent. He found this
treatment most effective.[57]

The prescription worked for Gerrit. Although he slept fitfully and
remained "utterly incoherent" for the first four nights, he soon began
to improve. On November 13 morphine was added to his nightly dose,
and the next day he felt better. He recited snatches of hymns, poetry,
and scripture, and though quite feeble, he tried to get out of bed. On
November 15 he took a little stroll by himself, recited entire poems,
and referred to a political meeting he had attended. Although his condition had improved markedly, he continued "to manifest depressing
delusions." He talked about going to hell and said that his wife Nancy
had "justly" left him for his transgressions, but he did not share with
anyone the source of these "delusions." By the end of November he
had gained strength and weight and was sleeping well into the day, and
Dr. Gray decreased the dosage of his medicine. His mind was still "feeble," he sometimes heard "sounds and voices" that no one else did, but
his "delusions" were "less vivid." Nancy joined him at the asylum for
Thanksgiving dinner, and Dr. Gray and his family began inviting him
to meals. On December 29 Gray accompanied Gerrit back to
Peterboro. Smith was still feeble "in mind and body," and Gray ordered him not to travel and "not to read or write or make any brain effort for six months."[58]

When Smith resumed writing in the summer of 1860, he was a
changed man. His breakdown and "delusions" of going to hell were the
outward manifestations of an inner rupture. This breakage stemmed
from his profound guilt over his participation in the Harpers Ferry raid
and, more generally, from his guilt over suspending his commitment to
Christian pacifism. One of the first letters he wrote in 1860 was to
Charles Sumner, who had, like Smith, just recovered from a severe illness linked to antislavery violence—Preston Brooks's attack on him in
1856. "I have gone through a sickness not as protracted as yours—but
more prostrating," Smith told Sumner. "Much of the year 1859 is a
black dream to me; and much of it hazy and uncertain." Smith had considered 1859 to be a particularly good year when he was living it; he

had felt sure that he and his comrades were closing the gap between blacks and whites, slaves and citizens, the present reality and their shared vision of America. Now the very idea of blackness seemed repulsive.[59]

Two weeks later he explicitly condemned the use of violence. "The shedding of blood is the poorest of all remedies for wrongs," he told Samuel Joseph May.[60] Violence had long served as a bridge connecting black and white, this world and the next. It had brought him closer to blacks and to his vision of a sin-free society. Kansas had been "saved" as a result of violence, as he often said. And the racial barriers separating himself from Douglass, McCune Smith, and other blacks seemed to dissolve when he became a revolutionary. Violence had been acceptable because it seemed to work. Brown's raid represented the first time that violent means had failed to achieve the desired ends. The guilt Smith suffered as a result of this failure now distanced him from blacks and from his sacred society. Although violence served as a short-term bridge, it ultimately became a barrier in his efforts to build a pluralist society and identify closely with African Americans.

The Harpers Ferry raid permanently affected Smith's worldview and reform visions. He was the only conspirator who, in the aftermath of the raid, considered it wrong and experienced profound guilt over his participation in it. He blamed his transgression of violence on two major sources: his close association with blacks and his belief in prophecy and a sacred vision of America. He never again identified so closely with blacks. He became considerably more moderate in his reform efforts. And for the rest of his life he denied his complicity in the Harpers Ferry raid. Before the Civil War officially began, he had become a casualty of his own inner war.[61]

Smith began denying his participation in Brown's raid—and thus denying his own history—immediately after recovering from his breakdown. In May 1860 he told William Goodell that although his "wildness" was "now gone," he had to "avoid looking back upon the year 1859" because it was "full of darkness to my eye" and "anguish to my heart." A few months later he wholly distanced himself from John Brown's violent methods. Although he agreed that Brown had been "sincere and self-sacrificing" in seeking to put weapons into the hands of the slaves, he said his "own ethics and education" were such that he "had rather live and die in slavery than shed blood to escape from it."

In an important sense, he *had* lived and died in bondage to his sin of violence. By denying his revolutionary past and not confessing his complicity in Brown's raid, he could neither free himself from his "black
dream" nor attain redemption from his sin. In 1872 Smith's co-
conspirator Franklin Sanborn wanted to publish a history of Brown's
raid and asked Smith "why the whole truth should not now be told."
Because, Smith responded, the truth threatened to unhinge him: "My
brain has continued to the present time to be sensitive in this John
Brown matter." Sanborn's proposition had given him "another sleepless turn," and "in every such turn I fear a recurrence of my insanity."[62]

Smith also renounced his future heaven on Earth. After recovering
from his breakdown he excoriated the belief in prophecy and miracles,
and the idea that God could enter and alter the affairs of the world. On
April 14, 1861, two days after Confederate guns opened fire on Fort
Sumter, he delivered a discourse in Peterboro in which he attacked all
supernatural acts in the Bible (especially the Old Testament) and
placed his faith instead on "the laws of Nature." Even creation, he said,
was not a miracle. He tried to reconcile Darwin's theory of "the origin
of species by natural selection" with the advent of man in the Bible by
saying that God "produced man from the original and eternal laws of
nature" rather than from the "absurdly" miraculous account in Gene-
sis. By the end of the war he was lamenting "how much the world has
lost by the deifying of Christ! . . . by the lifting of [Christ] up out of
manhood into Godhood, he comparatively ceases to be an example" to
humans. Smith was ridiculed by the mainstream press for his "materi-
alist" views and renunciation of most of the Bible. And he achieved a
cult following among some materialists and atheists. He stopped short
of disbelieving in God entirely. He simply kept him at arm's length.[63]

Smith did not oppose the war. He endorsed the war measures of the
Lincoln administration, but for reasons far different from his embrace
of John Brown's war. He had already fought and lost his own private
holy war, and his millennial dreams had been shattered. Now he simply
wanted to preserve an existing Union and end slavery in the process.
On February 6, 1861, while delegates from six southern states con-
vened at Montgomery, Alabama, to form the Confederacy, Smith
agreed to let states secede without resorting to "guns and swords" as
long as they left peacefully. But if the Confederacy drew blood first,
then retaliation by force was justified. At the end of April he organized

and spoke at a "war meeting" in Peterboro. He admitted that he was so averse to bloodshed that if he were a slave, he would prefer slavery to killing his master. He assembled the meeting as "an American" taking his stand "on the side of the Government" rather than on the side of rebellion. And he invoked John Quincy Adams to say that a war Congress (or president) had the right to enact a law abolishing American slavery. Two years earlier he had endorsed bloodshed as part of a revolutionary police state. Now he advocated it to put down a revolutionary government.[64]

Smith never renounced his opposition to slavery. But stopping the rebellion and preserving the Union now took precedence over ending slavery. "If a man cannot be a patriot whilst yet an abolitionist, he should cease to be an abolitionist," he said in an 1863 speech. "One should renounce his abolition if it at all hinders him from going for his country." The following year he said much the same thing to Elizabeth Cady Stanton: "I love the anti-slavery cause. Nevertheless, I would have the rebellion put down at whatever necessary expense to that cause." These were the views of Lincoln and the majority of Northern whites who opposed slavery. Despite his considerable backsliding, Smith was still part of the antislavery mainstream. But he was a long way from being at the forefront of reform.[65]

Smith came to believe that colonizing blacks would be the most effective way to end the problem of slavery in a deeply racist society. "In the right time and circumstances Colonization is a good thing. But it is not an adequate cure for the ills we are now suffering," he wrote Thaddeus Stevens in a December 1861 broadside. He wanted blacks to participate in the war effort, but also hoped they would follow their "nature" and find their own country once the war was over and the time was ripe. His advocacy of colonization was a far cry from his founding of North Elba, which represented an interracial form of colonization within the country. With his sacred vision of America shattered, so too were his hopes for a pluralist society.[66]

For the first time in his life, Smith began publicly to accept the prevailing belief among whites that blacks were innately inferior and thus incapable of attaining the kind of social rank and responsibility that whites enjoyed. In December 1861 he admitted to John Gurley in a broadside that in his "judgment, were the laws of nature allowed free play, the dark-skinned races would find their homes within and the

light-skinned races without the tropics." Four months later he said virtually the same thing to Postmaster General Montgomery Blair. Blair
was seeking government subsidies for black colonization in the "tropics" of Central America. Smith thought that the government should
not officially sponsor colonization, for such action would single out
blacks and depart from the principle that all Americans should be equal
in the eyes of the law. The government was not to act on these "theories" that "the blacks would move toward and the whites away from the
Equator," because "its one work [was] to protect those who for the
time being are its subjects." Blacks would soon migrate to the tropics
on their own, without government pressure, he assumed. In other
words, forced colonization was not essential for the achievement of an
all-white America. He also began to replace his long-held belief that
the government's role was to "protect" its subjects for one stipulating
that "the duty of Government [is] to control its subjects." Governmen-
tal control over its subjects opened the way for civil laws that accommodated natural laws and encouraged (but did not require) colonization, migration, and segregation.[67]

Smith's attitude toward the use of black troops highlights his considerable retrogression after Harpers Ferry. He urged black participation
in the war as early as August 1861, but for tactical reasons as much as
for egalitarian ones. "The party that gets the blacks to fight for it gets
the victory," he asserted. Although he believed that arming blacks
would facilitate the cause of equal rights, he also compared blacks (and
Indians) to the devil, suggesting that putting "down a base, brutal,
abominable, causeless, accursed Rebellion" required the use of dark-
skinned, base, and brutal savages: "Common-sense teaches us that we
should get the negro to help us if we can; and the Indian also if we can;
and the devil himself if we can. I would that we could succeed in getting our harness upon his back and in making him work for us. It
would, by the way, be doing a great favor to the old rascal to make him
serve a good cause once in his life." As a revolutionary Smith had believed that one needed to fight savagery with savage means. Now he
distinguished himself and other whites from blacks, Indians, and devils.
They were the savage ones, not whites. And they needed to be controlled. Smith invoked the slave metaphor of a domesticated beast; he
sought to harness blacks, Indians, and the devil to make them "work
for us."[68]

These were shocking words, especially for a man who, with John Brown, had stood apart from almost every other white reformer on record in the quest to break down racial barriers and resolve cultural dichotomies. No less shocking was his moderate position on Reconstruction. Initially he refused to support the Thirteenth Amendment because he felt it would detract from the war effort, but he eventually endorsed it. Similarly, he initially advocated literacy as a condition of voting for both blacks and whites, and then later accepted universal black suffrage. Throughout Reconstruction he sought amnesty for rebels and used his wealth to help redeem white Southerners. Perhaps the act that marks the greatest plunge from his militancy in the 1840s and 1850s occurred in 1867, when he alienated himself from most abolitionists by signing Jefferson Davis' bail bond—along with Horace Greeley and Cornelius Vanderbilt.[69] His collaboration with these two racist and power-hungry leaders in a project to free and forgive the former Confederate president is telling: it suggests that he could be as kind and generous to his enemies as he was hard on himself. He could forgive Jefferson Davis for leading a rebel nation, conceived in slavery, in a war for independence. Yet he could not forgive himself for financing a rebel army, conceived in racial equality, in a scheme to liberate slaves. Instead of forgiving himself, he assuaged his guilt about using violence by embracing racism. In this sense he was no different from most of his countrymen[70]

Even during the 1850s, Smith periodically experienced guilt about his sanction of violence. It was not chronic, and he did not publicize it; but when he did express his guilt, he exposed his private fears about identifying with blacks. The most vivid statement of his distress over violent means appeared in the form of a short story. It is his only work of fiction and it is highly revealing, for it uncovers Smith's innermost thoughts regarding his close identification with blacks and John Brown, and his embrace of violence.

The story is dated November 15, 1851, so it was written during the period when Smith had begun endorsing violence more than ever before. John Brown had been at North Elba for two years, he and Smith had become "kindred spirits," and Brown had already shared with Smith his plan to establish a "Subterranean Pass Way" in the Alleghenies for freeing slaves. In mid-October 1851, one month before he wrote the story, Smith had urged free blacks to "have the manliness and courage 'stand for their life.'" If they did, "the whites will stand by them." The principle of resistance—whether "with weapons" or not, "active or passive"—was the most effective way to abolish slavery and racial oppression. Publicly, Smith felt sure of this.[71]

Privately, he had serious reservations about violent means. His story, titled "A Story: The Ruinous Visit to Monkeyville," attests to these reservations. It is about a nine-year-old boy named John Brown, who could hear but could not speak.[72] His family "all prayed very earnestly that God would give him the faculty of speech." "God heard their prayers, and on a pleasant" morning in May, "at the breakfast table, John, to the surprise and joy of all around him, said his first words: 'Mother, I love you.'

"The whole family burst into tears, and joined in prayer, and thanked God for having given power to little John to speak." His speech was "deliberate and beautiful." People came from all around "to witness the wonderful goodness of God to little John." They predicted that he would some day "make a great preacher," "a great statesman," or "a great lawyer. Never was there a happier family than that of which John Brown was a member. All that had been lacking to fill up the measure of their happiness was that little John should be able to speak what he thought and what he felt; and now, through the kindness of the Lord, this was no longer lacking.

"But alas, much disappointment and especially sorrow visited this happy family."

Little John had aunts and uncles who lived "a half-dozen miles" away in the village of Monkeyville, and John spent a few weeks there with his relatives. There also lived in Monkeyville "a set of rude, igno-rant, low-bred boys," who had "a dialect or language peculiar to them-selves." They "thought it very smart to say 'datch' for 'that,'" for in-stance, and "'nishe' for 'nice.'" John played with these "miserable boys," and "such is the speedy and pernicious effect of evil communica-tions" that he soon "caught the strange and disgusting speech of these Monkeyville boys." When his parents learned of the travesty, they rushed over to Monkeyville to take him home. But the damage had been done. As a result of his new habit, "his head and his heart began to sympathize with his crooked speech. His thoughts and affections be-came crooked also." He "misstated facts," "told untruths," "scarcely told" or learned "anything correctly." "In less than ten years from the time he visited Monkeyville, he was a ruined boy."

John Brown became a "great liar" at age twelve, a "notorious thief" by fifteen, and at eighteen he murdered a man. "He continued his Monkeyville dialect to the last. In the court where he was tried, he said to the grand jury: I am not kilty." He was sentenced to die, and when he was on the "gallows" and was told that "he had come to a bad end, he replied, 'I hash come to the gallows at lasht.'

"A stone was put upon his grave, on which were inscribed these words:

> Here lies the wicked boy,
> Whose lying and stealing and murdering,
> All began in his Monkeyville talk.
> May his fate be a warning
> to others——"

The story ends with an invocation: "Remember, Reader, is it not better never to have a voice, than to misuse it, as John Brown did? Remember, Reader, is it not better to have your voice taken away from you, than to have it left to you, and so impaired by you?"

"The Ruinous Visit to Monkeyville" is a remarkable parable of Gerrit Smith's abolitionism, his relationship to John Brown, his friendship and identification with blacks, and his embrace of violence. Smith projected himself—his feelings, fears, and forebodings—onto John Brown to form his fictive character. Much like the fictive (and the real) John Brown, Smith received the gift of abolitionist speech from God; by turning inward and embracing sacred self-sovereignty, he (and Brown) became public speakers in the abolitionist cause. Both Gerrit Smith and the fictive John Brown had thoughts as young men of becoming great preachers, great lawyers, and great statesmen. Both loved their mothers. And both were corrupted. The fictive John Brown visited Monkeyville, associated with the "rude, ignorant, low-bred boys" there, and acquired their "strange and disgusting speech." He began to talk their talk, and soon was lying, stealing, and killing. The real John Brown (from Gerrit's point of view) went to North Elba, settled among blacks, and soon acquired his own strange and disgusting speech: he talked of shedding blood and killing. As for Gerrit, he was the architect of North Elba and of his story. He had founded the "colored colony," or "Timbucto," as he and Brown called it, much as he had created "Monkeyville." And in befriending blacks, he had associated with the wrong crowd, and had acquired the strange and disgusting speech of violence.

As a parable, Smith's story is eerily prophetic. The fictive John Brown goes to Monkeyville, acquires the strange and disgusting speech of the inhabitants there, and soon his "head and his heart" begin to "sympathize with his crooked speech." Nine years later he commits murder, enters a plea of "not kilty," and denies any wrongdoing. He is hanged on the gallows and seems to enjoy, even revel, in his death: "I has come to the gallows at lasht," he says. The real John Brown goes to North Elba and makes a clean break from white laws and society. He acquires the language and thought of the black settlers, and his head and his heart become black, meaning that he views the world from a black perspective. He employs the speech of violence and insurrection, and in eight years (rather than nine) he commits murder (among other crimes). Like the fictive John Brown, he enters a plea of "not guilty" and feels no remorse for his actions. Like his fictive counterpart, he is hanged from the gallows and experiences greater happiness in his death than ever before. And similarly to the fictive boy, a tombstone is put upon his grave, with an epitaph that explains why he died. Tragically, the "art" of Smith's story, rather than his vision of a new age, became the reality.

The invocation at the end of the story is Smith's warning to himself not to misuse his public voice, not to endorse the violent means of John Brown. He is telling himself that it would be better not to speak out against slavery at all than to adulterate abolitionism by encouraging violence. But he does not listen to his own warnings. He found violent means to be effective in freeing slaves, and he was becoming more and more concerned with ends rather than means. Although he never lost his abolition voice, he lost his black heart, his vision of a heaven on Earth, and himself as a Radical Abolitionist. After John Brown died, he retreated to the comparative safety of his white identity.

While Smith's story as a whole is a parable, Monkeyville itself can be seen as a rich symbol—a symbol that means many things but in general conveys the deep recesses of Smith's racism, or what might be termed his "heart of darkness." Monkeyville symbolized for Smith the dark side of identifying with black culture and consciousness. There was a rife association in antebellum America of blacks with monkeys. The association accommodated beliefs in innate black inferiority, in heightened sexual passions among blacks, and in proslavery thought in general. A related view linked apes and blacks with devils and sin. But blacks had their own association with monkeys: The rebellious trickster monkey, or "signifying monkey," was a potent figure in black folklore.[73] Smith combined these black and white views. He integrated the white representations of blacks as apes and devils with the black association of the rebellious trickster monkey. It is in this sense that Monkeyville signified black culture and consciousness. Little John Brown's visit to Monkeyville pointed to Smith's (and Brown's) black identification and to their subsequent acts of rebellious and "trickster" methods to combat slavery. Smith presented that identification as depraved, sinful, and savage in his story. Only by identifying with the "Monkeyville boys" and by adopting their speech, manners, and customs did Smith and Brown abandon peaceful efforts to end slavery.

"The Ruinous Visit to Monkeyville" suggests that Smith privately feared his identification with blacks and corruption from his friendship with John Brown. He had often expressed his desire to become a black man, had told Frederick Douglass a year earlier that he had "identified" himself and "made" himself a "colored man" with Douglass.[74] But he privately worried that if he "made" himself into a "colored man," he would acquire the dialect and speech of these "rude, ignorant, low-bred" people. He had encouraged John Brown to settle at "Timbucto," and now Brown's speech was punctuated with talk of insurrection and bloodshed. There is thus great significance in the fact that Smith shared in his correspondence with McCune Smith and Douglass the "dialect" of Robert Burns's poetry. For Smith, a close link existed between words and actions, between how words sounded and how people acted: "Evil-speaking and evil-doing go together," he acknowledged after John Brown's death; "profane, polluting, shameless words" were evidence of "bad character." Even the wrong dialect led to evil actions and associations.[75]

It is also significant that the fictive John Brown was a nine-year-old boy. By casting John Brown as a boy and not a man, Smith underscores the crisis of manhood that he and his comrades faced. In this sense, the story suggests that Smith searched into the heart of manhood and found darkness, death, and destruction. In the white mind blacks were childlike and savage and unable to control the passions of their hearts. The fictive boy's rejection of authority mirrors Brown's and Smith's own rejection of white laws and authority. The story reveals Smith's private fears and worries about making himself into a black man and acquiring a black heart.[76]

There is also a historical reason why Smith cast his protagonist as a nine-year-old boy. Gerrit's only son, Greene Smith, was nine years old at the time and a student at Theodore Dwight Weld's school at Belleville, New Jersey. Gerrit probably wrote his story while visiting Greene at his school, which was known as the "Weld Institute." He stayed at the nearby South Orange, New Jersey, Water Cure, and scribbled the location, "South Orange, New Jersey," at the bottom of the story along with the date.[77]

Both Smith and Weld considered Greene Smith a problem child. A few months after Gerrit's visit to the school, Weld wrote him to say that Greene "has passed gravely through two *character-casting crises.*" The first had to do with the "polluting contact of the Peterboro boys," which "was fermenting within him and breaking out upon the surface in those sad personal experiences which filled us all with so much concern." Weld did not explain the precise nature of this "polluting contact," but it may have concerned Greene's habit of telling tall tales and exaggerating facts. Weld was much more specific in describing the second crisis of Greene's character: "the death struggle with *monkeyishness,*" including "groveling" and "buffoonery." Greene's "monkey talk" stemmed from his "passion" for "making himself a center of attraction," and it included "grimaces," "long-lipped words," and "cheap methods of exciting a laugh." According to Weld, Greene was acting like a monkey, and his description of the boy's behavior closely paralleled antiblack stereotypes. Greene's "monkey talk" resembled that of a blackface minstrel singer or stage performer who stood at the center of attention and caricatured black accents, grimaces, and "long-lipped words."[78]

Gerrit projected his anxieties about Greene's behavior into his "Monkeyville" story. He translated the "Peterboro boys" who "polluted" Greene Smith into "Monkeyville boys" who "polluted" little John Brown; and he gave these "Monkeyville boys" a decidedly racial cast. They were "rude, ignorant, and low-bred," and they "had a dialect or language peculiar to themselves." In one sense, Greene's crisis of character, as Weld relayed it to Gerrit, was in becoming black—in acting out white stereotypes of black behavior. In creating his fictive character, Gerrit projected his guilt about using violence onto John Brown, and his fears about his black identification onto his son, and he fused these two projections in creating the nine-year-old John Brown in his story.

In life Greene Smith and not John Brown bore the brunt of Gerrit's guilt over his use of violent means to end slavery. Gerrit projected his guilt onto his son, resulting in his treatment of Greene as a depraved criminal. A few months after writing the "Monkeyville" story, Gerrit worried that his son was being violent to the other students. "Never hurt any of your school fellows," he admonished Greene. "Never kick, bite or scratch them. You know how offensive and horrid is all such brutality in the eyes of your parents. Love, love, love—love all and love continually." His letters to Greene became increasingly censorious. "My dear son: I have not heard from you since I wrote you respecting your cruel and brutal treatment of little Willie," he accused Greene in November 1852. Whatever brutality his son had committed was never made clear. He simply hoped that "our Heavenly Father has brought you to repentance and atonement for it," and then he abruptly ended his letter with the words: "In haste and co. . . . your aff. father." When Greene followed his father's example in closing his own letter, he was harshly rebuked: "I see that you are in the practice of writing on your letters, 'In haste and co. . . ,'" Gerrit wrote him in 1853. "It is a foolish and vulgar practice. Give it up." In Gerrit's mind, his son was "wicked" and under the influence of "Satan." What made this incessant criticism especially painful for Greene was the fact that he could not read his father's handwriting, and thus had to listen to Theodore Weld recite Gerrit's letters to him, often in front of his classmates. To avoid such humiliation, Greene eventually told Weld that he could read his father's letters "with ease," and thus did not need them recited. Thereafter, when he received a letter from his father, he would stuff it in his pocket, unopened, and leave it there for days.[79]

Throughout the 1850s Gerrit projected his deep-seated insecurities about his reform efforts onto his son. In February 1859, while Gerrit was at work on his "new religion" and preparing for Brown's raid and the new age that would result from it, he wrote a poem about Greene called "The Reasonable Boy." The title is misleading, however, for the poem and its refrain concern Gerrit's fears that Greene was "not a reasonable boy." On April 14, 1859, Greene's seventeenth birthday, Gerrit wrote his son a birthday poem, in which he fretted about Greene's character and behavior. He worried that Greene would "prove" "false to truth," and would "give the rein to passions wild," despite "those who'd die to save their child":

> The way of vice will you then choose
> And let mad feeling sway your will?
> Not e'en the glass of death refuse,
> Nor word which helps that glass to kill?

The poem concerned Gerrit's fears that Greene was falling sway to his wild passions and would eventually drown himself in alcohol. Little did he realize that his poem had as much to do with himself as with his son. His own "vice" and "mad feeling" about ending slavery through bloodshed were intoxicating him; and he had not been able to refuse "the glass of death" that John Brown had offered him.[80]

Gerrit's fears, anxieties, and guilt over his use of violence and black identification in the 1850s betray the degree to which he had unwittingly absorbed prevailing beliefs about race and reform. He harbored deep-seated doubts over the possibility of racial equality, but he was able to keep them mostly hidden. They are revealed not in his correspondence and friendship with his black friends, nor in his public speeches and broadsides, but in his private writings: in his "Monkeyville" story, his poetry, and his letters to his son. The Harpers Ferry raid broke down the walls that had long kept those fears and anxieties hidden.

As for Greene Smith, he would indeed fulfill Gerrit's premonitions of him. By the outbreak of the Civil War he was a heavy drinker, a gambler, and cheated at cards as a way to help fund his lavish lifestyle and other "wild" habits. He spent most of the war years as a student in England, pretending to study but mostly living the life of a debauched aristocrat. He did not fight in the war, and never appeared much interested in abolition or the cause of the slave. Sometime after the war he seems to have at least curtailed his drinking. He became passionate about aviculture and acquired an elaborate aviary that housed a diverse assortment of rare and exotic wild birds. In one sense, then, while the father devoted his career to human liberation of all stripes, the son devoted his to containment and captivity. Perhaps the son was responding to the father's fear of a boundless world with no restraint and dominion, where one's spirit could soar toward the heavens.[81]

❧ "Dear Friend, Your handwriting was a most welcome sight to my wife and myself. We thank God for it," James McCune Smith wrote Gerrit on June 21, 1860. He was overjoyed to hear that Gerrit had recovered and was able to write again. He had been very concerned about Gerrit's health and well-being, had written a short article honoring the "Smith Family," and told Gerrit to look for it in the next issue of the *Anglo-African Magazine*. "I trust [it] will interest and amuse you and yours." McCune Smith had no inkling of Gerrit's change of heart regarding their shared vision of America and blacks' place in it. He had no way of knowing that Gerrit blamed *him* and other black comrades for his transgression to violence and breakdown.[82]

But McCune Smith would soon notice the change in Gerrit and would become quite frustrated with his friend's behavior. In September 1860 Gerrit visited New York but made no effort to see him and did not even tell him he was in town. McCune Smith had eagerly looked forward to communing with Gerrit, and when he found out about his visit, he was hurt and disappointed:

> I think you might have dropped me a note stating that you were in town; for you must know that it would have given me the greatest pleasure to have walked any distance to see and shake hands with you again. And there are so many things that I would rejoicingly have talked over with you and others sadly. Now please let it be understood in [the] future that I shall consider it almost unfriendly if you ever come to our city and fail to drop me a line to inform me of your whereabouts.

It was the first time in over a decade that Gerrit had visited New York without calling on McCune Smith or at least informing him of his visit.[83]

The following month Gerrit virtually ignored a New York State black suffrage drive that McCune Smith was organizing. The two men had together spearheaded the black suffrage drive in 1846. McCune

Smith asked Gerrit for $300 to support the new effort, and was hopeful that his friend would donate at least that amount. But Gerrit contributed only $130, gave no explanation for why he did not give more, and made no effort to distribute tracts or deliver speeches to support the campaign.[84]

In 1861 their relationship came to a head, and McCune Smith lashed out at Gerrit for abandoning the abolition cause. In August 1861, one month after the first battle of Bull Run, he told Gerrit that "a sort of Bull's Run phrenzy seems to have seized on you inasmuch as you are fleeing from a half won field." Like the Union soldiers who fled panic-stricken back to Washington after almost defeating Confederate troops at Manassas Junction, Gerrit was abandoning the cause of freedom when victory seemed near. He had recently voiced his support of the Lincoln administration in a pamphlet titled *No Terms with Traitors: The Submission of the Rebels the Sole Condition of Peace.* But he all but ignored the issue of emancipation, and McCune Smith was outraged: "I charge you . . . with being unequal to the exigency of the hour. After lives spent in signal devotion to the cause of the slave you fairly abandon that cause in the hour of its trial and triumph." Gerrit was no better than the "Garrison party," which had canceled its annual May meeting after concluding that antislavery would sweep the North. As Gerrit well knew, McCune Smith had long attacked Garrisonians for their white paternalistic attitude toward blacks. McCune Smith was telling him that he had suddenly descended to their level.[85]

Like a stern teacher rebuking his student, McCune Smith spelled out precisely what he expected of Gerrit in this hour of exigency. "First," the whole nation wanted to know "what shall we do to be Saved?" "Second," he reminded Gerrit of the great truth they had shared together for over twenty years: "The only salvation of this nation is *Immediate Emancipation.*" "Third," it was the responsibility of the people to "ordain and carry out *Immediate Emancipation.*" "Fourth: You are the man to convince the people of this great truth by shouting it in their ears throughout the land by voice and pen." He suggested that Gerrit rewrite his pamphlet, titling it "Slavery the sole cause, Emancipation the sole remedy for the Rebellion." And he wanted Gerrit to know that his criticisms were meant as a friendly push to bring him back to his former level of radicalism, for he closed with the words "Sincerely, your loving friend."[86]

Gerrit responded by not responding. Following this letter there was a lapse in their correspondence of almost three years, their longest silence by far in over fifteen years. When they did resume writing in early 1864, McCune was suffering from an "enlarged heart" and an "overworked nervous system" that compelled him to be quiet when there "was so much to do." He had been confined to his house for three months, he told Gerrit in an April 1864 letter, and because of his tired heart he slept most of the day. Gerrit was suffering from the opposite problem of "sleeplessness"; perhaps he feared having more of his "black dreams." McCune Smith tried to make light of the situation; he offered to give Gerrit six hours per day of his own sleep in exchange for the same amount of Gerrit's wakefulness. He "had been thinking much" of Gerrit "of late," and hoped his letter would help him sleep. McCune Smith was reaching out, hoping to resume their close friendship and connectedness. Again Gerrit did not respond. Ten months later, in February 1865, McCune Smith again rebuked him, for endorsing (along with Garrison) a plan of forced labor for freedmen and women that General Nathaniel Banks had implemented in Louisiana. McCune Smith likened the plan to serfdom and expressed his sorrow over Gerrit's approval of Banks's labor system. So long as Gerrit and Garrisonians endorsed the "serfdom of Banks's kind," McCune Smith said, he would never see "Negro Emancipation," even if he had "a century of life" before him. But he did not have even a year of life before him. He died nine months later at the age of fifty-two, of a failed heart.[87]

🥨 Frederick Douglass never confronted Gerrit over his backsliding in the way that James McCune Smith did. The two men continued to correspond until Gerrit's death in 1874, and their letters remained cordial, though much less frequent than they had been during the 1850s. They no longer relied on each other for emotional support, as McCune Smith sought to do until the end. And their shared passion for a radically new America no longer infused their letters. Before Brown's raid the two men had been close friends and allies; after, respectful colleagues. Their correspondence reveals their waning friendship and the growing chasm separating black from white. In 1862 Douglass gently chided Gerrit for his "silence of late" in their friendship. Over the next decade they saw each other less and less, and in 1871 Smith tried to place the burden of his estrangement from blacks on Douglass by asking him, "Are you never coming to see me again?" Two years later Smith acknowledged the racial gulf separating them in praising one of Douglass' speeches. He referred to "*your* oppressed people," and told Douglass that "the same speech from a white man would have been far less influential upon *your* [black] hearers." Gone were Smith's empathy with blacks, his efforts to collapse racial barriers, and his quest to see himself as one of the "oppressed people." Douglass captured the nature of their changed relationship in a line he added to McCune Smith's letter to Gerrit in January 1864. He was staying at McCune Smith's home in New York, and at the bottom of the letter Douglass wrote: "I can only join in loving remembrances." It was the "remembrances" more than anything else that he and Gerrit still shared, the memories of Radical Political Abolitionism, and their shared vision of a pluralist America that few others were able even to imagine.[88]

Douglass experienced his own retreat from a revolutionary ethos. Like Gerrit Smith, he had experienced firsthand the effects of Brown's apocalyptic war. He gradually came to realize that the costs of Brown's war, and especially of the Civil War, were enormous. While the war brought a legal end to slavery, the glorious new age without racism and sin was nowhere in sight. As a result, Douglass' vision of perfection and a heaven on Earth increasingly seemed to him a sentimental illusion. After the war he became, like Smith, more secular in his worldview, and no longer believed that God could change the world or affect the laws of nature. "All the prayers of Christendom cannot stop the force of a single bullet, divert arsenic of its poison, or suspend any law of nature," he concluded in 1884.[89]

Secession and the war allowed Douglass to seek reform through existing social structures and institutions. He became a Republican, encouraged Lincoln and his party to turn the war into an abolition war, helped to recruit black soldiers, and tried to reconcile blacks to the fact that their pay would be about 50 percent less than that of white troops. There was no more talk of insurrection and murder. The Radical Abolition party folded after Lincoln's election and secession. And in August 1863, after sixteen years as an editor, Douglass abandoned his radical and often militant newspaper. (*Douglass' Monthly* came out in 1858, and replaced *Frederick Douglass' Paper* in 1860.) The reason he gave was that he "was going South to assist Adjutant General [Lorenzo] Thomas in the organization of colored troops." But he never went. He had been promised a commission by the War Department, but it did not come through. With his newspaper now gone, Douglass increasingly published in the mainstream press, which endorsed the moderate positions he took toward reform. In this sense he followed the path of many other reformers. As the historian John Thomas notes, "The antislavery cause during the secession crisis and throughout the Civil War offered reformers an escape from alienation by providing a new identity with the very political institutions which they had so vigorously assailed." By the end of the war, Douglass was more of an insider than he had ever been. He was the most famous black man in America, virtually a household name. He had met with Lincoln in the White House three times, longed for a Republican appointment, and became, in the apt phrase of Benjamin Quarles, a "Republican Wheelhorse."[90]

In one respect, Douglass exchanged his faith in an active and immanent God for his reliance on the Republican party. In 1876, the very time when Republicans abandoned the project of Reconstruction by removing federal troops from the South, he finally received the presidential appointment he had long hoped for. He was named marshal of the District of Columbia by President-Elect Rutherford B. Hayes, thus becoming the first black man to receive an appointment that required Senate approval. But Douglass' visible role in the new administration masked the concessions Republicans had made to white supremacists to get Hayes elected. Douglass seemed oblivious to this fact, and refused to criticize Republicans for abandoning federal responsibility for the rights of freedmen and women. From Reconstruction until the end of his life, he urged African Americans to "stick to the Republican party." He acknowledged that Republicans were not perfect. But he was no longer concerned with the quest for a perfect society. "Government is better than anarchy, and patient reform is better than violent revolution," he said in 1883. It was a profound reversal of his stance as a Radical Abolitionist. His status as a famous black man often served the interests of the Republican party rather than those of black people or his earlier hopes to realize a millennialist and pluralist America.[91]

In one sense, then, Douglass followed Smith in abandoning his identity as a passionate outsider. For Smith, the retreat was comparatively abrupt and noticeable; for Douglass, it was gradual and subtle. Both men started to contain their assault against the sins of their world, much as conservative reformers had done before the war. In varying degrees, they began to separate slavery from other evil institutions, and used the existing structures of government to bring legal freedom to blacks, thus legitimating many mainstream conventions. During the debates over the Fifteenth Amendment, Douglass virtually abandoned his push for female suffrage along with black suffrage. "When women because they are women, are dragged from their homes and hung upon lampposts; when their children are torn from their arms . . . then they will have an urgency to obtain the ballot equal to the black man," he said, referring to crimes against blacks during the New York City draft riots of 1863. He also began to accept mainstream views of innate differences between blacks and whites, and concurred with Smith that blacks were naturally predisposed to warmer climates, and whites to more temperate zones. He opposed the black "exodus" to the North partly because he thought that blacks would be able to compete more effectively against whites in the South. The warm southern climate made physical labor uninviting to whites: "He [the white man] shuns the burning sun of the fields, and seeks the shade of the verandas. On the contrary, the Negro walks, labors and sleeps in the sunlight unharmed." Thirty years earlier, Douglass had enthusiastically endorsed the "exodus" of poor New York State blacks to the cold mountains of Timbucto. By opposing this new black exodus, he was ignoring not only his identity as Frederick Bailey, who had fled north in search of freedom, but his interracial alliance that had led to the creation of Timbucto.[92]

Douglass said more than once that John Brown began the war that ended American slavery.[93] What he did not know was that Brown's war was also the beginning of the end of Gerrit Smith's inner war, in which Smith lost his black heart. And it was the beginning of the end of Douglass' own revolutionary ethos, and a vision of America that would not reemerge until the civil rights movement in the next century.

The dissolution of these men's alliance points to the power of the surrounding white culture and its racist solution to America's great paradox. For over a decade, Gerrit Smith and his comrades were more or less able to burst free from white society. But after Harpers Ferry, Smith pulled back, and found refuge in the traditional racist answers to the American dilemma. Douglass, too, became unwilling to confront the white supremacists with the directness and power he had exercised in the 1850s. Culture once again defined the boundaries of Smith's and Douglass' racial and religious makeup. In a way, Smith's inability to empathize with blacks after Harpers Ferry foreshadowed the North's abandonment of freedmen and women after Reconstruction: the war itself became for the North what Brown's bloodletting was for Smith. It destroyed reformers' visions of a heaven on Earth, justified racism as a way to atone for the bloodshed, and created an existential crisis in people's hopes for reform. The apocalypse had come, but not salvation.

Epilogue

He succeeds, who, in the sight of heaven, does his duty, even though, in the sight of men, he has failed, utterly failed.

— GERRIT SMITH, *"To Thyself Be True!"* BROADSIDE (1874)

Such are the ways of all who get gain by violence; it takes away the life of its possessors.

— PROVERBS 1:19

In early June 1874 the city of Chicago hosted an extravagant four-day abolition reunion. The large auditorium of the Second Baptist Church on Monroe Street was filled with "men and women in the vale of years," according to the *Chicago Tribune*. "Gray beards, bald heads, and spectacles were the rule among the men, and sober, Quakerish garbs among the women." A large wreath of roses adorned the rear of the pulpit, and a life-sized marble bust of Charles Sumner, who had died that spring, was prominently displayed on the lecture platform. The reunion had been the idea of Allan Pinkerton, a former abolitionist and now head of the Pinkerton World-Wide Detective Agency, which had attained prominence through its wartime counterespionage. Pinkerton had known Gerrit Smith and John Brown, and had conceived of (but never acted on) a plan to free Brown after his arrest at Harpers Ferry. His agency now specialized in silencing the agitators of big business.[1]

The principal aim of the four-day affair was to bring together reformers of all persuasions to "relate their personal experiences of the Anti-Slavery movement," so that future generations would learn "what they did and endured for the cause." The *Chicago Tribune* gave generous coverage to the event. It provided a brief history of the antislavery movement, summarized the proceedings in detail, and devoted pages eulogizing "the most prominent men who took part in the work." Political abolitionists, Free-Soilers, and Garrisonians were all represented, but the convention focused, both in its eulogies and in the makeup of its participants, on white men. There were comparatively few women present, and virtually no blacks. The primary effect of the reunion was to characterize the abolition movement as a white man's movement. In this it was successful, for a century later, abolition narratives continued to downplay the presence and influence of blacks.[2]

The reunion totally ignored the Radical Abolition party and the interracial alliance of Gerrit Smith, James McCune Smith, Frederick Douglass, and John Brown. It also ignored or downplayed their individual efforts to end slavery and create a new America. James McCune Smith was never even mentioned. There was a very brief summary of John Brown's life and career, amounting to one short paragraph in the *Tribune*. The newspaper also reprinted a brief letter from two of Brown's sons—John Jr. and Owen Brown—who said simply that they would not be able to attend.[3]

What is particularly ironic about the omission of McCune Smith and the downplaying of Brown is that these two men were in one sense the only *true* revolutionaries—the only ones whose religious zeal held firm from the beginning of their alliance until their deaths. Neither man abandoned his faith in God, in Bible politics, or in the quest to realize a sacred and integrated society. Indeed Brown's zeal continued to grow, and he never once wavered in his belief in the millennium or in himself as a prophet. McCune Smith, too, remained faithful to Bible politics, despite having to confront such shocking facts as Gerrit Smith's retrogression, new scientific (especially evolutionary) theories that threatened his spiritual beliefs, and the war. The religiosity of all four men, manifested in their Bible politics, had been their litmus test of a true rebel. Bible politics had helped bring on the Civil War, but the end of the war and Reconstruction brought a secularizing spirit that masked the true fervor of these men. By dying when they did, McCune Smith and especially Brown did not have to face the doubts, the crises of faith, and the abandonment of Bible politics that came with this new secularizing spirit.

Frederick Douglass did not attend the convention. He had just been appointed president of the Freedman's Savings and Trust Company, a national savings bank chartered by the federal government to hold deposits and make loans to freedmen and women. His elegant office stood across the street from President Grant's White House. Despite the appearance of stability, the bank was insolvent, and its failure foreshadowed the closing of the Freedman's Bureau, its parent institution. Douglass sent a brief note of support that was read at the reunion. It constituted one of the few black voices that was heard over the four days of celebration. He called the meeting "supremely attractive" and said that abolitionists should feel proud of their victory: "No class of the American people can look toward the sun-set of life with a larger measure of satisfaction than the Abolitionists . . . They have done a great work—the great work of the century. They have given the American slaves their freedom and the American people the possibility of a country." The nostalgic tone of his letter betrayed his loss of hope in the possibility of reforming America. He increasingly looked to the past for solace and comfort. That very same year he confessed that although he still played his violin, the sound was not the same, for "the music of the past is sweeter than any my unpracticed and unskilled bow can produce. I lay my dear, old fiddle aside, and listen to the soft, silent, distant music of other days." Despite legal freedom, none of his dreams of Bible politics remained.[4]

Gerrit Smith did not attend the reunion and did not even bother to send his regrets. He was at home in Peterboro, dwelling on the sick state of his soul and of the country. He had little hope in the salvation of either and admitted that the "religious element" in him was "far from strong." He was still obsessed with the blackness of his sins. In fact he had designated March 15 of that year as "Black Friday," because the sins of his past had "pressed heavily upon my conscience, and I got very little sleep." When he read the *Tribune*'s coverage of the reunion, he became even more despairing. Although the convention detailed the antislavery movement in central New York, the only mention of Smith was in connection with his offer of his home to abolitionists in 1835, after the Utica mob broke up the inaugural meeting of the New York State Anti-Slavery Society. After reading the *Tribune*'s coverage, Smith picked up a sheet of paper, scribbled some notes about the reunion, and hastily added: "[My life] seems to me to have been hypocritical and hollow." His abolition efforts had been "deplorably lacking in earnestness." He totally ignored his revolutionary role in creating political abolitionism; befriending Douglass, McCune Smith, and other blacks as social equals; and establishing at Peterboro and Timbucto model interracial communities that he had hoped would spread throughout the country.[5]

Despite his despair, Smith continued to voice his frustrations about the present state of reform. In November 1874 he attacked the Republican party for failing in its duty to be "true to itself." Republicans had allowed Southern whites to enact "excessive and murderous cruelties" against blacks and had permitted the "Kuklux Klan" to go unpunished. He then offered a maxim of reform: "He succeeds who, in the sight of heaven, does his duty, even though, in the sight of men, he has failed, utterly failed." At one level, Smith knew that he, too, had failed. He had largely abandoned his black friends and had ignored his past. But during the 1850s, when heaven had been clearly in sight, he had courageously struggled to do his duty. He would soon encounter heaven, for one month later, on December 28, he died from a sudden "apoplectic shock." There was a simple funeral at Peterboro, with only close friends, neighbors, and family members present. Perhaps McCune Smith and Brown were there in spirit to receive their old friend. But Frederick Douglass, who was still very much in the world, did not attend.[6]

Abbreviations

NYHIST *New York History*
  NYR *New York Review of Books*
  NYSA New York State Archives, Albany
  NYT *New-York Tribune*
SULAC *Syracuse University Library Associates Courier*
  TFDP John Blassingame, ed., *The Frederick Douglass Papers*, Series One, vols.
          1–5 (New Haven: Yale University Press, 1979–1992)
    WL Widener Library, Harvard University
  YJLH *Yale Journal of Law and the Humanities*

Notes

❧

Introduction

1. James McCune Smith to Gerrit Smith, December 28, 1846, *BAP*, 3: 480.
2. On the idea of race, class, and gender as socially constructed concepts, see Barbara Jeanne Fields, "Race and Ideology in American History," in *Region, Race, and Reconstruction: Essays in Honor of C. Vann Woodward*, ed. J. Morgan Kousser and James M. McPherson (New York: Oxford University Press, 1982), pp. 143–178; Kwame Anthony Appiah and Henry Louis Gates Jr., eds., *Identities* (Chicago: University of Chicago Press, 1995); and Stuart Hall, "Cultural Identity and Diaspora," in *Identity: Community, Culture, Difference*, ed. Jonathan Rutherford (London: Lawrence & Wishart, 1990), pp. 222–237.
3. My decision to braid together the four lives has been influenced by Alan Taylor, *William Cooper's Town: Power and Persuasion on the Frontier of the Early American Republic* (New York: Alfred A. Knopf, 1995); J. Anthony Lukas, *Common Ground: A Turbulent Decade in the Lives of Three American Families* (New York: Vintage, 1986); Philip Hallie, *Lest Innocent Blood Be Shed* (1979; reprint, New York: Harper Perennial, 1994); Peter Brooks, *Reading for the Plot: Design and Intention in Narrative* (1984; reprint, Cambridge: Harvard University Press, 2000), pp. 3–61; M. M. Bakhtin, *The Dialogic Imagination: Four Essays*, ed. Michael Holquist, trans. Holquist and Caryl Emerson (Austin: University of Texas Press, 1981), pp. 259–422; Kenneth Burke, *The Philosophy of Literary Form: Studies in Symbolic Action* (1941; reprint, Berkeley: University of California Press, 1973), pp. 1–137; and Frank Kermode, *The Sense of an Ending: Studies in the Theory of Fiction* (1966; reprint, New York: Oxford University Press, 2000), pp. 93–126.
4. Gilbert Hobbs Barnes, *The Antislavery Impulse, 1830–1844* (New York: Appleton-Century, 1933).

5. Crummell, quoted in Vernon Loggins, *The Negro Author: His Development in America* (New York: Columbia University Press, 1931), p. 182; Douglass, *Life and Times of Frederick Douglass* (1892; reprint, New York: Collier, 1962), pp. 467–468; Douglass, "Dr. James McCune Smith," *DM*, March 1859.

6. The one, superb article on McCune Smith is David W. Blight, "In Search of Learning, Liberty, and Self Definition: James McCune Smith and the Ordeal of the Antebellum Black Intellectual," *AANYLH* 9 (July 1985): 7–25.

7. John R. McKivigan examines the Gerrit Smith–Frederick Douglass friendship in an excellent article, "The Frederick Douglass—Gerrit Smith Friendship and Political Abolitionism in the 1850s," in *Frederick Douglass: New Literary and Historical Essays*, ed. Eric J. Sundquist (Cambridge: Cambridge University Press, 1990), pp. 205–232.

8. David Blight emphasizes Douglass' millennialist views in *Frederick Douglass' Civil War: Keeping Faith in Jubilee* (Baton Rouge: Louisiana State University Press, 1989), pp. 1–25.

9. The writers who have acknowledged Brown's ability to blur racial categories are W. E. B. Du Bois, *John Brown* (1909; reprint, New York: International Publishers, 1962); Russell Banks, *Cloudsplitter: A Novel* (New York: HarperCollins, 1998); William E. Cain, "Violence, Revolution, and the Cost of Freedom: John Brown and W. E. B. Du Bois," *boundary* 2 (Spring 1990): 305–330.

One. The Radical Abolitionist Call to Arms

1. James M. McPherson, *The Struggle for Equality: Abolitionists and the Negro in the Civil War and Reconstruction* (Princeton: Princeton University Press, 1964), pp. 12–20.

2. James Redpath, *The Public Life of Capt. John Brown* (Boston: Thayer and Eldridge, 1860), p. 60. The expression "summer butter" is from Gerrit Smith to Cornelia Smith Cochrane, April 27, 1818, GSP. On weather conditions see Franklin B. Hough, *Results of a Series of Meteorological Observations* (Albany: Weed, Parsons, 1872), pp. 39, 114–115, 228–229, 257–258.

3. Brown, quoted in F. B. Sanborn, ed., *The Life and Letters of John Brown, Liberator of Kansas, and Martyr of Virginia* (Boston: Roberts Brothers, 1855), pp. 193–194, 110–111; Richard O. Boyer, *The Legend of John Brown: A Biography and a History* (New York: Alfred A. Knopf, 1973), pp. 460, 526–527.

4. *Proceedings of the Convention of Radical Political Abolitionists . . .* (New York: Central Abolition Board, 1855), pp. 57, 64–65, HL; Benjamin Quarles, *Frederick Douglass* (1948; reprint, New York: Da Capo, 1997), pp. 160–161.

5. *Proceedings of the Convention*, pp. 64–65. On the biracial group of wise men who discovered Christ, see Jean Devisse and Michel Mollet, *The Image of the Black in Western Art*, vol. 2/2: *Africans in the Christian Ordinance of the World (Fourteenth to the Sixteenth Centuries)*, trans. William Granger Ryan (New York: William R. Morrow, 1980), pp. 161–210.

6. *FDP*, July 6, 1855.

7. *RA* 1 (August 1855): 7; *FDP*, July 6, 1855; *NYT*, June 29, 1855; *LIB*, July 6, 1855; *NASS*, July 7, 1855.

8. James McCune Smith to Gerrit Smith, [May] 1855 and October 6, 1855, GSP; McCune Smith to Gerrit Smith, December 28, 1846, GSP; McCune Smith, "Civilization" and "The German Invasion," *AAM*, pp. 5–17, 44–52.

9. *Proceedings of the Convention*, pp. 3, 44–45.

10. Ibid., pp. 3–4; Douglass to Gerrit Smith, March 27, 1855, GSP; *FDP*, March 13, April 20, June 15 and 22, 1855. See also John R. McKivigan, *The War against Proslavery Religion: Abolitionism and the Northern Churches, 1830–1865* (Ithaca: Cornell University Press, 1984), pp. 81, 114, 141, 203–220; Bertram Wyatt-Brown, *Lewis Tappan and the Evangelical War against Slavery* (Cleveland: Press of Case Western Reserve University, 1969), pp. 287–338; Lawrence J. Friedman, *Gregarious Saints: Self and Community in American Abolitionism, 1830–1870* (Cambridge: Cambridge University Press, 1982), pp. 68–95. The eight delegates who signed their names to the "call" for the convention were Lewis Tappan, Willian Goodell, Gerrit Smith, Simeon S. Jocelyn, William E. Whiting, James McCune Smith, George Whipple, and Frederick Douglass. Four of the delegates (Tappan, Jocelyn, Whipple, and Whiting) had been prominent members of the American and Foreign Anti-Slavery Society, which had disbanded earlier in 1855; and three delegates (Tappan, Jocelyn, and Whipple) were officers of the American Missionary Association. The convention thus hoped to bring together diverse abolitionists into a united political front.

11. *Proceedings of the Convention*, pp. 5–9, 10–22, 23–51, 59–62.

12. John Brown and John Brown Jr., quoted in Boyer, *Legend of John Brown*, pp. 524–527; *Proceedings of the Convention*, pp. 62–63.

13. Hebrews 9:22; *NASS*, July 7, 1855; *LIB*, July 6, 1855; Boyer, *Legend of John Brown*, pp. 526–527; Richard J. Hinton, *John Brown and His Men* (New York: Funk and Wagnalls, 1894), p. 19; Quarles, *Douglass*, pp. 156–158; Frederick May Holland, *Frederick Douglass: The Colored Orator* (1891; reprint, New York: Haskell House, 1969), p. 247.

14. *LIB*, July 6, 1855; *NASS*, July 7, 1855; Hinton, *John Brown and His Men*, p. 19; Boyer, *Legend of John Brown*, pp. 526–527; and Oswald Garrison Villard, *John Brown, 1800–1859: A Biography Fifty Years After* (1910; reprint, New York: Alfred A. Knopf, 1943), pp. 84–85.

15. *LWFD* 2: 49–50; Gerrit Smith, quoted in *Fifth Annual Report of the Executive Committee of the American Anti-Slavery Society* (New York: William S. Dorr, 1838), p. 35; Smith to General John H. Cooke, August 29, 1839, GSP; Friedman, *Gregarious Saints*, pp. 193–194; Martin Delany, quoted in *FDP*, May 6, 1853; Jane H. Pease and William H. Pease, *They Who Would Be Free: Blacks' Search for Freedom, 1830–1861* (1974; reprint, Urbana: University of Illinois Press, 1990), p. 92; Joel Schor, *Henry Highland Garnet: A Voice of Black Radicalism in the Nineteenth Century* (Westport, Conn.: Greenwood Press, 1977), p. 100.

16. "Passionate outsiders" is my term, conceived with help from the following sources: R. Laurence Moore, *Religious Outsiders and the Making of Americans* (New York: Oxford University Press, 1986); Moore, "Insiders and Outsiders in American Historical Narrative and American History," *AHR* 87 (April 1982): 390–412; Clarence E. Walker, "The American Negro as Historical Outsider, 1836–1935," *Canadian Review of American Studies* 17 (Summer 1986): 137–154; Robert H. Abzug, *Passionate Liberator: Theodore Dwight Weld and the Dilemma of Reform* (New York: Oxford University Press, 1980); and Colin Wilson, *The Outsider* (1956; reprint, Los Angeles: J. P. Tarcher, 1982).

17. William R. Hutchison, *The Modernist Impulse in American Protestantism* (1976; reprint, Durham, N.C.: Duke University Press, 1992), p. 1; Aileen S. Kraditor, *Means and Ends in American Abolitionism: Garrison and His Critics on Strategy and Tactics, 1834–1850* (1969; reprint, Chicago: Ivan R. Dee, 1989), p. 237; Ann Braude, *Radical Spirits: Spiritualism and Women's Rights in Nineteenth-Century America* (Boston: Beacon Press, 1989), pp. 62–63; Ralph Waldo Emerson, "The Fugitive Slave Law," in *Emerson's Antislavery Writings*, ed. Len Gougeon and Joel Myerson (New Haven: Yale University Press, 1995), p. 84; *Walt Whitman's Leaves of Grass: The First (1855) Edition*, ed. Malcolm Cowley (New York: Penguin, 1959), pp. 49, 83; Gerrit Smith, "The Liberty Party," *FDP*, December 11, 1851; Lewis Perry, *Radical Abolitionism: Anarchy and the Government of God in Antislavery Thought* (Ithaca: Cornell University Press, 1973), pp. 55–91.

18. F. O. Matthieson, *American Renaissance: Art and Expression in the Age of Emerson and Whitman* (New York: Oxford University Press, 1941), pp. 9, 537.

19. Gerrit Smith, *Nathan to David*, broadside, December 4, 1841, GSP; Smith, *Religion of Reason* (Peterboro, N.Y.: C. A. Hammond, 1864), p. 97; Smith, *The Theologies* (Peterboro, N.Y.: C. A. Hammond, 1866), p. 11, GSP; David Brion Davis, *The Problem of Slavery in Western Culture* (New York: Oxford University Press, 1966), pp. 291–332, 483–493.

20. Norman Pettit, *The Heart Prepared: Grace and Conversion in Puritan Spiritual Life* (1966; reprint, Middletown, Conn.: Wesleyan University Press, 1989), pp. 1–21; Thomas Jefferson to Mrs. [Maria] Cosway, October 12,

1786, in *The Life and Selected Writings of Thomas Jefferson* ed. Adrienne Koch and William Peden (New York: Modern Library, 1944), pp. 395–407; John Jay Chapman, "Doctor Howe," in *Learning and Other Essays* (New York: Moffat, Yard, 1910), p. 131; Perry Miller, *The Life of the Mind in America: From the Revolution to the Civil War* (New York: Harcourt Brace Jovanovich, 1965), pp. 99–116; Garth M. Rosell, "Charles G. Finney: His Place in the Stream of American Evangelicalism," in *The Evangelical Tradition in America*, ed. Leonard Sweet (Macon, Ga.: Mercer University Press, 1984), pp. 131–147.

21. Gerrit Smith, "Address to the Slaves of the United States . . . ," *NASS*, February 24, 1842; *TFDP*, 1/3: 48; James McCune Smith, quoted in *FDP*, May 11, 1855; McCune Smith, quoted in *BAP*, 4: 259; *BAP*, 3: 479–480; McCune Smith to Gerrit Smith, December 28, 1846, GSP. See also Garry Wills, "A Tale of Three Leaders," *NYR*, September 19, 1996, pp. 64, 66–67.

22. Douglass, quoted in *LWFD*, 2: 363–366.

23. Robert H. Abzug, *Cosmos Crumbling: American Reform and the Religious Imagination* (New York: Oxford University Press, 1994), pp. 7–8, 228.

24. *NYH*, May 29–30, 1856; *Radical Abolitionist* 1 (July 1856): 98–104; John R. McKivigan, "The Frederick Douglass–Gerrit Smith Friendship and Political Abolitionism in the 1850s," in *Frederick Douglass: New Literary and Historical Essays*, ed. Eric J. Sundquist (Cambridge: Cambridge University Press, 1990), pp. 220–222; Quarles, *Douglass*, pp. 161–163. Although James McCune Smith signed the call and served as a delegate to the convention, he was unable to attend. Douglass canceled a number of previously scheduled speaking engagements in order to come. Three months later Douglass began to endorse the Republican nomination of John C. Frémont, believing that Radical Abolitionists were "too far ahead of these degenerate times to be well supported." His shift in allegiance reflected not so much frustration with the Radical Abolition party as fear that he could not sustain his paper.

25. *NYH*, May 29–30, 1856; *Radical Abolitionist* 1 (July 1856): 104; Richard H. Sewell, *Ballots for Freedom: Antislavery Politics in the United States, 1837–1860* (New York: Oxford University Press, 1976), p. 287; Quarles, *Douglass*, pp. 160–164; Charles H. Wesley, "The Participation of Negroes in Anti-Slavery Political Parties," *JNH* 29 (January 1944): 69–71; John R. McKivigan, "Vote as You Pray and Pray as You Vote: Church-Oriented Abolitionism and Antislavery Politics," in *Crusaders and Compromisers: Essays on the Relationship of the Antislavery Struggle to the Antebellum Party System*, ed. Alan M. Kraut (Westport, Conn.: Greenwood Press, 1983), p. 195; McKivigan, *War against Proslavery Religion*, p. 158; McPherson, *Struggle for Equality*, pp. 16–20.

26. David Donald, *Charles Sumner and the Coming of the Civil War* (1960; reprint, New York: Da Capo, 1996), p. 298; *NYT*, May 30–31, 1856.

27. *RA* 1 (July 1856): 97, 102; *NYH*, May 29, 1856; Quarles, *Douglass*, pp. 160–162; Wesley, "Participation," pp. 69–71.

28. Perhaps they were the same broadswords that Gerrit Smith had presented Brown with the year before at Syracuse, if Richard J. Hinton's account is correct. Villard, *Brown*, pp. 148–188; Steven B. Oates, *To Purge This Land with Blood: A Biography of John Brown* (1970; reprint, Amherst: University of Massachusetts Press, 1984), pp. 126–137; Louis Ruchames, ed., *John Brown: The Making of a Revolutionary* (New York: Grosset and Dunlap, 1969), pp. 30–31; *NYH*, June 8, 10, 1856.

29. Both Gerrit Smith and John Brown spoke about the efficacy of political action at a Republican party convention in Milwaukee in June 1857. See *Daily Sentinel* (Milwaukee), June 18–19, 1857, Wisconsin Historical Society, Madison; and Kenneth M. Stampp, *America in 1857: A Nation on the Brink* (New York: Oxford University Press, 1990), pp. 138–139.

30. Eric Foner, "The Causes of the American Civil War: Recent Interpretations and New Directions," in *Politics and Ideology in the Age of the Civil War* (New York: Oxford University Press, 1980), pp. 15–33; Peter Wallenstein, "Incendiaries All: Southern Politics and the Harpers Ferry Raid," in *His Soul Goes Marching On: Responses to John Brown and the Harper's Ferry Raid*, ed. Paul Finkelman (Charlottesville: University Press of Virginia, 1995), pp. 149–173.

31. *Proceedings of the Convention*, pp. 3–8; *Radical Abolitionist* 1 (August 1855): 6, 15–16.

32. *Proceedings of the Convention*, pp. 3–4; William M. Wiecek, *The Sources of Antislavery Constitutionalism in America, 1760–1848* (Ithaca: Cornell University Press, 1977), pp. 249–275; McKivigan, "Vote as You Pray," pp. 187–196; Garrison, quoted in James Brewer Stewart, *Holy Warriors: The Abolitionists and American Slavery* (New York: Hill and Wang, 1976), pp. 98–99; Henry Mayer, *All On Fire: William Lloyd Garrison and the Abolition of Slavery* (New York: St. Martin's Press, 1998), pp. 443–445; Smith to Garrison, May 6, 1852, GSP.

33. Jeffery Rossbach, *Ambivalent Conspirators: John Brown, the Secret Six, and a Theory of Slave Violence* (Philadelphia: University of Pennsylvania Press, 1982); Boyer, *Legend of John Brown*, pp. 1–44; Edward J. Renehan Jr., *The Secret Six: The True Tale of the Men Who Conspired with John Brown* (New York: Crown, 1995); Otto Scott, *The Secret Six: John Brown and the Abolitionist Movement* (New York: Times Books, 1979); Albert J. von Frank, *The Trials of Anthony Burns: Freedom and Slavery in Emerson's Boston* (Cambridge: Harvard University Press, 1998); Tilden G. Edelstein, *Strange Enthusiasm:*

A Life of Thomas Wentworth Higginson (New Haven: Yale University Press, 1968), pp. 84–253.

34. Sewell, *Ballots for Freedom*, pp. 43–130; Kraditor, *Means and Ends*, pp. 118–177; Wiecek, *Sources of Antislavery Constitutionalism*, pp. 249–275; Alan M. Kraut, "Partisanship and Principles: The Liberty Party in Antebellum Political Culture," in Kraut, *Crusaders and Compromisers*, pp. 71–99; McKivigan, "Vote as You Pray," pp. 187–203; McKivigan, *War against Proslavery Religion*, pp. 157–158; M. Leon Perkal, "American Abolition Society: A Viable Alternative to the Republican Party?" *JNH* 65 (Winter 1980): 57–71; Robert William Fogel, *Without Consent or Contract: The Rise and Fall of American Slavery* (New York: W. W. Norton, 1989), pp. 328–338; Smith, "Autobiographical Sketch of the Life of Gerrit Smith," holograph, n.d. [1856], GSP.

35. Benjamin Quarles, "Letters from Negro Leaders to Gerrit Smith," *JNH* 27 (October 1942): 433–434; Quarles, *Douglass*, pp. 151–165, quotation p. 156; Wesley, "Participation," pp. 68–74; McKivigan, "Douglass–Smith Friendship," pp. 205–232; *FDP*, September 21, 1855.

36. *Proceedings of the Convention*, pp. 8–9; *American Jubilee*, June 1854, p. 14.

37. Octavius Brooks Frothingham, *Gerrit Smith: A Biography* (New York: G. P. Putnam's Sons, 1878), p. 188; Wiecek, *Sources of Antislavery Constitutionalism*, pp. 249–275.

38. *Proceedings of the Convention*, pp. 27, 49.

39. Ibid., pp. 18–19.

40. John Quincy Adams, quoted in Samuel Flagg Bemis, *John Quincy Adams and the Union* (New York: Alfred A. Knopf, 1956), p. 338.

41. Ibid., pp. 420, 545; Sewell, *Ballots for Freedom*, pp. 121–123; William Lee Miller, *Arguing about Slavery: The Great Battle in the United States Congress* (New York: Alfred A. Knopf, 1996), pp. 153–193; Frederick J. Blue, *Salmon P. Chase: A Life in Politics* (Kent, Ohio: Kent State University Press, 1987), pp. 47–49; Vernon L. Volpe, *Forlorn Hope of Freedom: The Liberty Party in the Old Northwest, 1838–1848* (Kent, Ohio: Kent State University Press, 1990), pp. 56–57, 82–83; Fogel, *Without Consent or Contract*, pp. 334–338.

42. *Proceedings of the Convention*, pp. 17, 23, 52, quotations pp. 17, 52. See also Bemis, *Adams and Union*, pp. 446–447; and Wiecek, *Sources of Antislavery Constitutionalism*, pp. 271–272. John Locke had also argued that slavery was a state of war, but for him it was "the state of war continued between a lawful Conqueror and a Captive." Montesquieu, even more than Locke, argued that slavery represented a state of war that contradicted natural law. Radical Abolitionists did not mention Locke or Montesquieu in their platform or convention, and they obviously disagreed with Locke's notion of masters as "lawful conquerors." See Davis, *Problem of Slavery*, pp. 118–121,

402–408; Montesquieu, *The Spirit of the Laws*, trans. Thomas Nugent (New York: D. Appleton, 1900), book 15.

43. *Proceedings of the Convention*, pp. 44, 27, 33, 54, 62; Hinton, *John Brown and His Men*, p. 19; Samuel Flagg Bemis, *John Quincy Adams and the Foundations of American Foreign Policy* (New York: Alfred A. Knopf, 1969), p. 416; Villard, *Brown*, p. 334.

44. Donald, *Sumner and Coming of Civil War*, pp. 153–154, 388, quotation p. 388; W. L. Miller, *Arguing about Slavery*, pp. 207–208; Ira Berlin et al., *Slaves No More: Three Essays on Emancipation and the Civil War* (New York: Cambridge University Press, 1992), pp. 21–26, 36–44; James M. McPherson, *Battle Cry of Freedom: The Civil War Era* (New York: Ballantine, 1989), pp. 353–356, 499–502; Abraham Lincoln, "Final Emancipation Proclamation," in *Selected Speeches and Writings*, ed. Don E. Fehrenbacher (New York: Vintage/Library of America, 1992), p. 368.

45. Frederick Douglass, *My Bondage and My Freedom* (1855; reprint, Urbana: University of Illinois Press, 1987), pp. 103–104; Dickson J. Preston, *Young Frederick Douglass: The Maryland Years* (Baltimore: Johns Hopkins University Press, 1980), pp. 101–102; William S. McFeely, *Frederick Douglass* (New York: W. W. Norton, 1991), pp. 32–34, 96.

46. Douglass to Gerrit Smith, July 18, 1855, GSP.

47. Douglass, *Bondage*, pp. 103–104; Preston, *Young Frederick Douglass*, pp. 101–102; McFeely, *Douglass*, pp. 96, 203; *TFDP*, 1/1: 4, 8; 1/3: 287.

48. Frothingham, *Gerrit Smith*, pp. 161–162; Ralph Volney Harlow, *Gerrit Smith: Philanthropist and Reformer* (New York: Henry Holt, 1939), pp. 19–20; Smith, "Autobiographical Sketch."

49. Smith to Adams, February 3, 1837, GSP; Adams to Gerrit Smith, April 5, 1837, AP.

50. Adams to Smith, April 5, 1837, AP.

51. Leviticus 18:21; Milton, *Paradise Lost*, I.342.

52. Deuteronomy 8:19–20; Michael Walzer, *Exodus and Revolution* (New York: Basic Books, 1985), pp. 3–6, 141–144; Ernest Lee Tuveson, *Redeemer Nation: The Idea of America's Millennial Role* (Chicago: University of Chicago Press, 1968), pp. 137–186; John Quincy Adams, *Report No. 404, 28th Congress, 1st Session, House of Representatives: Massachusetts Resolutions, April 4, 1844*, pamphlet (1844) (hereafter cited as *Mr. Adams' Report*), pp. 3–12, HL.

53. Adams to Smith, April 5, 1837, AP. On Adams' receiving death threats, see Bemis, *Adams and Union*, pp. 348, 375–376, 435, 438. On ambition as the bane of republicanism see Gordon Wood, *The Radicalism of the American Revolution* (New York: Vintage, 1991), pp. 229–370.

54. Smith, *Speeches of Gerrit Smith in Congress* (New York: Mason Brothers, 1956), pp. 135, 136, 209.

55. Smith to Adams, July 16, 1839, GSP; Adams to Smith, July 31, 1839, AP; John Quincy Adams, *The Jubilee of the Constitution* . . . (New York: Samuel Colman, 1839), pp. 5–136; Charles Francis Adams, ed., *Memoirs of John Quincy Adams, Comprising Portions of His Diary from 1795 to 1848*, 12 vols. (Philadelphia: J. B. Lippincott, 1874–1877), 10: 119–123; *National Intelligencer* 27 (May 28, 1839); Bemis, *Adams and Union*, pp. 379–383; "Letter of J. Q. Adams, No. II, To the Citizens of the United States," *LIB*, June 7, 1839.

56. On slavery as America's original sin, see Davis, *Problem of Slavery*, pp. 3–28, 483–494; James Madison, quoted in Matthew T. Mellon, *Early American Views on Negro Slavery* (Boston: Meador Publishing, 1934), p. 158.

57. Smith to Adams, July 16, 1839, GSP.

58. Adams to Smith, July 31, 1839, AP.

59. On the messianic understanding of Christianity as it relates to America, see Tuveson, *Redeemer Nation*, pp. 1–25; David Brion Davis, *Slavery and Human Progress* (New York: Oxford University Press, 1984), pp. 128–129, 143–153; Abzug, *Cosmos Crumbling*, p. 7.

60. Adams to Smith, July 31, 1839, AP; Adams, *Memoirs*, 10: 345; *Mr. Adams' Report*, pp. 3–4; Greg Russell, "John Quincy Adams: Virtue and the Tragedy of the Statesman," *New England Quarterly* 69 (March 1996): 69; Bemis, *Adams and Union*, pp. 104–106, 115–118, 178–184; Paul C. Nagel, *John Quincy Adams: A Public Life, A Private Life* (New York: Alfred A. Knopf, 1998), pp. 56–65, 202–205, 327–335.

61. Gerrit Smith to Cassius Clay, February 28, 1845, GSP; Smith to Adams, July 16, 1839, GSP; *American Jubilee* 1 (March 1854): 1; James McCune Smith to Gerrit Smith, [n.d.] 1855 and October 6, 1855, GSP; Russell, "John Quincy Adams," p. 67. See also Abzug, *Cosmos Crumbling*, pp. 204–229. According to the philosopher Arthur Lovejoy, the "imperfection of man is indispensable for the fullness of the hierarchy of being"; *The Great Chain of Being* (New York: Oxford University Press, 1936), pp. 199–200.

62. Adams, *Memoirs*, 4: 492–493, 531; Bemis, *Adams and Foundations*, pp. 417–418; Nagel, *John Quincy Adams*, p. 64; Boyer, *Legend of John Brown*, pp. 290–300. On the sublime see Thomas Weiskel, *The Romantic Sublime: Studies in the Structure and Psychology of Transcendence* (Baltimore: Johns Hopkins University Press, 1976), pp. 3–23; Philip Fisher, *Wonder, the Rainbow, and the Aesthetics of Rare Experience* (Cambridge: Harvard University Press, 1998), pp. 1–32; and Richard Klein, *Cigarettes Are Sublime* (Durham, N.C.: Duke University Press, 1993), pp. ix–xiii, 1–4.

63. John Quincy Adams, "Misconceptions of Shakespeare upon the Stage," *New England Magazine* 9 (December 1835): 435–440; Adams, "The Character of Desdemona," *American Monthly Magazine*, March 1836, pp. 209–

217; Adams, *Memoirs*, 10: 437–438; Russell, "John Quincy Adams," p. 67; Bemis, *Adams and Foundations*, pp. 416–418; William Jerry MacLean, "Othello Scorned: The Racial Thought of John Quincy Adams," *JER* 4 (Summer 1994): 143–160; Leonard L. Richards, *The Life and Times of Congressman Adams* (New York: Oxford University Press, 1986), pp. 95–112, quotation p. 98; Lynn Hudson Parsons, "'A Perpetual Harrow upon My Feelings': John Quincy Adams and the American Indian," *New England Quarterly* 46 (September 1973): 339–379.

64. Russell, "John Quincy Adams," pp. 56–74; David Brion Davis, "The Emergence of Immediatism in British and American Antislavery Thought," in *From Homicide to Slavery: Studies in American Culture* (New York: Oxford University Press), p. 257.

65. Bryan Jay Wolf, *Romantic Re-Vision: Culture and Consciousness in Nineteenth-Century American Painting and Literature* (Chicago: University of Chicago Press, 1982), p. 177.

66. Thomas Mann, quoted in William Van O'Connor, *The Grotesque: An American Genre and Other Essays* (Carbondale: Southern Illinois University Press, 1962), p. 5. See also Peter Gay, *Naked Heart: The Bourgeois Experience, Victoria to Freud* (New York: W. W. Norton, 1995), pp. 88–102. Unlike Mann, Gay does not see the sublime and the bourgeois experience as incompatible.

67. Adams, *Memoirs*, 10: 344–345.

68. Gougeon and Myerson, *Emerson's Antislavery Writings*, pp. xi–lvi; Len Gougeon, *Virtue's Hero: Emerson, Antislavery, and Reform* (Athens: University of Georgia Press, 1990), pp. 138–216; Ralph H. Orth and Alfred R. Ferguson, eds., *The Journals and Miscellaneous Notebooks of Ralph Waldo Emerson*, vol. 13: *1852–1855* (Cambridge: Harvard University Press, 1977), p. 334; Emerson to Samuel Joseph May, August 26, 1856, Kroch Library, Cornell University.

69. Gerrit Smith, *Peace Better than War . . .* (Boston: American Peace Society, 1858), p. 5, GSP; Smith, *Religion of Reason*, pp. 53, 65; Emerson, *Nature* (1836) and "Self-Reliance" (1841), in *The Portable Emerson*, ed. Carl Bode (New York: Penguin, 1981), pp. 7–8, 138–139, 157–158, 160–164.

70. Smith's portraits of Emerson were part of a photography "Album" that included hundreds of *cartes-de-visite* of friends, reformers, and European royalty. The album is at MCHS.

71. Douglass, "Pictures," ca. 1864, DP. See also *TFDP*, 1/3: 540; *TFDP*, 1/4: 367; David W. Blight, *Frederick Douglass' Civil War: Keeping Faith in Jubilee* (Baton Rouge: Louisiana State University Press, 1989), pp. 113–114; Waldo Martin Jr., *The Mind of Frederick Douglass* (Chapel Hill: University

of North Carolina Press, 1984), pp. 223–224, 255–256, 263–266; McFeely, *Douglass*, pp. 115, 166, 325.

72. McCune Smith, "From Our New York Correspondent," *FDP*, December 15, 1854.

73. Sanborn, *Life and Letters of Brown*, p. 500; Villard, *Brown*, pp. 273, 278, 282; Oates, *To Purge This Land with Blood*, p. 197; Gilman M. Ostrander, "Emerson, Thoreau, and John Brown," *Mississippi Valley Historical Review* 34 (March 1953): 720; Robert A. Ferguson, "Story and Transcription in the Trial of John Brown," *YJLH* 6 (Winter 1994): 37–73.

74. Susan Sutton Smith and Harrison Hayford, eds., *The Journals and Miscellaneous Notebooks of Ralph Waldo Emerson*, vol. 14: *1854–1861* (Cambridge: Harvard University Press, 1968), pp. 125–126, 329–330, 333–334; Gougeon and Myerson, *Emerson's Antislavery Writings*, p. xlvii; James Elliot Cabot, ed., *The Works of Ralph Waldo Emerson*, vol. 11: *Miscellanies* (Boston: Houghton Mifflin, 1904), p. 208; Ostrander, "Emerson, Thoreau, and John Brown," p. 720.

75. Thomas Wortham, "Did Emerson Blackball Frederick Douglass From Membership in the Town and Country Club?" *New England Quarterly* 65 (1992): 295–302; Joel Porte, ed., *Emerson in His Journals* (Cambridge: Harvard University Press, 1982), p. 463.

76. Ralph L. Rusk, ed., *The Letters of Ralph Waldo Emerson*, vol. 5 (New York: Columbia University Press, 1939), p. 178; Orth and Ferguson, *Journals and Notebooks of Emerson*, 14: 108, 334; Emerson, "Fugitive Slave Law," p. 84; Emerson, "Self-Reliance"; Porte, *Emerson in His Journals*, pp. 452, 463.

77. Perry Miller, ed., *The American Transcendentalists: Their Prose and Poetry* (Garden City, N.Y.: Doubleday/Anchor, 1957), p. 217; Lewis Perry, *Boats against the Current: American Culture between Revolution and Modernity, 1820–1860* (New York: Oxford University Press, 1993), p. 221.

78. Daniel Joseph Singal, "Towards a Definition of American Modernism," *AQ* 39 (Spring 1987): 15; Davis, "Emergence of Immediatism," pp. 255–257; Marshall Berman, "All That Is Solid Melts into Air," *Dissent* 25 (Winter 1978): 54–73; Lionel Trilling, *Sincerity and Authenticity* (Cambridge: Harvard University Press, 1971), pp. 1–52, 106–117, 134–172.

79. On William James's connection to Emerson and Whitman, see Henry James, ed., *The Letters of William James*, vol. 2 (Boston: Atlantic Monthly Press, 1920), pp. 122–123, 187–194; William James, "The Will to Believe" and "On a Certain Blindness in Human Beings," in *William James: Writings, 1878–1899*, ed. Gerald Myers (New York: Library of America, 1992), pp. 457–479, 841–860; idem, "The Religion of Healthy-Mindedness," in *William James: Writings, 1902–1910*, ed. Bruce Kuklick (New York: Li-

brary of America, 1987), pp. 82–85; Frederic I. Carpenter, "William James and Emerson," in *On Emerson: The Best from American Literature*, ed. Edwin H. Cady and Louis J. Budd (Durham, N.C.: Duke University Press, 1988), pp. 42–61; R. W. B. Lewis, *The Jameses: A Family Narrative* (New York: Farrar, Straus and Giroux, 1991), pp. 559–561; Giles Gunn, *Thinking across the American Grain: Ideology, Intellect, and the New Pragmatism* (Chicago: University of Chicago Press, 1992), pp. 21–39.

80. Smith argued that the constitutionality of slavery was not "a historical question—but a legal question," a fact that allowed him to ignore historical precedent. See *Substance of the Speech Made by Gerrit Smith . . . March 11 & 12, 1850* (Albany, N.Y.: Jacob T. Hazen, 1850), p. 4, GSP.

81. Smith, *Religion of Reason*, pp. 20, 26, 28, 33; Isaiah Berlin, "My Intellectual Path," *NYR*, May 14, 1998, p. 57.

82. Hutchison, *Modernist Impulse*, pp. 1–9, 19–24, 141, 183–193, 206–211.

83. Charles Edward Gauss, "Empathy," in *Dictionary of the History of Ideas*, ed. Philip M. Wiener, vol. 2 (New York: Charles Scribner's Sons, 1973), pp. 85–89; Peter Loewenberg, "The Psychology of Racism," in *The Great Fear: Race in the Mind of America*, ed. Gary Nash and Richard Weiss (New York: Holt, Rinehart and Winston, 1970), pp. 186–201; Kraditor, *Means and Ends*, pp. 235–273; Perry, *Boats against the Current*, pp. 239–240; Isaiah Berlin, *The Proper Study of Mankind: An Anthology of Essays* (New York: Farrar, Straus and Giroux, 1998), pp. 389, 405, 426, 428; Toni Morrison, *Playing in the Dark: Whiteness and the Literary Imagination* (Cambridge: Harvard University Press, 1992), pp. 4–5; Thomas Bender, ed., *The Antislavery Debate: Capitalism and Abolitionism as a Problem in Historical Interpretation* (Berkeley: University of California Press, 1992), p. 179.

84. Davis, *Problem of Slavery*, pp. 3–90; Orlando Patterson, *The Ordeal of Integration: Progress and Resentment in America's "Racial" Crisis* (New York: Civitas, 1997), p. 10.

85. David Kuebrich, *Minor Prophecy: Walt Whitman's New American Religion* (Bloomington: Indiana University Press, 1989), pp. 27–65; Martin Klammer, *Whitman, Slavery, and the Emergence of Leaves of Grass* (University Park: Penn State University Press, 1995), pp. 115–140; David S. Reynolds, *Walt Whitman's America: A Cultural Biography* (New York: Alfred A. Knopf, 1995), pp. 306–338; Reynolds, *Beneath the American Renaissance: The Subversive Imagination in the Age of Emerson and Melville* (1988; reprint, Cambridge: Harvard University Press, 1995), pp. 105–110.

86. Whitman, *Leaves*, p. 5 (emphasis added).

87. Ibid., pp. 46, 48–49.

88. Whitman to Emerson, August 1856, in Sculley Bradley and Harold W. Blodgett, eds., *Leaves of Grass: A Norton Critical Edition* (New York: W. W. Norton, 1973), p. 732; Adams, *Memoirs*, 10: 345; Emerson, *Nature*, p. 7.

89. Reynolds, *Whitman's America*, pp. 383–384, 453; C. Vann Woodward, "John Brown's Private War," in *The Burden of Southern History* (Baton Rouge: Louisiana State University Press, 1960), pp. 53–55.

90. Reynolds, *Whitman's America*, pp. 383–384, 453; Jerome Loving, *Walt Whitman: The Song of Himself* (Berkeley: University of California Press, 1999), pp. 94, 110–113, 143, 239–241, 398, 408–409, 443, 471–472, 497; John R. McKivigan, ed., "The Reminiscences of William Wild Thayer, Boston Publisher and Abolitionist," *Proceedings of the Massachusetts Historical Society* 103 (1991): 138–156; Justin Kaplan, *Walt Whitman: A Life* (New York: Simon and Schuster, 1980), pp. 247, 255–256, 341; Rossbach, *Ambivalent Conspirators*, pp. 261–264.

91. F. B. Sanborn, "A Concord Note-Book: Gerrit Smith and John Brown," *The Critic and Literary World: An Illustrated Monthly Review of Literature, Art and Life* 47 (July–December 1905): 355; Horace Traubel, *With Walt Whitman in Camden*, vol. 2: *July 16, 1888–October 31, 1888* (New York: D. Appleton, 1908), pp. 488–489; Reynolds, *Beneath the American Renaissance*, p. 108.

92. Sewell, *Ballots for Freedom*, pp. 286–289.

93. *LIB*, September 7, 1855.

94. Garrison, quoted in Sewell, *Ballots for Freedom*, p. 287; Quarles, *Douglass*, p. 160.

95. John R. McKivigan and Madeleine Leveille, "The 'Black Dream' of Gerrit Smith, New York Abolitionist," *SULAC* 20 (Fall 1985): 64–65, 71; "Case Notes of Gerrit Smith," New York State Lunatic Asylum, book 16, holograph, NYSA; Richard Warch and Jonathan Fanton, eds., *John Brown* (Englewood Cliffs, N.J.: Prentice-Hall, 1973), p. 86; Villard, *Brown*, p. 472; Michael H. Stone, *Healing the Mind: A History of Psychiatry from Antiquity to the Present* (New York: W. W. Norton, 1997), pp. ix, 110; Edward Shorter, *A History of Psychiatry: From the Era of the Asylum to the Age of Prozac* (New York: John Wiley & Sons, 1997), p. 107; G. E. Berrios, "Obsessional Disorders during the Nineteenth Century: Terminological and Classificatory Issues," in *The Anatomy of Madness: Essays in the History of Psychiatry*, ed. W. F. Bynum, Roy Porter, and Michael Shepherd, vol. 1: *People and Ideas* (London: Tavistock, 1985), pp. 170–171; W. L. Miller, *Arguing about Slavery*, p. 423.

96. Frederick Douglass to Harriet Bailey, May 16, 1846, DP; quoted in W. L. Miller, *Arguing about Slavery*, p. 423.

Two. Creating an Image in Black

1. Henry Louis Gates Jr., *Figures in Black: Words, Signs, and the "Racial" Self* (New York: Oxford University Press, 1987), pp. 98–124; John Blassingame, "Introduction," *TFDP*, 1/1: xxi–lxix.

2. Elizabeth Cady Stanton, quoted in Frederick S. Voss, *Majestic in His Wrath: A Pictorial Life of Frederick Douglass* (Washington, D.C.: Smithsonian Institution Press, 1995), p. v. See also *TFDP*, 1/1: xxix.

3. On treating images as texts that reveal hidden or implied meanings, see Allan Sekula, "The Invention of Photographic Meaning," *Artforum* 13 (January 1975): 28; Alan Trachtenberg, *Reading American Photographs: Images as History, Mathew Brady to Walker Evans* (New York: Hill and Wang, 1989), pp. 3–20.

4. Frederick Douglass, *My Bondage and My Freedom* (1855; reprint, Urbana: University of Illinois Press, 1987), p. 28. Douglass estimates his birth year as 1817, whereas the historian Dickson Preston establishes the date as February 1818; *Young Frederick Douglass: The Maryland Years* (Baltimore: Johns Hopkins University Press, 1980), pp. 5–8.

5. Alan Trachtenberg, "The Daguerreotype: American Icon," in *American Daguerreotypes from the Matthew R. Isenburg Collection* (New Haven: Yale University Art Gallery, 1989), p. 16; Trachtenberg, *Reading American Photographs*, pp. 21–70; Trachtenberg, "Photography: The Emergence of a Keyword," and Barbara McCandless, "The Portrait Studio and the Celebrity: Promoting the Art," in *Photography in Nineteenth-Century America*, ed. Martha A. Sandweiss (New York: Harry N. Abrams, 1991), pp. 16–47, 48–75; Robert Taft, *Photography and the American Scene: A Social History, 1839–1889* (1938; reprint, New York: Dover, 1964), pp. 46–166; Mary Panzer, *Mathew Brady and the Image of History* (Washington, D.C.: Smithsonian Institution Press, 1997), pp. 23–38, 71–92; John Stauffer, "Daguerreotyping the National Soul: The Portraits of Southworth and Hawes," *Prospects* 22 (1997): 69–107; Karen Halttunen, *Confidence Men and Painted Women: A Study of Middle-Class Culture in America, 1830–1870* (New Haven: Yale University Press, 1982), pp. xiii–xvii; Benedict Anderson, *Imagined Communities* (New York: Verso, 1991); E. J. Hobsbawm, *Nations and Nationalism since 1780: Programme, Myth, Reality* (New York: Cambridge University Press, 1990), pp. 11, 47.

6. Madison County, New York, which had the highest percentage of abolitionists in the country during the 1850s, also had an unusually high number of daguerreotypists. See Carl Peterson, "19th Century Photographers and

Related Activity in Madison County, New York," *Madison County Heritage* 23 (1998): 15–25.

7. On Douglass' predilection for self-portraits, see Voss, *Majestic in His Wrath*. On Whitman's passion for self-portraiture, see Ed Folsom, *Walt Whitman's Native Representations* (New York: Cambridge University Press, 1994), pp. 99–126; David S. Reynolds, *Walt Whitman's America: A Cultural Biography* (New York: Alfred A. Knopf, 1995), pp. 279–305; Trachtenberg, *Reading American Photographs*, pp. 60–70; Miles Orvell, *The Real Thing: Imitation and Authenticity in American Culture, 1880–1940* (Chapel Hill: University of North Carolina Press, 1989), pp. 3–29.

8. *FDP*, August 30, 1855. My interpretation differs dramatically from that of Eric Lott, who acknowledges Douglass' blackness as "a potential source of political advantage" but downplays Douglass' emphasis on the sincere and authentic display of blackness. See Lott, *Love and Theft: Blackface Minstrelsy and the American Working Class* (New York: Oxford University Press, 1993), pp. 36–37; and Douglass, "Gavitt's Original Ethiopian Serenaders," in *LWFD*, 5: 142.

9. Wilson Armistead, *A Tribute for the Negro* . . . (Manchester: William Irwin, 1848), following p. 456; Voss, *Majestic in His Wrath*, pp. 22–23.

10. Douglass, quoted in *LWFD*, 1: 379–380. See also my analysis of Douglass in "Race and Contemporary Photography: Willie Robert Middlebrook and the Legacy of Frederick Douglass," *21st: The Journal of Contemporary Photography* 1 (1998): 55–60.

11. Douglass, "Pictures," holograph, n.d. [ca. late 1864], DP, unpaginated. Douglass' other speech on photography was on December 3, 1861; *TFDP*, 1/3: 452–473, 619–620. On portraits' constituting about 95 percent of all daguerreotypes, see Robert A. Sobieszek and Odette M. Appel, *The Daguerreotypes of Southworth and Hawes* (1976; reprint, New York: Dover Publications, 1980), p. x.

12. Douglass, "Pictures."

13. Ibid. In calling humans the only picturemaking animals in the world, Douglass was paraphrasing Aristotle. See W. J. T. Mitchell, "Representation," in *Critical Terms for Literary Study*, ed. Frank Lentricchia and Thomas McLaughlin (Chicago: University of Chicago Press, 1995), p. 11; Aristotle, *Poetics*, trans. Malcolm Heath (New York: Penguin, 1996), pp. 6–7.

14. George M. Fredrickson, *The Black Image in the White Mind: The Debate on Afro-American Character and Destiny, 1817–1914* (1971; reprint, Middletown, Conn.: Wesleyan University Press, 1987), pp. 71–164; Thomas F. Gossett, *Race: The History of an Idea in America* (1963; reprint, New York: Oxford University Press, 1997), pp. 54–83; William Stanton, *The Leopard's*

Spots: Scientific Attitudes toward Race in America, 1815–1819 (Chicago: University of Chicago Press, 1960), pp. 90–99; Stauffer, "Daguerreotyping," pp. 93–107.

15. J. C. Nott and George R. Gliddon, *Types of Mankind; or, Ethnological Researches* (Philadelphia: Lippincott, Grambo, 1855), p. 458; Stephen Jay Gould, *The Mismeasure of Man* (1966; reprint, New York: W. W. Norton, 1981), pp. 67, 380; Stanton, *Leopard's Spots*, pp. 161–173.

16. Douglass, "Pictures," DP; *TFDP*, 1/3: 456.

17. James McCune Smith, "Introduction," in Douglass, *Bondage*, pp. 17, 20–21; *TFDP*, 1/1: xxii–xv.

18. Douglass, *Bondage*, p. 205.

19. Richard J. Hinton, *John Brown and His Men* (New York: Funk and Wagnalls, 1894), pp. 48, 103, 107; James C. Malin, *John Brown and the Legend of Fifty-Six* (Philadelphia: American Philosophical Society, 1942), pp. 449–450; John Bowles, *The Stormy Petrel: An Historical Romance of the Civil War* (New York: Home Book, 1894), pp. 76–77, 85–86, 108–109. On portraits of Brown by black photographers, see Ann M. Shumard, *A Durable Memento: Portraits by Augustus Washington, African American Daguerreotypist* (Washington, D.C.: National Portrait Gallery, Smithsonian Institution, 2000), pp. 2–23; and Christopher Mahoney, "Augustus Washington," in *Photographs, Sotheby's New York, Wednesday, October 2, 1996* (New York: Sotheby's, 1996), p. 18.

20. Stauffer, "Daguerreotyping," pp. 83–85; Trachtenberg, *Reading American Photographs*, p. 46.

21. Richard Warch and Jonathan Fanton, eds., *John Brown* (Englewood Cliffs, N.J.: Prentice-Hall, 1973), p. 73; Herman Melville, *Moby-Dick; or, The Whale* (1851; reprint, New York: Penguin, 1992), pp. 135, 181.

22. Douglass, quoted in David S. Reynolds, *Beneath the American Renaissance: The Subversive Imagination in the Age of Emerson and Melville* (1988; reprint, Cambridge: Harvard University Press, 1995), p. 76.

23. Douglass, *Bondage*, pp. 88–89; David Herbert Donald, *Lincoln* (New York: Simon and Schuster, 1995), p. 15.

24. Douglass, *Bondage*, p. 83. See Figure 2 for a better view of Douglass' scar.

25. Len Gougeon and Joel Myerson, eds., *Emerson's Antislavery Writings* (New Haven: Yale University Press, 1995), p. xlvii; Henry David Thoreau, "A Plea for Captain John Brown," in *Norton Anthology of American Literature*, 3d ed., vol. 1 (New York: W. W. Norton, 1989), p. 1846. On Brown's performativity, see Robert A. Ferguson, "Story and Transcription in the Trial of John Brown," *YJLH* 6 (Winter 1994): 37–73.

26. Mary S. Bull, "Gerrit Smith," *Good Company* 6 (November 1880): 241, MCHS; Gerrit Smith, "Letter of 1868," in *Fifty Years Ago: The Half-*

Century Annalists' Letters to the Hamilton College Alumni Association, 1865–1900, ed. Melvin Gilbert Dodge (Kirkland, N.Y.: Hamilton College, 1900), p. 32, HCA; Charles A. Hammond, *Gerrit Smith: The Story of a Noble Man's Life* (Geneva, N.Y.: W. F. Humphrey, 1900), p. 8; Octavius Brooks Frothingham, *Gerrit Smith: A Biography* (New York: G. P. Putnam's Sons, 1878), pp. 23–24. In the 1850s men's shirt collars were typically turned down over the necktie, were of moderate size, and did not rise up high on the neck. See Joan Severa, *Dressed for the Photographer: Ordinary Americans and Fashion, 1840–1900* (Kent, Ohio: Kent State University Press, 1995), pp. 57, 79, 105.

27. Both McCune Smith and Douglass quote Lord Byron in Douglass, *Bondage,* pp. 15, 96, 153. On the cult of Byron see Anne Barton, "Not an Ideal Husband," *NYR,* November 18, 1999, pp. 46–51, quotation p. 46; Northrop Frye, *Fables of Identity: Studies in Poetic Mythology* (New York: Harcourt, Brace, 1951), pp. 188–189; Andrew Elfenbein, *Byron and the Victorians* (New York: Cambridge University Press, 1995), pp. 13–89; Frank Lentricchia, "Harriet Beecher Stowe and the Byron Whirlwind," *Bulletin of the New York Public Library,* 70 (April 1966): 218–228; Joan D. Hedrick, *Harriet Beecher Stowe: A Life* (New York: Oxford University Press, 1994), pp. 21, 353–377.

28. Smith, "Autobiographical Sketch of the Life of Gerrit Smith," holograph, n.d. [1856], GSP; Ralph Volney Harlow, *Gerrit Smith: Philanthropist and Reformer* (New York: Henry Holt, 1939), pp. 336–337; Trachtenberg, *Reading American Photographs,* p. 46; Smith to Charles Sumner, March 2, 1856, GSP.

29. Oswald Garrison Villard, *John Brown, 1800–1859: A Biography Fifty Years After* (1910; reprint, New York: Alfred A. Knopf, 1943), pp. 1–9. On the third-person narrative voice in autobiography, see Robert Folkenflik, "The Self as Other," in *The Culture of Autobiography: Constructions of Self-Representations,* ed. Folkenflik (Stanford: Stanford University Press, 1993), pp. 215–234; Philippe Lejeune, "Autobiography in the Third Person," *New Literary History* 9 (1977): 27–50; Diane Bjorklund, *Interpreting the Self: Two Hundred Years of American Autobiography* (Chicago: University of Chicago Press, 1998), pp. 89–123.

30. Smith, *Speeches of Gerrit Smith in Congress* (New York: Mason Brothers, 1856), p. 228; Smith, quoted in Lawrence J. Friedman, *Gregarious Saints: Self and Community in American Abolitionism, 1830–1870* (Cambridge: Cambridge University Press, 1982), pp. 193–194; John R. McKivigan, "The Frederick Douglass–Gerrit Smith Friendship and Political Abolitionism in the 1850s," in *Frederick Douglass: New Literary and Historical Essays,* ed. Eric J. Sundquist (Cambridge: Cambridge University Press, 1990), p. 213.

31. Mary Brown, quoted in *The Principia*, November 26, 1859, p. 6; Warch and Fanton, *Brown*, pp. 73, 83, 96; F. B. Sanborn, ed., *The Life and Letters of John Brown, Liberator of Kansas, and Martyr of Virginia* (Boston: Roberts Brothers, 1855), pp. 38–39.

32. McCune Smith, "Letter from Communipaw," *FDP*, August 12, 1858.

33. George Thomas, "Personal Recollections of Gerrit Smith," Utica, N.Y., January 5, 1878, typescript, MCHS; Gerrit Smith to P. M. Marshall, April 16, 1838, GSP.

34. Gerrit Smith to Elizabeth Livingston Smith, August 10, 1817, GSP; Smith to Frederick Douglass, February 18, 1852, GSP; Sarah Grimké to Smith, September 9, 185[?], GSP; Smith to the Postmaster of Sherburne, N.Y., March 4, 1852, GSP; John Beeson to Smith, November 14 1856, GSP. On Greene Smith's not being able to read his father's handwriting, see Theodore Dwight Weld to Gerrit Smith, March 4, 1852, GSP.

35. Smith, "Autobiographical Sketch."

36. Vernon Loggins, *The Negro Author: His Development in America* (New York: Columbia University Press, 1931), pp. 179–182; David W. Blight, "In Search of Learning, Liberty, and Self Definition: James McCune Smith and the Ordeal of the Antebellum Black Intellectual," *AANYLH* 9 (July 1985): 7–9; McCune Smith to Horace Greeley, January 29, 1844, *BAP*, 3: 430–431; *FDP*, March 18, 1852, December 15, 1854, March 7, 1856; Leslie A. Falk, "James McCune Smith: First Black American to Graduate from a Medical School: Abolitionist, Suffragist, and Feminist," manuscript, WL, pp. ix–xiii, 22, 82, 98–101; Douglass, "Dr. James McCune Smith," *DM*, March 1859.

37. McCune Smith, "Horoscope," *FDP*, March 7, 1856.

38. McCune Smith, quoted in *FDP*, January 8, 1852; Falk, "McCune Smith," pp. xii, 8.

39. McCune Smith, quoted in *FDP*, March 9, 1855.

40. McCune Smith, *The Destiny of the People of Color: A Lecture Delivered before the Philomathean Society and Hamilton Lyceum, in January, 1841* (New York, 1843), pp. 13–15, WL. On McCune Smith's "Letters of the Republic," see Chapter Seven.

41. McCune Smith, quoted in *TFDP*, 1/3: 74.

42. McCune Smith to Gerrit Smith, May 12, 1848, GSP.

43. "Ethiop" [William Wilson], *FDP*, January 26, 1855; Jane H. Pease and William H. Pease, *They Who Would Be Free: Blacks' Search for Freedom, 1830–1861* (1974; reprint, Urbana: University of Illinois Press, 1990), pp. 292–293.

Three. Glimpsing God's World on Earth

1. On men's neckties, collars, and coats, see Joan L. Severa, *Dressed for the Photographer: Ordinary Americans and Fashion, 1840–1900* (Kent, Ohio: Kent State University Press, 1995), pp. 18–21, 104–109. On the "Byron Collar" and hair see Melvin Gilbert Dodge, ed., *Fifty Years Ago: The Half-Century Annalists' Letters to the Hamilton College Alumni Association, 1865–1900* (Kirkland, N.Y.: Hamilton College Press, 1900), p. 32.

2. Gerrit Smith to Gent. of the Phoenix Society, December 15, 1818, in "Historical Account of the Phoenix Society," holograph, n.p., HCA; *Proceedings of the Convention of Radical Political Abolitionists . . .* (New York: Central Abolition Board, 1855), p. 60, HL.

3. Charles A. Hammond, *Gerrit Smith: The Story of a Noble Man's Life* (Geneva, N.Y.: W. F. Humphrey, 1900), p. 8; Octavius Brooks Frothingham, *Gerrit Smith: A Biography* (New York: G. P. Putnam's Sons, 1878), pp. 23–24; Mary S. Bull, "Gerrit Smith," *Good Company* 6 (November 1880): 241; Lord Byron, *The Siege of Corinth,* in *Lord Byron: Selected Poems* (New York: Penguin, 1996), p. 359.

4. Gerrit Smith to Elizabeth Livingston Smith, July 16, 1815, GSP.

5. Ibid.; Gerrit Smith to Peter Smith, November 3, 1816, GSP; Smith to Catherine Henry, October 24, 1846, GSP; Smith to Elizabeth Livingston Smith, September 3, 1817, GSP.

6. Ralph Volney Harlow, *Gerrit Smith: Philanthropist and Reformer* (New York: Henry Holt, 1939), pp. 1–4; Frothingham, *Gerrit Smith,* pp. 5–13; Kenneth Wiggins Porter, *John Jacob Astor: Business Man* (Cambridge: Harvard University Press, 1931), pp. 36–38, 48–50, 93–100; Hammond, *Gerrit Smith,* pp. 3–6; "Gerrit Smith," *Harper's Weekly,* January 16, 1875; Smith, "Autobiographical Sketch of the Life of Gerrit Smith," holograph, n.d. [1856], GSP.

7. Harlow, *Gerrit Smith,* pp. 1–4; Frothingham, *Gerrit Smith,* pp. 5–13, 137–142; Hammond, *Gerrit Smith,* pp. 3–6; Bull, "Gerrit Smith," p. 246; Donna Burdick, ed., *Peterboro, New York: A Walking Tour* (Smithfield, N.Y.: Smithfield Community Association); Rev. Silas E. Persons, "A Historical Sketch of the Religious Denominations of Madison County, New York, 1796–1896," typescript, MCHS, p. 14; Ulysses Prentiss Hedrick, *A History of Agriculture in the State of New York* (Albany: New York State Agricultural Society, 1933), pp. 282–283; George Thomas, "Personal Recollections of Gerrit Smith," January 5, 1875, typescript, MCHS; Edward J. Renehan Jr., *The Secret Six: The True Tale of the Men Who Conspired with John Brown* (New York: Crown, 1995), p. 15; Whitney R. Cross, *The Burned-Over Dis-*

trict: The Social and Intellectual History of Enthusiastic Religion in Western New York, 1800–1850 (Ithaca: Cornell University Press, 1950), pp. 55–65; L. M. Hammond, *History of Madison County, State of New York* (Syracuse: Truair, Smith, 1872), pp. 145, 695–727; Walter Pilkington, *Hamilton College, 1812–1962* (Clinton, N.Y.: Hamilton College, 1962), p. 45. In many respects Peter Smith's career as a land baron resembled that of his contemporary William Cooper, who founded the settlement of Ostego, New York. On Cooper see Alan Taylor, *William Cooper's Town: Power and Persuasion on the Early American Frontier* (New York: Alfred A. Knopf, 1995), pp. 86–114, 141–169, 199–228.

8. Frothingham, *Gerrit Smith*, p. 9; John Adams Smith to Peter Smith, January 15, 1821, GSP; Peter Smith to Gerrit Smith, November 20, 1819, GSP; Elizabeth Smith Miller, untitled reminiscences, n.d., MCHS; Thomas, "Personal Recollections"; Harlow, *Gerrit Smith*, pp. 3–5, 10.

9. "Letter from Gerrit Smith to Gov. Hunt, February 20, 1852," *FDP*, March 4, 1852; Smith, *Speeches of Gerrit Smith in Congress* (New York: Mason Brothers, 1856), p. 228; Thomas, "Personal Recollections." On the importance of northern abolitionists' memories of slavery, see Joanne Pope Melish, *Disowning Slavery: Gradual Emancipation and "Race" in New England, 1780–1860* (Ithaca: Cornell University Press, 1998), pp. 1–11, 224–225; James L. Huston, "The Experiential Basis of the Northern Antislavery Impulse," *Journal of Southern History* 56 (November 1990): 609–640.

10. Gerrit Smith to Elizabeth Livingston Smith, July 16, 1815, GSP; "Catalogue of the Faculty and Students of Hamilton College," November 25, 1814, holograph, HCS; Harlow, *Gerrit Smith*, pp. 5–6, 8–10; Frothingham, *Gerrit Smith*, pp. 22–24; Hammond, *Gerrit Smith*, pp. 7–8; Pilkington, *Hamilton College*, pp. 64–66, 68–69, 74–81; Thomas, "Personal Recollections."

11. "Board of Trustees of Hamilton College: Book of Minutes, 1812–1875," holograph, pp. 6, 15, HCA; Frothingham, *Gerrit Smith*, pp. 5–10; Hammond, *Gerrit Smith*, pp. 5–7; Harlow, *Gerrit Smith*, pp. 7–10; Taylor, *Cooper's Town*, pp. 13–14; Pilkington, *Hamilton College*, p. 59; Thomas, "Personal Recollections."

12. Frothingham, *Gerrit Smith*, pp. 5–10; Hammond, *Gerrit Smith*, pp. 5–7; Harlow, *Gerrit Smith*, pp. 7–10; Thomas, "Personal Recollections"; Peter Smith to Gerrit Smith, June 7, 1814, May 22, 1815, November 19, 1819, GSP.

13. Miller, untitled reminiscences; Hammond, *Gerrit Smith*, pp. 8–9; Frothingham, *Gerrit Smith*, pp. 20–21; Harlow, *Gerrit Smith*, pp. 5–10; Thomas, "Personal Recollections."

14. Thomas, "Personal Recollections"; Gerrit Smith to Elizabeth Livingston Smith, January 14, 1817, GSP; Frothingham, *Gerrit Smith*, pp. 27–28; Hammond, *Gerrit Smith*, pp. 8–9; Harlow, *Gerrit Smith*, pp. 12–13; Gerrit Smith, untitled poem, holograph, March 20, 1820, Elizabeth Smith Miller Common Place Book, GSP.

15. Frothingham, *Gerrit Smith*, pp. 27–28; Hammond, *Gerrit Smith*, pp. 8–9; Harlow, *Gerrit Smith*, pp. 12–14; Gerrit Smith, preface to his untitled poem, holograph, March 20, 1820, GSP.

16. Smith, untitled poem.

17. Ibid.

18. Ibid.

19. Ibid.

20. Poe, "A Dream within a Dream," in *Selected Writings of Edgar Allan Poe*, ed. Edward H. Davidson (Boston: Houghton Mifflin, 1956), p. 8; Raymond Foye, ed., *The Unknown Poe* (San Francisco: City Lights Books, 1980), p. 96; David S. Reynolds, *Beneath the American Renaissance: The Subversive Imagination in the Age of Emerson and Melville* (1988; reprint, Cambridge: Harvard University Press, 1995), p. 43.

21. Harlow, *Gerrit Smith*, pp. 10–11, 14–16, 47–48; Frothingham, *Gerrit Smith*, pp. 10–21; Cross, *Burned-Over District*, pp. 3–51; Mary P. Ryan, *Cradle of the Middle Class: The Family in Oneida County, New York, 1790–1865* (New York: Cambridge University Press, 1981), pp. 60–104.

22. Harlow, *Gerrit Smith*, pp. 10–11, 14–16; Frothingham, *Gerrit Smith*, pp. 10–21; Peter Smith to Gerrit Smith, November 20, 1819, January 7 1820, February 22, 1820, March 1820 (quotation), GSP; Miller, untitled reminiscences; William James, *The Varieties of Religious Experience: A Study in Human Nature* (1902; reprint, New York: Penguin, 1982), pp. 53–72.

23. Frothingham, *Gerrit Smith*, pp. 19–22, 27–28; Hammond, *Gerrit Smith*, pp. 8–9; Harlow, *Gerrit Smith*, pp. 3, 10, 13–15; Thomas, "Personal Recollections" (quotation}; Peter Smith to Gerrit Smith, November 20, 1819, January 7, 1820, March 11, 1820, April 6, 19, 1820, July 26, 1820, GSP.

24. Miller, untitled reminiscences; Harlow, *Gerrit Smith*, pp. 10, 14–16; Hammond, *Gerrit Smith*, p. 9; Thomas, "Personal Recollections." The land office is the only building on the Smith estate that is still standing (the mansion-house burned down in 1936). I am grateful to Beth Spokowsky for letting me inside.

25. Dickson J. Preston, *Young Frederick Douglass: The Maryland Years* (Baltimore: Johns Hopkins University Press, 1980), pp. 41–52, quotation p. 50; Lawrence J. Friedman, *Gregarious Saints: Self and Community in American Abolitionism, 1830–1870* (Cambridge: Cambridge University Press, 1982),

pp. 192–193; Douglass, *My Bondage and My Freedom* (1855; reprint, Urbana: University of Illinois Press, 1987), pp. 46, 70; Douglass, quoted in Robin Blackburn, *The Making of New World Slavery: From the Baroque to the Modern, 1492–1800* (New York: Verso, 1996), p. 1; Harriet Tubman, quoted in Judith Bentley, *Harriet Tubman* (New York: Franklin Watts, 1990), p. 79; "Letter from Gerrit Smith," *NS*, March 16, 1849; Frederick Douglass to Gerrit Smith, March 30, 1849, GSP; John R. McKivigan, "The Frederick Douglass–Gerrit Smith Friendship and Political Abolitionism in the 1850s," in *Frederick Douglass: New Literary and Historical Essays*, ed. Eric J. Sundquist (Cambridge: Cambridge University Press, 1990), pp. 213–216; Thomas, "Personal Recollections"; Frothingham, *Gerrit Smith*, pp. 137–139; Barbara J. Giambastiani, ed., *Country Roads Revisited* (Oneida: Madison County Historical Society, 1984), p. 68. The Smith mansion-house was remodeled in 1846 in the Greek Revival style, which is when the columns were added.

26. Orlando Patterson, *Slavery and Social Death: A Comparative Study* (Cambridge: Harvard University Press, 1982), pp. 1–16, 93, 334–342; David Brion Davis, "At the Heart of Slavery," *NYR*, October 17, 1996, pp. 51–54; Gerda Lerner, *The Creation of Patriarchy* (New York: Oxford University Press, 1986), pp. 76–100; Eugene D. Genovese, *Roll, Jordan, Roll: The World the Slaves Made* (New York: Vintage, 1972), pp. 3–49.

27. Patterson, *Slavery and Social Death*, pp. 39–44, 51, 63–65, 302; David Brion Davis, *Slavery and Human Progress* (New York: Oxford University Press, 1984), pp. 14–16; Davis, *The Problem of Slavery in the Age of Revolution, 1770–1823* (Ithaca: Cornell University Press, 1975), pp. 562–563.

28. In summarizing Douglass' early years, I rely heavily on his second autobiography, *My Bondage and My Freedom*, rather than on his first or third. I do this not only because I consider *My Bondage* superior to the other two autobiographies, but also because of its periodization. In *My Bondage* Douglass wrote about his past from the vantage point of who he was in 1855, and I am interested in understanding him from the same vantage point—specifically, how and why he forged the kinds of relationships he did with his three comrades during the 1850s.

29. Douglass, *Bondage*, pp. 27–30, quotation p. 29; Preston, *Young Douglass*, pp. xv, 3–30; William S. McFeely, *Frederick Douglass* (New York: W. W. Norton, 1991), pp. 5–9.

30. Douglass, *Bondage*, pp. 29–31; McFeely, *Douglass*, pp. 8–9.

31. Douglass, *Bondage*, pp. 34, 36–37; Preston, *Young Douglass*, pp. 37–40; McFeely, *Douglass*, pp. 9–10.

32. Douglass, *Bondage*, pp. 96, 99–101, 104–105, 116–117; Preston, *Young Douglass*, pp. 96–100; McFeely, *Douglass*, pp. 33–39.

33. Douglass, *Bondage*, pp. 96, 99–101; Preston, *Young Douglass*, p. 100; McFeely, *Douglass*, pp. 34–36; David W. Blight, ed., *The Columbian Orator* (New York: New York University Press, 1998), pp. xiii–xxvii.

34. Douglass, *Bondage*, pp. 104–105; Douglass, *Life and Times of Frederick Douglass* (1892; reprint, New York: Collier, 1962), pp. 90–94; Preston, *Young Douglass*, pp. 96–98; McFeely, *Douglass*, pp. 37–39; James, *Varieties of Religious Experience*, pp. 206–216, quotation p. 206.

35. Charles C. Andrews, *The History of the New-York African Free-Schools* (1830; reprint, New York: Negro Universities Press, 1969), pp. 50–53; Leslie A. Falk, "James McCune Smith, First Black American to Graduate from a Medical School: Abolitionist, Suffragist, and Feminist," typescript, pp. 7–8, WL; George W. Williams, *History of the Negro Race in America, from 1619 to 1880: Negroes as Slaves, as Soldiers, and as Citizens* (New York: G. P. Putnam's Sons, 1883), pp. 165–168; Roi Ottley and William J. Weatherby, eds., *The Negro in New York: An Informal Social History, 1626–1940* (New York: Praeger, 1967), pp. 44–45.

36. James McCune Smith, quoted in Carter Woodson, ed., *The Mind of the Negro as Reflected in Letters Written during the Crisis, 1800–1860* (New York: Russell & Russell, 1926), p. 270; McCune Smith, "Introduction," in *A Memorial Discourse; by Rev. Henry Highland Garnet . . .* (Philadelphia: Joseph M. Wilson, 1865), p. 24; McCune Smith, "Introduction," in Douglass, *Bondage*, p. 23; David W. Blight, "In Search of Learning, Liberty, and Self Definition: James McCune Smith and the Ordeal of the Antebellum Black Intellectual," *AANYLH* 9 (July 1985): 7–8; Williams, *History*, pp. 165–168. On slaves' de facto freedom, see Shane White, "'It Was a Proud Day': African Americans, Festivals, and Parades in the North, 1741–1834," *JAH* 81 (June 1994): 38; and Shane White and Graham White, *Stylin': African American Expressive Culture from Its Beginnings to the Zoot Suit* (Ithaca: Cornell University Press, 1998), pp. 86–87.

37. Arthur Zilversmit, *The First Emancipation: The Abolition of Slavery in the North* (Chicago: University of Chicago Press, 1967), pp. 181–182, 208–215, esp. 213–215.

38. McCune Smith, quoted in Williams, *History*, pp. 167–168.

39. White, "'Proud Day,'" pp. 38–39.

40. McCune Smith, "Introduction," in *Memorial Discourse*, pp. 24–25.

41. Ibid., pp. 21–24; James Weldon Johnson, *Black Manhattan* (1930; reprint, New York: Atheneum, 1968), pp. 21–26; Leo H. Hirsch Jr., "The Slave in New York," *JNH* 16 (1931): 429–436; Carleton Mabee, *Black Education in New York State: From Colonial to Modern Times* (Syracuse, N.Y.: Syracuse University Press, 1979), pp. 19–35; Andrews, *History of Free-Schools*, pp. 35–60.

42. "Reception of Dr. Smith," *CA*, October 28, 1837; Blight, "In Search of Learning," p. 8; *BAP*, 3: 3–5, 224–225, 350–351.

43. John Brown to Henry L. Stearns, July 15, 1857, in Oswald Garrison Villard, *John Brown, 1800–1859: A Biography Fifty Years After* (1910; reprint, New York: Alfred A. Knopf, 1943), pp. 1–5.

44. Brown, quoted in Villard, *Brown*, pp. 3–5; Steven B. Oates, *To Purge This Land with Blood: A Biography of John Brown* (1970; reprint, Amherst: University of Massachusetts Press, 1984), pp. 11–12.

45. Brown, quoted in Villard, *Brown*, pp. 4–5; Oates, *To Purge This Land*, pp. 11–15; F. B. Sanborn, ed., *The Life and Letters of John Brown . . .* (Boston: Roberts Brothers, 1885), pp. 36–41.

46. Oates, *To Purge This Land*, pp. 12–14; Sanborn, *Life and Letters of Brown*, pp. 31–34; Villard, *Brown*, pp. 16–18.

47. Brown, quoted in Villard, *Brown*, pp. 6–7; Villard, *Brown*, pp. 17–26, quotation p. 19; Oates, *To Purge This Land*, pp. 16–18, quotation p. 17; Sanborn, *Life and Letters of Brown*, pp. 33–35; *Proceedings of the Convention*, p. 45.

48. Harlow, *Gerrit Smith*, p. 16; Ryan, *Cradle of the Middle Class*, pp. 60–104.

49. Hammond, *Gerrit Smith*, pp. 9–10; Harlow, *Gerrit Smith*, pp. 15–16; Frothingham, *Gerrit Smith*, p. 27; Smith to Mr. Worthington, April 13, 1840, GSP; Smith to Samuel and Harriet Russell, October 1, 1841, GSP; Smith to John Thomson Mason, November 11, 1842, October 19, 1846, November 6, 1846, GSP; George Fitzhugh to Gerrit Smith, December 25, 1854, February 25, 1855, GSP; Smith, "Autobiographical Sketch."

50. Bull, "Gerrit Smith," pp. 247–248, quotation from Garrison p. 247.

51. Harlow, *Gerrit Smith*, pp. 16–17, 46–52; Daniel Cady to Gerrit Smith, June 25, July 8, 1822, GSP; Gerrit Smith to Ann Smith, September 12, 1825, GSP.

52. Frothingham, *Gerrit Smith*, pp. 44, 144–160; Harlow, *Gerrit Smith*, pp. 51–52; Ann Smith to Gerrit Smith, March 6, 1826, GSP; Gerrit Smith to Rev. Hewitt, 1829, GSP.

53. Gerrit Smith to the Editors of *Freedom's Journal*, March 21, 1827, GSP; Harlow, *Gerrit Smith*, pp. 55–56, 60–61; Ralph Gurley to Gerrit Smith, November 21, 1827, January 5, 1828, GSP. On the Colonization Society, see George M. Fredrickson, *The Black Image in the White Mind: The Debate on Afro-American Character and Destiny, 1817–1914* (1971; reprint, Middletown, Conn.: Wesleyan University Press, 1987), pp. 1–42; P. J. Staudenraus, *The African Colonization Movement, 1816–1865* (New York: Columbia University Press, 1961); and James Brewer Stewart, *Holy Warriors: The Abolitionists and American Slavery* (New York: Hill & Wang, 1976), pp. 29–32.

54. Gerrit Smith to the Editors of *Freedom's Journal*, March 21, 1827, GSP; Harlow, *Gerrit Smith*, pp. 55–56, 60–61; Ralph Gurley to Gerrit Smith, November 21, 1827, January 5, 1828, GSP.

55. Smith, quoted in Harlow, *Gerrit Smith*, pp. 67–68; Frothingham, *Gerrit Smith*, pp. 144–160.

56. David Brion Davis, *The Problem of Slavery in Western Culture* (New York: Oxford University Press, 1966), p. 292; Gerrit Smith to His Nieces and Nephews, April 27, 1829, GSP, Smith, *To the Religious Newspapers Reviewers of My Recent Discourse*, broadside, September 3, 1859, GSP.

Four. The Panic and the Making of Abolitionists

1. *Gerrit Smith to Edward C. Delevan, Esq., on the Reformation of the Intemperate*, pamphlet, September 11, 1833, GSP; Ralph Volney Harlow, *Gerrit Smith: Philanthropist and Reformer* (New York: Henry Holt, 1939), p. 74.

2. R. J. Rorabaugh, *The Alcoholic Republic: An American Tradition* (New York: Oxford University Press, 1979), pp. ix, 5–11, 149–156.

3. Leo Damrosch, *The Sorrows of the Quaker Jesus: James Nayler and the Puritan Crackdown on the Free Spirit* (Cambridge: Harvard University Press, 1996); Christopher Hill, *The World Turned Upside Down: Radical Ideas during the English Revolution* (London: Penguin, 1975), pp. 107–150; Hugh Barbour and J. William Frost, *The Quakers* (Richmond, Ind.: Friends United Press, 1988), pp. 11–38; David Brion Davis, *The Problem of Slavery in Western Culture* (New York: Oxford University Press, 1966), pp. 291–299; Davis, "At the Heart of Slavery," *NYR*, October 17, 1996, pp. 53–54. On Brown and Douglass' claiming Cromwell as a hero, see Bertram Wyatt Brown, "'A Volcano beneath a Mountain of Snow': John Brown and the Problem of Interpretation," in *His Soul Goes Marching On: Responses to John Brown and the Harper's Ferry Raid*, ed. Paul Finkelman (Charlottesville: University Press of Virginia, 1995), p. 21; Oswald Garrison Villard, *John Brown, 1800–1859: A Biography Fifty Years After* (1910; reprint, New York: Alfred A. Knopf, 1943), p. 16; *TFDP*, 1/3: 456; *TFDP*, 1/4: 379.

4. Lewis Perry, *Radical Abolitionism: Anarchy and the Government of God in Antislavery Thought* (Ithaca: Cornell University Press, 1973), p. 65.

5. Smith, "Autobiographical Sketch of the Life of Gerrit Smith," holograph, n.d. [1856], GSP; Smith to the Rev. Hewitt, 1829, GSP; Harlow, *Gerrit Smith*, pp. 51–60.

6. Smith, *Letter to Edward C. Delevan, Esq.*, November 6, 1837 (printed letter), pp. 4–7, GSP; John Stauffer, "Beyond Social Control: The Example of Gerrit Smith, Romantic Radical," *ATQ* 11 (September 1997): 249–252.

7. Smith, "Autobiographical Sketch"; Smith to Rev. Hewitt, 1829, GSP; Smith to Gen. John H. Cooke, December 11, 1840, GSP; Smith to Edwin Hale, June 26, 1841, GSP; Harlow, *Gerrit Smith*, pp. 46–66, 67–71, 113–127; Octavius Brooks Frothingham, *Gerrit Smith: A Biography* (New York: G. P. Putnam's Sons, 1878), pp. 144–151, 163–171; George Thomas, "Personal Recollections of Gerrit Smith," manuscript, January 5, 1875, MCHS.

8. On the rise of immediatism see David Brion Davis, "The Emergence of Immediatism in British and American Antislavery Thought," in *From Homicide to Slavery: Studies in American Culture* (New York: Oxford University Press, 1986), pp. 238–257; Anne C. Loveland, "Evangelicalism and 'Immediate Emancipation' in American Antislavery Thought," *Journal of Southern History* 32 (May 1966): 172–188; Robert H. Abzug, *Cosmos Crumbling: American Reform and the Religious Imagination* (New York: Oxford University Press, 1994), pp. 125–162.

9. Harlow, *Gerrit Smith*, pp. 113–120.

10. Gerrit Smith to Ann Smith, July 2, 1832, GSP; Gerrit Smith Diary, March 6, 1834, February 10, 1835, quoted in Frothingham, *Gerrit Smith*, p. 45; Ann Smith to Gerrit Smith, February 2, 1835, GSP; Harlow, *Gerrit Smith*, pp. 52–53.

11. Smith, quoted in Frothingham, *Gerrit Smith*, pp. 163–164; Smith to Elizur Wright, August 13, 1834, GSP. See also Elizur Wright to Gerrit Smith, August 6, 1834, GSP; and *Letter of Gerrit Smith to President Schmucker*, broadside, June 19, 1838, GSP.

12. Harlow, *Gerrit Smith*, p. 120; Smith, quoted in Frothingham, *Gerrit Smith*, p. 164. On Jacksonian-era mobs see Leonard L. Richards, *"Gentlemen of Property and Standing": Anti-Abolition Mobs in Jacksonian America* (New York: Oxford University Press, 1970), pp. 3–19, 84–93, 131–170; Lorman Ratner, *Powder Keg: Northern Opposition to the Antislavery Movement, 1831–1840* (New York: Basic Books, 1968); and James Brewer Stewart, "Peaceful Hopes and Violent Experiences: The Evolution of Reforming and Radical Abolitionism, 1831–1837," *CWH* 17 (December 1971): 293–309.

13. Harlow, *Gerrit Smith*, pp. 120–124; Frothingham, *Gerrit Smith*, pp. 164–166; Howard Alexander Morrison, "Gentlemen of Proper Understanding: A Closer Look at Utica's Anti-Abolitionist Mob," *NYHIST*, January 1981, pp. 61–62; and William Lee Miller, *Arguing about Slavery: The Great Battle in the United States Congress* (New York: Alfred A. Knopf, 1996), pp. 51–52.

14. Frothingham, *Gerrit Smith*, pp. 164–165, quotation p. 165; Harlow, *Gerrit Smith*, pp. 122–124; Gerrit Smith to Leonard Bacon, October 24, 1835, GSP; "Speech of Gerrit Smith," in *The Abolitionists: A Collection of Their Writings*, ed. Louis Ruchames (New York: G. P. Putnam's Sons, 1963), p. 114; Morrison, "Gentlemen of Proper Understanding," pp. 61–62, 81–

82; Benjamin Sevitch, "The Well-Planned Riot of October 21, 1835: Utica's Answer to Abolitionism," *NYHIST* 50 (April 1969): 251–263.

15. *Speech of Mr. Gerrit Smith, in the Meeting of the New-York Anti-Slavery Society . . . October 22, 1835*, broadside, GSP; Harlow, *Gerrit Smith*, pp. 120–124; Frothingham, *Gerrit Smith*, pp. 164–166.

16. Smith, quoted in Frothingham, *Gerrit Smith*, p. 166; Smith to Rev. R. R. Gurley, quoted in ibid., pp. 166–168.

17. Gerrit Smith to Lewis Tappan, April 1, 1836, GSP; *Third Annual Report of the American Anti-Slavery Society . . . on the 10th May, 1836* (New York: William S. Dorr, 1836), p. 14; *Speech of Smith in Meeting of New-York Anti-Slavery Society* (quotation); Gerrit Smith to Bro. Bailey, August 1, 1843, GSP.

18. On the deaths of Ann and Fitzhugh see Harlow, *Gerrit Smith*, pp. 16–17; Leonard Bacon to Gerrit Smith, February 24, 1837, GSP; Henry Fitzhugh to Gerrit Smith, April 28, 1835, GSP.

19. Harlow, *Gerrit Smith*, pp. 22–31; Frothingham, *Gerrit Smith*, pp. 30–37; Smith to David Jones, October 27, November 23, 1835, GSP; Thomas, "Personal Recollections," MCHS.

20. On the effects of the panic on Smith, see Smith to Richard Kingston, Esq., June 22, 1837, GSP; Smith to F. P. Tracy, June 9, 1840, GSP; Smith to Dr. Corliss, April 1, 1840, GSP; Smith to David Jones, February 28, 1840, GSP; Harlow, *Gerrit Smith*, pp. 22–31.

21. Smith, *Letter to Delevan*; *Letter of Smith to Schmucker*; Stauffer, "Beyond Social Control," pp. 248–253.

22. *Letter of Smith to Schmucker*; Smith to Mr. Edwards, August 14, 1837, GSP; Smith to Gen. John H. Cooke, August 26, 1839, GSP.

23. Bacon to Smith, February 24, 1837, GSP. See also Hugh Davis, "Northern Colonizationists and Free Blacks, 1823–1837: A Case Study of Leonard Bacon," *JER* 17 (Winter 1997): 651–675; and Davis, *Leonard Bacon: New England Reformer and Antislavery Moderate* (Baton Rouge: Louisiana State University Press, 1998), pp. 65–84.

24. Bacon to Smith, February 24, 1837, GSP. See also David Brion Davis, "Reconsidering the Colonization Movement: Leonard Bacon and the Problem of Evil," *Intellectual History Newsletter* 14 (1992): 12; and George M. Fredrickson, *The Black Image in the White Mind: The Debate on Afro-American Character and Destiny, 1817–1914* (1971; reprint, Middletown, Conn.: Wesleyan University Press, 1987), p. 101.

25. Gerrit Smith, *Nathan to David, December 4, 1841*, broadside, GSP.

26. Gerrit Smith to Rev. Scofield, February 1, 1843, GSP; Smith to Joshua V. Himes, January 16, 1843, GSP; Smith to My Dearly Beloved, October 21, 1844, quoted in Frothingham, *Gerrit Smith*, p. 48. On the Millerites see

Ronald L. Numbers and Jonathan M. Butler, eds., *The Disappointed: Millerism and Millenarianism in the Nineteenth Century* (Knoxville: University of Tennessee Press, 1993); R. Laurence Moore, *Religious Outsiders and the Making of Americans* (New York: Oxford University Press, 1986), pp. 128–149; and Whitney R. Cross, *The Burned-Over District: The Social and Intellectual History of Enthusiastic Religion in Western New York, 1800–1850* (Ithaca: Cornell University Press, 1950), pp. 287–321.

27. Smith, "Autobiographical Sketch."

28. Gerrit Smith to F. P. Tracy, June 6, 1840, GSP; Smith to Oliver Johnson, July 6, 1840, GSP; Smith to W. E. Channing, August 7, 1841, GSP.

29. Smith to James C. Fuller, November 12, 1841, GSP; Ralph Volney Harlow, "Gerrit Smith and the Free Church Movement," *Proceedings of the New York State Historical Association* 18 (1937): 269–287.

30. Gerrit Smith to Rev. R. R. Gurley, quoted in Harlow, *Gerrit Smith*, pp. 67–68; *Third Annual Report*, p. 14.

31. Smith, quoted in *Fifth Annual Report of the Executive Committee of the American Anti-Slavery Society . . . on the 8th May, 1838* (New York: William S. Dorr, 1838), p. 38.

32. Ibid., p. 32.

33. Thomas, "Personal Recollections"; Mary S. Bull, "Gerrit Smith," *Good Company* 6 (November 1880): 245, MCHS; Gerrit and Nancy Smith, untitled poem, in Untitled Common Place Book of poetry, GSP; Gerrit Smith, *Be Natural! A Discourse* (Peterboro, N.Y.: American News, 1864), pp. 1–5, 14–16, GSP; Smith, *Religion of Reason* (Peterboro, N.Y.: C. A. Hammond, 1864), pp. 20, 94–95, 107, 137, 145; Frederick Platt, "Perfection," in *Encyclopedia of Religion and Ethics*, ed. James Hastings (New York: Charles Scribner's Sons, 1917), p. 729.

34. *BAP*, 3: 49, 383–384, 403–412, quotations pp. 383 (Ward), 410 (Garnet); Gerrit Smith, "Address to the Slaves of the United States . . . ," *NASS*, February 24, 1842. On *Prigg v. Pennsylvania*, see Norman L. Rosenberg, "Personal Liberty Laws and Sectional Crisis: 1850–1861," *CWH* 17 (March 1971): 25–29.

35. Gerrit Smith to Bro. Bailey, August 1, 1843, GSP; Smith to Warner P. Clemens, February 16, 1846, GSP.

36. "Letter from Gerrit Smith to Henry Clarke Wright, April 20, 1839, in *LIB*, May 17, 1839.

37. Douglass, *Life and Times of Frederick Douglass* (1892; reprint, New York: Collier, 1962), p. 202; Douglass, *My Bondage and My Freedom* (1855; reprint, Urbana: University of Illinois Press, 1987), pp. 205–208.

38. Jane H. Pease and William H. Pease, "Negro Conventions and the Problem of Black Leadership," *Journal of Black Studies* 2 (September 1971): 29–

44; Pease and Pease, "Ends, Means, and Attitudes: Black-White Conflict in the Antislavery Movement," *CWH* 18 (1972): 117–128; Pease and Pease, *They Who Would Be Free: Blacks' Search for Freedom, 1830–1861* (1974; reprint, Urbana: University of Illinois Press, 1990), pp. 95–170; Benjamin Quarles, *Black Abolitionists* (New York: Oxford University Press, 1969), pp. 168–196; James Oliver Horton and Lois E. Horton, *In Hope of Liberty: Culture, Community and Protest among Northern Free Blacks, 1700–1860* (New York: Oxford University Press, 1997), pp. 237–268; Donald Yacovone, "The Transformation of the Black Temperance Movement, 1827–1854: An Interpretation," *JER* 8 (Fall 1988): 281–297; R. J. M. Blackett, *Building an Antislavery Wall: Black Americans in the Atlantic Abolitionist Movement, 1830–1860* (Ithaca: Cornell University Press, 1983), pp. 79–117; Phyllis F. Field, *The Politics of Race in New York: The Struggle for Black Suffrage in the Civil War Era* (Ithaca: Cornell University Press, 1982), pp. 43–97; Charles H. Wesley, "The Participation of Negroes in Anti-Slavery Political Parties," *JNH* 29 (January 1944): 32–74.

39. Douglass, *Bondage*, pp. 116–117.

40. Ibid., pp. 122, 132, 136; Davis, "At the Heart of Slavery," p. 51.

41. Douglass, *Bondage*, pp. 148–151.

42. Ibid., p. 151; Leonard Cassuto, "Frederick Douglass and the Work of Freedom: Hegel's Master-Slave Dialectic in the Fugitive Slave Narrative," *Prospects* 21 (1996): 229–259, quotations pp. 241, 243. On Douglass and the master-slave dialectic see also David Brion Davis, *The Problem of Slavery in the Age of Revolution, 1770–1823* (Ithaca: Cornell University Press, 1975), pp. 557–564; Cynthia Willet, "The Master-Slave Dialectic: Hegel vs. Douglass," in *Subjugation and Bondage: Critical Essays on Slavery and Social Philosophy*, ed. Tommy L. Lott (New York: Rowman & Littlefield, 1998), pp. 151–170; Paul Gilroy, *The Black Atlantic: Modernity and Double Consciousness* (Cambridge: Harvard University Press, 1993), pp. 58–64.

43. Douglass, *Bondage*, p. 153.

44. Ibid., pp. 166–184, quotation p. 152; Dickson J. Preston, *Young Frederick Douglass: The Maryland Years* (Baltimore: Johns Hopkins University Press, 1980), pp. 148–149.

45. Preston, *Young Douglass*, pp. 103–104, 143–155; Douglass C. North, *The Economic Growth of the United States, 1790–1860* (New York: W. W. Norton, 1966), pp. 195–203; Thomas C. Cochran and William Miller, *The Age of Enterprise: A Social History of Industrial America* (1942; reprint, New York: Harper & Row, 1961), pp. 44–51; Reginald Charles McGrane, *The Panic of 1837: Some Financial Problems of the Jacksonian Era* (New York: Russell & Russell, 1965), pp. 22–23, 112–113. Hugh Auld's drinking problem probably contributed to his business failure.

46. Preston, *Young Douglass*, pp. 142–156.

47. Samuel Rezneck, "The Social History of an American Depression, 1837–1843," *AHR* 40 (October 1934–July 1935): 662–687.

48. Alan Trachtenberg, "Photography: The Emergence of a Keyword," in *Photography in Nineteenth-Century America*, ed. Martha A. Sandweiss (New York: Harry N. Abrams, 1991), p. 30; North, *Economic Growth*, p. 201. See also Rezneck, "Social History," pp. 662–687; and Forber William Fogel, *Without Consent or Contract: The Rise and Fall of American Slavery* (New York: W. W. Norton, 1989), pp. 354–369.

49. North, *Economic Growth*, pp. 194–203; Rezneck, "Social History," pp. 662, 664; Sean Wilentz, *Chants Democratic: New York City and the Rise of the American Working Class, 1788–1850* (New York: Oxford University Press, 1984), pp. 299–301; Carl J. Guarneri, *The Utopian Alternative: Fourierism in Nineteenth-Century America* (Ithaca: Cornell University Press, 1991), pp. 66–79; Cochran and Miller, *Age of Enterprise*, pp. 43–51; Arthur M. Schlesinger Jr., *The Age of Jackson* (Boston: Little, Brown, 1945), pp. 216–226; Alice Felt Tyler, *Freedom's Ferment: Phases of American Social History from the Colonial Period to the Outbreak of the Civil War* (New York: Harper and Brothers, 1944), pp. 214–220; Bertram Wyatt-Brown, *Lewis Tappan and the Evangelical War against Slavery* (Cleveland: Press of Case Western Reserve University, 1969), p. 174; Peter Temin, *The Jacksonian Economy* (New York: W. W. Norton, 1969), pp. 113–171.

50. Tyler, *Freedom's Ferment*, pp. 215–216; Brisbane, quoted in Guarneri, *Utopian Alternative*, p. 66; Rezneck, "Social History," pp. 662, 676; Henry Ward Beecher, *Seven Lectures to Young Men, on Various Important Subjects . . .* (Indianapolis: Thomas B. Cutler, 1844), pp. 32–33, 38–39; Horace Greeley, *Recollections of a Busy Life* (New York: J. B. Ford, 1868), p. 96; Karen Halttunen, *Confidence Men and Painted Women: A Study of Middle-Class Culture in America, 1830–1870* (New Haven: Yale University Press, 1982), pp. 16–20.

51. Perry, *Radical Abolitionism*, p. 65.

52. Lawrence Foster, *Religion and Sexuality: The Shakers, the Mormons, and the Oneida Community* (Urbana: University of Illinois Press, 1984), pp. 72–74, 79–87; John L. Thomas, *The Liberator: William Lloyd Garrison, A Biography* (Boston: Little, Brown, 1963), pp. 221, 226–233, 317–328; Lewis Perry, *Childhood, Marriage, and Reform: Henry Clarke Wright, 1797–1870* (Chicago: University of Chicago Press, 1980), pp. 34–41, 239–241.

53. Abzug, *Cosmos Crumbling*, p. 220; Robert H. Abzug, *Passionate Liberator: Theodore Dwight Weld and the Dilemma of Reform* (New York: Oxford University Press, 1980), p. 152; James Brewer Stewart, *Wendell Phillips: Liberty's*

Hero (Baton Rouge: Louisiana State University Press, 1986), p. 63; Stewart, *Joshua Giddings and the Tactics of Radical Politics* (Cleveland: Press of Case Western Reserve University, 1970), pp. 15–17, 22–27; Douglas M. Strong, *Perfectionist Politics: Abolitionism and the Religious Tensions of American Democracy* (Syracuse, N.Y.: Syracuse University Press, 1999), pp. 29–38, 68–90.

54. Foster, *Religion and Sexuality*, pp. 62–65, 84, 139–142; Guarneri, *Utopian Alternative*, p. 68; Wilentz, *Chants Democratic*, pp. 306–314; Steven Mintz, *Moralists and Modernizers: America's Pre–Civil War Reformers* (Baltimore: Johns Hopkins University Press, 1995), p. 74; Mary P. Ryan, *Cradle of the Middle Class: The Family in Oneida County, New York, 1790–1865* (Cambridge: Cambridge University Press, 1981), p. 140.

55. "Millerism," *American Journal of Insanity* (January 1845): 250; New York State Lunatic Asylum, Case Books 1–2, NYSA; Numbers and Butler, *The Disappointed*, pp. 36–59, 92–118, 153–172; Guarneri, *Utopian Alternative*, pp. 70–71, 73–74, 117–118; Wilentz, *Chants Democratic*, p. 300; Cross, *Burned-Over District*, pp. 317–318; Michael Barkun, *Crucible of the Millennium: The Burned-Over District of New York in the 1840s* (Syracuse, N.Y.: Syracuse University Press, 1986), p. 115.

56. Robert D. Richardson Jr., *Emerson: The Mind on Fire* (Berkeley: University of California Press, 1995), pp. 245–251, 260, 268–274, 332–336; Len Gougeon and Joel Myerson, eds., *Emerson's Antislavery Writings* (New Haven: Yale University Press, 1995), pp. xv–xvii; Joel Porte, ed., *Emerson in His Journals* (Cambridge: Harvard University Press, 1982), pp. 161–177; David S. Reynolds, *Walt Whitman's America: A Cultural Biography* (New York: Alfred A. Knopf, 1995), pp. 52–61, quotations pp. 52, 61; William Charvat, *The Profession of Authorship in America, 1800–1870* (Columbus: Ohio State University Press, 1968), chap. 4.

57. Ratner, *Powder Keg*, pp. 131–141; David Brion Davis, *The Slave Power Conspiracy and the Paranoid Style* (Baton Rouge: Louisiana State University Press, 1969), pp. 14, 18; Fogel, *Without Consent or Contract*, pp. 338–354; Richard H. Sewell, *Ballots for Freedom: Antislavery Politics in the United States, 1837–1860* (New York: Oxford University Press, 1976), pp. 101–106; Hugh Davis, *Joshua Leavitt: Evangelical Abolitionist* (Baton Rouge: Louisiana State University Press, 1990), pp. 169–172.

58. Gerrit Smith, "Peril to the Free," *CA*, September 1, 1838; Smith, quoted in *Third Annual Report*, p. 17; Davis, *Joshua Leavitt*, p. 169; "Cause of Hard Times," *NASS*, February 24, 1842; Fogel, *Without Consent or Contract*, pp. 338–354; Sewell, *Ballots for Freedom*, pp. 101–106; Stewart, "Peaceful Hopes," pp. 298–309; Ratner, *Powder Keg*, p. 141; Davis, *Slave Power*, p. 30; David Brion Davis, "Some Themes of Counter-Subversion: An Analysis of

Anti-Masonic, Anti-Catholic, and Anti-Mormon Literature" and "Some Ideological Functions of Prejudice," in *From Homicide to Slavery*, pp. 137–165; Barkun, *Crucible of the Millennium*, pp. 114–123.

59. Stewart, *Wendell Phillips*, p. 56; Gerrit Smith, "From the Friend of Man," *CA*, January 13, 1838; Lawrence Friedman, *Gregarious Saints: Self and Community in American Abolitionism, 1830–1870* (Cambridge: Cambridge University Press, 1982), pp. 200–201; Merton L. Dillon, *Elijah P. Lovejoy, Abolitionist Editor* (Urbana: University of Illinois Press, 1961), pp. 89–91, 96–99, 105–142, 160–170; Valarie H. Ziegler, *The Advocates of Peace in Antebellum America* (Bloomington: Indiana University Press, 1992), pp. 61–63.

60. Justus Newton Brown, "Lovejoy's Influence on John Brown," *Magazine of History, with Notes and Queries* 23 (July–December 1916): 101; J. Newton Brown, "The Beginning of John Brown's Career," *The Nation* 98 (February 12, 1914): 157; Steven B. Oates, *To Purge This Land with Blood: A Biography of John Brown* (1970; reprint, Amherst: University of Massachusetts Press, 1984), pp. 41–42.

61. Oates, *To Purge This Land*, pp. 22–50.

62. Ibid., pp. 22–50, quotations p. 37.

63. John Brown Jr., quoted in F. B. Sanborn, ed., *The Life and Letters of John Brown* (Boston: Roberts Brothers, 1885), pp. 87–88; Oates, *To Purge This Land*, pp. 43–47.

64. Boyd B. Stutler, "John Brown and the Oberlin Lands," *West Virginia History* 12 (April 1951): 183–199; Oates, *To Purge This Land*, pp. 45–47; Benjamin Quarles, *Allies for Freedom: Blacks and John Brown* (New York: Oxford University Press, 1974), p. 23.

65. Richard O. Boyer, *The Legend of John Brown: A Biography and a History* (New York: Alfred A. Knopf, 1973), p. 413.

66. Oates, *To Purge This Land*, pp. 5–6, 8, 22–24; Sanborn, *Life and Letters of Brown*, pp. 93, 11; Villard, *Brown*, p. 16.

67. Oates, *To Purge This Land*, p. 32; Sydney E. Ahlstrom, *A Religious History of the American People* (New Haven: Yale University Press, 1972), pp. 301–313, quotation p. 303; George Wallingford Noyes, *The Religious Experience of John Humphrey Noyes* (New York: Macmillan, 1923), pp. 391–392, quotation p. 392; Platt, "Perfection," pp. 728–737; Joseph A. Conforti, *Jonathan Edwards, Religious Tradition, and American Culture* (Chapel Hill: University of North Carolina Press, 1995), pp. 36–61.

68. Timothy L. Smith, *Revivalism and Social Reform: American Protestantism on the Eve of the Civil War* (New York: Harper Torchbooks, 1965), p. 103; Perry, *Radical Abolitionism*, pp. 36–42, 56–58, 63–69; Noyes, *Religious Experience of Noyes*, pp. 89–125; Foster, *Religion and Sexuality*, pp. 75–78.

69. Oates, *To Purge This Land*, p. 30; John Brown, "Sambo's Mistakes," in *John Brown: The Making of a Revolutionary*, ed. Louis Ruchames (New York: Grosset and Dunlap, 1969), p. 72; Perry, *Radical Abolitionism*, pp. 55–70; Thomas, *Liberator*, pp. 224–235.

70. Brown, quoted in Oates, *To Purge This Land*, p. 44; Ahlstrom, *Religious History*, pp. 298–313; Brown, quoted in Ruchames, *Brown*, pp. 88, 144.

71. John Barras Hay, *Inaugural Addresses by Lords Rectors of the University of Glasgow* . . . (Glasgow: David Robertson, 1839), pp. liii–lvi, lxx–lxxi, lxxiv–lxxxii.

72. "Reception of Dr. Smith," *CA*, October 28, 1837; David W. Blight, "In Search of Learning, Liberty, and Self Definition: James McCune Smith and the Ordeal of the Antebellum Black Intellectual," *AANYLH* 9 (July 1985): 8; *BAP*, 1: 66. It is unclear whether McCune Smith graduated first in his class for the bachelor's or medical degree.

73. *BAP*, 1: 65–67, 68–69; "Farewell Dinner to Dr. James McCune Smith, A.M.," *CA*, September 9, 1837; James Brewer Stewart, "The Emergence of Racial Modernity and the Rise of the White North, 1790–1840," *JER* 18 (Summer 1998): 181–217; Horton and Horton, *In Hope of Liberty*, pp. 237–268; Pease and Pease, *They Who Would Be Free*, pp. 68–93.

74. *CA*, September 23, 30, October 28, 1837; *NS*, February 11, 1848.

75. *CA*, September 23, 30, October 28, 1837; *NS*, February 11, 1848; Blight, "In Search of Learning," p. 21; *BAP*, 4: 45; McCune Smith to Gerrit Smith, July 31, 1839, GSP.

76. *Fifth Annual Report*, pp. 25–28.

77. James McCune Smith, *A Lecture on the Haytien Revolutions; with a Sketch of the Character of Toussaint L'Ouverture* (New York: Daniel Fanshaw, 1841), pp. 4, 15, 17–20, 23.

78. James McCune Smith to Gerrit Smith, July 31, 1839, GSP; *BAP*, 3: 471–472. Crummell to Smith, December 23, 1839, GSP.

79. Smith to David Jones, February 28, 1840, GSP; Smith to Thomas Beckman, May 22, 1840, GSP; Smith to Oliver Johnson, July 6, 1840, GSP; Smith to John Cooke, June 30, 1841, GSP; Smith to O. S. Renslaw, April 18, 1842, GSP; Gerrit Smith to General Smith, May 23, 1842, GSP; Smith to Henry Cummings, September 22, 1842, GSP; Smith to Elder Hitchcock, November 1, 1842, GSP; Smith to John Scoble, February 1, 1843, GSP; Smith to Judge Jones, February 27, 1843, GSP; Smith to Charles and Elizabeth Miller, March 1, 1845, GSP; Smith to L. Chaplin, January 7, 1846, GSP. On "The Grove," see Frothingham, *Gerrit Smith*, pp. 30–31. I am grateful to Beth Spokowsky for showing me "The Grove," which is still standing.

80. Smith to O. S. Renslaw, April 18, 1842, GSP; Smith to Samuel Crothers, April 15, 1842, GSP; Smith to Seth Gates, March 19, 1842, GSP; Smith to Prof. Eaton, December 11, 1839, GSP; Smith to J. J. Astor, December 2, 1839, GSP; Smith to David S. Jones, December 23, 1839, GSP; Smith to J. M. Woodruff, March 16, 1840, GSP; Elizabeth Cady Stanton, *Eighty Years and More: Reminiscences, 1815–1897* (1898; reprint, New York: Schocken, 1971), pp. 62–64.

81. Smith to Mr. L. Chaplin, January 7, 1846, GSP.

82. E. P. Tanner, "Gerrit Smith: An Interpretation," *Proceedings of the New York State Historical Association* 22, no. 5 (1924): 26; Friedman, *Gregarious Saints*, p. 100; Thomas, "Personal Recollections," MCHS; Smith, "Autobiographical Sketch"; Harlow, *Gerrit Smith*, pp. 234–249.

83. Harlow, *Gerrit Smith*, pp. 449–492; *Gerrit Smith to George Thompson, January 26, 1862*, broadside, GSP; *Letter to Hon. D. C. Littlejohn from Gerrit Smith, January 14, 1864*, broadside, GSP; *Railroads: Gerrit Smith to John B. Edwards, October 10, 1867*, broadside, GSP; *Letter from Gerrit Smith to Mssrs. Scovell, Wilson, Fowler, April 13th, 1870*, broadside, GSP.

84. On translating 1850s dollars into 1990s currency I have relied on two sources: U.S. Bureau of the Census, *Historical Statistics of the United States: Colonial Times to 1970, Part I* (Washington, D.C.: U.S. Department of Commerce, 1975), p. 224; idem, *Statistical Abstract of the United States, 1994: The National Data Book* (Washington, D.C.: U.S. Department of Commerce, Economics and Statistics Administration, 1995), pp. 487–488. For the low-end estimate, I compare a skilled laborer's wage of roughly $500 in the 1840s to an average annual family income in the 1990s of around $36,000: $36,000 ÷ $500 × $8 million = $576 million (I rounded up to obtain $600 million). For the high-end estimate, I used an average of two numbers. Per-capita GNP in current prices increased from $170 per year in 1869 to $5,000 per year in 1970, an increase of 2900 percent. Three different sources (the consumer price index; cost-of-living index; and a chart showing the purchasing power of the dollar from 1970 to 1994 in *Statistical Abstract*) all suggest that the value of money increased by a factor of 3.5 from 1970 to 1994: 29 × 3.5 × $8 million = $823 million. The second high-end estimate stems from a chart showing disposable personal income (DPI), which also represents the money Smith had to give away. In 1897 (the earliest year that DPI was recorded), DPI was $14 per year, and in 1970 it was $700 per year. These figures suggest that the value of money available for philanthropy increased by 700 ÷ 14, or a factor of 50, from 1897 to 1970, and by 50 × 5 3.5, or a factor of 175, from 1970 to 1994, which would mean that Smith's $8 million equates to 175 × $8 million =

1.4 billion in 1994 dollars. The average of the two high-end figures ($1.4 billion and $823 million) is $1.1 billion.

85. Frothingham, *Gerrit Smith*, p. 375; Mr. Fay, quoted in *NYH*, November 2, 1859; Smith, quoted in Frothingham, pp. 140–141; Smith, "Autobiographical Sketch."

86. *New York Times*, December 29, 1874. See also Thomas, "Personal Recollections," MCHS; Bull, "Gerrit Smith," pp. 246–247; W. Freeman Galpin, "The Smiths of Peterboro," *Ninth Publication of the Oswego Historical Society*, 1945, p. 57; Stanton, *Eighty Years*, pp. 51–53, 64–68.

87. Smith, quoted in Frothingham, *Gerrit Smith*, p. 131.

88. Smith to John L. Vorton, December 7, 1840, GSP; Smith to Hon. M. Sanford, February 14, 1840, GSP; Smith to Rev. E. S. Barrows, June 16, 1840, GSP; *NYH*, November 2, 1859; Thomas, "Personal Recollections," MCHS; Benjamin Quarles, ed., "Letters from Negro Leaders to Gerrit Smith," *JNH* 27 (October 1942): 432–436; Alan Kraut, "The Forgotten Reformers: A Profile of Third Party Abolitionists in Antebellum New York," in *Antislavery Reconsidered: New Perspectives on the Abolitionists*, ed. Lewis Perry and Michael Fellman (Baton Rouge: Louisiana State University Press, 1979), pp. 119–148.

89. Gerrit Smith to David Dickey and George M. Ellingwood, March 21, 1845, GSP.

90. The New York census for 1835 shows Smithfield containing 2,750 people, but in 1836 a large portion of the eastern edge of the town was used to help form Stockbridge, a fact that is reflected in the census by a corresponding decrease in land from 1835 to 1845. My figures take into account Smithfield's loss of land and people to form Stockbridge. See *Census of the State of New York for 1835* (Albany: Croswell, Van Benthuysen and Burt, 1836); *Census of the State of New York for 1845* (Albany: Carroll and Cook, 1846); and L. M. Hammond, *History of Madison County, State of New York* (Syracuse, N.Y.: Truair, Smith, 1872), p. 711.

91. *Census of . . . New York for 1835, 1845; Census of the State of New York for 1875* (Albany: Weed, Parsons, 1877); Hammond, *History of Madison County*, pp. 695–728; *NYH*, November 2, 1859; Stauffer, "Beyond Social Control," pp. 240–244.

92. Donna Burdick, *Peterboro, New York: A Walking Tour* (Smithfield, N.Y.: Smithfield Community Association, n.d.); *NYH*, November 2, 1859; George W. Bungay, "Gerrit Smith," in *Crayon Sketches and Off-Hand Takings* (Boston: Stacy and Richardson, 1852), pp. 47–51; Frothingham, *Gerrit Smith*, pp. 137–139; *Census of . . . New-York for 1835, 1845, 1875*.

93. On John Humphrey Noyes and the Oneida Community see Foster, *Religion and Sexuality*, pp. 72–122; Spencer Klaw, *Without Sin: The Life and Death of the Oneida Community* (New York: Penguin, 1993); Noyes, *Religious Experience of Noyes;* Cross, *Burned-Over District*, pp. 245–248, 333–340; *Slavery and Marriage: A Dialogue* (1850; reprint, Sherrill, N.Y.: Oneida Community Mansion House, 1994); Tyler, *Freedom's Ferment*, pp. 184–195; Charles Nordhoff, *The Communistic Societies of the United States* (1875; reprint, New York: Hillary House, 1961), pp. 259–304.

94. Noyes, *Religious Experience of Noyes*, pp. 330–331.

95. Thomas, *Liberator*, pp. 227–231, quotation p. 231; Noyes, *Religious Experience of Noyes*, pp. 287–291.

96. Thomas, *Liberator*, pp. 227–231; Noyes, *Religious Experience of Noyes*, pp. 287–291, 384–395, quotations pp. 287, 394; Foster, *Religion and Sexuality*, pp. 75–79.

97. Thomas, *Liberator*, pp. 221–231, 316–328; Foster, *Religion and Sexuality*, pp. 72–87.

98. Thomas, *Liberator*, pp. 221, 230, 232, 317, 328; Perry, *Radical Abolitionism*, pp. 55–91.

99. Thomas, *Liberator*, p. 232.

100. Perry, *Radical Abolitionism*, pp. 158–187.

Five. Bible Politics and the Creation of the Alliance

1. Richard H. Sewell, *Ballots for Freedom: Antislavery Politics in the United States, 1837–1860* (New York: Oxford University Press, 1976), pp. 72–138; Lawrence J. Friedman, *Gregarious Saints: Self and Community in American Abolitionism, 1830–1870* (Cambridge: Cambridge University Press, 1982), pp. 96–128; Hugh Davis, *Joshua Leavitt: Evangelical Abolitionist* (Baton Rouge: Louisiana State University Press, 1990), pp. 218–220; Ralph Volney Harlow, *Gerrit Smith: Philanthropist and Reformer* (New York: Henry Holt, 1939), pp. 136–175; Octavius Brooks Frothingham, *Gerrit Smith: A Biography* (New York: G. P. Putnam's Sons, 1878), pp. 170–180.

2. Gerrit Smith, quoted in *LIB*, January 31, 1840; Harlow, *Gerrit Smith*, p. 136.

3. George Henry Evans, "To Gerrit Smith," *People's Rights*, July 7, 1844; "Gerrit Smith's Reply," *Working Man's Advocate*, July 20, 1844. On Evans and the National Reform Association (NRA), see Jamie L. Bronstein, *Land Reform and Working-Class Experience in Britain and the United States, 1800–1862* (Stanford: Stanford University Press, 1999), pp. 15–18, 40–43, 93–96, 119–22, 146–149; Sean Wilentz, *Chants Democratic: New York City and*

the Rise of the American Working Class, 1788–1850 (New York: Oxford University Press, 1984), pp. 335–343; Carl J. Guarneri, *Utopian Alternative: Fourierism in Nineteenth-Century America* (Ithaca: Cornell University Press, 1991), pp. 296–313.

4. "Gerrit Smith's Reply," *Working Man's Advocate*, July 20, 1844; and "Second Letter from Gerrit Smith," ibid., August 10, 1844.

5. On Douglass' response to labor reform see *TFDP*, 1/2: 291–310. On McCune Smith's response see "Letter from Communipaw," *FDP*, February 12 and 26, 1852. On Brown's response see Oswald Garrison Villard, *John Brown, 1800–1859: A Biography Fifty Years After* (1910; reprint, New York: Alfred A. Knopf, 1943), p. 663; Richard J. Hinton, *John Brown and His Men* (New York: Funk and Wagnalls Company, 1894), p. 594; Steven B. Oates, *To Purge This Land with Blood: A Biography of John Brown* (1970; reprint, Amherst: University of Massachusetts Press, 1984), pp. 36–39; F. B. Sanborn, ed., *The Life and Letters of John Brown* (Boston: Roberts Brothers, 1885), pp. 87–88; William A. Phillips, "Three Interviews with Old John Brown," *Atlantic Monthly* 44 (December 1879): 741.

6. "Second Letter from Gerrit Smith."

7. Gerrit Smith to George H. Evans, August 27, 1846, GSP; Bronstein, *Land Reform*, pp. 93–96, 275–276; Wilentz, *Chants Democratic*, pp. 340–341. Evans did not specify which office he wanted Smith to run for. Smith reluctantly accepted the National Liberty party nomination for president in 1848, two years after declining Evans' offer to run as an NRA candidate.

8. "Gerrit Smith's Reply."

9. *Gerrit Smith's Land Auction*, broadside, February 1, 1846, GSP; John B. Edwards to Gerrit Smith, February 21, June 1 and 5, 1846, GSP; Gerrit Smith to Daniel Cady, July 27, 1846, HCA; Harlow, *Gerrit Smith*, pp. 241–242, 248–249.

10. Gerrit Smith to the Rev. Theodore S. Wright, Rev. Charles B. Ray, and Dr. J. McCune Smith, August 1, 1846, GSP, quoted in full in Frothingham, *Gerrit Smith*, pp. 102–105; Harlow, *Gerrit Smith*, pp. 242–245.

11. Smith to Wright, Ray, and McCune Smith, August 1, 1846.

12. Ibid.; Harlow, *Gerrit Smith*, pp. 242–245.

13. Smith to Wright, Ray, and McCune Smith, August 1, 1846; Harlow, *Gerrit Smith*, pp. 242–245.

14. Thomas C. Holt, "'An Empire over the Mind': Emancipation, Race, and Ideology in the British West Indies and the American South," in *Region, Race, and Reconstruction*, ed. J. Morgan Kousser and James M. McPherson (New York: Oxford University Press, 1982), pp. 283–313; Holt, *The Problem of Freedom: Race, Labor, and Politics in Jamaica and Britain, 1832–1938* (Baltimore: Johns Hopkins University Press, 1992), pp. 3–178; David Brion

Davis, *The Problem of Slavery in the Age of Revolution, 1770–1823* (Ithaca: Cornell University Press, 1975), pp. 39–83; Davis, *Slavery and Human Progress* (New York: Oxford University Press, 1984), pp. 192–226, 231–279, quotation p. 219.

15. Smith to Gen. John H. Cooke, December 11, 1840, GSP; Robert William Fogel, *Without Consent or Contract: The Rise and Fall of American Slavery* (New York: W. W. Norton, 1989), pp. 388–417; Davis, *Slavery and Human Progress*, pp. 168–279.

16. Smith to Cooke, December 11, 1840.

17. Ibid.; Horace Miner, *The Primitive City of Timbuctoo*, rev. ed. (New York: Anchor, 1965), pp. xi–xviii, 1–31; Elias N. Saad, *Social History of Timbuktu: The Role of Muslim Scholars and Notables, 1400–1900* (Cambridge: Cambridge University Press, 1983), pp. 1–23; John Brown to Friend Hodges, January 22, 1849, quoted in Villard, *Brown*, pp. 72–73; Richard O. Boyer, *The Legend of John Brown: A Biography and a History* (New York: Alfred A. Knopf, 1973), pp. 390–394, 399–401; Harold W. Thompson, *Body, Boots, and Britches* (Philadelphia: J. B. Lippincott, 1940), p. 303; Alfred L. Donaldson, *A History of the Adirondacks*, vol. 2 (New York: Century, 1921), p. 6. Brown and the settlers typically wrote "Timbucto," though many subsequent writers have used "Timbuctoo" or "Timbukto."

18. Garnet and Bemen, quoted in *NS*, March 2, 1849.

19. James McCune Smith, *The Destiny of the People of Color: A Lecture Delivered before the Philomathean Society and Hamilton Lyceum, in January 1841* (New York, 1843), pp. 5–6. See also David Brion Davis, "Jews and Blacks in America," *NYR*, December 2, 1999, pp. 57–63.

20. Gerrit Smith to Wright, Ray, and McCune Smith, quoted in full in Frothingham, *Gerrit Smith*, p. 106.

21. Gerrit Smith, *Compensated Emancipation: A Speech by Gerrit Smith, in the National Compensation Convention . . .* , broadside, GSP; *NYT*, August 31, 1857; *NASS*, September 12, 1857. For other instances of Smith emphasizing land monopoly as the greater evil, see Smith to J. K. Ingalls, August 15, 1848, quoted in Bronstein, *Land Reform*, p. 94. On the 1857 National Compensation Convention see Kenneth M. Stampp, *America in 1857: A Nation on the Brink* (New York: Oxford University Press, 1990), pp. 128–129; James Brewer Stewart, *Joshua Giddings and the Tactics of Radical Politics* (Cleveland: Press of Case Western Reserve University, 1970), pp. 257–259.

22. Eric Foner, *Reconstruction: America's Unfinished Revolution, 1863–1877* (New York: Harper & Row, 1988), pp. 67–68, 235; Davis, *Slavery and Human Progress*, pp. 274–279; James M. McPherson, *The Struggle for Equality: Abolitionists and the Negro in the Civil War and Reconstruction* (Princeton: Princeton University Press, 1964), pp. 238–259. On Smith no longer advocating

land redistribution see Smith, *Thoughts for the People*, broadside, April 14, 1865, GSP; Smith, *Sermon in Peterboro*, broadside, May 21, 1865, GSP; Smith, *No Treason in Civil War: Gerrit Smith at Cooper Institute, June 8th, 1865* (New York: American News, 1865), MCHS.

23. Theodore S. Wright, Charles B. Ray, and James McCune Smith, *An Address to the Three Thousand Colored Citizens of New-York . . . September 1, 1846* (New York: 1846), pp. 3, 9, New York Public Library. See also Charles B. Ray to Gerrit Smith, May 24, 1847, GSP; McCune Smith to Gerrit Smith, December 17, 1846, GSP.

24. Wright, Ray, and McCune Smith, *Address to the Three Thousand*, pp. 10, 18.

25. Ibid., pp. 10–18.

26. McCune Smith to Gerrit Smith, December 17, 1846.

27. Ibid.

28. McCune Smith, "Letter from Communipaw," *FDP*, February 26, 1852, March 18, 1852.

29. McCune Smith, "Letter from Communipaw," February 26 and March 18, 1852. On the link between wealth and caste in America see Davis, *Human Slavery and Progress*, pp. 274–279; Theodore W. Allen, *The Invention of the White Race*, vol. 1: *Racial Oppression and Social Control* (London: Verso, 1994), pp. 27–51, 136–199; Eric Lott, *Love and Theft: Blackface Minstrelsy and the American Working Class* (New York: Oxford University Press, 1993), pp. 38–88; David R. Roediger, *The Wages of Whiteness: Race and the Making of the American Working Class* (London: Verso, 1991), pp. 43–94.

30. McCune Smith to Gerrit Smith, December 28, 1846, *BAP*, 3: 479–484, quotation p. 480; McCune Smith, "Letter from Communipaw," February 26, 1852.

31. McCune Smith to Gerrit Smith, December 17, 1846.

32. McCune Smith to Gerrit Smith, February 6, 1850, *BAP*, 4: 44.

33. Gerrit Smith to Rev. T. S. Wright, C. B. Ray, and Dr. James McCune Smith, November 14, 1846, GSP.

34. Paul Schneider, *The Adirondacks: A History of America's First Wilderness* (New York: Henry Holt, 1997), pp. xi, 105–113, 155–191, quotation p. xi; John L. Thomas, "Romantic Reform in America, 1815–1865," *AQ* 17 (Winter 1965): 667. See also Roderick Nash, *Wilderness and the American Mind* (New Haven: Yale University Press, 1982), pp. 84–95; Catherine L. Albanese, *Nature Religion in America, from the Algonkian Indians to the New Age* (Chicago: University of Chicago Press, 1991), pp. 80–116; Richard Slotkin, *Regeneration through Violence: The Mythology of the American Frontier, 1600–1860* (Middletown, Conn.: Wesleyan University Press, 1973); Slotkin, *The Fatal Environment: The Myth of the Frontier in the Age of Industrialization, 1800–1890* (Middletown, Conn.: Wesleyan University Press,

1985); Stanley Harrold, "Romanticizing Slave Revolt: Madison Washington, the *Creole* Mutiny, and Abolitionist Celebration of Violent Means," in *Antislavery Violence: Sectional, Racial, and Cultural Conflict in Antebellum America*, ed. Stanley Harrold and John R. McKivigan (Knoxville: University of Tennessee Press, 1999), pp. 89–107; Guarneri, *Utopian Alternative*, pp. 60–90; Paul Goodman, "The Manual Labor Movement and the Origins of Abolitionism," *JER* 13 (Fall 1993): 355–387; Walter Jackson Bate, *From Classic to Romantic: Premises of Taste in Eighteenth-Century England* (1946; reprint, New York: Harper & Row, 1961), pp. 160–192; Jacques Barzun, *Classic, Romantic, and Modern* (1943; reprint, Chicago: University of Chicago Press, 1961), pp. 58–95.

35. On the concept of domestication in relation to slavery and servility see David Brion Davis, "At the Heart of Slavery," *NYR*, October 17, 1996, pp. 51–54.

36. Gerrit Smith to McCune Smith, Wright, and Ray, November 14, 1846; McCune Smith to Gerrit Smith, December 17, 1846. For examples of other black abolitionists quoting Burns see *BAP*, 1: 185, 188; *BAP*, 3: 391.

37. *TFDP*, 1/2: 147–148; *LWFD*, 1: 65, 151–153, quotation p. 153.

38. *TFDP*, 1/2: 147–148; *TFDP*, 1/3: 543. For additional examples of Douglass' esteem for Burns, see *TFDP*, 1/2: 120, 295, 523; *TFDP*, 1/3: 298.

39. Gerrit Smith to Timothy Hudson, October 28, 1842, GSP; Smith to Ann [illegible last name], March 14, 1849, GSP. See also George W. Bungay, "Gerrit Smith," in *Crayon Sketches and Off-hand Takings . . .* (Boston: Stacy and Richardson, 1852), pp. 47–51; McCune Smith to Gerrit Smith, January 25, July 27, 1847, March 22, May 12, July 7, 1848, GSP; *BAP*, 3: 479–484; *BAP*, 4: 42–47, 274–277; and Goodman, "Manual Labor Movement," pp. 355–377.

40. McCune Smith to Gerrit Smith, March 31, 1855, GSP; McCune Smith, *Destiny of People of Color*, p. 7; David W. Blight, "In Search of Learning, Liberty, and Self Definition: James McCune Smith and the Ordeal of the Antebellum Black Intellectual," *AANYLH* 9 (July 1985): 15; *NASS*, November 14, 1844; Jane H. Pease and William H. Pease, *They Who Would Be Free: Blacks' Search for Freedom, 1830–1861* (1974; reprint, Urbana: University of Illinois Press, 1990), pp. 8, 13, 74, 80.

41. McCune Smith to Gerrit Smith, May 12, 1848.

42. McCune Smith, "Editorial," in *BAP*, 4: 261–262; McCune Smith, "From Our New York Correspondent," *FDP*, February 16, 1855; *NASS*, December 23, 1854; *FDP*, January 19, 1855; Pease and Pease, *They Who Would Be Free*, pp. 82–93; Blight, "In Search of Learning," p. 15.

43. McCune Smith, "Editorial," p. 260; McCune Smith, "From Our New York Correspondent," February 16, 1855.

44. McCune Smith, "Editorial," p. 259; McCune Smith, "From Our New York Correspondent," February 16, 1855; McCune Smith, "From Our New York Correspondent," *FDP*, October 5, 1855; McCune Smith, quoted in Pease and Pease, *They Who Would Be Free*, p. 91.

45. McCune Smith to Gerrit Smith, March 31, 1855, *BAP*, 4: 275; *American Jubilee* 12 (April 1855): 81–94; Pease and Pease, *They Who Would Be Free*, pp. 241–243.

46. Gerrit Smith to Frederick Douglass, December 8, 1847, *NS*, January 8, 1848; Douglass to Smith, February 18, 1852, GSP. Douglass probably sold the deed he received from Smith. See William S. McFeely, *Frederick Douglass* (New York: W. W. Norton, 1991), pp. 150–151.

47. [Douglass], "The Smith Land," *NS*, February 18, 1848; Douglass, quoted in Philip S. Foner, *Frederick Douglass* (1950; reprint, New York: Citadel, 1969), p. 138.

48. McCune Smith to Gerrit Smith, July 7, 1848; McCune Smith to Gerrit Smith, February 6, 1850, in *BAP*, 4: 42–45; Wright, Ray, and McCune Smith, *Address to the Three Thousand*, pp. 13–14.

49. Samuel J. May, Chas. A. Wheaton, and Abner Bates, *DO NOT LOSE YOUR LANDS!*, *March 1, 1853*, broadside, GSP; Gerrit Smith to Elder Charles B. Ray, November 16, 1848, *NS*, January 12, 1849; J. W. Loguen, "Gerrit Smith's Land," *NS*, March 24, 1848; Ruth Thompson, quoted in Sanborn, *Life and Letters of Brown*, p. 101.

50. Smith to Ray, November 16, 1848.

51. Douglass to William Lloyd Garrison, January 1, 1846, *LWFD*, 1: 126–127. On Douglass' trip to Great Britain and his break with Garrison see Benjamin Quarles, *Frederick Douglass* (1948; reprint, New York: Da Capo, 1997), pp. 141–153; Philip Foner, *Douglass*, pp. 137–154; Jane H. Pease and William H. Pease, "Boston Garrisonians and the Problem of Frederick Douglass," *Canadian Journal of History* 2 (September 1967): 29–48; Tyrone Tillery, "The Inevitability of the Douglass–Garrison Conflict," *Phylon* 37 (June 1976): 137–149; Friedman, *Gregarious Saints*, pp. 187–192; Waldo Martin Jr., *The Mind of Frederick Douglass* (Chapel Hill: University of North Carolina Press, 1984), pp. 18–55; David W. Blight, *Frederick Douglass' Civil War: Keeping Faith in Jubilee* (Baton Rouge: Louisiana State University Press, 1989), pp. 26–58; McFeely, *Douglass*, pp. 119–182; John R. McKivigan, "The Frederick Douglass–Gerrit Smith Friendship and Political Abolitionism in the 1850s," in *Frederick Douglass: New Literary and Historical Essays*, ed. Eric J. Sundquist (Cambridge: Cambridge University Press, 1990), pp. 205–232; Benjamin Soskis, "Heroic Exile: The Transatlantic Development of Frederick Douglass, 1845–1847" (Senior thesis, Yale University, 1998), pp. 2–52.

52. A. Brook to Maria Weston Chapman, October 5 and 10, 1843, Weston Papers, Boston Public Library; McFeely, *Douglass*, pp. 104–113; Pease and Pease, "Boston Garrisonians," pp. 30–34.

53. Douglass to Harriet Bailey, May 16, 1846, DP; Soskis, "Heroic Exile," pp. 37–38.

54. Blight, *Douglass' Civil War*, p. 30; McKivigan, "Douglass–Smith Friendship," pp. 211–224; McFeely, *Douglass*, pp. 50–57; McCune Smith to Gerrit Smith, July 28, 1848.

55. Communipaw [McCune Smith], "Frederick Douglass in New York," *FDP*, February 2, 1855; Douglass, "James McCune Smith," *FDP*, June 3, 1853; McKivigan, "Douglass–Smith Friendship," pp. 211–224. See also Douglass, "Dr. McCune Smith's Lecture," *FDP*, November 18, 1853; McCune Smith to Frederick Douglass, May 4, 1854, *BAP*, 4: 220–226.

56. Douglass to Gerrit Smith, March 30, 1849, GSP; Quarles, *Douglass*, pp. 85–91; McFeely, *Douglass*, pp. 49–57; Foner, *Douglass*, pp. 75–100; Robert S. Levine, *Martin Delany, Frederick Douglass, and the Politics of Representative Identity* (Chapel Hill: University of North Carolina Press, 1997), pp. 18–57.

57. Douglass, "Comments on Gerrit Smith's Address," *NS*, March 30, 1849; *NS*, March 16, 1849; Quarles, *Douglass*, pp. 145–146; McKivigan, "Douglass–Smith Friendship," pp. 214–220; McFeely, *Douglass*, pp. 150–151; Friedman, *Gregarious Saints*, pp. 192–193.

58. McKivigan, "Douglass–Smith Friendship," p. 216; McFeely, *Douglass*, pp. 154, 165–166.

59. Douglass, "At Home Again," *NS*, May 30, 1850; Smith to Douglass, *NS*, June 13, 1850; Douglass, *Life and Times of Frederick Douglass* (1892; reprint, New York: Collier Books, 1962), p. 453; McKivigan, "Douglass–Smith Friendship," pp. 213–214; McFeely, *Douglass*, pp. 164–165.

60. Hugh C. Humphreys, "'Agitate! Agitate! Agitate!': The Great Fugitive Slave Law Convention and Its Rare Daguerreotype," *Madison County Heritage* 19 (1994): 4–22, quotations pp. 21–22; Philip S. Foner and George E. Walker, eds., *Proceedings of the Black State Conventions, 1840–1865*, vol. 1 (Philadelphia: Temple University Press, 1979), pp. 43–53; Stanley W. Campbell, *The Slave Catchers: Enforcement of the Fugitive Slave Law, 1850–1860* (1968; reprint, New York: W. W. Norton, 1972), pp. 3–25; Allan Nevins, *Ordeal of the Union: Fruits of Manifest Destiny, 1847–1852* (1947; reprint, New York: Collier Books, 1992), pp. 341–343.

61. Humphreys, "'Agitate!" pp. 31, 35–36; *NS*, September 5, 1850.

62. Humphreys, "'Agitate!" pp. 32–33, 38–43.

63. Douglass, "The Constitution and Slavery," in *LWFD*, 1: 352; Douglass to Gerrit Smith, May 1, 1851, in *LWFD*, 2: 149–150. See also McKivigan, "Douglass–Smith Friendship," pp. 212–215; McFeely, *Douglass*, pp. 151–158.

64. Douglass to Gerrit Smith, May 1, 1851, in *LWFD*, 2: 151–154, quotation pp. 151–152; Douglass to Smith, May 28, 29 (quoted), June 4, 10, 11, 18, 1851, GSP. See also McKivigan, "Douglass–Smith Friendship," pp. 214–217; Quarles, *Douglass*, pp. 90–92; Foner, *Douglass*, pp. 88–90; McFeely, *Douglass*, pp. 167–169.

65. Frederick Douglass to Gerrit Smith, June 4, 1851, in *LWFD*, 5: 186; Douglass to Smith, July 4, 1852, in *LWFD*, 2: 205.

66. Douglass, "F. D.," *FDP*, June 26, 1851; McFeely, *Douglass*, p. 150.

67. McFeely, *Douglass*, pp. 81–82; McKivigan, "Douglass–Smith Friendship," pp. 214, 221; *TFDP*, 1/3: 80–81.

68. Douglass, "There Is Something in Dress," *FDP*, May 25, 1855; Fogel, *Without Consent or Contract*, pp. 354–362.

69. Oates, *To Purge This Land*, pp. 54–55; *John Brown: The Making of a Revolutionary*, ed. Louis Ruchames (New York: Grosset and Dunlap, 1969), pp. 26–27; Sanborn, *Life and Letters of Brown*, pp. 35, 43. Brown fathered twenty-one children in all, seven of whom reached maturity.

70. Oates, *To Purge This Land*, pp. 55–56.

71. Brown, quoted in Sanborn, *Life and Letters of Brown*, p. 97; John Brown to Owen Brown, January 10, 1849, quoted in Harlow, *Gerrit Smith*, p. 246; Villard, *Brown*, pp. 71–77; Oates, *To Purge This Land*, pp. 64–69.

72. Phillips, "Three Interviews with Brown," p. 741; Smith, *Speeches of Gerrit Smith in Congress* (New York: Mason Brothers, 1856), p. 9; Quarles, *Douglass*, p. 148; Sanborn, *Life and Letters of Brown*, pp. 99–105; Villard, *Brown*, pp. 71–75; Oates, *To Purge This Land*, pp. 64–69; McCune Smith to Gerrit Smith, February 6, 1850, in *BAP*, 4: 44; Dana, quoted in Hinton, *Brown and His Men*, p. 684.

73. Oates, *To Purge This Land*, pp. 61–64, 86; Foner, *Douglass*, pp. 137–140, 173–175; Douglass, *Life*, p. 273; Higginson, quoted in James Redpath, *The Public Life of Capt. John Brown* (Boston: Thayer and Eldridge, 1860), p. 71; Sotheby's, *Photographs, Wednesday, October 2, 1996* (New York, 1996), p. 18; Ruth Thompson, quoted in Sanborn, *Life and Letters of Brown*, p. 101.

74. Douglass, *Life*, pp. 273–275; Foner, *Douglass*, p. 138; Quarles, *Douglass*, pp. 169–170.

75. Douglass, *Life*, p. 275. See also Oates, *To Purge This Land*, pp. 58–64; McFeely, *Douglass*, pp. 186–188; Blight, *Douglass' Civil War*, pp. 95–99; Quarles, *Douglass*, pp. 169–185; Foner, *Douglass*, pp. 137–140; Leslie Friedman Goldstein, "Violence as an Instrument for Social Change: The Views of Frederick Douglass," *JNH* 61 (1976): 61–72.

76. *NS*, February 11, 1848; Foner, *Douglass*, pp. 137–138; Brown, "Sambo's Mistakes," in Ruchames, *Brown*, p. 71; Brown to Hodges, January 22, 1849, quoted in Villard, *Brown*, pp. 72–73; Willard B. Gatewood Jr., ed., *Free Man of Color: The Autobiography of Willis Augustus Hodges* (Knoxville: Uni-

versity of Tennessee Press, 1982), pp. xxxviii–xlviii, 74–82; *BAP*, 3: 482–483; Friedman, *Gregarious Saints*, pp. 193–194; Slotkin, *Fatal Environment*, pp. 265–266.

77. Villard, *Brown*, pp. 73–74, 560–564; Sanborn, *Life and Letters of Brown*, pp. 114, 375; Oates, *To Purge This Land*, pp. 199, 206–207; Donaldson, *History of the Adirondacks*, 2: 7–8; Schneider, *Adirondacks*, pp. 110, 112.

78. Douglass, quoted in Quarles, *Douglass*, p. 152; Foner, *Douglass*, p. 165; Douglass to Gerrit Smith, October 21, November 6, 1852, GSP; Harlow, *Gerrit Smith*, pp. 297–303. On the Jerry Rescue see also Samuel J. May, *Some Recollections of Our Antislavery Conflict* (1869; reprint, New York: Arno Press, 1968), pp. 373–384; Donald Yacovone, *Samuel Joseph May and the Dilemmas of the Liberal Persuasion* (Philadelphia: Temple University Press, 1991), pp. 88–101; Campbell, *Slave Catchers*, pp. 151–157; Benjamin Quarles, *Black Abolitionists* (New York: Oxford University Press, 1969), pp. 209–211; W. Freeman Galpin, "The Jerry Rescue," *NYHIST* 26 (1945): 19–34; *FDP*, February 11, 1853. In his *Recollections*, May identifies Jerry as "McHenry" (as do some later historians), but *Frederick Douglass' Paper* and other sources from the 1850s refer to him as "Henry."

79. Douglass, quoted in Quarles, *Douglass*, p. 152; Foner, *Douglass*, p. 165; Douglass to Smith, October 21, 1852, November 6, 1852 (quoted); McKivigan, "Douglass–Smith Friendship," p. 219; Garrison, quoted in *FDP*, November 19, 1852; Harlow, *Gerrit Smith*, pp. 312–315; Frothingham, *Gerrit Smith*, pp. 214–216.

80. Harlow, *Gerrit Smith*, pp. 312–313; J. B. Edwards to Smith, September 28, 1852, GSP; Smith, *Speeches*, pp. 9–11; McKivigan, "Douglass–Smith Friendship," p. 219; Foner, *Douglass*, p. 165; "Gerrit Smith for Congress," *FDP*, October 22, 1852; "Gerrit Smith at Home," *FDP*, October 29, 1852.

81. Harlow, *Gerrit Smith*, pp. 317–318; Robert A. Huff, "Anne Miller and the Geneva Political Equality Club, 1897–1912," *NYHIST*, October 1984, p. 333; William Lee Miller, *Arguing about Slavery: The Great Battle in the United States Congress* (New York: Alfred A. Knopf, 1996), pp. 42–46.

82. Douglass to Smith, August 18, 1853, *LWFD*, 2: 268–269; Smith to Douglass, June 12, 1854, DP. Smith later said he suffered from "vertigo" while in Congress, but one could interpret his vertigo as a fear of falling in status in Washington, or as a fear of failing as an abolitionist congressman. See "Case Notes of Gerrit Smith," New York State Lunatic Asylum, book 16, holograph, NYSA.

83. Smith, "Autobiographical Sketch of the Life of Gerrit Smith," holograph, n.d. [1856], GSP; Smith, *Speeches*, p. 228; Smith, *To the Abolitionists and Prohibitionists of the County of Madison*, broadside, August 16, 1858, GSP; Douglass to Gerrit Smith, December 23, 1853, GSP; "Gerrit Smith in

Congress," *FDP*, July 9, 1853; Frothingham, *Gerrit Smith*, pp. 215–224; Harlow, *Gerrit Smith*, pp. 319–327; Stewart, *Joshua Giddings*, p. 223; Angelina Grimké Weld to Gerrit Smith, January 6, 1854, GSP.

84. Smith, *Speeches*, pp. 35–36, 376–377, 411; *Mr. Gerrit Smith on the President's Message: The Currency and the Hard Times*, broadside, December 21, 1857, GSP; Frothingham, *Gerrit Smith*, pp. 217–224; Harlow, *Gerrit Smith*, pp. 331–335.

85. Smith, *Speeches*, pp. 202–206, 305–306, 401–404; Harlow, *Gerrit Smith*, pp. 319–320, 327, 331–332; Smith, quoted in Foner, *Douglass*, p. 165; Smith, *To the Abolitionists and Prohibitionists of Madison*.

86. Smith, *Speeches*, pp. 386–400; Smith, "The Humbled Congressman; or, The Triumphant Postmaster" (verse), GSP; Harlow, *Gerrit Smith*, pp. 321–339; Frothingham, *Gerrit Smith*, pp. 220–224; Friedman, *Gregarious Saints*, p. 124; Smith, "Congressional Term, Miscellaneous Papers," GSP; *Gerrit Smith to William Goodell*, broadside, November 1, 1854, GSP; "Goodell's Reply to Smith."

87. Smith, *Speeches*, p. 381; *Controversy between the New-York Tribune and Gerrit Smith* (New York: John A. Gray, 1855), GSP; *Gerrit Smith to the New-York Tribune*, broadside, July 17, 1855, GSP; Harlow, *Gerrit Smith*, pp. 330–335; *Gerrit Smith to William Goodell*; "Goodell's Reply to Smith"; McKivigan, "Douglass–Smith Friendship," p. 219.

88. Smith, *Speeches*, p. 381; Douglass, "The End of All Compromises With Slavery—Now and Forever," *LWFD*, 2: 283; Douglass to Gerrit Smith, August 22, 1854, *LWFD*, 2: 310; McCune Smith to Gerrit Smith, March 31, 1855, *BAP*, 4: 275; McCune Smith to Gerrit Smith, [no date] 1855, GSP.

Six. Learning from Indians

1. James McCune Smith, "From Our New York Correspondent," *FDP*, March 25, 1859. See also Garry Wills, "A Tale of Three Leaders," *NYR*, September 19, 1996, pp. 64–67; and Sterling Stuckey, *Slave Culture: Nationalist Theory and the Foundations of Black America* (New York: Oxford University Press, 1987), pp. 198–243.

2. Martin Delany, *Blake; or, the Huts of America: A Tale of the Mississippi Valley, the Southern United States, and Cuba* (1859), reprinted in *Violence in the Black Imagination: Essays and Documents*, ed. Ronald T. Takaki (New York: Oxford University Press, 1993), pp. 162–163, 179.

3. On the revolutionary ethos in Delany's novel see Eric J. Sundquist, *To Wake the Nations: Race in the Making of American Literature* (Cambridge: Harvard University Press, 1993), pp. 182–210; Robert S. Levine, *Martin*

Delany, Frederick Douglass, and the Politics of Representative Identity (Chapel Hill: University of North Carolina Press, 1997), pp. 177–223; Ronald T. Takaki, "War upon the Whites: Black Rage in the Fiction of Martin Delany," in *Violence in the Black Imagination*, pp. 79–101.

4. Jacques Barzun, *Classic, Romantic, and Modern* (1943; reprint, Chicago: University of Chicago Press, 1961), pp. 4–5, 71–77; Sundquist, *To Wake the Nations*, pp. 118, 124; Robert J. Berkhofer Jr., *The White Man's Indian: Images of the American Indian from Columbus to the Present* (New York: Vintage, 1979), pp. 72–112; David Brion Davis, *Slavery and Human Progress* (New York: Oxford University Press, 1984), pp. 231–278; Catherine L. Albanese, *Nature Religion in America: From the Algonkian Indians to the New Age* (Chicago: University of Chicago Press, 1990), pp. 43–94.

5. Richard Slotkin, *The Fatal Environment: The Myth of the Frontier in the Age of Industrialization, 1800–1890* (Middletown, Conn.: Wesleyan University Press, 1985), pp. 242–244, 262–278; Davis, *Slavery and Human Progress*, pp. 231–278; Michael Fellman, "Rehearsal for the Civil War: Antislavery and Proslavery at the Fighting Point in Kansas, 1854–56," in *Antislavery Reconsidered: New Perspectives on the Abolitionists*, ed. Michael Fellman and Lewis Perry (Baton Rouge: Louisiana State University Press, 1979), pp. 287–307, quotation p. 293; Fellman, *Inside War: The Guerrilla Conflict in Missouri during the American Civil War* (New York: Oxford University Press, 1989), pp. 11–22.

6. E. Anthony Rotundo, *American Manhood: Transformations in Masculinity from the Revolution to the Modern Era* (New York: Basic Books, 1993), pp. 222–239, quotation p. 223; Frederick Douglass, "Pictures," n.d. [ca. 1864], DP; James Oliver Horton and Lois E. Horton, "Violence, Protest, and Identity: Black Manhood in Antebellum America," in *Free People of Color: Inside the African American Community*, ed. James Oliver Horton (Washington, D.C.: Smithsonian Institution Press, 1993), pp. 80–96; David Leverenz, *Manhood and the American Renaissance* (Ithaca: Cornell University Press, 1989), pp. 4, 73, 98–100, 108–134.

7. Winthrop Jordan, *White over Black: American Attitudes toward the Negro, 1550–1812* (New York: W. W. Norton, 1968), pp. 475–481; Richard Slotkin, *Regeneration through Violence: The Mythology of the American Frontier, 1600–1860* (Middletown, Conn.: Wesleyan University Press, 1973), pp. 358, 466–516; Robert F. Sayre, *Thoreau and the American Indians* (Princeton: Princeton University Press, 1977), pp. 3–58, 123–154; Ed Folsom, *Walt Whitman's Native Representations* (Cambridge: Cambridge University Press, 1994), pp. 55–98.

8. *TFDP*, 1/2: 147–167, 337–341, quotation by Douglass pp. 340–341; Frederick Douglass, "Colored Americans, and Aliens—T. F. Meagher," quoted

in *LWFD*, 5: 365; William M. Wiecek, *The Sources of Antislavery Constitutionalism in America, 1760–1848* (Ithaca: Cornell University Press, 1977), pp. 248–275; Oswald Garrison Villard, *John Brown, 1800–1859: A Biography Fifty Years After* (1910; reprint, New York: Alfred A. Knopf, 1943), p. 1; Smith, "Autobiographical Sketch of the Life of Gerrit Smith, holograph, n.d. [1856], GSP; McCune Smith, "Letter from Communipaw," *FDP*, March 18, 1852.

9. Berkhofer, *White Man's Indian*, pp. 72, 76. See also *TFDP*, 1/3: 171–172. On abolitionists and Indians see also Linda K. Kerber, "The Abolitionist Perception of the Indian," *JAH* 62 (September 1975): 271–295; and Mary Hershberger, "Mobilizing Women, Anticipating Abolition: The Struggle against Indian Removal in the 1830s," *JAH* 86 (June 1999): 15–40.

10. Berkhofer, *White Man's Indian*, pp. 72–111.

11. McCune Smith, "Letter from Communipaw," *FDP*, March 18, 1852; McCune Smith, "[Letter to] Messrs. Editors," *FDP*, December 25, 1851; McCune Smith to Gerrit Smith, February 6, 1850, GSP; *BAP*, 4: 225; Washington Irving, *Diedrich Knickerbocker's History of New-York* (1809; reprint, New York: Heritage Press, 1940), pp. 50–75; Irving, "Communipaw," in *Biographies and Miscellanies*, ed. Pierre M. Irving (Philadelphia: J. B. Lippincott, 1871), pp. 452–462; John Romeyn Brodhead, *History of the State of New York* (New York: Harper & Brothers, 1872), pp. 642–643; James Grant Wilson, ed., *The Memorial History of the City of New-York* . . . , vol. 4 (New York: New-York History, 1893), pp. 26–28. McCune Smith occasionally called himself "Wapinummoc" in his editorials—Communipaw spelled backward.

12. McCune Smith, "To the Editor of the Tribune," in *BAP*, 3: 431.

13. McCune Smith, "Messrs. Editors," December 25, 1851. The description of the Byronic hero is from Sundquist, *To Wake the Nations*, pp. 118, 124.

14. McCune Smith, "Messrs. Editors," December 25, 1851.

15. Stephen Jay Gould, *The Mismeasure of Man*, rev. ed. (New York: W. W. Norton, 1996), pp. 62–141; William Stanton, *The Leopard's Spots: Scientific Attitudes toward Race in America, 1815–59* (Chicago: University of Chicago Press, 1960), pp. 1–44.

16. McCune Smith, "Civilization: Its Dependence on Physical Circumstances" (1944), *AAM*, pp. 5–12, quotation p. 5; Douglass, "The Claims of the Negro Ethnologically Considered," *TFDP*, 1/2: 522.

17. Lewis Douglass, quoted in Dickson J. Preston, *Young Frederick Douglass: The Maryland Years* (Baltimore: Johns Hopkins University Press, 1980), p. 9; Leverenz, *Manhood and American Renaissance*, pp. 128–129; Peter Walker, *Moral Choices: Memory, Desire, and Imagination in Nineteenth-*

Century American Abolition (Baton Rouge: Louisiana State University Press, 1978), pp. 207–228, 248–261.

18. Frederick Douglass, *My Bondage and My Freedom* (1855; reprint, Urbana: University of Illinois Press, 1987), p. 54; *TFDP*, 1/2: 266; Douglass, "Pictures." See also *TFDP*, 1/3: 452–473, 619–620; *TFDP*, 1/5: 545–575; Douglass, "Self-Made Men," DP.

19. Douglass, quoted in Waldo Martin Jr., *The Mind of Frederick Douglass* (Chapel Hill: University of North Carolina Press, 1984), p. 213; Douglass, "Claims of the Negro," p. 524.

20. *TFDP*, 1/2: 266. See also *TFDP*, 1/2: 242, 325; *TFDP*, 1/1: 243, 295. On Martin Delany's embrace of emigration and black nationalism see Dorothy Sterling, *The Making of an Afro-American: Martin Robison Delany, 1812–1885* (1971; reprint, New York: Da Capo, 1996); and Levine, *Martin Delany, Frederick Douglass*, pp. 1–17, 177–238.

21. *TFDP*, 1/2: 276–277; *TFDP*, 1/3: 419; Douglass, *Bondage*, pp. 150, 152.

22. Douglass, "The Heroic Slave," reprinted in Takaki, *Violence in the Black Imagination*, pp. 37–77. For other interpretations see Ronald T. Takaki, "Not Afraid to Die," ibid., pp. 17–36; Sundquist, *To Wake the Nations*, pp. 115–126; Levine, *Delany, Douglass*, pp. 83–85; Richard Yarborough, "Race, Violence, and Manhood: The Masculine Ideal in Frederick Douglass's 'The Heroic Slave,'" in *Frederick Douglass: New Literary and Historical Essays*, ed. Eric J. Sundquist (Cambridge: Cambridge University Press, 1990), pp. 166–188; Robert Stepto, "Storytelling in Early Afro-American Fiction: Frederick Douglass' 'The Heroic Slave,'" *Georgia Review* 36 (1982): 355–368; Maggie Montesinos Sale, *The Slumbering Volcano: American Slave Ship Revolts and the Production of Rebellious Masculinity* (Durham, N.C.: Duke University Press, 1977), pp. 173–197. On the actual *Creole* case see Howard Jones, "The Peculiar Institution and National Honor: The Case of the *Creole* Slave Revolt," *CWH* 21 (March 1975): 28–50.

23. Douglass, "Heroic Slave," p. 40.

24. Ibid.

25. Ibid., p. 48.

26. Ibid., p. 49.

27. Ibid., pp. 75–76.

28. Ibid., pp. 49, 76–77.

29. Ibid., pp. 74–75. See also Stepto, "Storytelling," p. 364.

30. Douglass, "Heroic Slave," pp. 75–77; Douglass, "Pictures."

31. Smith, *Speeches of Gerrit Smith in Congress* (New York: Mason Brothers, 1856), p. 228; Smith, quoted in Octavius Brooks Frothingham, *Gerrit Smith: A Biography* (New York: G. P. Putnam's Sons, 1878), pp. 233, 240. See also Smith, "Address to the Slaves of the United States . . . ," *NASS*,

February 24, 1842. On Smith's reference to the Great Spirit, see Smith, *Peace Better than War* . . . (Boston: American Peace Society, 1858), p. 5, GSP; Gerrit Smith, *Religion of Reason* (Peterboro: C. A. Hammond, 1864), pp. 21–34, 44–75.

32. Frothingham, *Gerrit Smith*, pp. 6–9; Ralph Volney Harlow, *Gerrit Smith: Philanthropist and Reformer* (New York: Henry Holt, 1939), pp. 1–6; Charles A. Hammond, *Gerrit Smith: The Story of a Noble Man's Life* (Geneva, N.Y.: W. F. Humphrey, 1900), pp. 3–8; Kenneth Wiggins Porter, *John Jacob Astor: Business Man* (Cambridge: Harvard University Press, 1931), pp. 36–38, 48–50, 93–100; L. M. Hammond, *History of Madison County, State of New York* (Syracuse: Truair, Smith, 1872), pp. 99–121, 717–722; James H. Smith, *History of Chenango and Madison Counties, New York* (Syracuse: D. Mason, 1881), p. 686; Smith, *To the Religious Newspaper Reviewers of my Recent Discourse*, Peterboro, broadside, September 3, 1859, GSP; *Gerrit Smith to Governor Chase, Ohio*, Peterboro, broadside, January 30, 1856, GSP.

33. Smith, "Letter From Gerrit Smith to Gov. Hunt," *FDP*, March 4, 1852; Brown, quoted in Villard, *Brown*, p. 362.

34. F. B. Sanborn, ed., *The Life and Letters of John Brown* (Boston: Roberts Brothers, 1885), pp. 97, 245–246, 252, 321–323, quotation p. 97; Villard, *Brown*, pp. 1–7, 89–90, quotations pp. 2, 90; Steven B. Oates, *To Purge This Land with Blood: A Biography of John Brown* (1970; reprint, Amherst: University of Massachusetts Press, 1984), pp. 58–64, 172; *Harper's Weekly*, October 29, 1859, p. 690; Douglass, *Life and Times of Frederick Douglass* (1892; reprint, New York: Collier, 1962), pp. 272–275.

35. *NYH*, June 8, 10, 1856 (emphasis added); Louis Ruchames, ed., *John Brown: The Making of a Revolutionary* (New York: Grosset and Dunlap, 1969), pp. 30–31. On Brown as a western hero in the Leatherstocking tradition see Slotkin, *Fatal Environment*, pp. 242–244, 262–278. On the Leatherstocking myth, see also Henry Nash Smith, *Virgin Land: The American West as Symbol and Myth* (Cambridge: Harvard University Press, 1950), pp. 51–111; and David Brion Davis, *Homicide in American Fiction* (1957; reprint, Ithaca: Cornell University Press, 1968), pp. 3–55.

36. William Phillips, *The Conquest of Kansas, by Missouri and Her Allies* (Boston: Phillips, Sampson, 1856), pp. 332–333; Daniel C. Littlefield, "Blacks, John Brown, and a Theory of Manhood," in *His Soul Goes Marching On: Responses to John Brown and the Harper's Ferry Raid*, ed. Paul Finkelman (Charlottesville: University Press of Virginia, 1995), pp. 67–97.

37. Frothingham, *Gerrit Smith*, pp. 364–365; Ralph Volney Harlow, "The Rise and Fall of the Kansas Aid Movement," *AHR*, October 1935, pp. 1–15. For other abolitionists' responses to Brown's savagery in Kansas see Thomas

Wentworth Higginson, *Cheerful Yesterdays* (1898; reprint, New York: Arno Press, 1968), pp. 207–208.

38. Bryant, quoted in Allan Nevins, *Ordeal of the Union*, vol. 1, pt. 2: *A House Dividing, 1852–1857* (1947; reprint, New York: Collier, 1992), p. 449; Oates, *To Purge This Land*, pp. 90–91, 129, 139; Slotkin, *Fatal Environment*, pp. 262–278; James C. Malin, *John Brown and the Legend of Fifty-six* (Philadelphia: American Philosophical Society, 1942), pp. 89–116; C. Vann Woodward, "John Brown's Private War," in *The Burden of Southern History* (Baton Rouge: Louisiana State University Press, 1960), pp. 42–45.

39. Douglass, *Life and Times*, p. 303; *Gerrit Smith to John Thomas, August 27, 1859*, broadside, GSP; *TFDP*, 1/3: 304.

40. Douglass, *Life and Times*, p. 302; Boyer, *Brown*, p. 460; Sanborn, *Life and Letters of Brown*, pp. 110–111; David M. Potter, *The Impending Crisis, 1848–1861* (New York: Harper & Row, 1976), pp. 199–200; Richard J. Hinton, *John Brown and His Men* (New York: Funk and Wagnalls, 1894), pp. 18–19; Douglass, "Our Plan for Making Kansas a Free State," in *LWFD*, 2: 311–315; McCune Smith to Gerrit Smith, March 13, 1856, GSP; McCune Smith, "Letter to the Editor," *FDP*, August 8, 1856.

41. McCune Smith to Gerrit Smith, March 1, 1855, GSP; Douglass to Gerrit Smith, March 22, 1856, in *LWFD*, 2: 384.

42. Smith, *To the Men Who Put Me in Nomination*, November 5, 1858, broadside, GSP; Smith, *To the Abolitionists and Prohibitionists of the County of Madison*, broadside, August 16, 1858, GSP; Ruchames, *Brown*, pp. 33–35; Oates, *To Purge This Land*, p. 172.

43. Smith, quoted in Harlow, "Kansas Aid Movement," p. 15; Smith, *To Abolitionists and Prohibitionists of Madison*; Smith, *To the Men Who Put Me in Nomination*; Douglass, *Life and Times*, pp. 301–302.

44. Mohawk [John Henri Kagi], "Kansas: Stanton's Speech at Lawrence . . . ," *NYT*, May 5, 1857. On Kagi's authorship of the "Mohawk" articles, see Richard J. Hinton, ed., *Richard Realf's Free-State Poems, with Personal Lyrics Written in Kansas* (Topeka: Crane, 1900), pp. 49–52. On patriots' use of the pseudonym "Mohawk" during the American Revolution, see Philip J. Deloria, *Playing Indian* (New Haven: Yale University Press, 1998), chap. 1.

45. Donald Yacovone, "Abolitionists and the 'Language of Fraternal Love,'" in *Meanings for Manhood: Constructions of Masculinity in Victorian America*, ed. Mark C. Carnes and Clyde Griffen (Chicago: University of Chicago Press, 1990), pp. 85–95; Douglass, *Bondage*, p. 2.

46. William A. Phillips, "Three Interviews with Old John Brown," *Atlantic Monthly* 44 (December 1879): 740, 744.

47. Leverenz, *Manhood and American Renaissance*, pp. 1–8, 72–134; Rotundo, *American Manhood*, pp. 222–239; Horton and Horton, "Violence, Protest,

and Identity," pp. 80–96, 212–215; Smith, quoted in Harlow, "Kansas Aid Movement," p. 15; Douglass, quoted in *LWFD*, 2: 283; McCune Smith, "Proceedings of the National Council of the Colored People . . . ," *TFDP*, 1/3: 55–59, quotation p. 58.

48. Rotundo, *American Manhood*, p. 222; Horton and Horton, "Violence, Protest, and Identity," pp. 80–96; William S. McFeely, *Frederick Douglass* (New York: W. W. Norton, 1991), p. 189; Villard, *Brown*, p. 153. See also Sanborn, *Life and Letters of Brown*, pp. 240, 444.

49. McCune Smith, "Civilization," p. 8; Gerrit Smith to Rev. Theodore S. Wright, Charles B. Ray, and Dr. James McCune Smith, November 14, 1846, GSP.

50. Thomas Wentworth Higginson, *Out-Door Papers* (Boston: Ticknor and Fields, 1863), pp. 3, 4, 6, 35, 108–109.

51. Ibid., pp. 128–130, 133, 143–144.

52. Ibid., pp. 134–135, 137–140, 144–145, 149 (emphasis added).

53. Ottilie Assing, "A Visit with Gerrit Smith," in *Radical Passion: Ottilie Assing's Reports from America and Letters to Frederick Douglass*, ed. and trans. Christoph Lohmann (New York: Peter Lang, 1999), pp. 158–162, quotation p. 161; Inventory of the Frederick Douglass National Historic Site, Anacostia, Washington, D.C.; Keith F. Davis, "'A Terrible Distinctness': Photography of the Civil War," in *Photography in Nineteenth-Century America*, ed. Martha A. Sandweiss (New York: Harry N. Abrams, 1991), p. 143.

54. Higginson, *Out-Door Papers*, p. 42; George M. Fredrickson, *The Black Image in the White Mind: The Debate on Afro-American Character and Destiny, 1817–1914* (1971; reprint, Middletown, Conn.: Wesleyan University Press, 1987), pp. 169–171, 200–201.

55. David Brion Davis, "At the Heart of Slavery," *NYR*, October 17, 1996, pp. 51–52.

56. Laurence M. Hauptman, *Between Two Fires: American Indians in the Civil War* (New York: Free Press, 1995), pp. 1, 68–69; Edward Stone, ed., *Incident at Harper's Ferry* (Englewood Cliffs, N.J.: Prentice-Hall, 1956), pp. 44, 93.

57. See Leon F. Litwack, *Trouble in Mind: Black Southerners in the Age of Jim Crow* (New York: Alfred A. Knopf, 1998).

Seven. Man Is Woman and Woman Is Man

1. *Gerrit Smith to Elizabeth C. Stanton, December 1, 1855,* broadside, GSP.

2. Malcolm Cowley, ed., *Walt Whitman's Leaves of Grass: The First (1855) Edition* (New York: Penguin, 1959), pp. 8, 43, 89.

3. *Gerrit Smith to Elizabeth C. Stanton, December 1, 1855; New York Mirror,* October 24, 1850, and *NYH,* September 12, 1852, quoted in *FDWR,* pp. 12, 18.

4. Elizabeth Cady Stanton, *Eighty Years and More: Reminiscences, 1815–1897* (1898; reprint, New York: Schocken, 1971), pp. 51–70, quotations pp. 52–53; Elisabeth Griffith, *In Her Own Right: The Life of Elizabeth Cady Stanton* (New York: Oxford University Press, 1984), pp. 24, 30, 33, 40, 66–67, 91–92, 226–227; Theodore Stanton and Harriot Stanton Blatch, *Elizabeth Cady Stanton,* vol. 2 (New York: Arno, 1969), pp. 28–35, 43–44.

5. Stanton, quoted in William Leach, *True Love and Perfect Union: The Feminist Reform of Sex and Society* (1980; reprint, Middletown, Conn.: Wesleyan University Press, 1989), pp. xiv, 246; Stanton to Elizabeth Smith Miller, September 20, 1855, in Stanton and Blatch, *Stanton,* p. 61; *FDWR,* p. 73.

6. Susan B. Anthony to Gerrit Smith, December 25, 1855, September 5, 1856, GSP; Frederick Douglass to Gerrit Smith, January 1, 1856, GSP; Leach, *True Love,* pp. 244–248; Nancy Isenberg, *Sex and Citizenship in Antebellum America* (Chapel Hill: University of North Carolina Press, 1998), pp. 48–55; Griffith, *In Her Own Right,* pp. 91–92.

7. *Gerrit Smith to Elizabeth Cady Stanton, December 1, 1855;* Leach, *True Love,* pp. 244; Alice Felt Tyler, *Freedom's Ferment: Phases of American Social History from the Colonial Period to the Outbreak of the Civil War* (1944; reprint, New York: Harper Torchbooks, 1962), p. 441.

8. Stanton to Elizabeth Smith Miller, September 11, 1862, in Stanton and Blatch, *Stanton,* p. 91.

9. Joel Porte, ed., *Emerson in His Journals* (Cambridge: Harvard University Press, 1982), pp. 403–404, 431–432, 463, 472; Ralph Waldo Emerson, "Woman: A Lecture . . . ," in *The Works of Ralph Waldo Emerson,* ed. James Elliot Cabot, vol. 11: *Miscellanies* (Boston: Houghton Mifflin, 1878), pp. 337–339.

10. Gerrit Smith, *Religion of Reason* (Peterboro: C. A. Hammond, 1864), p. 12; *Smith to Elizabeth Cady Stanton, December 1, 1855;* Douglass, quoted in *TFDP,* 1/2: 377. See also Smith, *To the Reform Dress Association, May 18, 1857,* GSP; Robert H. Abzug, *Cosmos Crumbling: American Reform and the Religious Imagination* (New York: Oxford University Press, 1980), pp. 204–229; Tyler, *Freedom's Ferment,* 430; David Brion Davis, "The Other Revolution," *NYR,* October 5, 2000, p. 44.

11. Leach, *True Love,* p. 244; Stanton to Elizabeth Smith Miller, July 2, 1851, in Stanton and Blatch, *Stanton,* p. 32; Arch Merrill, "Bloomers and Bugles," typescript, p. 6, MCHS; Harriet Stanton Blatch, "Mrs. Elizabeth Smith Miller," *American Magazine* 72 (July 1911): 308–309; Robert A. Huff, "Anne Miller and the Geneva Political Equality Club, 1897–1912," *NYHIST,* October 1984, pp. 326–328.

12. *Hamilton* [College] *Literary Monthly* 3 (September 1868): 69, HCA; "The Last Illustration of Woman's Rights—A Female Base-Ball Club at Peterboro," *It's the Day's Doings*, 1868, New York Public Library; Frank Lorenz, "Athletics at Hamilton: A Historical Sketch," HCA; *Oneida Dispatch*, August 21, 1868; Gai Ingham Berlage, *Women in Baseball: The Forgotten History* (Westport, Conn.: Praeger, 1994), pp. 28–29; personal communications from Donna Burdick, Smithfield town historian, November 27, 1996, April 8, 1997. Although the first women's baseball team did not begin until 1868 at Peterboro, the very emergence of such a phenomenon, coupled with the support it received, could not have occurred without a radical reconception of women's roles in the 1850s.

13. Ann C. Smith to Gerrit Smith, November 20, 22, 1852, January 4, 1853, GSP; Gerrit Smith, "Thirty-Second Wedding-Day" and "The Retraction," January 3, 1854, Letterbook of Poetry, GSP.

14. "Diary of Ann C. Fitzhugh Smith," 1852, holograph, MCHS; Gerrit Smith, "My Beloved Wife . . . ," June 3, 1855, Letterbook of Poetry; Ann Braude, *Radical Spirits: Spiritualism and Women's Rights in Nineteenth-Century America* (Boston: Beacon Press, 1989), p. 3.

15. "Diary of Ann C. Fitzhugh Smith," 1852, holograph, MCHS.

16. McCune Smith published his sketches under the heading "Heads of the Colored People" in *FDP*, in eleven installments (No. X was published in two parts), from March 25, 1852, through November 17, 1854.

17. James McCune Smith, "'Heads of the Colored People,' Done with a Whitewash Brush," *FDP*, March 25, 1852. On phrenology see Charles Colbert, *A Measure of Perfection: Phrenology and the Fine Arts in America* (Chapel Hill: University of North Carolina Press, 1997); and John Davies, *Phrenology: Fad and Science* (New Haven: Yale University Press, 1955).

18. James McCune Smith, "'Heads,'" March 25, 1852.

19. Herman Melville, *Moby-Dick; or, The Whale* (1851; reprint, New York: Penguin, 1992), p. 66.

20. McCune Smith, "'Heads,'" March 25, 1852. On the "Republic of Letters," see Michael Warner, *The Letters of the Republic: Publication and the Public Sphere in Eighteenth-Century America* (Cambridge: Harvard University Press, 1990).

21. McCune Smith, "'Heads of the Colored People'—No. VIII: The Whitewasher," *FDP*, September 30, 1853. McCune Smith's term "lamp black" refers to the finely powdered black soot used as a pigment in paints, enamels, and printing ink.

22. McCune Smith, "'Heads,'" March 25, 1852; McCune Smith to Gerrit Smith, May 12, 1848, GSP.

23. McCune Smith, "'Heads of the Colored People'—No. 2: The Boot-Black," *FDP*, April 15, 1852.

24. McCune Smith, "'Heads of the Colored People'—No. 3: The Washerwoman," *FDP*, June 17, 1852.

25. Ibid.

26. Ibid.

27. McCune Smith, "'Heads of the Colored People'—No. X: The Schoolmaster," *FDP*, November 3, 1854.

28. Ibid.

29. Ibid.

30. Ibid.; McCune Smith, "'Heads,'" March 25, 1852; Melville, *Moby-Dick*, p. 3.

31. McCune Smith, "From Our New York Correspondent," *FDP*, May 11, 1855; McCune Smith, "'Heads of the Colored People'—No. 4: The Sexton," *FDP*, July 16, 1852. See also Braude, *Radical Spirits*, pp. 28–29.

32. *FDWR*, pp. ix, 3–4, 10, 12–14; Tyler, *Freedom's Ferment*, 454–55; Waldo Martin Jr., *The Mind of Frederick Douglass* (Chapel Hill: University of North Carolina Press, 1984), pp. 136–140, 148.

33. *FDWR*, pp. 49–51, 55, 58–59, 68; Douglass to Gerrit Smith, January 1, 1856, GSP; Martin, *Mind of Douglass*, pp. 138–145.

34. Frederick Douglass, *Narrative of the Life of Frederick Douglass, An American Slave, Written by Himself* (1845; reprint, New York: Penguin, 1982), p. 52; Douglass, *My Bondage and My Freedom* (1855; reprint, Urbana: University of Illinois Press, 1987), pp. 57–59; Amy Dru Stanley, "'The Right to Possess All the Faculties That God Has Given': Possessive Individualism, Slave Women, and Abolitionist Thought," in *Moral Problems in American Life: New Perspectives on Cultural History*, ed. Karen Halttunen and Lewis Perry (Ithaca: Cornell University Press, 1998), pp. 123–130; Jenny Franchot, "The Punishment of Esther: Frederick Douglass and the Construction of the Feminine," in *Frederick Douglass: New Literary and Historical Essays*, ed. Eric J. Sundquist (Cambridge: Cambridge University Press, 1990), pp. 141–165; Karen Sánchez-Eppler, *Touching Liberty: Abolition, Feminism, and the Politics of the Body* (Berkeley: University of California Press, 1993), pp. 1–21; Jean Fagan Yellin, *Women and Sisters: The Antislavery Feminists in American Culture* (New Haven: Yale University Press, 1989), pp. 3–28; Gerda Lerner, *The Creation of Patriarchy* (New York: Oxford University Press, 1986), pp. 76–100; David Brion Davis, "At the Heart of Slavery," *NYR*, October 17, 1996, p. 52.

35. *FDWR*, pp. 19, 76.

36. Douglass, *Narrative*, pp. 78, 85–86, quotation p. 78; Douglass, *Bondage*, pp. 92–93, 103–104; *FDWR*, pp. 8–24; Martin, *Mind of Douglass*, pp. 137–138; Tyler, *Freedom's Ferment*, p. 429; William S. McFeely, *Frederick Douglass* (New York: W. W. Norton, 1991), pp. 26–30, 32–34, 66–73, 96,

162–182; Dickson J. Preston, *Young Frederick Douglass: The Maryland Years* (Baltimore: Johns Hopkins University Press, 1980), pp. 101–102.

37. Douglass, *Narrative*, p. 137; Douglass, *Bondage*, pp. 195–197; Douglass, *Life and Times of Frederick Douglass* (1892; reprint, New York: Collier, 1962), pp. 76–87; McFeely, *Douglass*, p. 66; David Leverenz, *Manhood and the American Renaissance* (Ithaca: Cornell University Press, 1989), pp. 128–129; Maria Diedrich, *Love across Color Lines: Ottilie Assing and Frederick Douglass* (New York: Hill and Wang, 1999), pp. 178–179.

38. Douglass, *Narrative*, p. 145; Douglass, *Bondage*, p. 208. See also Daniel Walker Howe, *Making the American Self: Jonathan Edwards to Abraham Lincoln* (New York: Oxford University Press, 1997), pp. 107–156; Linda Kerber, "Can A Woman Be an Individual? The Discourse of Self-Reliance," in *American Chameleon: Individualism in Trans-National Context*, ed. Richard O. Curry and B. Goodheart Lawrence (Kent, Ohio: Kent State University Press, 1991), pp. 151–166; Henry Louis Gates Jr., *Figures in Black: Words, Signs, and the "Racial" Self* (New York: Oxford University Press, 1987), pp. 98–124; Gates, "A Dangerous Literacy: The Legacy of Frederick Douglass," *New York Times Book Review*, May 28, 1995, pp. 3–4; Diedrich, *Love across Color Lines*, pp. 175–177.

39. Douglass, *Life*, p. 204.

40. McFeely, *Douglass*, pp. 65–73; Preston, *Young Douglass*, pp. 149, 151–152; Rosetta Douglass Sprague, "Anna Murray-Douglass—My Mother as I Recall Her," *JNH* 8 (January 1923): 93–101; Gates, "Dangerous Literacy," pp. 3–4; Diedrich, *Love across Color Lines*, pp. 169–198.

41. "Frederick Douglass to Mrs. Lydia Dennett," April 17, 1857, in *FDWR*, pp. 21–22; Diedrich, *Love across Color Lines*, pp. 176–185.

42. Diedrich, *Love across Color Lines*, pp. 175–194. See also Garry Wills, "A Reader's Guide to the Century," *NYR*, July 15, 1999, pp. 25–26.

43. Diedrich, *Love across Color Lines*, pp. 43–88; Gates, "Dangerous Literacy," pp. 3–4; Assing, quoted in *Radical Passion: Ottilie Assing's Reports from America and Letters to Frederick Douglass*, ed. and trans. Christoph Lohmann (New York: Peter Lang, 1999), p. 70.

44. Assing, quoted in Gates, "Dangerous Literacy," p. 4; Diedrich, *Love across Color Lines*, pp. xv–xxix, 169–198; Lohmann, "Introduction," in *Radical Passion*, pp. xiii–xxxvii.

45. Assing, quoted in Gates, "Dangerous Literacy," p. 4; Diedrich, *Love across Color Lines*, pp. xv–xxix, 169–198; Lohmann, "Introduction," in *Radical Passion*, pp. xvi–xxvi.

46. *TFDP*, 1/2: 438; *TFDP*, 1/3: 552; Diedrich, *Love across Color Lines*, pp. 33–34, 104, 227–230; Assing quotation p. 227.

47. Douglass, quoted in Gates, "Dangerous Legacy," p. 4.

48. Assing, quoted in Lohmann, *Radical Passion*, pp. 158–160; McFeely, *Douglass*, p. 154; Diedrich, *Love across Color Lines*, pp. 210–214; Assing to Mrs. Gerrit Smith, October 1867, GSP; Assing to Mr. Smith, October 3, 1867, GSP.

49. Annie Brown, quoted in Oswald Garrison Villard, *John Brown, 1800–1859: A Biography Fifty Years After* (1910; reprint, New York: Alfred A. Knopf, 1943), p. 50; Stanton to Elizabeth Smith Miller, November 15, 1856, in Stanton and Blatch, *Stanton*, p. 69. See also Wendy Hamand Venet, "'Cry Aloud and Spare Not': Northern Antislavery Women and John Brown's Raid," in *His Soul Goes Marching On: Responses to John Brown and the Harper's Ferry Raid*, ed. Paul Finkelman (Charlottesville: University Press of Virginia, 1995), pp. 98–115. On Lydia Maria Child's close relationship with John Brown, see Carolyn L. Karcher, *The First Woman in the Republic: A Cultural Biography of Lydia Maria Child* (Durham, N.C.: Duke University Press, 1994), pp. 416–442.

50. Brown, "Provisional Constitution," in Richard J. Hinton, *John Brown and His Men* (New York: Funk and Wagnalls, 1894), pp. 619–620, 629, 632; Daniel Rosenberg, "Mary Brown: From Harpers Ferry to California," *American Institute for Marxist Studies*, 1975, pp. 7–9, 12, quotation p. 9, WL; Venet, "'Cry Aloud,'" p. 99. See also Brown, quoted in James Redpath, *The Public Life of Capt. John Brown* (Boston: Thayer and Eldridge, 1860), p. 192; F. B. Sanborn, ed., *The Life and Letters of John Brown* (Boston: Roberts Brothers, 1885), pp. 529–530; Villard, *Brown*, pp. 404–405.

51. Richard J. Hinton, ed., *Richard Realf's Free-State Poems, with Personal Lyrics Written in Kansas* (Topeka: Crane, 1900), pp. 77–80; Villard, *Brown*, pp. 294–309, 674–675; James Redpath, *Echoes of Harper's Ferry* (1860; reprint, New York: Arno, 1969), pp. 393, 422, quotation p. 393.

52. Frederick Douglass, "Woman and the Ballot," quoted in *FDWR*, pp. 96, 98; Douglass, *Life*, p. 470; *Gerrit Smith to Susan B. Anthony, February 5th, 1873*, broadside, GSP; Martin, *Mind of Douglass*, pp. 138–145.

Eight. The Alliance Ends and the War Begins

1. *NYH*, November 2, 1859.

2. Steven B. Oates, *To Purge This Land with Blood: A Biography of John Brown* (1970; reprint, Amherst: University of Massachusetts Press, 1984), pp. 274–279, 290–301; Oswald Garrison Villard, *John Brown, 1800–1859: A Biography Fifty Years After* (1910; reprint, New York: Alfred A. Knopf, 1943), pp. 426–455; Edward Stone, *Incident at Harper's Ferry* (Englewood Cliffs, N.J.: Prentice-Hall, 1956), pp. 21–42, 166–185.

3. *NYH*, November 2, 1859.
4. Smith, quoted in *LIB*, January 31, 1840; Ralph Volney Harlow, *Gerrit Smith: Philanthropist and Reformer* (New York: Henry Holt, 1939), p. 136.
5. *NYH*, November 2, 1859.
6. Ibid.
7. Ibid.
8. Smith, quoted in Harlow, *Gerrit Smith*, p. 399; Edward J. Renehan Jr., *The Secret Six: The True Tale of the Men Who Conspired with John Brown* (New York: Crown, 1995), pp. 146–147; James Brewer Stewart, *Joshua Giddings and the Tactics of Radical Politics* (Cleveland: Press of Case Western Reserve University, 1970), pp. 256–262, 269–270. The other five members of the "secret six" were all Massachusetts abolitionists: Thomas Wentworth Higginson, Franklin Sanborn, Theodore Parker, Samuel Gridley Howe, and Geogre Luther Stearns.
9. Renehan, *Secret Six*, pp. 150–165; F. B. Sanborn, ed., *The Life and Letters of John Brown* (Boston: Roberts Brothers, 1885), pp. 462–464; Harlow, *Gerrit Smith*, pp. 400–402; Jeffery Rossbach, *Ambivalent Conspirators: John Brown, the Secret Six, and a Theory of Slave Violence* (Philadelphia: University of Pennsylvania Press, 1982), pp. 136, 142, 160–181.
10. Gerrit Smith, *Peace Better than War* . . . (Boston: American Peace Society, 1858), pp. 10–20, 30–32, quotations pp. 10–20, GSP; George C. Beckwith to Gerrit Smith, quoted in Harlow, *Gerrit Smith*, p. 401; Richard J. Hinton, *John Brown and His Men* (New York: Funk and Wagnalls, 1894), pp. 592–597, 601–602, 619–637.
11. *Gerrit Smith to John Thomas, Esq., Peterboro*, broadside, August 27, 1859, GSP.
12. *NYH*, October 18, 19, 20, 21; Harlow, *Gerrit Smith*, pp. 403–409.
13. Dr. John P. Gray, quoted in Octavius Brooks Frothingham, *Gerrit Smith: A Biography* (New York: G. P. Putnam's Sons, 1878), p. 244; John Brown Jr. to J. H. Kagi, August 11, 1859, quoted in Harlow, *Gerrit Smith*, p. 404; Gray, quoted in ibid., p. 412; "Case Notes of Gerrit Smith," New York State Lunatic Asylum, Book 16, holograph, NYSA.
14. Gerrit Smith, *Religion of Reason* (Peterboro: C. A. Hammond, 1864), pp. 20, 53; Harlow, *Gerrit Smith*, pp. 382–390; Jack P. Maddex Jr., "'The Southern Apostasy' Revisited: The Significance of Proslavery Christianity," in *Religion and Slavery*, ed. Paul Finkelman (New York: Garland, 1989), pp. 462–471; Larry E. Tise, *Proslavery: A History of the Defense of Slavery in America, 1701–1840* (Athens: University of Georgia Press, 1987); Forrest G. Wood, *The Arrogance of Faith: Christianity and Race in America from the*

Colonial Era to the Twentieth Century (New York: Alfred A. Knopf, 1990), pp. 38–83.

15. Smith, quoted in Frothingham, *Smith*, pp. 237–238; Harlow, *Gerrit Smith*, pp. 403–404; Villard, *Brown*, pp. 676–678.

16. *NYH*, November 12, 1859; Harlow, *Gerrit Smith*, pp. 401–404; Sanborn, *Life and Letters of Brown*, pp. 466–467; Renehan, *Secret Six*, pp. 162–163; John R. McKivigan and Madeleine Leveille, "The 'Black Dream' of Gerrit Smith, New York Abolitionist," *SULAC* 20 (Fall 1985): 56; Rossbach, *Ambivalent Conspirators*, pp. 128–129, 139–145.

17. *NYH*, October 20, 27, November 11, 12, 1859, quotation from November 12; "Case Notes of Smith"; Charles A. Hammond, *Gerrit Smith: The Story of a Noble Man's Life* (Geneva, N.Y.: W. F. Humphrey, 1900), pp. 48–49; Frothingham, *Smith*, pp. 244–245; Harlow, *Gerrit Smith*, pp. 408–413; McKivigan and Leveille, "'Black Dream' of Smith," pp. 60–62.

18. *NYH*, November 2, 11, 12, 1859, quotations from November 11, 12; Frothingham, *Smith*, p. 245; Harlow, *Gerrit Smith*, pp. 412–414; "Case Notes of Smith."

19. *NYH*, November 11, 12, 1859; Frothingham, *Smith*, pp. 243–245; Harlow, *Gerrit Smith*, pp. 410–413; McKivigan and Leveille, "'Black Dream' of Smith," pp. 61–62.

20. Henry A. Wise to Honorable John Cochrane, November 16, 1859, GSP. Wise showed less compassion for Smith in a letter he wrote Andrew Hunter the very same day: "Gerrit Smith is a stark madman, no doubt! God, what a moral, what a lesson. Whom the gods wish to make mad they first set to setting others to destroying"; Wise to Andrew Hunter, November 16, 1859, reprinted in Villard, *Brown*, p. 522.

21. Oates, *To Purge This Land*, pp. 307–308; Villard, *Brown*, pp. 455–463, 477–486; Robert E. McGlone, "John Brown, Henry Wise, and the Politics of Insanity," in *His Soul Goes Marching On: Responses to John Brown and the Harper's Ferry Raid*, ed. Paul Finkelman (Charlottesville: University Press of Virginia, 1995), pp. 218–219. By prosecuting Brown in a Virginia court, Wise also sought to enhance the prestige of Virginia and further his own political career.

22. Wise, quoted in Villard, *Brown*, p. 455; Wise, quoted in Sanborn, *Life and Letters of Brown*, pp. 571–572.

23. Wise, quoted in Villard, *Brown*, p. 455. See also Edmund Morgan, "The Big American Crime," *NYR*, December 3, 1998, p. 16; McGlone, "Brown, Wise, and Politics of Insanity," pp. 218–252.

24. Douglass, quoted in William S. McFeely, *Frederick Douglass* (New York: W. W. Norton, 1991), p. 198; Douglass, *Life and Times of Frederick Douglass*

(1892; reprint, New York: Collier, 1962), p. 309; *NYH*, October 20, 1859; Philip S. Foner, *Frederick Douglass* (1950; reprint, New York: Citadel Press, 1969), pp. 178–180.

25. Douglass, *Life*, pp. 307–313, 314–323; Foner, *Douglass*, pp. 174–182; Benjamin Quarles, *Frederick Douglass* (1948; reprint, New York: Da Capo, 1997), pp. 170–182; McFeely, *Douglass*, pp. 194–195; Frothingham, *Smith*, p. 233.

26. Gerrit Smith to Nancy Smith, January 10, 1859, GSP; *LWFD*, 5: 429–430; Douglass, *Life*, pp. 307–313, 314–323; Foner, *Douglass*, pp. 174–182; Quarles, *Douglass*, pp. 170–182; McFeely, *Douglass*, pp. 194–195; Harlow, *Gerrit Smith*, p. 403.

27. Douglass, *Life*, pp. 315–321, quotations pp. 316, 319; Foner, *Douglass*, pp. 177–179; McFeely, *Douglass*, pp. 195–197; Quarles, *Douglass*, pp. 177–179; Oates, *To Purge This Land*, pp. 282–283; Villard, *Brown*, pp. 412–413.

28. Douglass, *Life*, pp. 319–320; *LWFD*, 2: 462.

29. On slaves' lacking honor, see Orlando Patterson, *Slavery and Social Death: A Comparative Study* (Cambridge: Harvard University Press, 1982), pp. 1–16, 77–104.

30. Douglass, *Life*, p. 20; *Aesop, The Complete Fables*, trans. Olivia and Robert Temple (New York: Penguin, 1998), p. 173; Keith Hopkins, "Novel Evidence for Roman Slavery," *Past and Present* 138 (February 1993): 3–27. On Brown's familiarity with Aesop's fables, see Sanborn, *Life and Letters of Brown*, p. 93.

31. McFeely, *Douglass*, pp. 197–199; Douglass, *Life*, p. 319.

32. *TFDP*, 1/3: 290–291. Douglass' "Self-Made Men" speech at Philadelphia in October 1859 was never published, so I am quoting from the same speech that he gave in Halifax, England, on January 4, 1860.

33. McFeely, *Douglass*, pp. 198–204; Douglass, *Life*, pp. 321–332.

34. *LWFD*, 2: 458–459.

35. *LWFD*, 5: 467; Foner, *Douglass*, p. 182; McFeely, *Douglass*, pp. 198–204; Douglass, *Life*, pp. 321–332.

36. McCune Smith to Gerrit Smith, September 20, 1859, GSP; McFeely, *Douglass*, p. 195.

37. *Weekly Anglo-African*, July 30, 1859; Jane H. Pease and William H. Pease, *They Who Would Be Free: Blacks' Search for Freedom, 1830–1861* (1974; reprint, Urbana: University of Illinois Press, 1990), pp. 119, 243.

38. McCune Smith, quoted in *FDP*, March 14, 1856; *FDP*, March 7, 1856; McCune Smith to Gerrit Smith, March 13, 1856, GSP; Leon F. Litwack, *North of Slavery: The Negro in the Free States, 1790–1860* (Chicago: University of Chicago Press, 1961), p. 263; Eugene H. Berwanger, *The Frontier*

against Slavery: Western Anti-Negro Prejudice and the Slavery Extension Controversy (Urbana: University of Illinois Press, 1971), pp. 30–59.

39. McCune Smith, quoted in *FDP*, August 8, 1856, January 3, 1857.

40. McCune Smith, quoted in *FDP*, April 16, 1858. See also *FDP*, March 6, 1857, August 12, 1858.

41. Brown, quoted in Hinton, *Brown and His Men*, p. 26.

42. "The Nat Turner Insurrection," *AAM*, p. 386. See also the article immediately following, titled "The Execution of John Brown," pp. 398–399; Pease and Pease, *They Who Would Be Free*, p. 119; *BAP*, 5: 27; *FDP*, March 25, 1859; McCune Smith to Gerrit Smith, June 21, 1860, GSP.

43. James McCune Smith, quoted in *FDP*, October 28, 1859.

44. Hannah N. Geffert, "The Local Black Community's Response to John Brown's Raid," presentation at the conference "John Brown: The Man, the Legend, the Legacy," Pennsylvania State University, Mont Alto, July 24–27, 1996; Villard, *Brown*, pp. 54–55, 313–315, 331–335; Oates, *To Purge This Land*, p. 244; Hinton, *Brown and His Men*, pp. 25, 30–31, 34, 72, 83, 178–180, 513, 715; Benjamin Quarles, *Allies for Freedom: Blacks and John Brown* (New York: Oxford University Press, 1974), p. 111; W. E. B. Du Bois, *John Brown* (1909; reprint; New York: International Publishers, 1962), pp. 97, 110, 254–255, 294; Sanborn, *Life and Letters of Brown*, p. 468; James Redpath, *The Public Life of Capt. John Brown* (Boston: Thayer and Eldridge, 1860), pp. 203–205.

45. Sanborn, *Life and Letters of Brown*, p. 468; F. B. Sanborn, *Recollections of Seventy Years*, vol. 1 (Boston: Ticknor and Fields, 1909), p. 184; Geffert, "Local Black Community's Response"; Rossbach, *Ambivalent Conspirators*, pp. 4, 132–134, 200; Quarles, *Allies for Freedom*, pp. 79–83; Hinton, *Brown and His Men*, pp. 257, 272–73, 674; Osborne Anderson, *A Voice from Harper's Ferry: A Narrative of Events of Harper's Ferry . . .* (Boston: Printed for the author, 1861), p. 21.

46. Anderson, *Voice from Harper's Ferry*, pp. 34–39, quotation p. 37; Hinton, *Brown and His Men*, pp. 262, 272–273, 288, 293–295, 298, 300, 305, 314–315, 550, quotations pp. 272–273; Quarles, *Allies for Freedom*, p. 79; A. R. H. Ranson, "Reminiscences of the Civil War by a Confederate Staff Officer," *Shawnee Review* 21 (October 1913): 439; Brown, quoted in Sanborn, *Life and Letters of Brown*, p. 572; Geffert, "Local Black Community's Response."

47. Quarles, *Allies for Freedom*, p. 108; Geffert, "Local Black Community's Response"; Villard, *Brown*, p. 520.

48. D. H. Strother, quoted in Quarles, *Allies for Freedom*, p. 104; *LWFD*, 2: 464–465; Hinton, *Brown and His Men*, pp. 507–508; Geffert, "Local Black Community's Response."

49. Brown, quoted in Sanborn, *Life and Letters of Brown*, p. 572.
50. Brown, "Provisional Constitution," in Hinton, *Brown and His Men*, p. 619; Henry Kagi, quoted in ibid., p. 453; Brown to Sanborn, quoted in Oates, *To Purge This Land*, p. 289; McFeely, *Douglass*, p. 187; Villard, *Brown*, p. 334; Judges 16:28–30.
51. Anderson, *Voice from Harper's Ferry*, p. 24; Douglass, quoting Shields Green, in *TFDP*, 1/5: 32; Hinton, *Brown and His Men*, pp. 507–508.
52. Brown, quoted in Sanborn, *Life and Letters of Brown*, pp. 573, 579.
53. Brown, quoted in Richard Warch and Jonathan Fanton, eds., *John Brown* (Englewood Cliffs, N.J.: Prentice-Hall, 1973), pp. 91, 94, 96, 99.
54. Brown to Dearly Beloved Wife, Sons: & Daughters, November 30, 1859, reprinted in Louis Ruchames, ed., *John Brown: The Making of a Revolutionary* (New York: Grosset and Dunlap, 1969), p. 164.
55. Villard, *Brown*, pp. 554–555; Ruchames, *Brown*, p. 167; Oates, *To Purge This Land*, pp. 349–352; *The Life, Trial and Execution of Captain John Brown, Known as "Old Brown of Ossawatomie," Compiled from Official and Authentic Sources* (1859; reprint, New York: Da Capo, 1969), pp. 100–101.
56. "Case Notes of Smith."
57. McKivigan and Leveille, "'Black Dream' of Smith," pp. 67–68, 75, quotation p. 68; "Case Notes of Smith"; "Definition of Insanity—Nature of the Disease," *American Journal of Insanity*, October 1844, pp. 97–115. On Gray's use of marijuana, brandy, and morphine in cases of mania, see Case Books 1–16, New York State Lunatic Asylum, Utica, NYSA.
58. "Case Notes of Smith"; McKivigan and Leveille, "'Black Dream' of Smith," pp. 69–70; Harlow, *Gerrit Smith*, p. 413; Gray to Mrs. Smith, December 19, 1859, GSP. Smith's illness prevented him from testifying at the Senate investigation of the Harpers Ferry invasion, which began in January 1860 and ended in June.
59. Smith to Charles Sumner, June 7, 1860, GSP.
60. Smith to Samuel Joseph May, August 22, 1860, GSP.
61. My use of the term "inner war" comes from George M. Fredrickson, *The Inner Civil War: Northern Intellectuals and the Crisis of the Union* (1965; reprint, Urbana: University of Illinois Press, 1993), pp. xv–xvi, 1–4.
62. Smith to William Goodell, May 1, 1860, reprinted in *DM*, June 1860; Smith, *Religion of Reason*, pp. 118–119; Smith, quoted in F. B. Sanborn, "A Concord Note-Book: Gerrit Smith and John Brown," *Critic and Literary World: An Illustrated Monthly Review of Literature, Art and Life* 47 (October 1905): 351–352.
63. Smith, *Religion of Reason*, p. 126; Smith, *Be Natural! A Discourse in Peterboro, November 20, 1864* (New York: American News, 1864), pp. 3–22, GSP; Smith, *The Theologies* (Peterboro: C. A. Hammond, 1866), p. 18, GSP;

Smith, *Nature the Basis of a True Theology* . . . (Peterboro: Rev. J. W. West, 1867), GSP; *Correspondence of Gerrit Smith with Albert Barnes* (New York: American News, 1868); N. Goodsell to Gerrit Smith, New Haven, Conn., February 25, March 4, December 6, 17, 1867, GSP; Edward R. Wood to Gerrit Smith, November 25, 1861, GSP; Smith, *To the Religious Newspaper Reviewers of My Recent Discourse*, broadside, September 3, 1859, GSP.

64. Gerrit Smith, *Speech for Human Rights, February 6, 1861*, broadside, GSP; Smith, *War Meeting In Peterboro, April 27, 1861*, broadside, GSP; *Gerrit Smith to Thaddeus Stevens, December 6, 1861*, broadside, GSP.

65. *Speech of Gerrit Smith in Oswego, on the Rebellion and the Draft*, July 29, 1863, broadside, GSP. See also Smith, "Letter to Mrs. Stanton on the Presidential Question," June 6, 1864, in *Speeches and Letters of Gerrit Smith on the Rebellion*, vol. 2 (New York: American News, 1865), p. 15, GSP.

66. *Smith to Stevens, December 6, 1861*. See also George M. Fredrickson, *The Black Image in the White Mind: The Debate on Afro-American Character and Destiny, 1817–1914* (1971; reprint, Middletown, Conn.: Wesleyan University Press, 1987), pp. 130–164; James M. McPherson, *The Struggle for Equality: Abolitionists and the Negro in the Civil War and Reconstruction* (Princeton: Princeton University Press, 1964), pp. 154–156.

67. *Gerrit Smith to John A. Gurley, December 16, 1861*, broadside, GSP; *Gerrit Smith to Montgomery Blair, April 5, 1862*, broadside, GSP; *Gerrit Smith to George Thompson, January 25, 1862*, broadside, GSP. See also Gerrit Smith, *Stand by the Government, February 27, 1863*, broadside, GSP; Smith, *Letter to Hon. D. C. Littlejohn . . . on the Country, January 14, 1864*, broadside, GSP; *Gerrit Smith to John C. Churchill, December 22, 1870*, broadside, GSP; Fredrickson, *Black Image in White Mind*, pp. 149–153.

68. Smith, *Letter to the President from Gerrit Smith, August 31, 1861*, broadside, GSP; Smith, *Speech at Young Men's Mass Convention, September 3, 1863*, broadside, GSP.

69. Harlow, *Gerrit Smith*, pp. 423–448.

70. Morgan, "Big American Crime," p. 16.

71. Quarles, *Allies for Freedom*, pp. 22–24, quotation p. 22; Gerrit Smith, *To the Members of the Liberty Party in the County of Madison, October 10, 1851*, broadside, GSP; Villard, *Brown*, pp. 71–74; Sanborn, *Life and Letters of Brown*, pp. 99–102.

72. Gerrit Smith, "A Story: The Ruinous Visit to Monkeyville," November 15, 1851, holograph, GSP.

73. Winthrop D. Jordan, *White over Black: American Attitudes toward the Negro, 1550–1812* (1968; reprint, New York: W. W. Norton, 1977), pp. 30–31, 228–231; Fredrickson, *Black Image in White Mind*, pp. 71–96; Henry Louis Gates Jr., *The Signifying Monkey: A Theory of Afro-American Literary Criti-*

cism (New York: Oxford University Press, 1988), pp. 3–88. Gerrit Smith suggested in 1867 that a monkey represented the "embodiment" of "trickery"; *Gerrit Smith on Free Moral Agency, February 1867*, GSP.

74. Smith to Douglass, June 1, 1850, in *NS*, June 13, 1850.

75. Smith, *Religion of Reason*, p. 81.

76. Fredrickson, *Black Image in White Mind*, pp. 43–96; Ronald Takaki, "The Black Child-Savage in Ante-Bellum America," in *The Great Fear: Race in the Mind of America*, ed. Gary B. Nash and Richard Weiss (New York: Holt, Rinehart and Winston, 1970), pp. 27–44.

77. Smith, "Monkeyville"; Robert H. Abzug, *Passionate Liberator: Theodore Dwight Weld and the Dilemma of Reform* (New York: Oxford University Press, 1980), pp. 250–255.

Historians typically refer to Gerrit's son as "Green" rather than "Greene." Gerrit named him after his abolitionist friend Beriah Green, and when he announced his son's birth, he wrote "Green." But sometime around 1850, perhaps as a result of a falling out with Beriah Green, he added an "e" to his son's name. A passport from 1861 shows him as "Greene." See Gerrit Smith to Beriah Green, April 14, 1842, GSP; Gerrit Smith to O. S. Renslaw, April 18, 1842, GSP. On Gerrit Smith's falling out with Green see Milton C. Sernett, *Abolition's Axe: Beriah Green, Oneida Institute, and the Black Freedom Struggle* (Syracuse, N.Y.: Syracuse University Press, 1986), pp. 127–132, 138–139.

78. Theodore Dwight Weld to Gerrit Smith, March 4, 1852, Belleville, N.J., GSP.

79. Gerrit Smith to Greene Smith, April 5, 1851, November 29, 1852, January 9, 1853, February 25, 1853, GSP; Weld to Gerrit Smith, March 4, August 14, December 22, 1852, February 5, 1853, GSP.

80. Gerrit Smith, "The Reasonable Boy," February 15, 1859, GSP; Gerrit Smith to Greene Smith, on His Birthday, April 14, 1859, GSP.

81. Greene Smith to Ann Smith, February 5, 1860, MCHS; Greene Smith to Brother[-in-law, probably Gerrit Smith Miller], February 22, 1860, MCHS; Greene Smith to Gerrit Smith, September 8, November 23, 1861, March 7, May 11, 1862, March 28, 1866, December 5, 1866, MCHS; Greene Smith, "To My Mother," poem, holograph, April 14, 1863, MCHS; Greene Smith, "Copy of dissertation on Prof. Frothingham's Life [of] Father," holograph, June 2, 1878, Greene Smith Papers, Syracuse University; Harlow, *Gerrit Smith*, pp. 489–490.

82. McCune Smith to Gerrit Smith, June 21, 1860, GSP.

83. McCune Smith to Gerrit Smith, September 22, 1860, GSP.

84. McCune Smith to Gerrit Smith, June 21, August 9, September 22, 29 1860, GSP; McCune Smith to Gerrit Smith, October 20, 1860, in *BAP*, 5: 84–87.

85. McCune Smith to Gerrit Smith, August 22, 1861, in *BAP*, 5: 113; Gerrit Smith, *No Terms with Traitors: The Submission of the Rebels the Sole Condition of Peace*, reprinted in *LIB*, August 26, 1861. See also McPherson, *Struggle for Equality*, pp. 55–65.

86. McCune Smith to Gerrit Smith, August 22, 1861, in *BAP*, 5: 114.

87. McCune Smith to Gerrit Smith, January 13, April 26, 1864, February 17, 1865, GSP; McPherson, *Struggle*, pp. 289–293.

88. Douglass to Gerrit Smith, September 8, 1862, in *LWFD*, 3: 260; Smith to Douglass, August 26, 1871, DP; Smith to Douglass, September 23, 1873, DP (emphasis added); Douglass, in McCune Smith to Gerrit Smith, January 13, 1864, GSP.

   Douglass and Smith did collaborate briefly in helping to arm black troops during the war. Yet he also chastised Smith's emphasis on preserving the Union rather than on ending slavery, saying: "you seem to admit that some abolitionists have shown a disposition to *pervert* the war to abolitionism. You and I know that the natural use of this war is to abolish slavery"; Douglass, quoted in *LWFD*, 3: 408; Douglass to Smith, March 9, June 19, 1863, GSP; Smith to Douglass, March 10, 1863, DP.

89. Douglass, quoted in Quarles, *Douglass*, p. 295.

90. Quarles, *Douglass*, pp. 95, 202–282, quotations pp. 212–213, 252; McFeely, *Douglass*, pp. 201–237; David W. Blight, *Frederick Douglass' Civil War: Keeping Faith in Jubilee* (Baton Rouge: Louisiana State University Press, 1989), pp. 101–121, 175–188; John L. Thomas, "Romantic Reform in America, 1815–1865," *AQ* 17 (Winter 1965): 679; Fredrickson, *Inner Civil War*, pp. 183–198; Maria Diedrich, *Love across Color Lines: Ottilie Assing and Frederick Douglass* (New York: Hill and Wang, 1999), pp. 226–229, 259–300.

91. Douglass, quoted in McFeely, *Douglass*, pp. 317, 318; *LWFD*, 4: 393–396.

92. Douglass, quoted in Quarles, *Douglass*, pp. 246, 288; *FDWR*, pp. 86–90; McFeely, *Douglass*, pp. 291–304, quotation p. 302; Douglass, "The Negro Exodus from the Gulf States," *Journal of Social Science* 11 (May 1880): 1–2. On Douglass and the black "exodus" movement see also Nell Irvin Painter, *Exodusters: Black Migration to Kansas after Reconstruction* (New York: Alfred A. Knopf, 1976), p. 249; Leon F. Litwack, *Trouble in Mind: Black Southerners in the Age of Jim Crow* (New York: Alfred A. Knopf, 1998), pp. 484–485.

93. *TFDP*, 1/5: 35, 634–635.

Epilogue

1. *CT*, June 9, 10, 1874; James D. Horan, *The Pinkertons: The Detective Dynasty That Made History* (New York: Crown, 1967), pp. 37–42; Allan Pinkerton,

The Spy of the Rebellion . . . (1883; reprint, Lincoln: University of Nebraska Press, 1989), pp. 25–27; Gerrit Smith to Allan Pinkerton, May 1, 1851, GSP.

2. *CT*, June 9, 10, 1874, quotation from June 9; Larry Gara, "A Glorious Time: The 1874 Abolitionist Reunion in Chicago," *Journal of the Illinois State Historical Society* 65 (Autumn 1972): 280–292; Lawrence J. Friedman, *Gregarious Saints: Self and Community in American Abolitionism, 1830–1870* (Cambridge: Cambridge University Press, 1982), pp. 277–280.

3. *CT*, June 11–12, 1874.

4. *CT*, June 11, 1874; Douglass, quoted in Benjamin Quarles, *Frederick Douglass* (1948; reprint, New York: Da Capo, 1997), p. 272; Friedman, *Gregarious Saints*, p. 278; William S. McFeely, *Frederick Douglass* (New York: W. W. Norton, 1991), pp. 280–287.

5. *CT*, June 10, 11, 1874; Gerrit Smith, quoted in Octavius Brooks Frothingham, *Gerrit Smith: A Biography* (New York: G. P. Putnam's Sons, 1878), p. 46; Smith, "Reunion of Abolitionists at Chicago," June 17, 1874, holograph, GSP.

6. Gerrit Smith, *"To Thyself Be True!"* broadside, November 23, 1874, GSP; *New York Times*, December 29, 1874; Frothingham, *Gerrit Smith*, pp. 353–361; Ralph Volney Harlow, *Gerrit Smith: Philanthropist and Reformer* (New York: Henry Holt, 1939), pp. 490–491.

Acknowledgments

—— ❧ ——

This book began as a dissertation in American studies at Yale, and it could not have been conceived, researched, or written without extraordinary support from a number of people. My greatest debt goes to my adviser, David Brion Davis, to whom this book is dedicated. He is intellectually, emotionally, and spiritually the most generous person I know. In his writing, teaching, mentoring, and criticism, he has not only expanded my mind and heart, but has inspired me in ways I never thought possible before I met him. I also had the opportunity to work closely with Alan Trachtenberg, and his support and friendship have been similarly invaluable in my development as a scholar and individual. In fact these two mentors influenced me even before I met them, for it was after reading their works that I decided to apply to Yale to pursue a Ph.D. degree. Jon Butler also played a central role in my development as a scholar and individual. His guidance and advice about writing, teaching, and the academic profession marked another high point in my graduate education. At times, I felt as though these three mentors had more confidence in me than I had in myself, and for that too, I am immensely grateful.

A number of people at Yale and in New Haven helped bring the project to light. Casey King read the entire manuscript, offered superb criticism, and has served as a steady source of inspiration and friendship. Richard Brodhead read a chapter and shared with me some of his own extraordinary work on the American prophetic tradition. Eric Papenfuse and Catherine Lawrence lent their well-tuned ears to the project in its early stages, and were always there when I needed them. John Demos expanded my understanding of narrative in writing history and criticism. Jon Baer, Susie Blumenthal, Nancy Cott, Robert Forbes, Ben Karp, Jackie Robinson, Joe Thompson, and Bryan Wolf provided sources, advice, and support. A number of undergraduates shared their research and helped me develop arguments: Debbie Dinner, Kiera Levine, Seth Oltman, Daniel Pollack-Pelzner, and Ben Soskis. Barbara Sherod and Mark Steinhardt served as a kind of surrogate family, opening their home and hearts. These mentors, colleagues, students, and friends were largely responsible for making my five years in New Haven a wonderfully nurturing and rewarding environment.

I completed and revised the project at Harvard, and a number of colleagues there have been incredibly generous with their advice and recommendations. Larry Buell in particular has been extremely helpful; he gave me some excellent advice on the manuscript and has guided me through various revisions and the publication process. Robert Ferguson, Tim McCarthy, and James Brewer Stewart also read the entire manuscript and provided very detailed and often brilliant criticism. Several other scholars went out of their way to read some or all of the manuscript, providing excellent suggestions and insights: Bob Abzug, Steve Biel, Cathy Corman, Susan Curtis, Neal Dolan, Stanley Harrold, Richard Johns, Bill Kenney, and Steven Mintz. At Harvard University Press, Aida Donald, Ann Hawthorne, and Joyce Seltzer have been wonderfully supportive, straightforward, and patient editors and have made the book far better than it otherwise would have been. The readers for the Press, David Blight and Jack McKivigan, were extremely helpful and generous in their comments.

A number of abolition aficionados, critics, and writers also helped shape the project. Joel Fleishman, Shan Holt, Deborah Hornblow, and John Wood inspired me with their own writings, conversation, and friendship. Tim Adriance, Donna Burdick, Dean Grodzins, Hannah Geffert, Carolyn Karcher, Jean Libby, Christoph Lohmann, Bob Shear, and Beth Spokowsky helped me better understand Gerrit Smith. James Folts, Amy Greenberg, Mary Panzer, Martha Sachs, Stephanie Shaiman, Rachel Stuhlman, and Damon Whelchel followed through with needed assistance.

The librarians and staff at the following libraries and archives greatly facilitated my research: the Sterling and Beinecke Libraries, Yale University (especially the Microfilm Room and Manuscripts and Archives at Sterling Library); the Department of Special Collections, Bird Library, Syracuse University; the Madison County (New York) Historical Society; the Houghton and Widener Libraries, Harvard University; the New York Public Library; the New York State Archives, Albany; the Library of Congress, Washington, D.C.; the National Portrait Gallery, Smithsonian Institute; the Gilder Lehrman Institute of American History in New York City; the Department of Manuscripts and Archives, Hamilton College; and the Wisconsin State Historical Society, Madison.

I received generous financial assistance from the following foundations, funds, and institutions: the National Endowment for the Humanities; the Woodrow Wilson National Fellowship Foundation; the American Studies Association; the Pew Program in Religion and American History; Yale University; the Yale History and American Studies Research Fellowship; the John F. Enders Research Fund; the Marcia Brady Tucker Fellowship; the Gilder Lehrman Institute of American History; a Harvard University Faculty research grant; and a Robinson Rollins research grant.

Two close friends, Kevin Parks and Wendell Gibson, have been a wellspring of good sense and encouragement. Even though they live in Chicago and have careers outside academia, they have known me since high school, have sustained me in the good times and bad, and have taken a keen interest in this project. Finally, I owe an enormous debt of gratitude to my parents and family, Bill and Jean Stauffer, Mark and Becky LaFavre, and Rachel Windsor. They have been unwavering in their love and understanding.

Index